T0178912

Enterprise Interoperability

Enterprise Interoperability

*Smart Services and Business Impact
of Enterprise Interoperability*

Edited by

Martin Zelm
Frank-Walter Jaekel
Guy Doumeingts
Martin Wollschlaeger

WILEY

First published 2018 in Great Britain and the United States by ISTE Ltd and John Wiley & Sons, Inc.

ISTE Ltd
27–37 St George's Road
London SW19 4EU
UK

www.iste.co.uk

John Wiley & Sons, Inc.
111 River Street
Hoboken, NJ 07030
USA

www.wiley.com

Library of Congress Control Number: 2018955679

British Library Cataloguing-in-Publication Data
A CIP record for this book is available from the British Library
ISBN 978-1-78630-373-8

Contents

Introduction

The works in this book stem from research presented during 11 workshops and a doctrol symposium which were organized in the frame of the International Conference on Enterprise Interoperability (I-ESA 2018).

Most of the papers presented in this book originate from European or national research projects. One major goal of the I-ESA workshops is the exchange of knowledge to encourage an active debate of results between the presenters and the audience, which could inspire further research. The results of the discussions are reflected in the papers finalized after the conference and documented in the workshop reports.

With the conference subtitle "Smart services and business impact of enterprise interoperability", the workshops elaborate results of research and industry transfer in the area of smart service-related technologies like next generation Internet, IoT, cloud-based platforms, artificial intelligence and advanced enterprise modeling for future manufacturing.

The I-ESA workshops were organized in three tracks, each track moving from research-oriented topics of wider scope towards particular application topics focusing on real benefits for industry.

Track A was composed of four workshops. The first workshop addressed embedded intelligence in manufacturing decision support, and elaborated on the business requirements of ICT solutions for directed trans-disciplinary information and knowledge-sharing capability. The second workshop elaborated the business impact of application use cases of enterprise interoperability (EI). In the third workshop, recent research on an operating system for virtual factory (vf-OS) was presented. The last workshop addressed issues in EI standardization management.

Track B consisted of four workshops. The first two workshops elaborated on smart services to enable semantic interoperability for industrial Big Data platforms to support digital transformation. Included was a position paper regarding the European Big Data Value Association for Smart Manufacturing Industry. The last two workshops addressed methodologies for predictive maintenance in Industry 4.0 and issues of higher education.

Track C was composed of three workshops. The first workshop focused on modeling and simulation for the design of advanced manufacturing systems including an ontology for enterprise modeling and the presentation of the first implementation of a new architecture, MDSEA for Industrie 4.0. The second workshop addressed methods and tools for product service systems (PSS) by proposing an innovation process and the use of a tool called the product service concept tree. The third workshop provided an outlook of the research into how interoperability solutions for crisis management could increase the resilience of smart cities.

The doctoral symposium presented the results of three dissertations in the field of flexible shop floor management. The results concern information systems for network organisations in the context of enterprise interoperability. The goal of the symposium was to discuss interactively the findings, issues or ideas between the participating PhD students and experienced participants from research and industry.

We would like to acknowledge the professional contribution of Andrea Koch to organize the papers for the delivery to the publisher.

Preface

Markets, stakeholders and information technologies will constantly evolve, making it challenging for a single organization to keep up with the competition. Modern production enterprises are responding to this challenge with Industries 4.0 and interoperable solutions in collaborative networks to become more reactive and innovative in both their organization and their production systems.

The International Conference on Enterprise Interoperability (I-ESA 2018) presented interoperable solutions for enterprises from the viewpoints of research and innovation (business impact). The workshops addressed Smart Services and new technologies like next generation internet (Internet of Things, cloud-based platforms, and artificial intelligence) applied in future manufacturing systems using digital transformation.

This book contains work that stemmed from 11 workshops and a doctoral symposium. One particular method used for each workshop was to exchange knowledge about actual research and applications and to interactively discuss issues and new ideas between the presenters and the audience of experts from research and industry.

Martin ZELM
Frank-Walter JAEKEL
Guy DOUMEINGTS
Martin WOLLSCHLAEGER
August 2018

PART 1

Embedded Intelligence

Part 1 Summary: Embedded Intelligence Discussion

Introduction

The research presented in this workshop involved 22 participants. The supporting presentations provided an in-factory perspective, a supply chain perspective, a technology perspective and a solution provider's perspective. The workshop contributors proposed the most important issues that should be addressed which were then discussed against four topics: (1) how do we best empower people?; (2) how do we enable effective knowledge sharing across multiple users with different viewpoints?; (3) what analytics techniques are needed/essential? and (4) how do we deploy and maintain ICT solutions to suit dynamic business environments? The results of the discussion are provided below against each of these topic areas.

How do we best empower people?

Within this area contributors identified the following topics: trust, skills and training, presenting decision support data, and integration of humans in the system.

Trust: *"How will operators accept new technology and culture change?"*

For successful automation and model building, a significant amount of data is required about the entire system. A large portion of this data should be obtained from the work force, including tacit knowledge. Trust would be essential to gain workforce involvement and ensure accurate data provision. Automated systems,

Chapter written by Bob YOUNG, Paul GOODALL, Richard SHARPE, Kate VAN-LOPIK, Sarogini PEASE and Gash BHULLAR.

autonomous agents and system models should provide a user with visibility of decisions. This should be easy to understand and interrogate.

Skills and training: *"How will we train people with no experience themselves to be good decision makers?"*

Dynamic embedded management will continue to be required. A human retains responsibility, and must have the ability to respond appropriately and intervene *when* exceptions, errors and emergency situations occur. Due to the reduced lifecycle of products and increased variability in processes, it would not be easy for someone to gain necessary or significant experience. Training should be provided for changing manual roles and strategic decision-making.

Presenting data for decision support: *"What are the tools required to make human decisions the right ones?"*

Complex, multi-system architectures should be easier to maintain and be user friendly, but how this could be achieved remained unclear. With complex systems that include autonomous and human elements it would be necessary for process and system models to be understood by human and machine. Process models for such systems could be excessively large and incomprehensible. Presenting processes in a manner easily understood by people would be necessary to support the generation of interoperable systems. Data presented for decision support should be simplified, potentially a summary of events and include both provenance and be easily interrogated. Interface to these data should be user friendly, visually pleasing and provide additional metadata to facilitate understanding.

A human in the system: *"How can we support/integrate the human worker?"*

The portion and abstraction of the system presented to the user should relate to the role they are expected to undertake. Interoperability will depend on successful communication and understandings between different organizations, groups and between the human and the system. Wearable technologies could be used to help support humans within these systems if they were ergonomically suitable. Legal and ethical questions arise if such tools are used to gather data about their users. Wearable technologies present an opportunity to develop a "digital human twin" however this concept presented concerns regarding ownership of such a twin and ethical use of the data.

How do we enable effective knowledge sharing across multiple users with different viewpoints?

Within this area contributors addressed three topics, with key findings listed as points below each topic.

The key features of an effective knowledge-sharing platform are for it to:

– support multiple users from various disciplines;

– use a common knowledge management language;

– be easily usable;

– be used and updated (user buy-in to managing and accessing the knowledge);

– be developed by experts, not developers;

– be easy to change and flexible to modification;

– define standards (e.g. for specific processes) and stick to them;

– have standard interfaces with interoperable layers;

– be a smart space for ontology sharing (using a semantic broker).

What tools and methods are currently used to store, manage, access and share knowledge?

– Databases	– Product Catalogues
– System models	– ISO Standards
– Wikis (often noted to be out of date)	– IBM Watson (AI)
– Ontologies	– INDUSTREWEB
– Human interaction (discussion and training)	– Solidworks PDM
– Scientific literature searches	– Written grant applications
– RDF triples	– Textbooks

What problems should a future knowledge-sharing platform solve?

Note: all of the discussions in this area hinged on trust in the sources of knowledge where face-to-face interaction was considered of particular importance. In order to solve problems, a future knowledge-sharing platform should aim to:

– guarantee trust in sources of knowledge;

– ensure only experts ask the right (appropriate) questions;

– embed decision-making to provide the most useful solution;

– handle multi-process questions; respond to follow-up questions in light of previous questions;

– share knowledge only with trusted entities (security and data privacy);

– manage ownership of knowledge; ensure it is up to date and trusted;

– reflect the interactive process of learning (conversational).

What analytics techniques are needed/essential?

A broad discussion was held around the topic of data analysis, modeling, simulation and decision support for manufacturing with the aim of exploring the state of the art, identifying research challenges and suggesting routes to tackle these challenges. Listed below is a summary of the discussion areas and points raised.

Data and information uncertainty:

– it should not be assumed that the data is correct. Methods, measures and standards should be employed to assess if data is fit for purpose;

– how can we validate the analysis to determine if correlations are causations;

– can we include the scientific process?

– feedback data into models to enable continuous improvement;

– how should we determine if a sensor has failed or requires calibration?

People, skills and tools:

– domain experts need to be better integrated with the analysis team;

– good engineers need to be trained to ask the right questions;

– currently we can ask questions and use analytics to help answer them, but how can we be proactive – how do you know what you don't know?

– new software tools are being developed all the time; keeping up-to-date with the market is a challenge to ensure you are not reinventing the wheel;

– better integration is required to enable "plug and play'" functionality.

Interoperability and sharing data within and between businesses:

– knowledge is wealth, so businesses are unlikely to freely share information;

– data represents a new opportunity for business;

– better tools and methods are required to utilize historical data for data analysis.

How do we design, deploy and maintain ICT solutions to suit dynamic business environments?

In this area the contributors discussed (1) what are the barriers to adopting cyber-physical systems (CPSs) for Industry 4.0 and interoperability?; (2) how can the challenges of design, development and adoption be dealt with? and (3) how can longevity within these systems be created, that is, how can you future-proof them?

From the discussions four main barriers to success were identified as a recurring focus in the group: (1) *flexibility*, (2) *culture*, (3) *awareness* and (4) *providers*.

There were concerns that the *flexibility* required to both interact with legacy components and cope with evolving systems was not currently achievable in systems. The lack of flexibility was attributed mainly to the numerous legacy components using numerous communication standards and protocols and the investment which would be required to not only interoperate with them but to adapt to any new components.

The second barrier of *culture* was discussed in terms of a business' unwillingness to share data. Reasons for this unease included the concern that a single supply chain member might become dominant by holding all other members' data and that there would likely be a lack of visibility of who would be using their data, how they would be using it and why.

The third barrier, which formed a common theme throughout the discussions, was industrialist *awareness*. This included their awareness of existing systems and benefits as well as the costs involved in development and deployment. Encompassed within this barrier is the concept of trust and the extent to which industrialists accept and agree with a presented system's benefits and costs.

The final discussed barrier to an interoperable environment, in which systems from different suppliers can interact, is whether or not major *providers* actually want to develop this functionality within their systems. Major providers may prefer not to allow third-party integration to their systems to keep customers investing in their in-house solutions.

Exploiting Embedded Intelligence in Manufacturing Decision Support

1.1. Introduction

There have been many advances in the ability to embed intelligence into products and manufacturing equipment in order to collect important data using wireless, intelligent systems of radio frequency identification (RFID) tags and networked sensors [XU 14]. Similarly, the ICT industries that support manufacturing businesses continue to expand and develop their range of decision support software across the full range of business requirements from shop floor systems, manufacturing execution systems, enterprise resource planning, product lifecycle management and supply chain management and so on. However, while each of these systems provide important capabilities, the ability to effectively interconnect them in a meaningful trans-disciplinary way is limited [HUB 14] and must be overcome if the visions of Industry 4.0, the fourth industrial revolution (4IR) and smart manufacturing are to be met.

In the continual need for manufacturing industry to strive for a competitive edge, the ICT industry should have the potential to deliver great benefit. Given the potential of ICT, a company's multiple decision makers should have ready access to high quality, timely information directed to meet their needs, on which to base critical business decisions. This paper highlights the technological progress that has been made towards meeting this manufacturing requirement and discusses the issues that still need to be resolved.

Chapter written by Paul GOODALL, Heinz LUGO, Richard SHARPE, Kate VAN-LOPIK, Sarogini PEASE, Andrew WEST and Bob YOUNG.

1.2. Key technologies

In this section the key technologies that we consider to be of major importance are highlighted and discussed in turn in terms of their current capabilities for manufacturing decision support. If we start from a decision support perspective the base level requirements are simply to (1) be able to collect the required data, (2) to direct the appropriate aggregated data to suit the needs of a range of users and (3) to define data analysis techniques to be able to answer specific sets of multi-user questions. However, meeting these needs is not straightforward and a range of issues must be resolved. There is a need to ensure that we can communicate up-to-date high quality information against an understanding of business knowledge across a range of business activities and to be able to build software platforms that can offer a dynamic way of directing information to support the trans-disciplinary needs of multiple users. In addition to the capabilities of embedded components to collect high quality real-time data, the main requirements of such a platform are proposed as falling into the following four key categories: (1) analytics technologies, (2) application services, (3) toolkits to empower workers and (4) interoperable knowledge environments, as illustrated in Figure 1.1. Each of these areas are discussed in turn in the following sections.

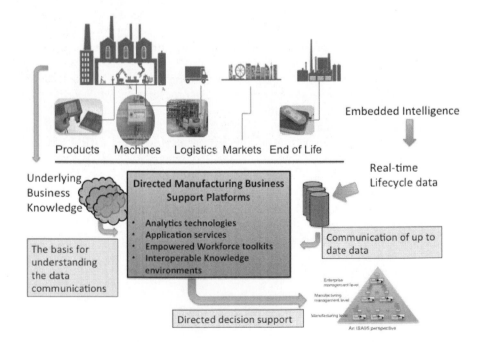

Figure 1.1. *Overview of technologies for directed decision support.*
For a color version of this figure, see www.iste.co.uk/zelm/enterprise.zip

1.2.1. *Embedded Systems*

A critical issue for any embedded system is the link between the physical world and the cyber world. The robustness of this link determines whether the system can be provided with accurate and timely measurements of the real world. In manufacturing, non-intrusive monitoring is significantly valued as it reduces requirements to pause a production line to maintain or scale infrastructure, avoiding associated productivity losses. Summarizing and extracting information from various sources of monitored contextual data, for example machine power consumption, tool vibration and asset location, then provides intelligent monitoring such as the ability to identify which components have been machined by a worn or damaged tool.

The identification of a physical object is the basis of any cyber–physical link and the methods of identification and continuous monitoring need to be appropriate to manufacturing environments, that is, they must be able to operate in harsh environments and be cost effective. Commonly used technologies are passive UHF RFID tags and wireless sensor networks (WSN) which to operate robustly may require a custom design, down to the selection of appropriate substrate, chip selection, antenna design and choice of sensors. Once physical objects can be identified, the level of intelligence can be extended to aspects such as problem notification, for example monitoring environmental conditions and decision making, such as requesting resources. As a physical object or product becomes more intelligent it must be able to access more processing power to be able to extract features from potentially numerous sensors (e.g. position, temperature, acceleration and humidity) and to interpret the results.

An example of an intelligent product's potential output is its location. Asset positioning precision increases with number of sensors, packets sent and traffic rate but is compromised by wireless packet loss that can inevitably be reduced by limiting the wireless transmissions in range of each other [PEA 17]. At the same time, an architecture of embedded sensors combined with prediction and optimization models can reduce the need for this type of continuous monitoring [PEA 18]. With an increasing demand on a product to be intelligent, the product's demand for power, internal storage and reliable and more frequent communication also increases. As intelligent products become more widespread within manufacturing, the requirement for security is also a key concern.

1.2.2. *Analytics technologies*

Data analytics refers to the process of examining and analyzing data with variable types to uncover hidden patterns, correlations and trends. The outcome of this process is to uncover a business' valuable knowledge in order to increase operational efficiency and explore new market opportunities. Within manufacturing, data analytics is often reported as a machine learning solution to a business problem [ECK 17], disregarding the fact that data analytics exploits knowledge and tools from areas such as data mining, statistical analysis and data modeling.

The usefulness of data analytics is correlated with the time span covered by the gathered data and its analysis. In the first instance, the data regarding an immediate snapshot is useful in answering questions regarding what is currently happening. The second instance drawson historical data to answer what has happened via the detection of trends and correlations. At this point the understanding of why something happened is not yet achieved through data analytics. The understanding and abstraction of knowledge is the focus of the third instance of data analytics and this is where machine learning and data modeling fit in. Once an understanding of why something has occurred has been achieved it is necessary to understand its impact on the business. Tools such as process mining are appropriate at this stage [VAN 07]. Improving and expanding the results of data analytics across a range of instances requires an understanding of the increased complexity in the volume of data required, the integration between different data types and sources of data and the improved complexity of the analysis.

1.2.3. *Application services*

While analytics technologies provide techniques that can be generally applied to identify useful information, application services package these techniques in a reusable and on-going manner to support particular business needs. The process starts from a user application perspective and defines services that can support their needs. Examples of the sorts of services that can be defined are product/workpiece traceability, process monitoring, product/workpiece monitoring, logistics monitoring and performance assessment.

For these sorts of services to be effective it is necessary to have a clear understanding of the attributes, processes, resources and constraints that they must model and simulate in order to provide useful outputs. This can be challenging within real world manufacturing environments that are highly integrated into a supply chain, and are dynamic and constantly refining and updating their products, processes and resources. Challenges for application services include the ability to adapt to changing manufacturing environments, ensure they can scale to the needs of production and provide horizontal and vertical interoperability.

1.2.4. *Empowered workforce toolkits*

An important part of directed decision support is being able to present information to suit the needs of a range of decision makers throughout the business [JAR 17]. While it can be argued that the most important decisions are ensuring that the business makes the correct long-term strategic decisions, these are only effective if the short-term operational decisions are also made effectively and the data gathered are representative of the processes being completed. A problem associated with both small and "big" data is one of ensuring veracity [WHI 12]. Veracity may be affected by factors such as choice of sensors or filtering algorithms, and the users of the devices or processes being monitored. This human input can be supported by adopting a user-centric approach. When stakeholders are involved in changes they are more likely to adopt new processes and technology and develop the shared mental models that contribute to positive behavior.

While offering effective graphical user interfaces to suit strategic- and tactical-level decision makers are important, potentially the most important are those that enable rapid reaction to real-time data changes such as anomaly detection. The provision of appropriate real-time data may also be used to develop and supplement operator skills and abilities to improve efficiency and reduce operator stress.

The role of augmented reality in empowering the workforce is potentially where rapid benefits can be achieved. These toolkits can enable workers to: access information hands free, exploit digital twins to locate resources, products and people, be made aware of critical manufacturing issues that need immediate attention or maintenance or access online resources or be connected with an expert to advise on problem solutions.

1.2.5. *Interoperable knowledge environments*

There is a wide range of trans-disciplinary knowledge and expertise that must be brought together in a successful manufacturing business. Capturing the knowledge of each discipline, the relationships that exist between them, the different semantics that different groups use and ensuring that core knowledge remains secure are just a few of the problems that knowledge environments must achieve.

However, a key requirement for knowledge to be effective is for it to be sharable. It must therefore be captured within an interoperable knowledge environment. However, at the same time, a business' core knowledge is critical to its success and needs to be secure so that it is only shared when appropriate.

A great deal of research effort has been targeted at formal ontologies as a route to knowledge exchange but has not produced the flexibility in knowledge base development that is needed. A new approach defining reusable reference ontologies is beginning to show potential [PAL 17] and is being further researched [MOR 17].

1.3. Concluding discussion

There are clearly huge business benefits to be gained from providing decision makers with high quality, accurate and timely information on which to base their decisions and inform their actions. Each of the areas mentioned above needs to be improved and enhanced for the full range of manufacturing business users to benefit.

At a basic level, real-time data can be communicated effectively. However, we are far short of the understanding needed to offer up the multiple different aggregations of information needed to satisfy the needs of trans-disciplinary business personnel. Just as importantly, the software platforms that start to offer solutions must be dynamically reconfigurable to match the rapid change requirements of manufacturing business.

1.4. References

[ECK 17] Eckart U., Abdelhakim L., Claudio G., Hohwieler E., "Decentralized data analytics for maintenance", *Procedia Manufacturing*, vol. 11, pp. 1120–1126, 2017.

[HUB 14] Huber A., Presentation by Siemens CEO, World Manufacturing Forum, Milan, http://www.ims.org/2014/07/world-manufacturing-forum-2014/, July 2014.

[JAR 17] Jardim-Goncalves R., Romero D., Grilo A., "Factories of the future: challenges and leading innovations in intelligent manufacturing", *International Journal of Computer Integrated Manufacturing*, vol. 30, no. 1, pp. 4–14, 2017.

[MOR 17] Morris K.C., Kulvatunyou S., Working towards an industrial ontology foundry to facilitate interoperability, Online, available at: http://blog.mesa.org/2017/03/working-towards-industrial-ontology.html, 2017.

[PAL 17] Palmer C., Usman Z., Canciglieri Junior O., Malucelli A., Young R.I.M., "Interoperable manufacturing knowledge systems", *International Journal of Production Research*, pp. 1-20, October 2017.

[PEA 17] Pease S.G., Conway P.P., West A.A., "Hybrid ToF and RSSI real-time semantic tracking with an adaptive industrial Internet of Things architecture", *Journal of Network and Computer Applications*, vol. 99, pp. 98–109, 2017.

[PEA 18] Pease S.G., Trueman R., Davies C., Grosberg J., Yau K.H., Kaur N., Conway P.P., West A.A., "An intelligent real-time cyber-physical toolset for energy and process prediction and optimisation in the future industrial Internet of Things", *Future Generation Computer Systems*, vol. 79, pp. 815–829, 2018.

[VAN 07] van der Aalst W.M.P., Reijers H.A., Weijters A.J.M.M., van Dongen B.F., Alves de Medeiros A.K., Song M., Verbeek H.M.W., "Business process mining: an industrial application", *Information Systems*, vol. 32, no. 5, pp. 713–732, 2007.

[WHI 12] White M., "Digital workplaces: vision and reality", *Business Information Review*, available at: http://doi.org/10.1177/0266382112470412, vol. 29, no. 4, pp. 205–214, 2012.

[XU 14] Xu L. D., He W., Li S., "Internet of Things in industries: a survey," *IEEE Transactions on Industrial Informatics*, vol. 10, no. 4, pp. 2233–2243, 2014.

Test of the Industrial Internet of Things: Opening the Black Box

2.1. Introduction

The Internet of Things (IoT) is well known in the context of smart homes, smart cities and general consumer goods. Examples include refrigerators, coffee makers and heaters equipped with smart components and which are connected to the internet. Industry IoT raises especially in the context of smart factory and Industry 4.0. It has become an essential part in terms of the digital transformation in most of the business areas.

For example, in the manufacturing industry an approach is to have manufacture capabilities represented in terms of services accessible via intranet or even via cloud [JAE 17]. This creates questions like the following: is the cloud safe or is it accessible to everyone? Are the used cyber physical systems (CPS) and IoT compliant to the whole infrastructure? Is compliance to specific standards enough for real implementation?

With an industry focus, the expectations related to robustness, interoperability and especially security increases. However, IoT approaches remain similar comparing with the consumer area [WON 16, POL 17]. On the consumer side, the focus is much more related to low cost and therefore lower security and robustness. In contrast, IoT elements used in industry are not necessarily more mature in these aspects. In fact, currently they are more used in terms of a "black box" because of missing detailed knowledge and tools to prove the IoT components. This might be gateways but also protocols, machine controllers and software applications. Finally, the user has to rely on the supplier.

Chapter written by Frank-Walter JAEKEL and Jan TORKA.

Industrial cases have been identified that even if components are proved to be compliant to protocols such as OPC-UA [OPC 17], they do not work together with others because the standard can be implemented in different ways (see section 2.4). This can block the implementation of new manufacturing components such as machinery, monitors or sensors.

IoT test software and related labels or certificates are proposed to improve the situation such as in the German IoT-Test project [PRO 17]. This project uses standards for test software as well as IoT requirements such as described in ISO/IEC JTC 1. This has been combined with use cases and specific test requirements from IoT providers and end users [PRO 18] to get a clear view on the demands for such test features, also called testware [REN 16]. The objective is to provide the end users with more knowledge about the used IoT components to avoid unpleasant surprises as far as possible.

The paper focuses on emulating industrial scenarios and use cases to test and sharpen the testware because the testware developers usually do not have direct access to manufacturing lines. Moreover, the execution of a specific scenario can influence the real manufacturing process. Therefore, environments are proposed to demonstrate specific test cases to show the power of the testware. Moreover, an adaptor is presented to test CPS/IoT interfaces related to specific configurations of shop-floor-IT infrastructures.

2.2. Scoping

Regarding IoT tests and validations the following different cases can be distinguished (Figure 2.1):

1) providing a label or certificate illustrating a specific level of compliance to security, robustness and implementation of standards;

2) generic tests to prove an IoT element against a specific infrastructure. This relates to the check of a CPS network;

3) monitoring and runtime tests, which need to be setup within an IoT infrastructure such as a virus scanner.

Points one and two are the current targets of the IoT-T project. The IoT-T project works on a testlab [TES 18] to realize point one. However, for the industrial emulator and validation adaptor it is intended to focus on all three cases.

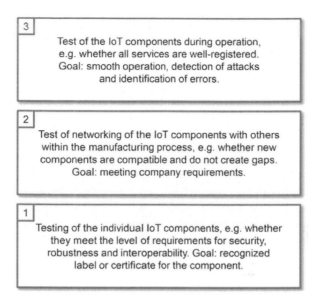

Figure 2.1. *Scopes related to potential testware and for the emulation*

2.3. Architecture of the industrial emulator

The industrial emulator aims to simulate different test cases to test the IoT test-ware as well as to demonstrate the relevance of the IoT test especially for industrial usage. The emulator should be usable by developers of IoT testware, independent of hardware components such as robots. This requires the emulation of the hardware components. In the best case scenario, machinery providers directly deliver these emulations of cyber physical systems (CPS). In any case, an adaptor is used to bridge different formats, specific implementations and provide a service interface. This approach allows an easy transformation from the emulated CPS to the real machinery. Moreover, the configuration of the adaptor will allow for the validation of interoperability demands.

The industry emulator follows the idea of manufacturing services, which can be combined to realize manufacturing processes as well as networks of manufacturing processes. The basis of the emulator is the model based on a modular shop floor IT system [JAE 17, RIE 14]. This allows that the specific configuration of a test case is designed by an enterprise model and afterwards executed by an execution engine. The execution requires an emulation of the manufacturing processes. CPS emulators provide the specific machinery data and behavior. To support the interoperability on the service side a CPS adaptor is used (Figures 2.2 and 2.3).

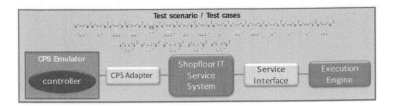

Figure 2.2. *Concept of the industrial emulation. For a color version of this figure, see www.iste.co.uk/zelm/enterprise.zip*

The CPS adaptor converts the specific formats and functionality of the CPS to a shop floor IT service system that allows the definition of specific services for the shop floor. Together with the service interface, it delivers the services to an execution engine.

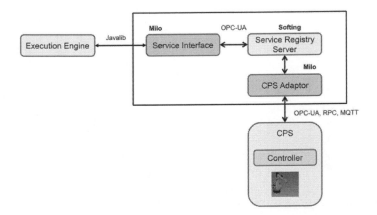

Figure 2.3. *Current technical realization. For a color version of this figure, see www.iste.co.uk/zelm/enterprise.zip*

In fact, to add a new CPS emulator or a real CPS only the interface between the CPS adaptor and the CPS needs to be realized. The execution engine enables the connection of the different CPS to realize the manufacturing network of cyber physical systems.

Figure 2.4 illustrates a test configuration for an availability test of services for an IoT system (here a robot). This test is intended to ensure that the specified services are available. This test must be fulfilled by a plant or system supplier and is based on precise specifications, which could be standardized in the future. Among other things, the aim is to ensure that new IoT systems can be safely integrated into existing IoT infrastructures and networks.

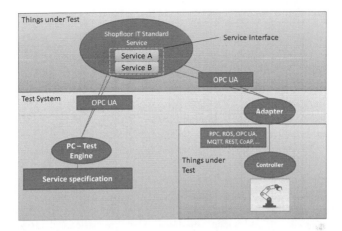

Figure 2.4. *Concept of the test scenario. For a color version of this figure, see www.iste.co.uk/zelm/enterprise.zip*

2.4. Application case

An industrial scenario derived from challenges related to the setup of smart new shop floor IT infrastructures illustrates the demand. Each of the equipment and machinery acts in terms of IoT with digital components (controllers) connected to the network (intra- or internet). Different machinery suppliers provide the equipment and machinery. They confirm them to be compliant to specific standards such as OPC-UA. However, during the setup of the infrastructure they appear non-interoperable because of specific interface configurations. One challenge is that OPC-UA can provide different security approaches. If the CPS uses different ones they might not work properly in the IT infrastructure. Furthermore, the set of supported functions could be different. Related to a report of the German Federal Office for Information Security (Bundesamt für Sicherheit in der Informationstechnik) [BSI 17] the security level of OPC-UA can be variable depending on the configuration. Therefore, it is also important to test potential security issues to create robustness against IT attacks.

2.5. Future work and conclusion

The aim is to support the "plug and produce" behavior of machine–tool interfaces. It becomes important in the context of smart and digital factory because it ensures a seamless plug and produce of new equipment into the shop floor IT infrastructure. It needs to cover different protocol aspects such as compliance tests for OPC-UA, MQTT, DDS, CoAP by using mostly existing open source tests. More importantly it needs to validate machine–tool interfaces against specific interoperability, performance and security demands. This requires a configuration method of formats and demands. The configuration needs to be executable by a validation service. A CPS adaptor and an execution service will comprise the interface capability validation. The CPS adaptor will cover specific aspects of frameworks and protocols (OPC-UA, DDS, CoAP, MQTT, TCP/IP, etc.). The execution service runs the validation. Related to OPC-UA, both services are available as prototypes. At the time of writing, the configuration is in development and will be tested in summer 2018.

2.6. References

[BSI 17] Federal Office for Information Security (Bundesamt für Sicherheit in der Informationstechnik; BSI), Open Platform Communications Unified Architecture Security Analysis, available at: https://www.bsi.bund.de/Shared Docs/Downloads/EN/BSI/ Publications/Studies/OPCUA/OPCUA.htm, 2017.

[JAE 17] Jaekel F.-W., Torka J., Eppelein M. *et al.*, "Model based, modular configuration of cyber physical systems for the information management on shop-floor", in Ciuciu I., Debruyne C., Panetto H. *et al.* (eds), *LNCS, OTM 2017 Workshops*, Springer, 2017.

[OPC 17] OPC-UA, available at: https://opcfoundation.org/about/opc-technologies/opc-ua, 2017.

[POL 17] Poleg Y., "Consumer IoT vs. Industrial IoT – What are the Differences?", *IoTforall*, available at: https://www.iotforall.com/consumer-iot-vs-industrial-iot, July 2 2017.

[PRO 17] Projekt IoT-T, available at: http://www.iot-t.de/, 2017.

[PRO 18] Projekt IoT-T: Resources, available at: http://www.iot-t.de/en/resources/, 2018.

[REN 16] Rennoch A., Wagner M., "Challenges and ideas for IoT testing", *Internet des Objects*, Genie Logiciel, no. 119, pp. 26–30, December 2016.

[RIE 14] Riedel O., Margraf T., Stölzle S. *et al.*, Modellbasierte modulare Shopfloor IT – Integration in die Werkzeuge der Digitalen Fabrik, Study, Electronic Publication, available at: http://publica.fraunhofer.de/eprints/urn_nbn_de_0011-n-3162488.pdf, accessed July 31, 2017, 2014.

[TES 18] Testlabor, available at: http://www.iot-testlab.de/en/, 2018.

[WON 16] Wong W., "What's the difference between consumer and industrial IoT?", Electronic Design, September 21, available at www.electronicdesign.com/iot/what-s-difference-between-consumer-and-industrial-iot, 2016.

3

Intelligent Decision-support Systems in Supply Chains: Requirements Identification

The research area on artificial intelligence and machine learning is pushing a trigger effect for the appearance of a new generation of intelligent decision-support systems (iDSS), which aim at achieving more efficient, agile and sustainable industrial systems. The implementation of intelligent DSS is conceived as a challenging issue for managing sustainable operations among the enterprises taking part in supply chains (SC), in an environment characterized by rapid changes and uncertainty. This paper establishes the state of the art and identifies new research challenges and trends for designing intelligent DSS, within the SC context (iDSS-SC).

3.1. Introduction

Current markets, globally operating, must work in an environment that demands agility and resilience of the enterprises; in which the decision-making process has to be as quick as possible, by considering all the information available that may affect the decision. The consideration of DSS has been widely addressed in the context of individual enterprises [GOU 17]. Nevertheless, enterprises are more and more aware about the establishment of collaborative relationships, and business, among its downstream and upstream partners [AND 16]. It is because of this that the DSS research area needs to extend individual DSS towards an extended DSS that covers the decision-making process performed within the supply chain (SC) [BOZ 09]. Moreover, novel SC-DDSs have to be profitable and include the

Chapter written by Eduardo SAIZ, Raul POLER and Beatriz ANDRES.

new trends and advances achieved in the research areas of artificial intelligence and machine learning. Adapting these new solutions and approaches will create intelligent supply chain DSSs (iDSS-SC) with the aim of supporting the decision-making process in collaborative environments between SC partners.

It is also a reality that iDSS-SC should facilitate the inclusion of interoperability functionalities between SC partners, willing to carry out collaborative decision-making. Providing interoperability functionalities, when designing intelligent DSS, is the basis on which iDSS-SC must be built [PAN 07, CHE 08].

Working on this research line, the European Commission [EU 18] has launched several calls in the scope of H2020, that have resulted in the emergence of multi-country projects to address the object of discussion: intelligent and interoperable DSS in the SC context. To that extent, it is worth mentioning the following projects: C2NET, CREMA, MANTIS and vf-OS [C2N 15, CRE 15, MAN 15 and VFO 16]. Particularly, C2NET intends to be an intelligent DSS that covers all the planning processes of the supply chain, including replenishment, production and delivery planning. The collaborative, optimization and data collection framework modules developed allow individual enterprises and SCs to perform collaborative decisions based on real time information and in an automated way. The three aforementioned modules of C2NET are embedded in a cloud service and developed considering interoperability features. Regarding the CREMA and MANTIS projects, they are focused on developing intelligent DSS in the context of maintenance planning and proactive maintenance prediction. CREMA aims to simplify the establishment, management, adaptation, and monitoring of dynamic, cross-organizational manufacturing processes following Cloud manufacturing principles. MANTIS retrieves information from physical systems (e.g. industrial machines, vehicles, renewable energy assets), which are monitored continuously by a broad and diverse range of intelligent sensors, resulting in massive amounts of data. Intelligent systems are part of a larger network of heterogeneous and collaborative systems connected via robust communication mechanisms able to operate in challenging environments. In this context, MANTIS seeks to transform raw data into knowledge to create a new process of decision-making. Finally, the vf-OS project is more transversal in terms of its application as an iDSS-SC. vf-OS provides a portable, multitasking and multi-user operating system, which enables the creation of APIs to connect software, drivers to connect machines, and apps that contain modules such as data analytics, optimizers and so on. Apps are developed for their use as a DSS to facilitate the connection between different legacy systems, basing their deployment in interoperable functions; so that the developers do not have to deal with specific connection details and the heterogeneity of hardware and software systems that characterizes SC.

3.2. State of the art

This section introduces some concepts that could serve as a background for the design of intelligent DSSs in supply chains, namely business analytics, supply chain analytics, key performance indicators, machine learning, and data managing.

Business analytics (BA) and business intelligence (BI) are viewed as similar terms, which refer to different analytical capabilities for organizational business processes and decision support systems [CHA 13]. According to [ROB 10] BA enables the accomplishment of business objectives through reporting of data to analyse trends, creating predictive models for forecasting and optimizing business processes to achieve improved performance. BA aims to find "intelligence" within large volumes of the enterprise data (products, services, customers, manufacturing, sales, etc.).

Supply chain analytics (SCA) and supply chain intelligence (SCI) refer to BA for supply chain management, in uncertain business environments [TEE 97]. Seeing the SC as a set of four kinds of processes: plan, source, produce and deliver [API 17], SCI empowers decision makers with real-time performance insight across the extended supply chain. In this way, it allows continuous, KPI-based supply chain improvement. SCI helps organizations tackle the increased global complexity that impacts supply chains. It collects and presents crucial data from all trading partners in easy-to-use, customizable dashboards on a computer or tablet. SCI metrics illustrate where performance is weak or strong, allowing executives to make smart and strategic decisions [GT 18].

In all the above concepts, it is crucial to use key performance indicators (KPIs) and other metrics to monitor the enterprise and supply chain performance in several areas such as finance, production systems, marketing or planning. Therefore, technologies for gathering, storing and analyzing data are required for the proper measurement of KPIs. Accordingly, managing data stored in the enterprises' database's is a relevant challenge and becomes an important technical issue, especially when these data have to be exchanged with other SC partners. The need of technologies for addressing real time data gathering and analysis, catalyses research activities regarding sensors, IoT, CPS, linked data, data privacy, federated identity, big data, data mining, sensing technologies and so on.

Machine learning (ML) or intelligent machines (IM) refers to a specific area of artificial intelligence the objective of which is to develop techniques that allow machines to learn. It is applied to machine and sensor networks that analyze performance in predefined processes. It also explores the study and construction of learning methods and algorithms that can learn from and make predictions based on input data [CAM 09].

3.3. Trends in the research area of iDSS-SC

Taking as a starting point the state of the art described above, this section is devoted to identifying the next trends and concepts to be addressed in order to design and implement an iDSS-SC. A summary of the requirements needed to develop these kinds of iDSS-SCs that apply novel trends such as business analytics, business intelligence, supply chain analytics, key performance indicators, machine learning and data managing, is proposed. The requirements have been identified using a panel of experts working in the research area. iDSS-SCs must be accessible for all the partners of the supply chain. In this regard, systems and technologies in the cloud will favor the ubiquitous connection of all enterprises regardless of their location, as the previously noted H2020 projects demonstrate.

As stated before, SC intelligence (business analytics, supply chain analytics and machine learning) is based on data analysis processes, and transforms simple data into usable information, which is capable of supporting decision making by the analysis and prediction of the enterprise or SC behavior when different events occur. Therefore, data exchange among enterprises of the SC and the iDSS-SC is a key factor. Thus, data security and trust are two relevant concepts to address. In order to achieve SC visibility in all areas security issues – for example access rights – must be addressed.

Moreover, enterprises seek the easy facilitation of a connection between their legacy systems and the iDSS-SC. One important requirement is to design user-friendly cloud services that allow connection in real time, communication technologies to carry out teleconferences, or technologies that allow sending messages. In this research field, it is crucial to design and implement systems that generate alert messages when the iDSS-SC detects deviations. For the detection of deviations, the SC needs to define KPIs and their corresponding threshold values. An iDSS-SC will be able to monitor the defined KPIs, analyze potential deviations, and ultimately predict potential behaviors in the SC operations; these deviations and predictions will be communicated to the SC decision maker, via notifications from the cloud service in which the iDSS-SC is deployed. The notifications will be communicated to the subscribed SC stakeholders, making the security process more sustainable and considering the need to maintain high security and privacy controls.

iDSS-SC will be also able to create alternative decision-making scenarios, according to data gathered and processed for the KPIs identified. The generation of such scenarios will enable the decision maker to simulate different options of operating within the SC, taking into account diverse inter and intra-enterprise characteristics for more accurate decision making.

3.4. New research challenges

Considering the identified trends, new challenges and areas requiring further research in iDSS-SC, within the SC context, are identified:

– Automatic generation of not only *predefined* rules but also *predictive* rules. The aimed predictive rules can be created applying artificial intelligence technologies taking analytics as base data. Predictive analysis will allow the generation of predictive rules to figure out the future behavior of the SC system based on the current aggregated values extracted from the monitoring and measurement of KPIs. Predictive rules will enable the decision maker to identify how deviations can create new future scenarios. In this regard, the iDSS-SC must be able to identify that something not specifically modeled (predefined rules) can occur (predictive rules).

– Big Data, Data Analytics, and Machine Learning technologies have to be used for the *identification of patterns* and for the generation of potential scenarios when predictive rules are created, based on *KPI analysis*. The use of machine learning technologies should work with aggregated information and analyze *aggregate values* for *simulating patterns* with different scenarios, and make analytic predictions. SC decision makers will be able to anticipate future changes, or deal with current uncertainties, through the predictive functionalities of the iDSS-SC. Prediction will be handled taking into account the current behavior of KPIs and analyzing past behaviors that occurred in a given time period.

– Supply chain analytics must deal with lot of information gathered from SC stakeholders. In this regard, *data security* is a key factor when designing DSS in cloud platforms. Security when using artificial intelligence systems could be dealt with by analyzing all the information generated in the SC, and gathering sets of key variables that will be used to carry out learning and prediction processes. Moreover, data security and privacy that comes from the different companies that form the SC is also a key research area.

– Data aggregation can be faced with the definition of master KPIs to gather information (from the past and the present). SCAs must work within current master KPI values that will allow the identification of future potential behaviors. The designed iDSS-SC will support decision-makers about which decision to carry out and will provide an insight into the future effects of the decision made.

3.5. Conclusions

This paper carries out the state of the art and identifies new research challenges and trends for designing iDSS-SCs. Future work will be devoted to completing the list of requirements needed to develop new iDSS-SCs according to the opinion of experts and industrial users.

3.6. References

[AND 16] Andres B., Poler R., "A decision support system for the collaborative selection of strategies in enterprise networks", *Decision Support Systems*, vol. 91, pp. 113–123, 2016.

[API 17] APICS, Supply Chain Operations Reference (SCOR) model, Online, available at: http://www.apics.org/apics-for-business/products-and-services/apics-scc-frameworks/scor, 2017.

[BOZ 09] Boza A., Ortiz A., Vicens E. *et al.*, "A framework for a decision support system in a hierarchical extended enterprise decision context", *Enterprise Interoperability*, vol. 38, pp. 113–124, 2009.

[C2N 15] C2NET, Cloud Collaborative Manufacturing Networks, available at: http://cordis.europa.eu/project/rcn/193440_es.html, 2015.

[CAM 09] Camarinha-Matos L.M., "Collaborative networked organizations: status and trends in manufacturing", *Annual Reviews in Control*, vol. 33, pp. 199–208, 2009.

[CHA 13] Chae B.K., Olson D.L., "Business analytics for supply chain: a dynamic-capabilities framework", *International Journal of Information Technology and Decision Making*, vol. 12, no. 1, pp. 9–26, 2013.

[CHE 08] Chen D., Doumeingts G., Vernadat F., "Architectures for enterprise integration and interoperability: past, present and future", *Computers in Industry*, vol. 59, no. 7, pp. 647–659, 2008.

[CRE 15] CREMA, Cloud-based Rapid Elastic Manufacturing, available at: http://cordis.europa.eu/ project/rcn/193459_en.html, 2015.

[EU 18] European Commission, European Research Council, Online, available at: https://ec.europa.eu/programmes/horizon2020/en/h2020-section/european-research-council, 2018.

[GOU 07] Goul M., Corral K., "Enterprise model management and next generation decision support", *Decision Support Systems*, vol. 43, pp. 915–932, 2007.

[GT 18] GT Nexus Commerce Networks Solutions, available at: http://www.gtnexus.com/solutions/supply-chain-intelligence, 2018.

[MAN 15] MANTIS, Cyber Physical System based Proactive Collaborative Maintenance, available at: http://cordis.europa.eu/project/rcn/198079_en.html, 2015.

[PAN 07] Panetto H., "Towards a classification framework for interoperability of enterprise applications", *International Journal of Computer Integrated Manufacturing*, vol. 20, no. 8, pp. 727–740, 2007.

[ROB 10] Robinson A., Levis J., Bennett G., "INFORMS to officially join analytics movement", *OR/MS Today*, vol. 37, no. 5, p. 59, 2010.

[TEE 97] Teece D., Pisano G., Shuen A., "Dynamic capabilities and strategic management", *Strategic Management Journal*, vol. 18, pp. 509–533, 1997.

[VFO 16] vf-OS, Virtual Factory Open Operating System, available at: http://cordis.europa.eu/project/rcn/205550_es.html, 2016.

A Total Solution Provider's Perspective on Embedded Intelligence in Manufacturing Decision-support Systems

4.1. Introduction

"Embedded Intelligence" is being extracted from manufacturing equipment to generate information that improves productivity by reducing breakdown times and provides operators with effective knowledge to do their jobs more efficiently. It also supports engineers by storing knowledge on frequently occurring faults and breakdowns through the collection and analysis of captured data. The key to providing effective data for decision-support systems is a multifaceted approach to data collection. Multiple sources of data are pulled from shop floor devices and fed up to populate decision making systems at the enterprise level. The ability to collect this multi-process data is a major challenge considering that most companies (especially tiers 1 and 2 automotive suppliers, for example) have multivendor machines with a variety of control systems; this lack of interoperability makes the connectivity and collection of data difficult.

The challenge is to create an overarching system that can "glue" all the data sources together to give a coherent and meaningful single source of data that can be passed up the knowledge chain to provide valuable enterprise knowledge. This knowledge can of course be fed back down the chain to optimize processes on the shop floor.

This paper offers an approach to creating the "glue" that binds the knowledge chain.

Chapter written by Gash BHULLAR.

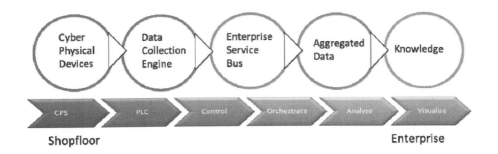

Figure 4.1. *Knowledge chain of pulled data from the shop floor. For a color version of this figure, see www.iste.co.uk/zelm/enterprise.zip*

4.2. Presenting knowledge for decision makers

In the manufacturing domain, as the roll-out of Industry 4.0 gathers momentum, the focus of increasing production, efficiency and reducing waste remains the "holy grail" for all manufacturing companies. To achieve this, it is vital to understand the connectivity aspects of an enterprise with respect to business processes, life-cycle management and understanding of the processes involved in the production process. The more "connected" an enterprise becomes, the better their chances of achieving the reduction of costs and increasing profits. The goal of connecting systems is to collect data for decision-support systems that can present themselves at many parts of the company. Taking a simplistic view, taking the production team for example, the usual focus of engineers and managers is to adopt a "pull" approach which takes data from shop-floor systems and presents it to management at board level to follow key performance indicators (KPIs) which are usually derived at this level. As can be seen in Figure 4.1, many defined layers are crossed to present the data required for the decision makers. These layers are normally points of hardware and infrastructure change. So generally, the cyber physical devices (CPDs) can be anything from proximity sensors to intelligent monitoring devices typically supplied by a wide variety of vendors with differing interface requirements such as voltage or current loop connections. These traditionally always interface with programable logic controllers (PLCs and control systems) at the shop-floor level which again can come from a variety of vendors such as Siemens, Rockwell, Omron, Schneider Electric and so on. The orchestration software starts to link from the shop floor to IT systems which are normally office-based systems and usually linked to enterprise resource planning (ERP) systems. These systems are again provided by different vendors such as SAP or Oracle. Finally, the analysis and visualization is carried out at the intranet, edge (fog) or cloud level depending on the company's data management policies but very much at the office level and again this could be provided by third party operators using Amazon Web Services (AWS), Microsoft Azure, Siemens MindSphere or IBM Watson, amongst others.

This situation certainly hinders the connectivity challenges faced by the enterprise and of course ideally it would be great to have a single vendor that can connect the shop floor to the outer limits of the enterprise. For a brand-new enterprise setting up from scratch, it may be possible to contract a specific vendor to completely install a plant using only their own hardware and software, but usually this is not a possibility. It would also leave the organization vulnerable to single-source provider issues. A novel approach to this dilemma is to create an overarching platform and architecture that will allow connection points to be made at strategic points in the chain. A platform called Industreweb 4.0 (www.industreweb.com) can do just this task.

4.3. Modeling the connectivity of products and services

When considering all the connectivity challenges present in an organization, a deeper understanding is required to model the organization. Such a model exists in the form of the Reference Architectural Model Industry 4.0 [HAN 15], which is abbreviated to RAMI 4.0. It consists of a three-dimensional coordinate system that describes all crucial aspects of Industry 4.0. In this way, complex interrelations can be broken down into smaller and simpler clusters. This paper assumes the reader will familiarize themselves with the general concepts of the model which is well documented by the German Electrical and Electronic Manufacturers' Association (ZVEI), one of the most important manufacturers' associations in Germany. Their product portfolio is available at https://www.zvei.org which also includes presentations by their members [HAN 15], which are used as a basis for this paper.

The RAMI 4.0 model offers vendors, suppliers, customers a way to map their processes and products onto a three-dimensional grid which has three axes:

Axis 1: The "Hierarchy Levels" axis – Indicated on the right horizontal axis are hierarchy levels from IEC 62264, the international standards series for enterprise IT and control systems. These hierarchy levels represent the different functionalities within factories or facilities. To represent the Industry 4.0 environment, these functionalities have been expanded to include workpieces, labeled "Product", and the connection to the Internet of Things and Services, labeled "Connected World" or in this paper, "Cloud Services".

Axis 2: The "OSI Layers" – The seven layers on the vertical axis serve to describe the decomposition of a machine into its properties structured layer by layer, that is, the virtual mapping of a machine. Such representations originate from information and communication technology, where properties of complex systems are commonly broken down into layers.

Axis 3: The "Life Cycle and Value Stream" axis is the left horizontal axis representing the life-cycle of facilities and products, based on IEC 62890 for life-cycle management. Furthermore, a distinction is made between "types" and "instances". A "type" becomes an "instance" when design and prototyping have been completed and the actual product is being manufactured.

Within these three axes, all crucial aspects of Industry 4.0 can be mapped, allowing objects and machines to be classified according to the model. Highly flexible Industry 4.0 concepts can thus be described and implemented using RAMI 4.0. It also allows solution providers to map the requirements of embedded intelligence in manufacturing decision support systems so that the knowledge chain depicted in Figure 4.1 can be broadened out to identify the connectivity points. In the case of Industreweb 4.0, the connectivity elements of the knowledge chain are mapped onto this reference architecture model showing a typical implementation for a manufacturing in a three-dimensional way. Figure 4.2 shows the individual components of Industreweb 4.0 such as the Collect engine (IW Collect) which is used to pick up data from sensors and PLCs on the shop floor the data can then be presented using Industreweb Global (IW Global) onto any web browser.

Figure 4.2. *Industreweb 4.0 Mapped to RAMI 4.0 Model. For a color version of this figure, see www.iste.co.uk/zelm/enterprise.zip*

Figure 4.2 also shows up-and-coming communications protocols such as OPC-UA and the areas these protocols are extending to from product to the work center and also linking the application layer down to the internet protocols. These connections are further extended using Industreweb 4.0 which can carry the data to cloud-based systems using the AMQP/MQTT protocols that the OPC-UA PUB-SUB services look to provide.

The mapping is essential to allow intelligent products to be interconnected so they can provide useful information such as location, temperature or fault data to wider parts of the organization which ultimately eliminates repeated or duplicate data in the system and allows near-time information to be reported further up the knowledge chain.

4.4. Business knowledge generation

Once any connectivity issues are overcome, opportunities arise for novel ways to present the gathered data. Connectivity mapping allows isolated software packages to be interconnected. A simple example would be Statistical Process Control (SPC) which is used in multiple areas of production to keep the processes within tolerance. As standalone systems they serve their intended purpose. So an organization could typically deploy multiple applications across the shop floor which would keep the localized production of parts to a set quality standard but the data generated by the processes would not be correlated to other areas of the plant to find the root causes of the deviation. Siemens (amongst other vendors) provide shop floor connectivity through "MindSphere" to processes that are analyzed in the cloud and give valuable data to those who wish to monitor the trends. But whilst these vertical connections from "shop floor to cloud" can provide relevant data, there still needs to be horizontal connectivity to link different knowledge sources to show a wider correlation of data that would ensure business support systems can be made effective. This allows the data analytics tools to pass data to the relevant departments and potentially allow self-corrections and adaptions to processes to be suggested to the operators of the processes and even back down the integrated supply chain. Industreweb 4.0 provides data via web browsers so with the correct login credentials, anyone worldwide can get access to this dynamic knowledge.

4.5. Presenting data in a "human" way

Once you have access to enterprise data, the next challenge is to present it in a way that is meaningful to the recipient of those data. If the data are presented in a more "human friendly" way then users of the data can make far more informed decisions based on a better understanding of the data. Gaming technology has made its way to the manufacturing shop floor but the world of operators and machinery is far removed from the normal "shoot'em up" games that many play on gaming consoles. It's not the technology that inhibits the right type of software being deployed, it's the knowledge needed to enable the crossover from control systems to IT systems and ultimately web technologies. Industreweb 4.0 again addresses this, especially if it looks like decision support is able to present information to suit the needs of a range of decision makers throughout the business.

Figure 4.3. *Presenting data back down the knowledge chain. For a color version of this figure, see www.iste.co.uk/zelm/enterprise.zip*

4.6. Conclusions

To provide decision makers with high quality, accurate and timely data, total enterprise connectivity is essential. Enterprises have been collecting data for decades but if it not presented usefully and in context then data collection systems will continue to collate data forever. Industry 4.0 offers a way to do business radically different and offers the opportunity to use business data in new and interesting ways. The secret is having a "glue" that can link all the different datapoints together to provide business intelligence for decision-support systems.

4.7. References

[HAN 15] Hankel M., Rexroth B., "The Reference Architectural Model Industrie 4.0 (RAMI 4.0)", Report, ZVEI, available at: http://www.zvei.org/en/press-media/publications/the-reference-architectural-model-industrie-40-rami-40/, 2015.

Business Impact of Enterprise Interoperability

Part 2 Summary: Business Impact of Applications of Enterprise Interoperability

Discussion

The topic of interoperability has become more common in industrial parlance. Work appears in several industrial research and development projects on vertical as well as horizontal interoperability fostered by the digital transformation. The topics considered include:

– seamless cooperation between strategy, tactic and operation;

– flexibility in value networks;

– implementation of new IT technologies such as Cyber Physical systems and the Internet of Things;

– use of IT service provision and Cloud technologies.

This calls for a mechanism that supports the management of all of this information as well as the structured documentation and retrieval of data and mechanism related to the interoperability of an organization. It incorporates exchange protocols, standards followed by the organization, system landscape and the processes related to managing interoperability with other organizations. This will not only improve the federation in global production networks but also improve cycles within the organizations. See also Interop-VLAB TG9 Enterprise Interoperability Management, available at: http://interop-vlab.eu/tg9-enterprise-interoperability-management/.

Based on enterprise interoperability (EI) use cases, the workshop aimed to identify the business impact by externalizing artifacts of methods and procedures to

Chapter written by Frank-Walter JAEKEL.

achieve EI in current approaches and applications. The presentations given in the workshop delivered examples of interoperability challenges together with potential solutions and savings regarding cost and time as well as quality improvements:

– enterprise interoperability management and artifacts;

– challenges for adaptable energy-efficient production processes;

– interoperability requirements for an adaptive production system-of-systems;

– platforms for the industrial Internet of Things: enhancing business models through interoperability.

Following the presentations, a set of questions were discussed using meta-plan techniques:

– what are the business effects of interoperability?

– what are your expectations from the workshop?

– do you see specific artifacts related to enterprise interoperability?

– do you have application cases related to interoperability, especially enterprise interoperability?

– how can we manage enterprise interoperability?

A general question discussed, was "does the term interoperability sell". The workshop participants stated that even though the term has become more normal in large organizations, it does not sell or at least not sell enough. It requires business cases to point out benefits. In fact, interoperability sells much better under different umbrellas such as industrial IoT, global cooperation, self-controlled manufacturing or cloud services.

5

Enterprise Interoperability Management and Artifacts

5.1. Introduction

"In a world of converging yet diverse technologies, complex ICT systems must communicate and interwork on all levels" is the definition of interoperability according to the European Telecommunications Standards Institute (ETSI) [ETS 18]. Digital transformation, Industrie 4.0, smart factories and the Internet of Things (IoT) are demanding interoperability of the systems involved independent of whether they are physical, cyber physical or just software. It requires a foundation for seamless, clear and secure communication called "interoperability". Moreover, the cooperation between different organizations such as manufacturers, service providers, and government, requires "enterprise interoperability".

Interoperability of organizations (horizontal enterprise interoperability) and within the organization from business to operation (vertical enterprise interoperability) is a major issue when it comes to success in the digital transformation. Interoperability is a key factor when smart services inside organizations and autonomous factories have to cooperate. Currently the responsibility for the related interoperability is distributed in different departments and working groups and is quite often seen in IT departments. It makes it difficult to have a comprehensive view related to the interoperability standards and capabilities of an organization. This is a risk for the implementation of new strategies and technologies because new systems might not fit into the target infrastructures. It could be the interface of a Cyber Physical System (CPS) which does not fit onto the shop floor or a new machinery

Chapter written by Frank-Walter JAEKEL.

supplier not requesting remote maintenance independent of the security policies of the organization.

5.2. Situation and motivation

In recent years the topic of interoperability has become more common in industry. Related work appears in several industrial research and development projects from strategic aspects over organizational projects from joint venture implementation to IT system implementation, and shop-floor integration into IT systems to service-based IT configuration in a federated environment.

Self-organizing production networks will have an enormous impact on companies and their networks, and require management of interoperability in smart service infrastructures. Interoperability assumptions appear on an operational as well as business level. For example, if a system can directly decide to order goods, it acts not only on a communication level sending orders but also on a contractual level related to the payments and legal regulations.

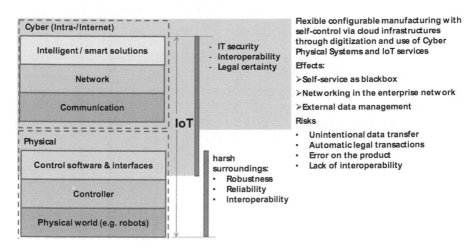

Figure 5.1. *Example of demands [IOT 18]*

In general, interoperability becomes mandatory for the digital transformation between and inside organizations. Self-controlled manufacturing in the scope of smart factories requires networking of everything involved in the production including cyber physical systems, application services, manufacturing services and IoT components. This opens fields previously disconnected from the term "interoperability", like manufacturing and shop-floor management. Therefore, the management of interoperability constraints becomes important such as protocols, architectures, security demands and semantic aspects related to the required interfaces.

The example in Figure 5.1 illustrates constrains in a CPS infrastructure. The challenges of interoperability, security and legal certainty are dependent; for example different security levels will block the communication. If the processes and responsibilities are not well understood, risks are underestimated or overseen.

This calls for a mechanism that supports the management of this information and also the structured documentation and retrieval of data and mechanisms related to the interoperability demands of an organization. This will improve the federation in global production networks and require improvement cycles within the organizations.

Enterprise modeling techniques have been used for decades to document and implement workflows for management systems [JAE 16], such as ISO9001 [ISO 18]. Artifacts exist in the interoperability domain to use similar technologies to create an information basis for the management in an organization.

5.3. Approach

The main directions of the management of interoperability are:

1) reference models for the interoperability management expressing the way to manage interoperability within and across organizations. This needs to cover the recording or development of management methods, procedures and processes;

2) indications for the enterprise interoperability in terms of key performance indicators expressing the quality and providing guidance for its management;

3) comprehensive and operational description of the interoperability artifacts and their interrelation with other aspects of the organization such as processes, organization, services and machinery.

What is an artifact in this context? An artifact in the context of this chapter is any method or approach that should compose interoperability management. In the last few decades, European projects developed several artifacts such as maturity and assessment models, standard frameworks and protocols, ontologies, reference models, enterprise-modeling technologies. INTEROP-NoE and ATHENA-IP was a starting point but INTEROP-VLAB still collects project results related to interoperability aspects [INT 18]. This conglomerate of different artifacts is available to work on methods for enterprise interoperability management and industrial applications. The application can start from the integrated management system (IMS) concept. Enterprises use IMS to survive audits such as quality management audits (ISO9001) as well as to achieve and assure certificates. IMS also supports the implementation of new processes and standards into organizations. "An integrated management system (IMS) integrates all of an organization's systems and processes in to one complete framework, enabling an organization to work as a single unit with unified objectives" [ISS 18].

The state of the art about IMS is its generation from an enterprise model. An example is the integrated enterprise modeling supported by MO²GO system [MOO 18] and the Process Assistant (PA) [PRO 18]. The steps are drafted below:

– training of the organization in the management system and the use of IEM, MO²GO and the PA;

– creation of the information model and process model of an enterprise by the organization;

– transference of the enterprise model into the PA in terms of an IMS representation which interlinks responsibilities, documents, organizations and processes;

– publishing of the IMS within the PA through the organization, accessible via the intranet;

– performance of audits and use of the PA as an information base for processes, responsibilities and data.

Technologies such as IoT, Industrie 4.0, Cloud and Fog computing and so on require interoperability which needs rules, structures, processes, policies and the management of said technologies and information.

The current IMS covers usually processes, documents, risks, organizational structures, IT systems, KPIs and its interrelation. This is the foundation to extend it with interoperability artifacts. Data, protocols and semantic and business aspects can be related to communication standards such as OPC-UA or DDS (Data Distribution Service), interface descriptions, processes and responsibilities and the use of specific ontologies. This will also include company standards for interoperability (e.g. automotive sector) in relation to international standards or extending international standards. The principle was published in 2010; see Figure 5.2. But at this time knowledge about interoperability demands in industry was less matured. This has now changed. In communication with industry interoperability counts as an important topic. However, from these experiences the interoperability is often seen as a local issue. Therefore, islands of interoperability solutions are created. A general overview of what is in use and where the white areas are is missing. Furthermore, the technology and available solutions in terms of IMS mature. The enterprise model generated IMS is available and powerful in terms of extensions of data and functionalities.

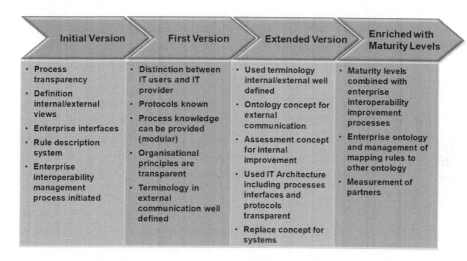

Initial Version	First Version	Extended Version	Enriched with Maturity Levels
• Process transparency • Definition internal/external views • Enterprise interfaces • Rule description system • Enterprise interoperability management process initiated	• Distinction between IT users and IT provider • Protocols known • Process knowledge can be provided (modular) • Organisational principles are transparent • Terminology in external communication well defined	• Used terminology internal/external well defined • Ontology concept for external communication • Assessment concept for internal improvement • Used IT Architecture including processes interfaces and protocols transparent • Replace concept for systems	• Maturity levels combined with enterprise interoperability improvement processes • Enterprise ontology and management of mapping rules to other ontology • Measurement of partners

Figure 5.2. *Concept for enterprise interoperability management system. Source: [JOC 10]*

The integration of enterprise interoperability into a management framework and an integrated management system will provide the following benefits:

– comprehensive view of the interoperability capability of the organization;

– identification of white areas related to interoperability;

– reduction of interoperability barriers in terms of missing information about interfaces and protocols;

– acceleration of the introduction of new technologies, machinery and business cooperation;

– cost reduction related to sufficient interoperability and reduction of interoperability barriers.

5.4. Future work and conclusion

Many areas, such as seamless connection from business to operation, industrial Internet of Things, cyber physical systems, Smart Factory and self-controlled production, demand interoperability. It targets infrastructure, protocols, communication, organization and process as well as shop-floor and service provision. Approaches such as Industrie 4.0, Smart Factory, industrial Internet of Things (IIoT) and industrial web drive the demand of interoperability. Today, interoperability is a hot topic but needs wider communication in terms of benefits and business models. The return of investment needs to be better understood and communicated. Tasks are:

– identification of the industry demands and requirements by case studies;

– definition of a minimum information framework;

– description of business cases and solutions;

– extension of the management systems by further interoperability aspects for research and industry.

5.5. References

[ETS 18] EUROPEAN TELECOMMUNICATIONS STANDARDS INSTITUTE (ETSI), available at: http://www.etsi.org/standards/why-we-need-standards/interoperability, accessed March 13, 2018.

[INT 18] INTEROP-VLAB, available at: http://interop-vlab.eu/deliverables/, accessed March 13, 2018.

[IOT 18] IoT-T, available at: http://www.iot-t.de/wp-content/uploads/sites/11/2017/06/IoT-T_R1.1.pdf, accessed March 15, 2018.

[ISO 18] INTERNATIONAL ORGANIZATION FOR STANDARDIZATION, available at: https://www.iso.org/iso-9001-quality-management.html, accessed March 15, 2018.

[ISS 18] INTEGRATED STANDARDS STORE, What is an integrated management system, available at: http://integrated-standards.com/articles/what-is-integrated-management-system/, 2018.

[JAE 16] JAEKEL F.-W., GERING P., WINTRICH N. et al., Integration of risk and interoperability into integrated management systems, IESA, 2016.

[JOC 10] JOCHEM R., ZELM M., JAEKEL F.-W., Enterprise interoperability enabling support of traceability along the product lifecycle, PLM, 2010.

[MOO 18] MO²GO, available at: http://www.moogo.de, accessed February 16, 2018.

[PRO 18] PROZESSASSISTENT, available at: http://www.prozessassistent.de, accessed February 16, 2018.

6

Challenges for Adaptable Energy-efficient Production Processes

The informatization of current production environments through Industry 4.0-based technologies enables information-driven services. As an outcome, all physical, virtual and human entities are able to communicate with each other. In doing so, the different terminologies, data formats and challenges are barriers for an efficient collaboration within a system. This chapter demonstrates which challenges occur and how to solve the data integration barriers to achieve the interoperability and intended collaboration. Furthermore, the chapter motivates how to use the achieved interoperability to gain an added value and to increase the energy efficiency of production processes. For that purpose, the integration of information-driven methods from an expert system will be presented. Finally, the interplay between interoperability and expert systems to achieve the required energy efficiency is shown by means of a use case in a production environment.

6.1. Introduction

The actual development of data exchange and automation in manufacturing technologies is summarized under the term Industry 4.0. The increase of digitalization in economy and society deeply changes production in Germany. It all started with the steam machine, followed by electricity, mass production, electronics and IT, and the fourth generation is dictated by smart factories [PI4 18]. It includes cyber-physical systems, cloud computing and the Internet

Chapter written by Kay Burow, Marc Allan Redecker, Alena V. Fedotova, Quan Deng, Marco Franke, Zied Ghrairi and Klaus-Dieter Thoben.

of Things (IoT). At this point, the actual production environments are far too complex to be handled by human decision alone. Connecting physical, virtual and human entities and giving them the ability to communicate with each other, allows a system to make decentralized decisions for a customer. This chapter picks up this topic and introduces an AI-supported model for the assistance of production control with its focus on energy efficiency. Within a production environment, production processes are often driven by the control of different machines. In order to reach an optimized production process, critical control decisions on machines have to be made based on a clear understanding of the current situation. For that purpose, it is essential to have a holistic logical view on information flows with information extracted from diverse sources. However, there are still major gaps to be filled to reach the holistic logical view on information flows in a production environment. For the support of production processes, diverse production information in various domains are handled in many different IT systems, which are often syntactically or semantically incompatible with each other. This kind of diversity leads to information silos and makes information interoperability challengeable. With the boundary limits of systems, fluent information flows as well as a clear linkage between the information flows and material flows are hard to achieve.

According to the direction of production processes, information flows can be classified as either vertical or horizontal. At first, at each stage of a production process, many systems are involved vertically with information in different levels and from different aspects. Then, along the production process, horizontal information flows are generated. Unlike the vertical information flow, information in the horizontal information flows is usually captured at different timestamps. It is still challengeable to synchronize the information, which is in distinct abstract levels, from various perspectives and at different timestamps. To enable a seamless collaboration, it emphasizes a sustainable information exchange between the physical parts and the information-based services. The information view describes the information flows independently of the deployed hardware and software. Therefore, it can be handled as an additional resource from the management perspective with respect to gaining benefits and optimizing the information quality. Furthermore, new sensors and analyzers can be integrated in the system by adapting the existing model.

As an outcome, a possible application shall be an energy-efficient production environment since current energy management systems are only able to capture the energy data and determine key indicators. With this model and by extending it with an expert system (ES) it will be possible to define automated measures which allow us to lower the primary energy demand.

6.2. Approach

To digitalize a production environment and to achieve a seamless connection between all entities, homogeneous data is required. Therefore, it will be the basis for the collaboration for each entity and is described as interoperability. The term "interoperability" is understood as the ability of a system to work with other products or systems without any restrictions [DOI 18]. The necessary interoperability between and within production environments is considered by ATHENA Interoperability Framework on four levels [BER 07]:

– data/information (for information interoperability);

– services (for flexible execution and composition of services);

– processes (for cross-organizational processes);

– enterprise/business (for collaborative enterprise operations).

The interoperability on the first level enables the interoperability on the other three levels. To achieve the interoperability on the data information layer, a broad variety of data sources representing machines, assembly lines, pps and erp solutions have to be considered. To enable a flexible and adaptable information flow within a production environment, one of the key challenges is to exchange information and not only data in order to prevent a false interpretation of the data between the stakeholders. [BEL 04] defines information as "...data that has been given meaning by way of relational connection...". In this chapter, the information according to expected behaviour of a product should be represented as exchangeable unambiguous information within the product lifecycle management (PLM) of a product. The unambiguous interpretation of the transferred information can be achieved on different levels. Oren et al. [ORE 05] defined different levels of understanding, which are: lexical understanding, syntactical understanding, morphological understanding, semantic understanding and pragmatic understanding. Lexical, syntactical and morphological understanding enables the recognition of the structure of the information and the grouping of relevant entities, but the meaning is still unclear. The semantic understanding is the key to understanding the meaning of the data and closing the gap from a data view to an information view. The interoperability shall be achieved by using a canonical model. At current stage, the best-known technique to enable the canonical model is reconciliation using ontology [CHE 04]. To integrate the heterogeneous data formats, information systems can be used [LEN 02]. Current solutions can transform data from a wide range of heterogeneous data sources like CSV, XML, SQL, etc. into an ontology [FRA 16, SHA 17]. An ontology is applicable as a global information view within the production environment. In modern computer science and artificial intelligence the term "ontology" stands for clear and formal specification of a domain. According to

T.R. Gruber, it is often referred to as an explicit specification of shared conceptualization [GRU 93]. In other words, ontology is a conceptualization of a domain into a format that is not only human understandable, but also machine readable. A formal definition of conceptualization has been given in [GEN 87]. [GUA 95] defines ontology as a logical theory that specifies some conceptualization; it includes for example some basic terms for forming taxonomy, describing attributes and related axioms. Therefore, it can play the role of knowledge representation and enable on top information-driven applications. With respect to the application of artificial methods, an ontology enables the application of artificial methods without considering the underlying data formats and tools. Moreover, artificial methods can capture the domain knowledge as if from the mind of an expert instead of how it is stored. This simplifies the setting up of personalized analyses (semantic network and rules) by domain experts. Complex decisions require a great deal of information and applied knowledge. Such decisions have to be made quickly and reliably. Using ontologies in artificial methods helps us to enable reuse of domain knowledge, to make domain assumptions explicit, to provide interoperability with legacy and future intelligent systems [NOI 01]. The following use case demonstrates the benefits of using an ontology-supported expert system.

6.3. Use case

The addressed use case consists of the use of ES for compound feed production processes (Figure 6.1), helping producers in this sector to deal with uncertainties on natural raw material and energy flows. These uncertainties, which could fall in energy-intensive production steps, make a significantly impact on the energy consumption during the processing of natural raw materials, because the raw material is subject to changeable properties like moisture and grain size distribution.

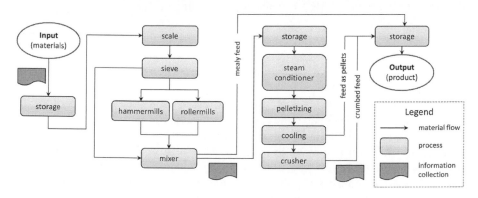

Figure 6.1. *Process flow of compound feed production*

The main objective for compound feed producers is to perform an entire process optimization including high production rates with the required product quality by searching for an optimal operating condition of the operating variables (rpm, pressure, temperature, etc.). The interpretation of these uncertainties is mandatory and will enhance a better understanding of energy problems and therefore generate action plans [TOP 09] that an employee (expert) may perform. This could be realized using ES that are able to emulate the decision-making ability of a human expert [GOV 13] and to solve complex problems by reasoning. Due to the fact that the production environment includes a great deal of IT-Systems data acquisition, processing/storage and process control, which are generating different data formats at different times, the integration of an ES into a production environment will face many challenges such as gaining access to diverse systems and the aggregation of a huge amount of information needed for generating a specific measure defined as a rule. The adopted interoperability approach consists of the use of a middleware (Figure 6.2) dealing with access to heterogeneous systems, aggregation of different information, synchronization and linkage between information flows.

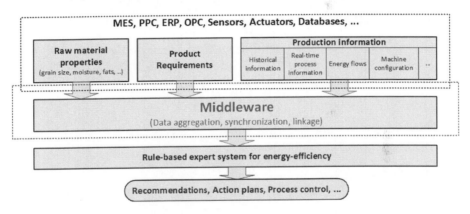

Figure 6.2. *Overall concept*

The ontology-based middleware should have the ability to share and exchange information by using common syntax and semantics to meet an application-specific functional relationship across a common interface. Compared to traditional approaches, where different data sources are linked directly to an ES, all data processing tasks will be performed at middleware level. Any changes within the process such as new machines, machine descriptions or new product requirements will take place at middleware level. This concept will reduce the complexity by the ES and ensure its transferability to other production scenarios. The users of ES have only to define/import the process-related rules such as IF grain_size_distribution>2 THEN steam_conditioner=1. The definition of the rules will be supported by the information provided within the ontology. Additional rules can be automatically generated from historical information. For the implementation of the presented approach, a related effort which has been conducted in [DAS 08] will be investigated in order to assess the extent up to which the mentioned aspects can be fulfilled.

6.4. Conclusion and outlook

This chapter has shown the importance of interoperability to achieve a seamless collaboration by means of a use case. Furthermore, it has demonstrated the necessity of a collaboration of all entities to optimize a system, especially in an AI-supported production environment to reduce the energy consumption. The next steps will be a concrete implementation with the help of further use cases in an industrial environment to generalize the started approach.

6.5. Acknowledgments

The authors from the University of Bremen thank the German Federal Ministry for Economic Affairs and Energy (BMWi) for funding the current research project KIPro.

6.6. References

[AFU 18] AFUL Definition of Interoperability, available at: http://interoperability-definition.info/en/, 2018.

[BEL 04] BELLINGER G., CASTRO D., MILLS A., *Data, Information, Knowledge, and Wisdom*, 2004.

[BER 07] BERRE A.J., ELVESÆTER B., FIGAY N. *et al.*, "The ATHENA interoperability framework", in JARDIM-GONÇALVES R., MÜLLER J.P., MERTINS K. *et al.* (eds), *Enterprise Interoperability II*, Springer, London, 2007.

[CHE 04] CHEN D., VERNADAT F., "Standards on enterprise integration and engineering – A state of the art", *International Journal of Computer Integrated Manufacturing (IJCIM)*, vol. 17, no. 3, pp. 235–225, 2004.

[DAS 08] DASSISTI M., PANETTO H., TURSI A. *et al.*, "Ontology-based model for production-control systems interoperability", *The 5th CIRP Digital Enterprise Technology Conference*, pp. 527–543, 2008.

[FRA 16] FRANKE M., KLEIN K., HRIBERNIK K.A. *et al.*, "Semantic data integration approach for the vision of a digital factory", in MERTINS K., JARDIM-GONÇALVES R., POPPLEWELL K. *et al.* (eds), *Enterprise Interoperability VII*, Springer International Publishing, 2016.

[GEN 87] GENESERETH M.R., NILSSON N.J., *Logical Foundation of Artificial Intelligence*, Morgan Kaufmann, Los Altos, 1987.

[GOV 13] GOVINDA RAO S., ESWARA RAO M., SIVA PRASAD D., "Fever diagnosis rule-based expert systems", *International Journal of Engineering Research & Technology (IJERT)*, vol. 2, no. 8, 2013.

[GRU 93] GRUBER T.R., "A translation approach to portable ontologies", *Knowledge Acquisition*, vol. 5, no. 2, pp. 199–220, 1993.

[GUA 95] GUARINO N., "Formal ontology, conceptual analysis and knowledge representation", *International Journal of Human-Computer Studies*, vol. 43, nos 5–6, 1995.

[LEN 02] LENZERINI M., "Data integration: A theoretical perspective", *Proceedings of the 21st ACM SIGMOD-SIGACT-SIGART symposium on Principles of database systems*, pp. 233–246, 2002.

[NOY 01] NOY N., MCGUINNESS D., Ontology Development 101: A Guide to Creating your first ontology, Stanford Knowledge Systems Laboratory Technical Report KSL-01-05 and Stanford Medical Informatics Technical Report SMI-2001-0880, 2001.

[ORE 07] OREN T., GHASSAM-AGHAEE N., YILMAZ L., "An ontology-based dictionary of understanding as a basis for software agents with understanding abilities", *Proceedings 2007 Spring Simulation Multiconference*, IEEE Press, 2007.

[PI4 18] PLATTFORM INDUSTRIE 4.0, available at: http://www.plattform-i40.de/I40/Navigation /DE/Industrie40/WasIndustrie40/was-ist-industrie-40.html, 2018.

[SHA 17] SHANI U., FRANKE M., HRIBERNIK K.A. *et al.*, Ontology mediation to rule them all: Managing the plurality in product service systems, *Systems Conference (SysCon), 2017 Annual IEEE International*, pp. 1–7, 2017.

[TOP 09] TOPAC V. *et al.*, "A software solution for reducing energy consumption in domestic sector", *3rd International Workshop on Soft Computing Applications*, 2009.

7

Interoperability Requirements for Adaptive Production System-of-Systems

The Cognitive Robotics and Shop Floors research area of the newly established research center Pro²Future focuses on modular and interoperable production systems. The research combines the engineering of production machines and their runtime behavior in production systems-of-systems (PSoS). In contrast with other systems, our focus is on the production process spanning multiple machines (systems) under the assumption that these machines are from different manufacturers, as is commonly the case. Enterprise interoperability in general and process interoperability in particular play a fundamental role. Machines are autonomous, developed by different manufacturers, and form a larger system on demand – the assembly lines and other shop floors. In this chapter, we present a conceptual vision and business considerations which we want to cover with our industrial partners in the research center. The presented approach builds on existing approaches which are included in the discussion.

7.1. Introduction

The economic potential enabled through the use of ICT for production systems is overwhelming. Gartner lists current technology trends in their Hype Cycle 2017 (see table below). Most, if not all, technologies that reach the plateau of productivity within the next 10 years are highly relevant for production.

To estimate an economic impact, McKinsey [MCK 15] investigated one of the most fundamental technologies supporting the production domain: the Internet of Things platforms. For this technology, McKinsey estimates an economic potential of

Chapter written by Georg WEICHHART and Alexander EGYED.

$1.2 to $3.7 trillion in the factory domain alone. Compared to other settings where economic benefits are realized (like cities, retail, logistics and self-driving vehicles), the factory has by far the greatest share of the total sum of $4 – $11 trillion economic impact of IoT [MCK 15].

Hype Cycle Phase	Plateau of Productivity will be reached in	
	2–5 years	5–10 years
Innovation Trigger	Serverless PaaS; Augmented Data Discovery; Edge Computing	Deep Reinforcement Learning; Neuromorphic Hardware; 5G; Digital Twin; Conversational User Interfaces; Smart Workspace
Peak of Inflated Expectations	IoT Platform; Deep Learning; Machine Learning; Commercial UAVs (Drones)	Smart Robots; Virtual Assistants; Connected Home; Nanotube Electronics; Cognitive Computing; Blockchain
Trough of Disillusionment	Cognitive Expert Advisors; Software-Defined Security	Enterprise Taxonomy and Ontology Management; Augmented Reality
Slope of Enlightenment	Virtual Reality	

Table 7.1. *2017 Gartner Hype Cycle for technologies expected to be productive in 2–10 years [GAR 17]*

The process of digitalization will not stop in producing isolated cyber-physical artifacts (e.g. Virtual Assistants, Augmented Reality, Smart Robots). Connecting these artifacts will provide an enormous business impact. Network and connection technologies are on the rise (e.g. Connected Home, 5G, IoT, Smart Workplace).

IoT platforms focus on the aspect of collecting data and preparing it in edge computing platforms for cloud computing. In order to be usable in production, technologies need to be capable of acting along and implementing parts of the production process. The physics of the production process requires that all involved machines (systems) are synchronized and that a consistent *world view* on the production process is guaranteed among all involved machines. However, since these machines are independently built, deployed and maintained by their respective manufacturers, a consistent world view can be only established by the shop floor. The shop floors are the factories, assembly lines and other production facilities that use these machines. This chapter argues that a consistent world view can be captured in enterprise models or enterprise ontologies.

One key challenge to be solved is interoperability. The technologies used in machines have to be interoperable with the production process and with each other.

Even more importantly, the technologies have to be adapted to quickly adapt the machines to changing production needs.

The chapter is organized as follows. We first briefly identify the strategic direction of the project within the research center with respect to interoperable and modular production systems. We then highlight requirements and needs for the engineering parts for such an environment. We present the outlook of the research work in the given $Pro^2Future$ area on Cognitive Robotics and Shop Floors.

7.2. Process interoperability requirements addressed

In this section we discuss interoperability requirements for production systems-of-systems partly identified in previous projects, and partly in $Pro^2Future$ (a new competence center for smart production) together with industrial partners.

As indicated above, we identified a trend towards modularization of systems in manufacturing. The foremost business goal is adaptability. Machines need to be enhanced over time to add new capabilities. This can be done by altering the hardware of the machines (i.e. with physical modules) and/or by altering the software of the machines (i.e. the same, existing hardware but with changed behavior characteristics) to better interact with other machines. The main motivation for adaptive shop floors is about adaptive production processes so that "lot size one" production goals become economically feasible. Another motivation is about resilient supply networks where partners come and go and continuous logistic uncertainties are reflected in the productions process.

No matter the reason, the goal is to adapt the production process – and with it to adapt the machines. We see different needs and different priorities for functions. Foremost, there are time-constraints. On the machine level we see the need for real-time adaptability. The process here is the behavior of the machines modifying a work piece. On the shop-floor level, humans, machines and logistic modules need to be coordinated. Real-time constraints are a bit more relaxed, with the notable exception of the safety of humans taking part in the production process (e.g. emergency stop). On the shop-floor level, security becomes more important and the interaction of machines needs to be consistent during the execution of a process. The grippers for two robotic arms may not be at the same place at the same time and so on. On the supply chain level, timing is less of an issue, but security requirements are of high priority. When executing the production process on this level, emphasis is placed on logistical aspects.

Machines are systems and a shop floor is a system of systems. The adaptability of such a system-of-systems requires interoperability of different kinds. For example, machines may have different software versions (even if from the same manufacturers) and still need to be interoperable. Products are adapted over time. Moreover, machines may undergo periodic changes. This implies changes in the production process. However, at the same time, a process may also be changed, for example in order to make it more efficient or optimize it to changing environmental conditions.

To cover these constraints and requirements we have sketched a three-layer system-of-systems with a communication-enabling middleware on each layer. The following figure gives an abstract overview of two of the three layers.

All systems are aware of process fragments to which they contribute even if they do not understand the complete production process. To have a correct and efficient production process, these fragments need to be chained together; either manually or through intelligent reasoning algorithms. The communication infrastructure and middleware has to be capable of supporting the discovery of (new) machines (or adapted machines capabilities) participating in the production system.

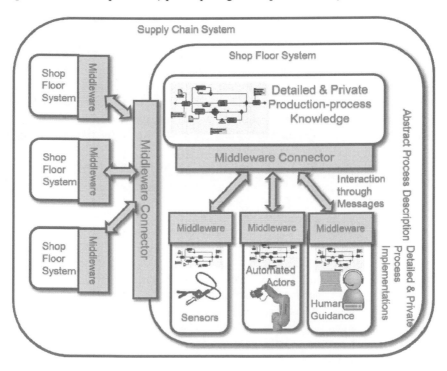

Figure 7.1. *Conceptual process centric middleware on shop-floor level and supply-chain level*

For realizing this vision and prototype, we are building on existing standards and approaches. In particular, Industry 4.0-related interface standards and information models are on the rise. We plan to leverage standards around OPC UA and other machine communication norms.

Research-wise, there are several elements missing that support system-of-systems aspects. Systems have a certain independence that allows multiple systems to form larger systems. Sometimes these are referred to as super- and sub- systems. Systems have and keep their purpose and function even when the organization of the systems changes. This implies that in their nature systems are not controllable from the outside (as passive elements would be). With respect to adaptability of the overall system, this allows us to (ex)change sub-systems over time. Exchange in this particular context refers to the replacement of hardware as well as SW updates.

Basic services required are, for example, the discovery of machines and their capabilities (e.g. directories or multi-cast services), lifetime services for HW/SW modules plugged into the shop floor, working modules and modules that are broken. Here, different strategies from the production process point of view also need to be realizable.

7.3. Engineering and design requirements addressed

In this section we identify requirements for engineering complex and adaptive systems in a collaborative manner.

That is, if multiple heterogeneous domains are combined then there is an interoperability gap that needs to be bridged [WEI 17a, WEI 17b]. In the given production context, there are not only software but also hardware requirements for machines to consider. Moreover, there are different IoT, Edge and Cloud systems that can be included. In addition to that we have production processes and the respective knowledge base. The project-specific interoperability gap in this context does involve technical aspects as well as process aspects. The technical aspects are data and document types specific to the domain. This involved for example CAD drawings, source code, XML files (SysML, AutomationML), spreadsheets, text documents for configuration and so on.

To support these many kinds of artifacts, we have created the DesignSpace for hardware/software co-design [EGY 18]. The DesignSpace supports multiple user groups (e.g. engineers in manufacturing and engineering) and is capable of connecting engineering and production artifacts in the form of explicit links. In doing so, it also supports change management. This is how hardware changes affect the software or machine changes affect the production [DEM 16]. Of course this does not support establishing interoperability, but it supports signaling potential non-interoperability due to changes.

We also believe that reuse will play a very fundamental role in production. Today, manufacturers often already define reusable product lines for machines. However, there is still potential to explore reuse among production processes based on the idea that production processes are likely similar if the products produced are similar. Therefore, we have created ECCO for the automated reuse of artifacts which could be applied to reuse machines and shop-floor processes [FIS 15].

Still missing here is the overall production process point of view, which is implemented using existing systems. The process (as coordination mechanism) also involves different existing HW/SW systems. So far the engineering support misses this cross-system interoperability support.

7.4. Expected impact

From our experiences and talks with industry, we conclude with the following. Enterprises are working on modularization at different levels, resulting in production systems-of-systems. Some standards emerge or exist that provide APIs for connecting machines. Information models for exchanging data are also on the rise.

The focus of many of these developments is on enabling information flows among machines. However, interoperability on the production process level and organization level will not come by simply enabling machines to communicate. Some ideas for future research directions on modular and interoperable enterprise are presented under the framing idea of the "enterprise operating system" [CHE 15, WEI 18]. This includes debugging, engineering support and support for the lifetimes of systems. Our work is aligned with these ideas and go beyond. We are planning on creating models not only about the machines (their capabilities and behavior) but also the interaction among these machines. We are planning on introducing a production process as a coordination mechanism that spans these machines and holds production know-how tied together with engineering abilities. Representation schemata will be required to support interoperable functionalities.

7.5. Next steps

It is important to mention that our research work will leverage the hardware, software and production domain knowledge base. Interoperability in (research) projects like the proposed work within Pro²Future also has interoperability requirements in itself [WEI 17a, WEI 17b]. The path to a successful implementation of the modular and interoperable enterprise has to bring together two currently disconnected worlds. On the one hand, there is the existing automation pyramid, supporting stable processes but therefore rigid. On the other hand, there is a fully flexible, service-oriented architecture where any service calls any service at any time. The envisioned work will stay away from both worlds by making the concept of a process a top-level concept. We hope to allow both stable, consistent processes and modular, flexible production systems.

7.6. Acknowledgements

This research is partly funded by Pro²Future. Pro²Future is funded within the Austrian COMET Program – Competence centers for excellent technologies – under the auspices of the Austrian Federal Ministry of Transport, Innovation and technology, the Austrian Federal Ministry for Digital and Economic Affairs and of the Provinces of Upper Austria and Styria. COMET is managed by the Austrian Research Promotion Agency FFG (contract no. 854184).

7.7. References

[CHE 15] CHEN D., YOUSSEF J.R., ZACHAREWICZ G., "Towards an enterprise operating system-requirements for standardisation", *Proc. 6th Workshop on Enterprise Interoperability (IWEI)*, 2015.

[DEM 16] DEMUTH A., KRETSCHMER R., EGYED A. *et al.*, "Introducing traceability and consistency checking for change impact analysis across engineering tools in an automation solution company: An experience report", *International Conference on Software Maintenance and Evolution (ICSME)*, pp. 529–538, 2016.

[EGY 18] EGYED A., ZEMAN K., HEHENBERGER P. *et al.*, "Maintaining consistency across engineering artifacts", *IEEE Computer*, vol. 51, no. 2, pp. 28–35, 2018.

[FIS 15] FISCHER S., LINSBAUER L., LOPEZ-HERREJON R.E. *et al.*, "The ECCO tool: extraction and composition for clone-and-own", *International Conference on Software Maintenance and Evolution (ICSME)*, pp. 665–668, 2015.

[GAR 17] GARTNER INC., available at: https://www.gartner.com/smarterwithgartner/top-trends-in-the-gartner-hype-cycle-for-emerging-technologies-2017/, 2017.

[MCK 15] MCKINSEY GLOBAL INSTITUTE, available at: https://www.mckinsey.com/business-functions/digital-mckinsey/our-insights/the-internet-of-things-the-value-of-digitizing-the-physical-world, 2015.

[WEI 17a] WEICHHART G., ROLJIC B., BEHAM A. *et al.*, "Enterprise interoperability as framework for project knowledge management", *On the Move to Meaningful Internet Systems: OTM 2016 Workshops*, pp. 190–199, 2017.

[WEI 17b] WEICHHART G., STARY C., "Project-based learning for complex adaptive enterprise systems", *IFAC-PapersOnLine*, vol. 50, pp. 12991–12996, 2017.

[WEI 18] WEICHHART G., STARY C., VERNADAT F., "Enterprise modelling for interoperable and knowledge-based enterprises", *International Journal of Production Research*, vol. 56, no. 8, pp. 2818–2840, 2018.

Platforms for the Industrial Internet of Things: Enhancing Business Models through Interoperability

8.1. Introduction

Currently, the world is undergoing a decisive change in information technology. Billions of new connection points will be added to the Internet, with the majority being small sensors that are attached to new and existing devices for collecting various types of data. In industrial facilities, the integration of new information technology services is complicated by existing infrastructure of machines and operational technology (OT) like machine control systems [REI 14]. Digital platforms for the Industrial Internet of Things (IIoT) help with overcoming these hurdles through enabling connectivity between devices, storage of machine data, and analytics for operational insights. In addition, they facilitate the development of complementary applications and enable the design of novel business models.

A current framework for business models for the IoT is derived from Fleisch *et al.* [1]. It provides components of business models that operate in siloed applications and a pattern that describes collecting data for open application enablement. On the subject of the latter, the authors state that there is much room for innovation. A facilitating factor is the emerging shift from value chains to value networks in the industrial domain [1]. IIoT platforms can thus leverage their ecosystems for value creation [3], which is particularly enabled by interoperability between different IIoT platforms [4]. Through expert interviews, our research objective is to augment the existing framework with new business

Chapter written by David Soto Setzke, Nicolas Scheidl, Tobias Riasanow, Markus Böhm and Helmut Krcmar.

model components. To derive this scenario, it is paramount to understand the aspects of interoperability between IIoT platforms. Hence, we first develop scenarios of interoperability and subsequently we derive new business model components. The outcomes can help companies to better shape their ecosystems. To sharpen our results, we focus our research on manufacturing as the most prevalent industrial domain [5].

8.2. Theoretical background

8.2.1. *Business models for the Internet of Things and ecosystems*

Based on the Business Model Navigator from Gassmann *et al.* [7], [1] identified two new business model patterns that are enabled through the IoT. First, there is the Digitally-charged Product pattern which describes the joint offering of a physical product and a digital service. Several components represent variations thereof, for example Predictive Maintenance and Guaranteed Availability. On the other hand, the Sensor-as-a-Service pattern represents the capture of data and provision of application enablement for the customer. In this case, data is made available for many potential applications within an ecosystem.

Further research focuses on industrial ecosystems. Findings about ecosystems, in particular in the industrial domain, show how single entities therein increase their value creation through connection with others [7]. Through aligned collaboration, multiple new services for the end user are possible [8]. While being confronted with many new threats, especially in the manufacturing domain, this trend is evident [9]. IIoT platforms take a central position in their ecosystem. However, there is still a lack of research about concrete business model components that utilize this administrative role. To fill this gap, we use the patterns Digitally-Charged Product and Sensor-as-a-Service as described above.

8.2.2. *Interoperability in industrial ecosystems*

Interoperability is the paramount means to increase the ecosystems' value creation capacity [9], and thus leverage the position of IIoT platforms. Hence, it is important to understand the fundamentals thereof. Currently, many organizations are trying to establish standards on various levels and domains [10], but it is still unclear which of these will prevail. Nevertheless, there are several categories for interoperability. First, there is hierarchy which represents the technical, syntactic, semantic and organizational levels [11]. At the technical level, information models are used to transfer data in a machine-readable way [12]. While the syntactic level specifies the exchange format, semantics are necessary for the interpretation of data [11]. Organizational interoperability ensures automation of processes between different systems [13]. Due to the increased number of devices, self-configuration within systems has become ever more important [14]. Overall, there is a lack of research on interoperability possibilities in industrial ecosystems, specifically in the inter-domain area. Therefore, we aim to develop new business model components that are enabled by interoperability.

8.3. Research approach

By augmenting existing IoT business model patterns with the opportunities of interoperability, new business model components are possible. For that matter, we used a three-step research process. First, we identified business model components through conducting semi-structured expert interviews about interoperability opportunities. Second, we validated our results with business model experts from the IIoT industry.

For the first step, we designed a questionnaire to address what opportunities for IIoT platform business models will emerge through interoperability. The interviews were conducted with experts from industrial corporates and technology consultancies. For the analysis, we conducted a structured content analysis [15] by coding first platform instances, then connections to the IIoT platform and finally opportunities. In a second step, we conducted interviews with two business model experts who specialized in the IIoT in order to get feedback about the logic and feasibility of our results.

8.4. Business models component based on interoperability

Following the framework of Gawer [16], we identified six business model components. Therefore, the value proposition types Revenue Increase (R) and Operations Improvement (O) respectively contain two and four items. Regarding the platform instances, we identified 10 categories. Internal instances are (1) ERP/Business, (2) MES and (3) shop floor. Supply-chain instances are (4) Material/upstream product/services supplier and (5) labor supply platform. Ecosystem instances are (6) customer IoT platform, (7) other manufacturing IIoT platforms, (8) other IIoT domains, (9) application provider and (10) non-IIoT instances. In addition, Table 8.1 shows the connections between an IIoT platform and its instances for each business model component.

New business model component	Internal instances	Supply-chain instances	Ecosystem instances
(R): Monetization of operation data	(3): Collection of operation data		(10): Sale of operation data
(R): Co-development of products	(3): Provision of production parameters		(6): Collection of usage data
(O): Synchronization with end customer ecosystem	(2): Collection of scheduled operation data	(4): Collection of delivery times for components	(6): Provision of scheduled operation data and collection of required end customer data
(O): Information integration	(1): Provision of operation forecasts	(4): Collection of quoted delivery prices (5): Collection of forecasted labor salaries	(6): Collection of quoted sale prices
(O): Co-usage enablement	(1): Provision of usage data		(7): Collection and provision of machinery usage data
(O): Automated procurement and vending operations	(1): Provision of purchased and sold units (2): Collection of operation data and provision of orders	(4): Ordering of units (5): Contraction of labor	(6): Negotiation of orders considering capability and capacity

Table 8.1. *Platform types and instances. (R) – revenue increase, (O) – operations improvement*

Monetization of operation data allows the customer to sell data to interested third parties. These can be financial services companies that use this information to get live market data in certain industries. IIoT platforms serve as an intermediator and their operators earn a commission or a fixed fee depending on the revenue model.

Co-development of products enables the automated development of customized products for the end customer. It is accomplished by collecting specific usage data and deriving individualized components for spare parts or succeeding products. Thereby, customer data is leveraged not only for general development purposes but also for user-designed parts.

Synchronization with end customer ecosystem aligns the own production operations with the ecosystem of the customer, specifically in the ever more important after-sales market. A case in point is scheduling maintenance. Through product usage data, repair requirements can be predicted. Repair appointments are then made based on the availability of the customer and production planning of spare parts. IIoT platforms thereby serve as a connector.

Information integration consolidates supply-chain and ecosystem information into the planning process. For example, in lifecycle management for either plants or products, it is possible to project financials based on quoted data from external parties early on. There are different possible revenue models like commission or fixed fees.

Co-usage enablement signifies the provision of machinery to multiple customers at the same time. The IIoT platform enables billing based on real usage and solving of warranty issues. Revenue models are either commission or fixed fees.

Automated procurement and vending operations facilitate the negotiations of input and output in vendor networks. With predicted supply needs IIoT platforms submit purchase orders for the company. It is also possible to hire labor based on flexible contracts. By providing capacity and capability information to other companies in the network, sales orders are generated.

While our validation partners were optimistic about the feasibility of our results, they stated that some of them are only applicable in niche industries. For example, automated procurement and vending operations expose great transparency. Many companies are not willing to share extensive information about their operations. In addition, it is still unclear how the structure and functionality of IIoT platforms themselves will evolve, especially in manufacturing. It is possible that they will adopt more functions of MES or that some even evolve into one combined system. Thus, connections and even business model components can change. Another factor is the type of the IIoT platform customer. To machine builders, different aspects apply compared to assembly factories since end customers are one step further away in the value chain.

8.5. Conclusion and outlook

We introduce six new business model components that are enhanced through interoperability identified by a structured content analysis of expert interviews. We show that interoperability offers great potential for IIoT platform business models. An existing framework for IoT business models could be applied in this context. As the technical architecture for interoperability in the IIoT is not fixed yet, it is unclear how roles will be assigned in the future. Thus, IIoT platforms may adopt functions in the areas of ERP and MES. We validated our results with two strategy consultants and reviewed public information. However, since we conducted our research about manufacturing, our findings might not be directly transferable to other IIoT domains. Our research has shown that information security is very important for some companies. Therefore, we suggest investigating the possibility of basing business models on this aspect. As IIoT platform providers are dependent on customer data for further development of their algorithms, it would be valuable to know how they prize the ability to use that data. Furthermore, a complete case study of a concrete implementation of an interoperability-enabled business model would be especially valuable, as it would highlight designing the technical structure.

8.6. References

[1] Fleisch E., Weinberger M., Wortmann F., Geschäftsmodelle im Internet der Dinge, Schmalenbachs Zeitschrift für betriebswirtschaftliche Forschung, pp. 444–464, 2015.

[2] Vermesan O., Friess P. (eds.), *Building the Hyperconnected Society: IoT Research and Innovation Value Chains, Ecosystems and Markets*, River Publishers, 2016.

[3] Schladofsky W., Mitic J., Megner A.P. *et al.*, "Business Models for Interoperable IoT Ecosystems", in Podnar Žarko I., Broering A., Soursos S. *et al.* (eds), *Interoperability and Open-Source Solutions for the Internet of Things*, Springer International Publishing, Cham, 2017.

[4] Broring A., Schmid S., Schindhelm C.-K. *et al.*, "Enabling IoT ecosystems through platform interoperability", *IEEE Software*, vol. 34, pp. 54–61, 2017.

[5] Chungoora N., Young R.I., Gunendran G. *et al.*, "A model-driven ontology approach for manufacturing system interoperability and knowledge sharing", *Computers in Industry*, vol. 64, pp. 392–401, 2013.

[6] Gassmann O., Frankenberger K., Csik M., *Geschäftsmodelle entwickeln: 55 innovative Konzepte mit dem St. Galler Business Model Navigator*, Hanser, München, 2013.

[7] Leminen S., Rajahonka M., Westerlund M. *et al.*, "Ecosystem business models for the Internet of Things", in Varjonen S. (ed.), *Internet of Things Finland*, pp. 10–13, 2015.

[8] Ehret M., Wirtz J., "Unlocking value from machines: Business models and the industrial internet of things", *Journal of Marketing Management*, vol. 33, pp. 111–130, 2016.

[9] Herzog R., Jacoby M., Podnar Žarko I., "Semantic interoperability in IoT-based automation infrastructures", *Automatisierungstechnik*, vol. 64, pp. 742–749, 2016.

[10] Kovacs E., Bauer M., Kim J. *et al.*, "Standards-based worldwide semantic interoperability for IoT", *IEEE Communications Magazine*, vol. 54, pp. 40–46, 2016.

[11] Kubicek H., Cimander R., "Three dimensions of organizational interoperability: Insights from recent studies for improving interoperability frame-works", *European Journal of ePractice*, vol. 6, pp. 1–12, 2009.

[12] Pfrommer J., "Semantic interoperability at big-data scale with the open62541 OPC UA implementation", in Podnar Žarko I., Broering A., Soursos S. *et al.* (eds), *Interoperability and Open-Source Solutions for the Internet of Things*, Springer International Publishing, Cham, 2017.

[13] Chen Y.-K., "Manageability challenges for the Internet of Things", *Electronic Device Failure Analysis*, vol. 18, pp. 18–21, 2016.

[14] Prazeres C., Serrano M., "SOFT-IoT: Self-Organizing FOG of Things", in BAROLLI L. (ed.), *IEEE 30th International Conference on Advanced Information Networking and Applications Workshops*, Piscataway, pp. 803–808, 2016.

[15] Miles M.B., Huberman A.M., Saldaña J., *Qualitative data analysis: A methods sourcebook*, Sage, 2014.

[16] Gawer A., "Bridging differing perspectives on technological platforms: Toward an integrative framework", *Research Policy*, vol. 43, pp. 1239–1249, 2014.

Virtual Factory

Part 3 Summary: Virtual Factory Operating System

The world is facing the fourth industrial revolution based on ICT, specifically architectures and services, as key innovation drivers for manufacturing companies. Traditional factories will increasingly be transformed into smart digital manufacturing environments. Currently, however, the full potential for ICT in manufacturing is far from being fully exploited. Factories are complex systems of systems and there is a need to develop a platform on which future manufacturing applications can be built.

European SMEs' needs around ICT solutions are far off from being satisfied at affordable costs and time. Some of these are: to reduce integration overheads for ICT, to provide mobile devices that are intuitive, to provide traceability from cradle to grave through the supply chain and to facilitate monitoring, optimization and predictive maintenance to enhance availability and productivity.

Over the last decades, manufacturing companies have been implementing point-solutions, each bringing a specific feature or fixing a specific issue. Resulting from this approach is a highly heterogeneous manufacturing IT landscape. While these IT landscapes are already costly to administer, further addition of capabilities becomes even more costly because they have to be fitted into the heterogeneous IT landscape already existing. There is a need for a homogeneous manufacturing IT landscape offering manufacturing IT solutions to support manufacturing companies, especially SMEs, in successfully responding to the challenge to be flexible and offer highly customized products, and without daunting implementation costs, thereby maintaining and boosting their competitiveness locally and in the increasingly globalized markets they participate in.

Chapter written by Raul POLER and Ricardo JARDIM-GONÇALVES.

As an answer to these needs, an H2020 European project called "Virtual Factory Open Operating System" (vf-OS) funded under the topic FoF-11-2016 "Digital Automation", subtopic "Collaborative Manufacturing and Logistics", started in October 2016 with a duration of three years. The aim of this section is to demonstrate the research undertaken with the project during its first year. The six chapters included here were developed from papers presented at the vf-OS workshop:

– "vf-OS Architecture": this chapter describes the vf-OS software architecture. Information and requirements of the real world are included in the structural planning of the complex software system.

– "Enablers Framework: Developing Applications using FIWARE": this chapter proposes the Enablers Framework, a component of the vf-OS project that acts as a bridge between applications and enablers, granting programmers an easy access to the services they need.

– "vf-OS IO Toolkit": this chapter describes the IO Toolkit, which provides tools for on-premises facilitation of the access to manufacturing devices and existing business software, while also facilitating the interaction with the rest of the vf-OS infrastructure.

– "Data Management Component for Virtual Factories Systems": this chapter envisages the vf-OS middleware platform and the Data Management Component for covering the issues related to data handling, pre-processing, extracting, and data flows management for Virtual Factories.

"An Open Environment for Development of Manufacturing Applications on vf-OS": this chapter describes a novel environment that was envisioned for providing software developers with an advanced editor with syntax highlighting, providing a large set of artifacts and libraries including standard connectors and extension points, debuggers, and tools to optimize the performance of developed Apps.

"A Novel Approach to Software Development in the Microservice Environment of vf-OS": this chapter describes the vf-OS approach consisting of "Docker"-based microservices, orchestrated through common REST services with special attention given to the challenge of running resources OnPremise versus purely InCloud[1].

1 The "Virtual Factory Operating System" workshop chairs kindly acknowledge all the members of the program committee. In particular, they thank Stuart Campbell, Eduardo Saiz, Nejib Moalla and Raquel Almeida for their support in the scientific success of the event. The research leading to the results presented in these chapters received funding from the European Union H2020 Program under grant agreement No. 723710 "Virtual Factory Open Operating System" (vf-OS).

vf-OS Architecture

This chapter discusses the software planning of the Industry 4.0 project vf-OS. Information and requirements of the real world are included in the structural planning of the complex software system. The waterfall model is used, in which several phases of the planning build on each other. Starting with the system architecture, the individual components are defined in vf-OS and the individual connections to each other and to the outside world are specified. The application of various technical solutions is also dealt with in this phase. Based on this, the functional and technical specifications are drawn up, which describe the internal processes in more detail and also define the communication level. In today's industry 4.0 the emphasis is on security, since sensitive data in particular must be protected and the risk of abuse has increased as a result of the connection of industrial processes to the Internet. In order to minimize or avert these dangers, vf-OS has developed a concept for security and privacy that lists the main sources of danger and their solutions.

9.1. Global architecture definition

vf-OS uses a Service Oriented Architecture (SOA) approach in which the different vf-OS components implement individual functionalities and thus the composition of all these inter-related components form the complete vf-OS architecture to ground the vf-OS ecosystem. In order to apply this approach, all components implement and publish a REST interface allowing the exchange of data (primarily) with the messaging bus to be implemented within the project. vf-OS will support Event Driven SOA features so that the different components can decide their interaction pattern and react to internal and external events. Following this approach,

Chapter written by Danny PAPE, Tobias HINZ, Oscar GARCIA PERALES, Francisco FRAILE, José Luis FLORES and Oscar J. RUBIO.

the components of vf-OS can behave either as services or as event producers and consumers.

Figure 9.1 provides an overview of the high-level architecture of vf-OS and provides a formal split of functional components. This diagram classifies the components based on their role to vf-OS (design, runtime, etc.) and its relationship with external resources. The "Kernel box", situated at the top-left of the diagram, indicates that all the components marked with the same color can be deployed within the vf-OS Kernel when vf-OS is installed as an OnPremise solution.

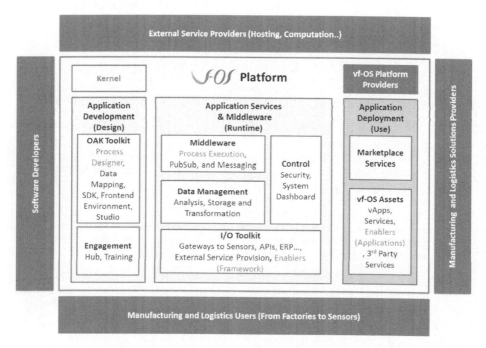

Figure 9.1. *vf-OS Global Architecture Definition. For a color version of this figure, see www.iste.co.uk/zelm/enterprise.zip*

Thus, the architectural building blocks are the following:

– Environment Block: the vf-OS Platform acts as an executing environment of vf-OS architecture. It acts as a container, which includes all other components;

– Application Development Block aka design time comprises the different vf-OS components that will be used for the development of vf-OS Manufacturing Assets/vApps;

– Application Services & Middleware Block aka Runtime includes the vf-OS components that will be used by the Assets/vApps, when they are requesting vf-OS resources;

– Application-Deployment Block includes all vf-OS components that will be taken into consideration when the vf-OS environment is going to be in use.

vf-OS Assets are the different elements that are executed within, or interact with, the vf-OS ecosystem. Intrinsically speaking, a vApp (a Manufacturing Smart Application) is the first example of what a vf-OS Asset can be, but it is not the only one. As such, a vf-OS Asset consists of several Solution Building Blocks (SBB). In summary, the Solution Building Blocks are prioritized as follows:

FIWARE Enablers > Specific Enablers > Open Source Solutions > Existing Solutions > New Development.

9.2. Functional specification

The functional specification describes how the vf-OS platform works from the perspective of the user. More specifically, for every component, the functional specifications contain a description of the functionality and behavior from the perspective of the user, the sequence of actions taking place during the execution of the component to satisfy its functionality and the mockups of the user interfaces that support the interactions with different vf-OS users.

The behavior and functionality of the components is described using story maps [PAT 14]. Story maps organize user stories for software development in a matrix, following the user workflow from left to right and the user priority from top to bottom. This visualization helps users and developers to build a common understanding of the behavior of the component and the expected functionality of the different software releases. User stories capture the functionality that needs to be developed with enough granularity to identify inconsistencies or overlapping of functionalities between components. The same methodology is applied to the pilot applications. This provides an effective feedback mechanism from the pilots to the individual components.

The story maps are linked to UML sequence diagrams used to depict the interactions between components and to UI mockups that describe the interaction with users. This way, every activity in the story map sequence has a high level description of the interaction with external components and/or users.

Finally, the models used in the component and the inner interactions of the component are described using UML class diagrams and a detailed component architecture diagram to enrich the high-level description provided in the global architecture definition.

9.3. Technical specification

The technical specification is the primary document detailing the communication amongst vf-OS components. It defines and describes the API endpoints and data models to be used in vf-OS. Therefore, it takes into account the knowledge of the Functional Specification and builds the foundation for development efforts.

The target group of the technical specification are developers who need to build software that interacts with vf-OS components. To ease this approach the outfacing interfaces of each component are accessible in a RESTful manner [RIC 08]. An online documentation tool has been used to do this where each vf-OS component describes its endpoints and data models. This approach keeps the documentation flexible and update-able for later use during the development or if there need to be changes in a later phase.

To provide all information needed by the developer each API endpoint is separated into three parts:

– description: API endpoints are introduced with a short description to show the purpose of the related endpoint;

– request: contains the endpoint URI and the necessary parameters (information and data) to be transmitted to the endpoint component for a successful response;

– response: describes both cases of responses (success and error). In case of success, it describes the expected data and the corresponding standardized HTTP status code (e.g. HTTP/1.1 200 OK), in case of an error a description is returned including a HTTP status code (e.g. HTTP/1.1 404 Not Found).

9.4. Holistic security and privacy concept

The main aim of the vf-OS infrastructure is to provide a set of information services enabling industrial processes. From the security point of view, protecting industrial processes is very challenging, due to the high economic incentives for hackers to interfere with them (e.g. stop, corrupt, spy). This has resulted in a rising wave of cyber-attacks (e.g. denial of service, ransomware, espionage) targeting industrial services. Therefore, the vf-OS infrastructure must be adequately protected before it is deployed in production. This is not a trivial task, since vf-OS is composed of a variety of inter-related components and services that may expose large attack surfaces.

Hence, guaranteeing continuous and appropriate availability, integrity and confidentiality (AIC) levels along the whole vf-OS infrastructure calls for a solid, holistic security and privacy model. This model elicits know-how from reference software development life cycles, applicable regulations (General Data Protection Regulations), key industrial IT standards (mainly ISA-62443) and recommendations from top-class security institutions (e.g. NSA, NIST). The objectives pursued are to minimize attack surfaces, maintain security risks at acceptable levels and keep security threats at bay, while minimizing the negative impact of security measures on the functionality and performance of vf-OS services.

Mainly inspired by SELinux, NSA's Open Source Security Enhanced Linux, the vf-OS holistic security model integrates five simple, ruling principles:

– the security component shall act as a security proxy, intercepting, authenticating and authorizing all actions on the platform in order to guarantee the protection of the vf-OS resources;

– following the example of Marketplaces such as Google Play or iOS Store, every external software development shall be provided as an Asset so that they can be examined and controlled in a uniform manner;

– most security processes (credentials exchange, tokenization, cryptographic verifications) are automated and transparent, but there may be humans in the loop. Particularly, the process of vApp installation will typically involve granting vApp access permissions (to resources) by the administrator(s) of the vf-OS Platform instance. These access permission policies are managed by using a central console;

– there is sandboxing by default. Any access (to a resource) that is not explicitly permitted, because it has been authorized, is prohibited;

– authorization policies follow a mixed system based on Role-Based Access Control (RBAC) and Attribute-Based Access Control (ABAC) called RABAC model. This will be addressed by means of XACML, and can be extended to support ABAC as well.

The holistic security model envisioned above translates into a vf-OS security component, whose architecture is defined by the following components:

– a Primary Security Component: comprised of a Security Command Center that concentrates the majority of security processes (authentication, authorization, and continuous security monitoring), an Installer Broker Service, to download and install vf-OS asset, an Identity Service to provide authentication, and an authorization Service to provide global security policies. This component is the main target for cyber-attacks and represents the largest attack surface.

– Marketplace Identity Manager: located in the vf-OS Marketplace, it is intended as the dependable source of applications, external packages, components and so on;

– Marketplace PKI: located in the vf-OS Marketplace, it carries out the creation, delivery, and renewal of digital certificates for vf-OS in order to guarantee the authenticity and authorship of the vf-OS Assets;

– OAK Studio/Toolkit: includes a set of tools for assessing the security of any development following a Software Development Life Cycle;

– Engagement Hub: responsible for providing required security information to the OAK Studio. This service is focused on providing check lists, threats lists and so on.

9.5. Conclusions

This paper describes the overall architecture and the specifications of vf-OS which are needed for the subsequent programming work. It ensures that the selected vf-OS technologies fit the requirements and that interfaces for all vf-OS software components are defined. Important security and privacy issues are promoted to their own focused task as they are cross-cutting concerns which largely need to be fulfilled by all vf-OS software components but of course they will be integrated with the overall specification stack. With the following completed core phases of software planning, the programming work of the individual components can begin:

– architecture to define relations and data streams between vf-OS components and excluding APIs;

– functional specification to define and prioritize functionalities depending on the requirements analysis;

– technical specification to define the access rules of each component;

– holistic privacy and security concept to prevent the system from misuse.

9.6. Acknowledgements

The research leading to these results received funding from the European Union H2020 Program under grant agreement No. 723710.

9.7. References

[JAL 12] JALOTE P., *An integrated approach to software engineering*, Springer Science & Business Media, 2012.

[PAT 14] PATTON J., ECONOMY P., *User story mapping: discover the whole story, build the right product*, O'Reilly Media, Inc., 2014.

[RIC 08] RICHARDSON L., RUBY S., *RESTful web services*, O'Reilly Media, Inc., 2008.

10

Enablers Framework: Developing Applications Using FIWARE

Industry is moving towards smart systems and automation, which leads modern factories to demand a set of tools capable of sustaining their needs. Generic and specifics sets of enablers are emerging as core industry 4.0 components, as they provide the software services that factories of the future require. Although enablers can be at the FoF foundation, a system able to integrate them together in an interoperable way does not exist. To integrate the several enablers with their matching applications, it is necessary to create an adaptable system able to overcome this gap. This article proposes the Enablers Framework, a component of the vf-OS project that acts as a bridge between applications and enablers, granting programmers an easy access to the services they need. This framework will thus open the possibility for several business opportunities to arise, since the integration of such versatile components is an alternative to the heterogeneous components used in the industrial panorama.

10.1. Introduction

The world is facing the fourth industrial revolution based on ICT, specifically architectures and services, as key innovation drivers for manufacturing companies. Traditional factories will increasingly be transformed into smart digital manufacturing environments but currently the full potential of ICT in manufacturing is far from being fully exploited. Factories are complex systems of systems and there is a need to develop a platform on which future manufacturing applications can be built. Examples of platforms exist in some industrial sectors but there is a lack of cross-cutting platforms based on open standards for creating an ecosystem for

Chapter written by Pedro Corista, Joao Giao, Joao Sarraipa, Oscar Garcia Perales, Raquel Almeida and Nejib Moalla.

cooperative innovation. The approaches that have been used in industry rely on point-to-point solutions that compete, by providing new specific features or fixing specific issues. Using these solutions results in having a highly heterogeneous industrial IT panorama, where each factory may have similar solutions with different architectures and programming languages. Having such heterogeneous solutions creates problems for adapting current solutions from an existing factory to another, as a specific solution is developed to a specific end. There is the need for a homogeneous solution that allows the support of the needs from manufacturing companies and fills current approaches' gaps. vf-OS (virtual factory Operating System) aims to be that solution. The goal of the vf-OS project is to develop an Open Operating System for Virtual Factories, responsible for managing factory-related computer hardware and software resources and providing common services for factory computational programs. This system will be the component in a real factory system where all factory application programs will run. To fulfill this objective, the system must have a component which follows the kernel's principles and logic. A kernel is a component that acts as a resource manager by taking care of the various programs that are running concurrently in the system [MAU 08]. As seen in [GAR 10] one of a kernel's functions is to interface all the applications, granting the bridge between them and the resources they need. Following this concept, vf-OS has a component called Enablers Framework (EF) that interfaces the applications (vApps) and the services they require. Such a component allows the integration of necessary tools, without the user needing to experience the associated installation complexity. This paper proposes a definition for the EF. The first section highlights the EF's purpose and its role as a wrapper; it also explains and details its main components. The second section is related to the business opportunities that EF provides, considering software developers, manufacturing users and ICT providers.

10.2. Enablers framework

EF is the component that acts as a bridge between service providers and service consumers. There already exist approaches to work with FIWARE that allow one to integrate enablers with applications; as seen in [COL 15], EF aims to provide support for enabler integration and also installing and managing instances of an enabler. To understand the overall functionality of EF's, it is necessary to define what the service providers for the applications that consume them are (vApps).

The service providers were chosen from the set of solutions adopted from the FIWARE project [FIW 18a] and are classified as generic enablers (GEs) or specific enablers (SEs). GEs can be found in [FIW 18b] and provide functionalities that ease the connection to Internet of Things (IoT) technologies and devices, process data and media in real-time at large scale, perform Big Data analytics or incorporate advanced features for the interaction with users. SEs can be found in [FIT 13] and provide functionalities which are more specific to the manufacturing domains such as manufacturing assets virtualization, collaborative manufacturing asset management, 3D scanning and virtualization, social data analysis and so on. Using the functionalities of the several GEs and SEs, a programmer can have a high range of tools that can act as core software components while designing the vApps. How EF integrates the existing enablers is explained in the next sections.

10.2.1. *EF as a bridge*

The EF component provides a solution for integration, exposition of and uniform access to functionalities of the different enablers in a single service-based component. The enablers, specifically GE and SE, can expose heterogeneous sets of service interfaces that could be used by vApp developers posing a need to understand and implement them. The EF component acts as a wrapper engine for the different enablers and the vApps consume its services. Such an approach presents high interoperability advantages, as any enabler can be accessed through the platform, and integrated in any developed application. The developer doesn't have to worry about the enablers' installation process in the target machine, as the EF oversees its whole process. This way they can focus on the development process, saving time and resources. The first step to use an enabler is to register it through EF's interface. From that moment on, the user can create an instance of the enabler and use it. The instantiation process allows users to choose whether the enabler instance is public or private.

The instance creation and installation are processed by creating a Docker container from an enabler image, as seen in [MER 14]. To run an enabler on a personal computer or public server it is necessary to have access to its virtual instance. The Docker solution allows the instantiation of enablers, following an approach similar to the one done in [STU 15] for microservices, presenting an alternative to actual Virtual Machines (VM). Docker is a platform that lets the user run an application in an isolated environment meaning that it is possible to run multiple containers at the same time on the same host. Using such an approach allows any enabler to be packaged into isolated containers with necessary code, runtime environment, system tools, system libraries and settings bundled all together. This strategy can lead towards the realization of efficient, lightweight, self-contained software packages and guarantees that software always runs the same way, regardless of where it is deployed. A Docker-based approach secures the enablers instantiation, granting that all enablers can be installed, thus contributing to the integration process.

10.2.2. *Component functionalities*

After an instance is created, a user can access the enabler he needs through the EF. The access to each enabler is granted by following an approach analogous to proxy communication. Whenever an application needs a service it communicates with the framework which contacts the corresponding enabler, performing the necessary request and delivering its result to the vApp. The communication between the applications and the framework can be made using Messaging and Pub/Sub components, all through the Process Execution. Between the applications and EF a Process Executor exists that orchestrates what the application will need. Communication between enablers and the framework is performed using IoT protocols such as REST and NGSI. To perform the enablers' integration, EF uses two main modules: Request Handler (RH) and Enabler Registry Lookup Services (ERLS) (see Figure 10.1).

The RH abstracts and implements all necessary functionalities for translating requests to/from vApps and enablers that are served by the EF. The internal components of this module parse the requests and create a suitable communication channel for accessing the functionalities of the enablers and build necessary response messages, based on the result of the function invocation. This module uses the technical details of the enablers from the ERLS and relies on suitable proxies to invoke the method requested by vApp. ERLS abstracts all the data models corresponding to registrations details and provides functionalities for performing Create, Read, Upgrade and Delete (CRUD) operations on them. This module is also responsible for providing service details of the enabler to the RH.

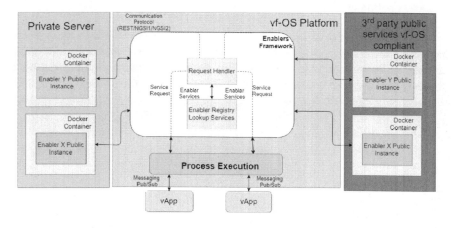

Figure 10.1. *Enablers integration using Enablers Framework. For a color version of this figure, see www.iste.co.uk/zelm/enterprise.zip*

The two presented module interactions grant the enablers integration. After receiving a service request from an application, the RH contacts ERLS to verify if such an enabler is registered in the framework. Upon verifying it, ERLS informs RH about the target enabler's services and this information is then used to exchange information between the framework and the enabler. The framework then informs the vApp on the service's response or delivers an error if the target enabler or service are unreachable.

10.3. Implementation scenario

This section provides a scenario that explains how the vApps can consume the enabler's services they need. The implementation scenario uses the EF's components presented in section 2.2, along with the Process Enabler (PE) (Figure 10.2). The PE is a tool used to orchestrate the diffProerent tasks that a vApp will carry out. When developing a vApp (Design Time), the Process Designer (the designer side of the Process Enabler) will be used to define the different sub-tasks (e.g. call an analytics algorithm) and/or sub-processes (e.g. retain data in the storage) that will be necessary for executing the vApp, and assign the necessary EF libraries to achieve integration. This process model, in the form of a BPMN, will be then incorporated to the vApp source code so vf-OS is able to execute the different process steps. Thus, the cess Designer will contact the vf- OS Marketplace, vf- Store, to access the definition and the services of the different assets that the vApp developer wants to make use of. These assets could indeed be an enabler which offers certain services and then this enabler will be accessed through the EF at runtime. At runtime, when the vApp is being executed, the vf-OS Platform will call the Process Execution (PEX) PE. This way, any vApp will be executed following the same pattern. Then, the PEX will open the BPMN definition of the vApp and orchestrate the calls to the different assets specified in this definition. When it is time to call the services offered by an enabler, regardless of whether it is a GE, SE or vf-OS Enabler, the PEX will call the EF that will be in charge of relaying the call to the enabler specified. Then, when the enabler replies, the EF will take its response, pack it and send it to the PEX so the response packet can continue its route in the BPMN flow of the vApp.

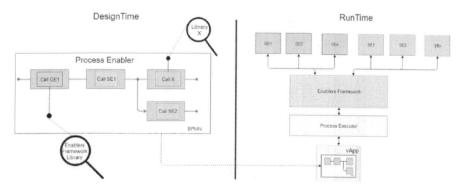

Figure 10.2. *Application scenario. For a color version of this figure, see www.iste.co.uk/zelm/enterprise.zip*

10.4. Business opportunities

vf-OS aims to become a business multi-side platform enabling value by creating interactions between external producers and consumers. This approach provides an open, participative infrastructure for these interactions and sets governance conditions for them. Its main goal is to make producers' and consumers' information available to each other, in a timely, accurate and transparent way, diminishing their information asymmetry, and making the digital exchange of products and services a better interaction experience for both. The EF and its underlying enablers are a significant part of the added value of vf-OS, which business value relates to: (1) end user enablers that could be directly utilized in the development of vApps (design time), or solely to facilitate an easy plug and play of other resources (CPS, APIs etc.); (2) scalable services through enablers that can provide services, which vApps or other components can consume; (3) the vf-OS Ecosystem where the EF as the bridge between service providers and consumers facilitates their integration with the vf-OS platform and its associated services.

Being developed under FIWARE guidelines, enablers must follow an open source approach, but this doesn't exactly mean that the enabler services execution through the EF should be taken for free. On top of this free approach, enablers' developers could sell support contracts on top of enablers' deployment for continuous maintenance, specially customization. Thus, it is expected that all these transactions occur through vf-OS Store, it being the platform and the main sponsor of the marketing and selling activities of all its vApps and enablers specific services.

10.5. Conclusions and future work

Modern industry demands new tools capable of providing resources for its needs. Generic and specific enablers provide the services that factories of the future require. This article presented a framework, part of the vf-OS project, able to integrate enablers with the applications, acting as a bridge between them. By relying on a Docker-based approach the framework provides several instances of the desired enabler, without the user having to pass through its installation process. The enabler can then be accessed through the framework that provides the means to access the enabler's services. The orchestration of the services can be achieved through Process Enabler which assigns the necessary tasks that the application will carry out. The PE will then generate a BPMN which will be integrated in the vApp to execute the defined tasks. The integration of the enablers implies new business opportunities as it opens new business opportunities for its customer segments directly. Additionally, enablers can be used directly in shop floors for easy establishment of IoT connections or indirectly by enrichment of the vApps functionalities.

10.6. Acknowledgements

The research leading to these results received funding from the European Union H2020 Program under grant agreement No. 723710 "Virtual Factory Open Operating System" (vf-OS).

10.7. References

[COL 15] DI COLA S., TRAN C., LAU K. *et al.*, "A Heterogeneous Approach for Developing Applications with FIWARE GEs", *Eur. Conf. Serv. Cloud Comput.*, vol. 2, pp. 65–79, 2015.

[FIT 13] FITMAN, "FITMAN Manufacturing Enablers", available at: http://catalogue. fitman.atosresearch.eu/catalogue.fitman.atosresearch.eu/enablers.html, 2013.

[FIW 18a] FIWARE, "FIWARE Project", available at: https://forge.fiware.org/projects/ fiware/., 2018.

[FIW 18b] FIWARE, "Generic Enablers", available at: https://catalogue.fiware.org/ enablers, 2018.

[GAR 10] GARRISON J., "What is the Linux Kernel and What Does It Do?", *How-To Geek*, 2010.

[MAU 08] MAUERER W., Linux ® Kernel Architecture, 2008.

[MER 14] MERKEL D., "Docker: lightweight Linux containers for consistent development and deployment", *Linux Journal*, vol. 239, no. 2, 2014.

[STU 15] STUBBS J., "Distributed Systems of Microservices Using Docker and Serfnode", *7th International Workshop on Science Gateways*, Budapest, Hungary, 2015.

vf-OS IO Toolkit

The growing variety of programming languages in software engineering feeds the permanent need of interoperability enablers between IT solutions. In agile and integrated software development, it is vital to ensure the communication between existing IT system and new ones. In addition, the connected smart factories paradigm extends the perimeter of enterprise information systems to cover the direct integration of sensors and machines. vf-OS is an H2020 European project aimed at providing a development environment with an integrated, virtual view on manufacturing processes. Within vf-OS, the IO Toolkit provides tools for on-premises facilitation of access to manufacturing devices and existing business software, while also facilitating the interaction with the rest of the vf-OS infrastructure. As such it allows developers to build secure and controlled gateways into the factories, as part of the capability set for their applications.

11.1. Introduction

vf-OS, virtual factory Open Operating System is an Open Operating System for Virtual Factories composed of a kernel, application programming interface, and middleware specifically designed for the factory of the future. The purpose is to attract talent from solution developers and to provide accessible manufacturing smart applications to European SMEs.

Enterprise interoperability [JAK 12] remains the common research umbrella for software-oriented initiatives aiming to provide development frameworks and

Chapter written by Víctor ANAYA, Nejib MOALLA, Ludo STELLINGWERFF, José Luis FLORES and Francisco FRAILE.

toolkits. To ensure engineering efficiency, structured interoperability methodologies are requested to improve the sustainability of software-oriented initiatives and solutions.

11.2. vf-OS IO Toolkit

The IO Toolkit is the development framework provided by vf-OS to Manufacturing and Service Providers wanting to generate new device drivers and API Connectors with the purpose of widening the range of shop floor devices and line of business systems that can be connected to applications developed for the vf-OS platform (called vApps).

Any new developed device driver or API connector (generically called IO component) can be published to the Marketplace (see top-right part of Figure 11.1).

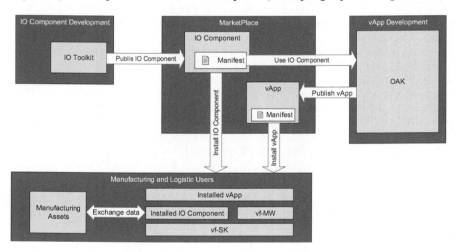

Figure 11.1. *IO Toolkit Positioning*

If a vApp uses a specific IO component, then the Manifest file of the vApp describes this dependency, so that users can be informed before installing the vApp. Software Developers can thus develop functionalities that interact with any manufacturing asset that is connected to vf-OS via an IO component.

11.3. IO components

An IO component is a generic term to refer to Device Drivers or API connectors. A Device Driver is a kind of IO component that interacts with physical industrial devices to integrate sensors' data and send commands to devices. An example is a driver for consuming data from devices supporting the OPC UA protocol. On the other hand, API Connectors are IO components that interact with legacy software in factories (such as ERPs, databases or tailored ICT solutions).

The common structure followed by every IO component is shown in the next layered schema:

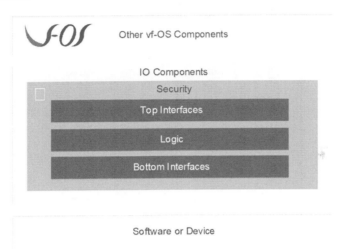

Figure 11.2. *I/O components functionalities*

11.3.1. *Top interfaces*

Top interfaces are the interfaces that any IO component must implement to be vf-OS compliant. Those interfaces, bootstrapped by the IO toolkit, provide a mechanism to invoke and consume data and functionality provided by drivers and APIS. The different interfaces are:

– REST API Server Composition: provides specific REST APIs that new drivers and API connectors must follow to be called by the vf-OS platform components;

– messaging endpoints: provides drivers and connectors with ways to interact with the vf-OS Messaging component when sending and receiving new messages;

– Pub/Sub endpoints: provides ways to interact with the vf-OS Pub/Sub component, providing triggers, events and subscription functionalities;

– metadata template composition: generates a metadata template file used by vApp developers;

– registration endpoints: provides functionality to drivers and API connectors to be registered themselves in the Platform and the Marketplace;

– logging endpoints: registers logs that will be consumed by the System Dashboard and the Marketplace.

11.3.2. *Logic*

The IO Toolkit will provide a set of functionalities available when developing the internal logic of a driver or API connector. Every new driver and component will have available a set of libraries when developing its internal logic. Those libraries are functionally aggregated as:

– internal Storage: connects and queries the internal databases used to store configuration and operational data, both relational and non-relational databases;

– key-value store: accesses key-value stores to manage associative key-value pairs;

– edge computing: processes sensor data as close to the data source as possible, instead of processing raw sensor data in the cloud;

– API Access Control: for authentication and security, which can be used alone or in combination to issue credentials and control access;

– API Lifecycle management: the IO Toolkit must provide API lifecycle management tools (prototype, publish, deprecate, and block).

11.3.3. *Bottom interfaces*

Bottom interfaces are the proprietary interfaces which are part of well-known communication standards used by devices and business applications in manufacturing companies.

The IO Toolkit will provide the bottom interfaces out-of-the-box (Table 11.1).

Protocol	Description
OPC UA	OPC UA is a machine-to-machine communication protocol for industrial automation developed by the OPC Foundation.
MQTT	ISO standard (ISO/IEC PRF 20922) publish-subscribe-based "lightweight" messaging protocol for use on top of the TCP/IP protocol.

Modbus	Ethernet serial communication protocol extensively used in SCADA.
GPIO	Generic hardware interface integrated in single board computers (e.g. Raspberry Pi) widely used in fast prototyping.
MTConnect	Protocol to exchange data between industrial network components.
MS Excel	Spreadsheets are widely used in SMEs to build simple data analysis and reporting applications.
STEP	STEP is a file format used in CAD to work with 3D models. The STEP file format is widely used in the design of mechanical parts and is supported by the most popular CAD software tools.
ODBC	Standard API to access database management systems.
OData	REST protocol to build API Connectors with leading business software applications and systems (e.g. IBM WebSphere, Microsoft Dynamics CRM, Acumatica ERP, SAP ERP).
SAP ERP	OData-based API Connector.
NAV ERP	Microsoft Dynamics NAV is an ERP system developed by Microsoft.

Table 11.1. *Drivers and API connectors to be supported by vf-OS platform (extract)*

11.3.4. *IO Toolkit Security*

The IO Toolkit Security incorporates a mapped set of security requirements and a documented unit testing plan in security for the development of new vf-OS IO Components. This set of security requirements are based on the recommendations of the most relevant and authoritative organizations in the field of security such as SysAdmin Audit, Networking and Security Institute (SANS), OpenWeb Application Security Project, or National Institute of Standards and Technology.

Based on these recommendations, the requirements are created and provided as a set of checklists. These will require concrete specifications of aspects such as the use of the corresponding libraries for implementing OpenID [OPE 17] for fulfilling the holistic authentication and authorization model of vf-OS (XACML [OAS 17]) or the specification of valid time periods of sessions, error management, or memory management policies.

Finally, the IO Toolkit Security will provide endpoints for the vf-OS Security Command Centre REST APIs (Identity Service, Policy Administration, and Continuous Security Monitoring).

11.4. Containerization

The vf-OS platform technical infrastructure [VFO 17] is based on microservices, and Docker [DOC 17] is the core technology used with that purpose.

Developed drivers and API connectors will be deployed by the vf-OS marketplace as Docker containers. The benefits that Docker provides the IO Toolkit Execution Services are a Standardized API for connecting various services, the possibility to port applications to different environments and adapt to several deployment patterns, and several security features such as signed containers, through the Docker Trust feature.

11.5. Conclusions

The vf-OS IO Toolkit is the core component in the vf-OS platform providing the functionality to consume and interact with physical device drivers and existing business software solution. The IO Toolkit will provide a containerization solution to run drivers and API connects as microservices in the context of the vf-OS technical architecture. The driver could be run in a specific webserver on a docker machine providing very flexible deployment alternatives. The IO toolkit will provide a catalog of driver and connector templates that will empower developers on the development of new Device drivers and API connectors on the vf-OS Platform. The IO Toolkit will provide a convenient development documentation, along with a standard versioning scheme for the Toolkit and the produced components. Finally, vf-OS requires new drivers and connectors to be properly validated. With that purpose, the IO Toolkit will provide a testing framework to check the compliance of the IO component development.

11.6. Acknowledgements

The research leading to these results received funding from the European Union H2020 Program under grant agreement No. 723710 "Virtual Factory Open Operating System" (vf-OS).

11.7. References

[DOC 17] DOCKER INC., Docker, available at: https://www.docker.com/, accessed October 30, 2017.

[JAK 12] JAKOLE P., *An integrated approach to software engineering*, Springer Science & Business Media, 2012.

[OAS 17] OASIS, eXtensible Access Control Markup Language (XACML) Version 3.0, available at: http://docs.oasis-open.org/xacml/3.0/xacml-3.0-core-spec-os-en.html, accessed October 30, 2017.

[OPE 17] OPENID, OpenID Specifications, available at: http://openid.net/developers/specs/, accessed October 30, 2017.

[VFO 17] vf-OS CONSORTIUM, D11.5: Technical Set Up and Quality Toolset v1.2, 2017.

12

Data Management Component for Virtual Factories Systems

The vf-OS project aims to develop a middleware platform for the virtual factory of the future. The vf-OS is composed of several modules providing interoperability mechanisms for systems to exchange real-time data. Moreover, it enables the managing of data flows, transforming data, providing open APIs to ease the integration process. The proposed Data Management Component (DMC) intends to cover the issues related to data handling, pre-processing, extracting, and data flows management for virtual factories. It integrates four subcomponents: a data infrastructure middleware element that handles the data communications; a data storage mechanism able to work with high loads and triples; a semantic and mapping function to establish model information integration; and an analytical module composed by machine learning and prediction mechanisms to enable knowledge extraction from the vast amount of data generated by the associated virtual factory system.

12.1. Introduction

The modern Internet of Things (IoT) and Cyber-Physical Systems developed to cover the needs of the manufacturing domain are facing difficulties related not only to the amounts of data generated which need to be properly stored, transmitted and delivered on demand, but also to the challenges of structuring and analyzing data in order to create additional value. The vf-OS project, tightly related to concepts of IoT and CPS, aims at provision of an open platform for virtual factories (VF) and collaborative environments for different entities on different levels of the

Chapter written by Artem A. NAZARENKO, Joao GIAO, Joao SARRAIPA, Oscar J. SAIZ, Oscar GARCIA PERALES and Ricardo JARDIM-GONÇALVES.

manufacturing process. The vf-OS ecosystem will also inherit the problem of handling enormous ascending and descending data flows. Some of these challenges are covered by other vf-OS platform components, where one of them is responsible for the data connection (I/O functionality) and data movement which comes from its corresponding middleware module. However, before data are absorbed or consumed by applications, they need to be mapped from input to output type – this will be facilitated via semantic harmonization and transformation techniques. Finally, for data consumption analytics interfaces provided by the infrastructure must scale to extract relevant data subsets according to user's expectations in the simplest possible way. To access the data, the proposed component also includes all the elements required for data stream management: reading, cleaning, storing, indexing, enrichment, search and retrieval, fusion, maintenance, and correspondence of open APIs. This data infrastructure will serve analytic and decision-making services to the Virtual Factory Open Operating System.

12.2. Virtual factory data and connect

The focus of the proposed DMC [n.1] is on providing a set of semi-independent but related services taking the inputs of a variety data at large scale, with different characteristics such as transmission speed and so on, and providing a set of nontrivial analytic operators. It is composed of four subcomponents: the data infrastructure middleware; data storage; data harmonization; and data analytics. The data infrastructure middleware provides the core access that utilizes data storage functions for permanent and cross-application access. Data harmonization provides transformation services, based on semantics, and is particularly connected to the first subcomponent for data connectivity. All these four will be supported by the data analytics.

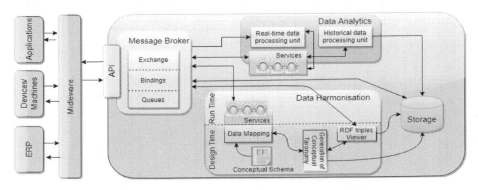

Figure 12.1. *DMC architecture. For a color version of this figure, see www.iste.co.uk/zelm/enterprise.zip*

12.2.1. *Data infrastructure middleware*

This component specifies and implements a data bus that will support the other subcomponents and the overall vf-OS application for data storage, transformation, and analytic operations. The data infrastructure will contain adapters in order to aggregate data from various enterprise information sources including: machines, hardware sensors (which might include high-precision camera data, accelerometers, vibration, and temperature sensors), software sensors from Enterprise Resource Planner (ERP) systems and external business context data and so on, and make use of other vf-OS activities. Since sensorial data typically generates large amounts of micro-measurements, the supporting data infrastructure needs to provide a high throughput technology pipeline for acquisition, pre-processing and aggregation of collected data [VFO 17].

At the early stage two main concepts for middleware were considered: REST and message-oriented (AMQP). In terms of advantages and disadvantages, the first to be mentioned is that REST has a synchronous nature while the AMQP broker implies rather asynchronous processing: for instance, a message might be requested right after it has been published in the queue or later, as it is kept until being consumed. REST has the advantage that the web-kind behavior can be transmitted to its resources. In some cases, when direct client-server communication is not possible, the REST approach will be completely useless, while AMQP allows ignoring mutual awareness between exchange parties. Another clear advantage, considering the IoT domain, is that AMQP supports both point-to-point as well as publish/subscribe patterns, while REST implies only point-to-point connections. Considering two ways of implementation, with broker or broker-less, the first was chosen due to characteristics extremely relevant for vf-OS: history logging, traceability, message queuing and reordering.

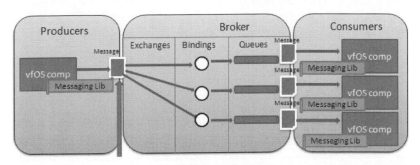

Figure 12.2. *Messaging model for vf-OS components using RabbitMQ broker. For a color version of this figure, see www.iste.co.uk/zelm/enterprise.zip*

To implement the above-mentioned functionality a message-oriented approach or middleware was selected: the AMQP protocol implemented by RabbitMQ message broker. According to the definition provided by designer of AMQP architecture [OHA 07] it is: "a binary wire protocol and well-defined set of behaviours for transmitting application messages between systems using a combination of store-and-forward, publish-and-subscribe, and other techniques". It is based on four basic definitions:

1) *Message*: basic unit of transmitted data, the main part of which is not interpreted by the server (only headers are processed);

2) *Exchange point*: delivery service for messages. All messages are sent into this point to be then distributed into different queues (Figure 12.2). There are three main types of exchange points:

Direct Exchange: sending a message directly at a single queue;

Topic Exchange: producing the copies of the message and sending to all clients;

Headers Exchange: checking all headers are matching with query predicates from interested clients;

3) *Queue*: here the messages are kept until the client request;

4) *Bindings*: deliver necessary information about routing, in different types of exchange it is provided by different entities.

The main components represented in Figure 12.2 are as follows: message broker (RabbitMQ) deployed on the server side implementing the AMQP protocol for message exchange and, on the client side, both message producers as well as message consumers. The client side is only responsible for creating or requiring messages and also adding some headers with relevant information about the type of exchange and target node/nodes. The rest is being performed by broker. A publish-subscribe middleware will help to implement Event Driven Architecture (EDA) and is fully compatible with major industry standards (i.e. JBI, SCA, BPEL or WSDL).

12.2.2. *Data storage*

This component implements the storage services for vf-OS assets. It supports three major dimensions of "Big Data" when dealing with intensive streaming data, namely: volume (scale of data being processed), velocity (data transmission speed and optimized reaction time), and variety (supporting heterogeneous types of data). It implements a scalable data storage system, capable of handling real-time sensor data and events, based on an underlying infrastructure that transparently absorbs very large amounts of data, as well as other types of non-real-time heterogeneous data. The vf-OS Platform has different needs for data storage, for example, sensor data, events, alarms, time series, maps, models, data files, log files and structured data. Each of them has its own requirements in terms of velocity of storage and querying, volume and updateability of the data, consistency, availability, partition tolerance, and other dimensions. So, it is not possible to think of a solution based on a single storage system. Here is where *polyglot persistence* comes into play.

In 2006, Neal Ford coined the term "polyglot programming"[1], to express the idea that applications should be written in a mix of languages to take advantage of the fact that different languages are suitable for tackling different problems. The same concept can be applied to databases; thus applications utilize different databases using each for what they are best at to achieve an end goal. This is called polyglot persistence[2]. vf-OS storage is based on this polyglot persistence paradigm. So, following this paradigm, four different storage services are provided:

1) Relational data: to store relational data from vApps as well as other relational information of the vf-OS Platform itself;

2) Time Series data: to allow storage and querying time series data;

3) Document-Oriented data: to store, retrieve and manage document-oriented information, also known as semi-structured data;

4) RDF data: to store and query subject-predicate-object triples.

12.2.3. *Data harmonization*

Data harmonization aims at (1) extracting more information from incoming data, and (2) preparing the data in a form/schema suitable for other vf-OS components and vf-OS Assets. It will enable semantic enrichment with background knowledge and data mining on real-time streams, received through the Messaging component. The data enrichment objective is to generate from the observed data additional derived attributes/features, either using external background knowledge or internal relationships within data. This could include the use of external ontologies, statistical properties, (models) of data and/or temporal characteristics of data. The key aim is to encode functional transformations of data to help the data (pre-) processing as long as the vApp needs it; as an example, by carrying out analytic techniques of T5.4 to detect non-linear and other nontrivial patterns within the data (otherwise non-detectable by traditional analytic techniques).

Issues related to data extraction from heterogeneous sources with further transformation of them are solved by so called Extract-Transform-Load (ETL) Systems. The main goal of ETL systems is to make data more useful for further processing and analytics. This might be achieved through linking data and creating

---

1 http://nealford.com/memeagora/2006/12/05/Polyglot_Programming.html.
2 https://martinfowler.com/bliki/PolyglotPersistence.html.

triples or semantic triples, which can be described as a statement of the subject-predicate-object form. ETL workflow consists of three main phases, as it follows from the definition: extraction, transformation and load. According to [BAN 14], data extraction aims at getting data from the source, which can be presented in the form of flat file or data base source. Transformation is a process of "cleaning" data or bringing them to the form corresponding to the scheme, including some actions such as: normalization, filtering and so on. And the last stage is loading them to the data storage.

Since vf-OS is oriented towards the software developers wanting to develop vApps for the Manufacturing Industry, it is expected that the ETLs would be part of the execution of a vApp. However, vf-OS follows a different approach: instead of programming the ETLs directly in the source code of the vApp, the ETLs will be programmed as independent services and, thus, deployed as standalone services that could be re-used by other vApps and launch several instances of the same service if deemed necessary. As such, the data harmonization is divided in two components: one for design-time, data mapping, and another for run-time, data transformation. Thus, the ETLs will be "programmed" under the data mapping component and deployed as these standalone services and executed within the vApp as part of the data transformation component.

12.2.4. *Data analytics*

This sub-component covers the creation of building blocks for offline analytical processing of inputs coming from the manufacturing environment. This will include machine learning algorithms supporting supervised and unsupervised scenarios. The core of the analytic algorithms will be based on the combination of the modern statistical machine learning linear algebra-based algorithms (e.g. SVM, CRF, LDA, Mixture-Models) and traditional data-mining algorithms (e.g. decision trees and rules, k-means, association rules). This will cover typical classification and segmentation scenarios for enriched representations coming from semantic based ontological descriptions to capture nonlinearities in data. The key research innovation will be provided by using "multi-level" analysis on the top of more traditional machine learning algorithms simultaneously observing the data on multiple aggregation levels [VFO 17].

In a factory there will be two different types of analytics tasks to be performed: those depending on historical data sources, for example readings of sensors for a given period of time in the past, and those that need to be calculated in real-time as they will be involved in triggering alarms conducive to time-(or spend-) critical actions. As such, two different modules will be integrated into the data analytics component focusing each of them in these two, although complementary, areas.

Similarly to the data harmonization, the data analytics will be composed of analytics libraries so that the vf-OS user, that is the developer of vApps, would be able to re-use the existing analytics libraries that will be provided by vf-OS. This means that there will be a set of libraries each of which covering complementary functionality. There will be libraries for the various analytics approaches as for modeling and training like Random Forest predictors, which will be built on top of a SOTA analytics tool [H2O 18] that offers an API to access to such different algorithms.

12.3. Conclusions and future work

Current research work represents the DMC as the part of vf-OS project's being performed within Horizon 2020 initiative. The proposed solution being developed to satisfy both basic as well as more complex needs of VF's in managing data flows. This includes organization of data exchange based on message-oriented middleware, extracting, transforming and representing data with data harmonization and data analytics subcomponents and storage of heterogeneous data both in terms of content and format. Important requirements for VF's such as vast amount of data being produced as well as consumed, scalability and adaptability of infrastructure, need to cope with different data in terms of formats, origin, heterogeneity and distributiveness of data sources are also considered. The main efforts are directed towards providing a scalable, open-source, modular platform for developing various industrial applications within a shared VF ecosystem. The resulting component, in fact an independent platform, will be able to solve relevant issues related to quick and agile deployment of smart applications through enabling of necessary tools and software modules around data flows handling. Further work will include implementation of DMC within vf-OS for different manufacturing scenarios. However, DMC can also be used as an independent component being integrated with already exciting solutions and thus offering the wide range of possible implementations as a part of other systems and solutions.

12.4. Acknowledgements

The research leading to these results received funding from the European Union H2020 Program under grant agreement No. 723710 "Virtual Factory Open Operating System" (vf-OS).

12.5. References

[BAN 14] BANSAL S.K., "Towards a Semantic Extract-Transform-Load (ETL) framework for Big Data Integration", *IEEE International Congress on Big Data*, pp. 522–529, 2014.

[H2O 18] H2O.AI, https://www.h2o.ai, Accessed Jan 29, 2018.

[OHA 07] O'HARA J., "Toward a Commodity Enterprise Middleware", *ACM Queue*, vol. 5, no. 4, pp. 48–55, 2007.

[VFO 17] vf-OS, Virtual Factory Open Operating System, Technical Annex, 2017.

13

An Open Environment for Development of Manufacturing Applications on vf-OS

Developing a project aimed at providing an Operating System to a manufacturing system requires having a suite of tools that can specify, develop, build and distribute the applications that will be at the heart of this manufacturing system. These applications shall be able to receive stimuli from, and to provide actuation over, the manufacturing assets, combining this virtualized manufacturing system with the power of the novel ICT resources, enablers and state-of-the-art techniques for development and building of systems and applications that have been used in industry, which involve WYSIWYG editors with syntax highlighting, SDKs which provide a large set of artifacts and libraries including standard connectors and extension points, but also debuggers, tools to optimize the performance and make the best use of the latest technology. Additionally, innovative methodologies for development promote strong involvement of the development community and the developers' engagement. This paper describes a novel environment that was envisioned for this purpose, involved in the scope of the H2020 European Project vf-OS.

13.1. Introduction

The upcoming new industrial revolution "Industry 4.0" [IND 18] presents a new paradigm for the development of manufacturing services, tightly aligned with the most advanced ICT innovations. At the very heart of this development are new techniques that promote the collection of data from multiple sensors and sources of

Chapter written by Carlos Coutinho, Luís Lopes, Vítor Viana, Danny Pape, Gerrit Klasen, Bastian von Halem, Oscar Garcia Perales, Ludo Stellingwerff and Andries Stam.

input information and the ability to infer knowledge from them (Internet of Things – IoT), and virtualization of the manufacturing assets. The new smart digital manufacturing environments will allow the development of applications that are able to interact with the virtual factory assets, receiving inputs and actuating on the real factory systems. This will allow them to benefit from the advances in the methodologies and development of software applications that traditionally were not applicable to the manufacturing domain, with multi-purposed agile dashboards and frontends that deal with accessibility and that are more responsive and provide more valuable information. New methodologies include agile techniques, the use of popular and proven development frameworks and the support of development communities that provide manpower for testing and for innovative ideas, suggestions and bug corrections. Additionally, the development of applications shall be more pleasant, with a set of tools like IDEs and editors with code syntax highlighting, debuggers, drag and drop features, integration with version control, issue trackers and other mechanisms that engage and motivate the developer into the creation of applications, a set of libraries accessible through the development SDK that will provide access to innovative features such as new enablers, dependencies analysis, dashboards and especially the connection to the internet and to a whole new level of ICT assets.

The developers will be able to produce "what you see is what you get" (WYSIWYG) applications that use frontend elements commonly used on web-based applications, based on the latest technologies and best practices of the market.

The H2020 project vf-OS [VFO 18] proposes to create an operating system targeted to the manufacturing business. This naturally involves the development of mechanisms that interact with the real factory assets, enablers for connecting to internet and web features, and an environment that fosters the development of applications for the manufacturing business. The vf-OS development framework is named the Virtual Factory Open Application Development Kit (OAK) [VFO 17]. It is composed of a set of libraries, assets and tools which are described next.

13.2. vf-OAK SDK

The vf-OAK Software Development Kit (SDK) is a centralized environment for the development of applications and, generically, for centralized access to the vf-OS assets and functionalities. The SDK itself will not have a user interface per se, instead, it will be accessed as a set of APIs to access the main development resources. That way, the SDK will be able to provide to the vf-OAK Studio (see section 13.3) and to other Application/Development components the resources and services that they require.

The vf-OAK SDK comprises an extensive fully-documented API framework that provides to developers the means to easily generate applications (vApps) and services. It also includes the development of a service API which offers methods to access functionalities of all technical components in the vf-OS environment that the service developers need, such as the easy integration of data from the Cloud-based information infrastructure and the storage of service-specific data within the Cloud.

The basis for the development of the SDK is to provide a component or framework of elements that foster and improve the development of solutions and vApps for vf-OS. The idea is to be able to help a developer to create vApps with this framework such that the SDK will provide what needs to be included in the vApp, and then other OAK components will be responsible for defining behaviors, process flows and other application definitions, in a user-friendly interface, based on Frontend customized elements, that aims to promote and foster development.

Particularly speaking, the SDK is divided into several parts considering the components that are to be connected: the SDK core is responsible for handling and exporting the communication layer between the OAK Studio or other components for actions, for example publish/subscribe, messages, or security. The SDK for vApps has a process interpreter which can transform the results from the Process Designer tool (XML files) to JavaScript language. And the SDK for the I/O Toolkit accesses the real manufacturing devices, sensors and other mechanisms via the vf-IO interfaces.

13.3. vf-OAK Studio

The vf-OAK Studio provides an Integrated Development Environment (IDE) with a Graphical User Interface (GUI) for users that want to develop vApps for the vf-OS platform. It also provides all the necessary tools and means for developing a vApp, and supports the application deployment on end-user devices, and its publication in multiple marketplaces. Besides including tools for code development, with editors that include features like Business Process Management Notation (BPMN), syntax highlighting and drag-and-drop, debugging and analysis of the developed code, the vf-OAK Studio includes the interfaces for Process Designer, Frontend Composer, and provides access to the vf-Store marketplace.

The vApp creation starts by setting the necessary configuration which includes dependencies, marketplaces and permissions that are going to be used by the vApp. Then the vf-OAK Studio provides a working space composed by a Process Designer (see section 13.4) and a list of services and processes available in the vf-Store marketplace which are specified during the project configuration.

The implementation of vApps will be based on the composition of pre-built blocks, where the developer can select an available process/service from the marketplace, and drag-and-drop it as a block to the Process Designer. Each block can be configured by the user. If a process or service needed by the user is not available in the list, the user can create and develop a new customized block. The logic for the implementation of this custom block can be done by using or composing other blocks or code. When finished, the custom block can be saved locally, so it can be used on the vApp, or deployed to one or more marketplaces, so that other developers can make use of it.

The vf-OAK Studio also includes a Frontend composer (see section 13.5) which manages the user interfaces used by the vApp. From this tool, the user can use the available templates, for example default login page, or create new ones. This User Interface (UI) composer also supports logic implementation used by the UI, for example filtering the received data and showing the results or having the inputs entered by the user.

13.4. Process designer

vf-OS will use a Process Designer for complementing the development of the vApps. The Process Designer is responsible for allowing users to model multiple manufacturing workflows for orchestrating the various assets available within a collaborative framework. The tool will be an online workspace supporting a BPMN-like model and will be usable by vApps whenever process design and orchestration is appropriate.

The Process Designer will be a visual online reactive canvas, allowing the developer to pull in existing models from a library representing the virtualized manufacturing assets and all the elements which will be necessary for the correct development of a vApp. These elements can be any of the vf-OS Assets: Generic FIWARE Enablers (Application, Services, e.g. single-sign-on (SSO), but also Specification/Methodology), Manufacturing Enablers (Applications, Services and Specification/Methodology), vf-OS Services (e.g. Transformation), vf-OS Component (e.g., Process Engine [VFO 18a]), and of course, other vApps.

Each asset may support additional properties that can be defined. The defined workflow can include other sub-workflows and be saved and versioned within the Data Storage as BPMN-model definitions. This will allow a developer to design an *ad hoc* workflow that will model and shape the desired vApp. Examples of vApps could be the execution of a specific business process or the integration of both intra-plant and cross-company data exchange processes. These services, which will be orchestrated at runtime, will be augmented with additional information needed to define the required processes.

The vf-OS Process Designer will be a web-based BPMN tool accessible through the vf-OS OAK. It will take advantage of cutting-edge web technologies. The foundations of the Process Designer will make use of an open source BPMN modeler framework such as BPMN-IO, which is a rendering toolkit and web modeler for BPMN. It allows easy creation of BPMN2.0 diagrams using a web-based modeling library which can be extended to add the functionality for vf-OS.

The toolbox inside the Process Designer will offer vf-OS manufacturing assets (Services) that are available from the vf-Store. From this repository, a process designer can then select and drag from the Toolbox onto the design canvas to begin modeling a process. It will contain all the standard BPMN modeling elements, such as Parallel or Exclusive Gateways, Processes, and many others needed to create a BPMN diagram.

13.5. Frontend

The Frontend Environment is part of vf-OAK and builds a library of graphical elements that are optionally linked to simple functionalities. These elements are cross-platform compatible and they serve as a help for developers to quickly and safely create consistent looking vApps. The libraries from the Frontend Environment are integrated into the vf-OAK Studio, and can be used directly, by using the elements in the shape of classes. By using the Frontend Environment, the developers can choose between the following repositories:

– UI Element Repository contains single UI elements following the style guide of vf-OS that can be used during vApp development. Particular attention was paid to the corporate holistic layout of vf-OS for branding purposes;

– UI Template Repository provides compositions of UI elements from the UI Element Repository. Each template appears as a single UI element but is composed of several UI predefined elements. A lightweight example of a UI template is a login form, which is composed of a grid, textbox, password-textbox, and action buttons;

– Behavior Repository contains several default behaviors for activities, which are related to UI interactions. Those behaviors are easy to integrate and applicable, for example forms, downloads, registration, and notifications;

– Behavior Template Repository provides a composition of several behavior templates. A single behavior template consists of lined-up behaviors that are processed synchronously. Lined-up behaviors ease the use of handling events and support developers with additional default events;

– Holistic Template Repository provides holistic templates that unite UI templates and behavior templates. Those templates follow the style guide and include logic to handle user interactions automatically.

Furthermore, in vf-OS, the Frontend Environment is used both in design and at runtime. In design time the developer can choose elements from the library and can integrate them in their vApps with help of the vf-Studio. But, in runtime, demanded user interactions can call simple functionalities from public vf-OS interfaces, such as the analytics component or the vf-SDK.

13.6. System dashboard

The vf-OS System Dashboard is a runtime, central dashboard and task manager, aimed at monitoring, warning, configuring, and adapting system resources. As such, it provides information on the runtime behavior of the vf-Apps, useful for both the end user and the developers of the apps.

The primary component of the dashboard is a web-based user interface, in which the status of all user accessible vf-OS components and deployed assets can be monitored and controlled.

Behind this UI, a controller service is provided which aims to collect the required information for the dashboard and which contacts the execution services for the starting and stopping of vf-Apps and their dependencies.

A notification service is also part of the dashboard, allowing the user (and/or developer) to be informed of off-nominal issues or other triggers. The Notification Engine stores and manages notifications, and applies several external messaging mechanisms (e.g. email, messaging, notification icon) to warn users of such issues.

13.7. Developers engagement hub

To complement the actions of development, creation, debugging and integration, the modern methodologies for supporting the development advocate that as good or better than having a great development team is to have an active and engaged community of users, partners, customers and developers that contribute to the success of the projects.

Hence, the team proposed the inclusion of a centralized hub which has the purpose of gathering and promoting the contact, interaction, collaboration and discussion of interested stakeholders. These communities often help with their requirements, their suggestions and ideas, but also greatly with their own development or testing of the developed vApps. This is the largely successful philosophy around Open Source, but to be able to do this in a correct way, these communities need to be correctly biased and engaged with the developing project. The vf-OAK suite therefore includes a platform that has as sole purpose the capitalization of the developing project, providing mechanisms that promote a clear and straightforward description of what is being developed and its surrounding concepts, methodologies, requirements, and as much more information as possible.

The vf-OS Developers Engagement Hub will promote the dissemination of the developed code and its evolution using source code control (e.g. Git repositories), and tools which will mostly deal with dissemination and communication (collaboration), which may include wikis, templates, tutorials, multimedia, forums, mechanisms for capturing and describing new features and bugs (issue trackers), management tools, and many others which may support the development and make it simpler, like business and continuous integration, connections to larger ERP and CRM tools, statistics and other tools which may both facilitate the development, its documentation and dissemination.

13.8. Conclusion

The purpose of the H2020 vf-OS European Project is to provide manufacturing businesses with an open Operating System that will allow them to – similarly to what happens in a regular computer – create, develop, build and load applications that span and cover the whole manufacturing operation and process, enabling the capture of the business knowledge and promoting its analysis and potential to achieve greater value.

13.9. Acknowledgements

The research leading to these results received funding from the European Union H2020 Program under grant agreement No. 723710 "Virtual Factory Open Operating System" (vf-OS).

13.10. References

[IND   18] INDUSTRIE 4.0, http://www.plattform-i40.de/I40/Navigation/EN/Industrie40/ WhatIsIndustrie40/what-is-industrie40.html, Federal Ministry for Economic Affairs and Energy, Germany, Accessed on January 10, 2018.

[VFO 18] vf-OS http://vf-os.eu, Accessed January 10, 2018.

[VFO 18a] vf-OS CONSORTIUM, vf-OS Process Execution Engine, http://158.42.105.151/ mediawiki/index.php/Process_Engine, Accessed January 10, 2018.

[VFO 17] vf-OS CONSORTIUM, D2.1 Global Architecture Definition, 2017.

14

A Novel Approach to Software Development in the Microservice Environment of vf-OS

Within the vf-OS project, a common approach is taken for the deployment of computing resources and data models. As such vf-OS represents a modern approach to the software middleware layer, specifically aimed at the manufacturing domain. The approach consists of "Docker"-based microservices, orchestrated through common REST services. Because of the domain, special attention is given to the challenge of running resources OnPremise versus purely InCloud, and the challenges of letting such heterogeneous environments work together. As this environment poses challenges for the development process of applications, a novel approach to the development of such applications is needed. In this paper, this approach is described. During the vf-OS project, experience will be obtained, validating this approach.

14.1. Introduction

vf-OS, virtual factory Open Operating System, is an Open Operating System for Virtual Factories composed of a kernel, application programming interface, and middleware specifically designed for the factory of the future. The purpose is to attract talent from solution developers and to provide accessible manufacturing smart applications to European SMEs.

Chapter written by Luís Manteigas Da Cunha, Ludo Stellingwerff and Andries Stam.

vf-OS offers a manufacturing-oriented cloud platform, supporting a multi-sided market ecosystem that provides a range of services for the connected factory of the future, allowing manufacturing companies to develop and integrate better manufacturing and logistics processes [VFO 18].

Due to the highly distributed microservices architecture used in vf-OS, such an environment poses some challenges for the software development process which will produce the assets. This paper describes the approach taken to handle these challenges and describes how this can be evaluated over the lifetime of the project.

14.2. vf-OS platform

The design of the vf-OS platform environment is formed based on the requirements set out in the public requirements document D1.5 [VFR 18]. It provides the environment in which vf-OS assets are installed, run and accessed. These assets encompass services, tools and applications. In the case of end-user visible applications, these are called vApps. Such assets interact with each other through web-technologies, such as REST-services, web-based GUIs and modern message busses (see Figure 14.1).

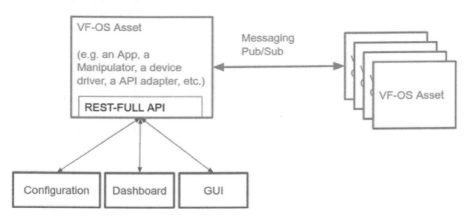

Figure 14.1. *vf-OS asset interaction. For a color version of this figure, see www.iste.co.uk/zelm/enterprise.zip*

The platform allows the assets to run both InCloud or OnPremise. This heterogeneous model is the result of the specific requirements for the manufacturing domain. In most use-cases there is data produced within the factories and through the legacy systems of the end-users. This data can be used within cloud applications.

This introduces quite stringent security challenges to allow the users to control their data dissemination. Similarly it requires security measures to prevent undesired access to machinery and other local resources. The manufacturing domain poses several unique privacy and control issues, especially due to the inter-corporate interactions. The relationship between a factory, its subcontractors and its customers is complex, with many contracts on liability, guarantees, services and time constraints.

Within vf-OS this is solved by introducing a model where there are multiple vf-OS platform instances, with a strict inter-platform communication model. One of the implementation options for this model is shown in Figure 14.2. It shows a factory, which will run a platform instance locally, which will communicate with a cloud platform instance, through a controlled proxy asset. The customer application will then run in the cloud platform and only get highly controlled access to the data from the factory's premises. The SCC component in the platform is the Security Contact Center, part of the security model of vf-OS.

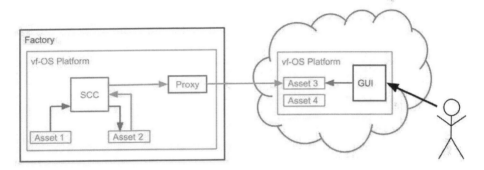

Figure 14.2. *vf-OS inter-platform communication. For a color version of this figure, see www.iste.co.uk/zelm/enterprise.zip*

The vf-OS assets will have a standardized structure and packaging format. The basic executable entity will be based on Docker images [DOC 17]. This Docker image will be enveloped in a wrapper structure, containing metadata, like access rules, dependency information and security signatures. The assets will be storable in the vf-OS Marketplace and can be bought and deployed into the Execution environment, provided by the Platform.

This distributed environment makes it harder to create consistent, coherent applications, especially with regard to debugging, versioning and other software life-cycle aspects. An important goal of the vf-OS project is aimed at providing an answer to these challenges.

14.3. Development approach

The vApp development is the most visible asset development process, as facilitating this process is the stated goal of the project. But the development of the other assets within the vf-OS environment is very similar. It is therefore a good approach to use a single development model for both application development and for the development of other assets. This means that different types of developers will interact with the development model, requiring some flexibility in supporting tools and building blocks.

To tackle this challenge of building consistent, coherent applications within the highly distributed environment of vf-OS, an integrated development environment has been chosen. This environment is called the vf-OS Studio. As with all parts of the vf-OS project, it will be available as a set of assets, forming an IDE-like application. An overview of the building blocks of the studio is given in Figure 14.3.

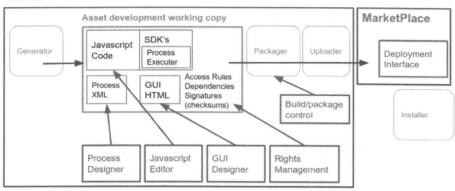

Figure 14.3. *vf-OS Studio components. For a color version of this figure, see www.iste.co.uk/zelm/enterprise.zip*

As can be seen, the main assets are Javascript-based services. Each service will run in its own docker container, providing some generic APIs for system interacting. For example, each asset will provide data for the vf-OS Dashboard. Similarly, each asset exposes an API for interacting with the Execution environment. Assets may choose to also carry a web-based GUI, in the form of containing a web server (e.g. an NGINX host [NGI 18]). Several SDKs and JavaScript libraries are provided by the project for interacting with other assets. Examples of such libraries are the publish/subscribe mechanism, the messaging framework and access to storage facilities.

To support the distribution and marketing of the developed vApps, the project offers a Marketplace. This Marketplace has several tasks in the software development process: 1) a marketing and sales channel; 2) a services registry; and 3) hosting of the assets for deployment. Because of the single development model, incorporating this marketplace, these tasks all contribute to the ease of developing vApps.

External services can be represented in the single development model as well, by encapsulating them into vf-OS Assets. For this purpose the project provides a support module, called the External Services Provisioning framework.

14.4. Conclusions

We have explained a solution to a particularly interesting problem, arising from the manufacturing domain and the micro-services architecture which vf-OS employs to handle the domain. The described approach of standardized packaging, marketing, deployment and interaction between micro-services, is quite novel. Future steps are evaluating this approach, using the projects intermediate releases, use-cases and experimentation. The results of this evaluation will be reported in similar publications.

14.5. Acknowledgments

This paper presents work developed in the scope of the project vf-OS. This project received funding from the European Union's Horizon 2020 research and innovation programme under grant agreement no. 723710. The content of this paper does not reflect the official opinion of the European Union. Responsibility for the information and views expressed in this paper lies entirely with the authors.

14.6. References

[DOC 17] DOCKER Inc., Docker – Build, Ship, and Run Any App, Anywhere, https://www.docker.com, 2017.

[NGI 18] NGINX Inc., NGINX | High Performance Load Balancer, Web Server, & Reverse Proxy, https://www.nginx.com/, 2018.

[VFO 18] VF-OS CONSORTIUM, vf-OS | virtual factory Operating System, http://www.vf-os.eu/, 2018.

[VFR 18] VF-OS CONSORTIUM, D1.5: Requirements Specification (M6), Version 1.0.1, http://www.vf-os.eu/results, 2018.

Standardization

Part 4 Summary: Corporate Standardization Management

This workshop, made up of the next five chapters, aimed to address some of the aspects associated with the management of standardization, looking at both the corporate and the public sectors. Regarding the former, the potential tensions that may result from different corporate priorities were discussed, as was a novel approach to standards lifecycle management. This was complemented by a discussion of government-specific problems and issues, which stand in the way of a one-to-one adoption of corporate best practices. A newly developed framework should help overcome some of these problems. Finally, specific IPR and licensing issues related to standardization, which affect companies and government alike, were discussed.

The first presentation, entitled "Standardization and Innovation: a Multipriority Approach" is given by Eitan Naveh from Technion, the Israel Institute of Technology. He discusses how tensions that result from different and potentially contradictory company-internal priorities may affect process standardization in organizations. Focusing on the potential conflict between standardization and innovation, he shows how firms can manage and possibly even benefit from tensions that may exist between these different priorities. Specifically, he discusses a number of approaches from the literature showing how managers may balance standardization and innovation. The ensuing discussion focused on the "rigidity" of a process standard and how it can be determined up-front. It turned out that the "human side" is important, that is, employees' perception of a standard's rigidity and complexity

Staying in the corporate realm, but looking at a very different problem, Nenad Ivezic and Boonserm Kulvatunyou, from NIST's Systems Integration Division, pose the question "Why Should Interoperability R&D Work be Driven by Agile

Integration and Message Standards Concerns?". They argue that interoperability R&D must consider the need for standards development and deployment from the outset in order to enable agile reconfiguration of smart services and applications, particularly in the manufacturing sector. Using the example of message standards, the chapter shows the need for new and agile standards lifecycle management capabilities. Subsequently, the question of whether to enable broad dissemination and use of such message standards is discussed. A good, verifiable tool that effectively supports agile lifecycle management would be most helpful; such a tool is now (almost) available (according to Nenad). It was also mentioned that this problem has been around for over 30 years now, starting with EDI.

Moving on to the e-government realm, Dian Balta, who is with the fortiss research center, presents two interrelated chapters. The first is "Managing IT Standardization in Government: Towards a Descriptive Reference Model"; the presented model defines three levels of interoperability and five categories of standardization artifacts. Applying this framework to an e-government project shows that said project almost exclusively focuses on the technical/syntactic layer rather than semantic concepts.

The analysis framework applied in Balta's second chapter (Chapter 18), entitled "Review: What are the Strategies for and Benefits of Effective IT Standardization in Government?", identifies three types of standardization strategies ("anticipatory standardization", "integrated solutions" and "flexible generification"; with increasing levels of pragmatism), three categories of determinants and three categories of potential benefits. In addition, three standards development stages are identified. It turns out that most standardization projects implement a mixture of strategy types and that standards are adapted pragmatically if and when necessary. Discussing the specific characteristics of government entities versus companies showed that the lack of any external pressure on government entities significantly contributes to both the numerous e-government projects that fail to work properly and the lack of proper standardization (management). Political issues that may also play a role do not seem to help either.

The final chapter, written by Matt Heckman, is entitled "Licensing Terms for IoT Standard Setting: Do we Need 'End-User' or 'Licence-for-All' Concepts?" relates to a topic that is of general relevance to standardization management – intellectual property. Here, it focuses on the valuation of standards essential patents, which may be based on the 'license for all' or the 'end-user' concept. The paper shows that standards setting organization's endorsement of one of these concepts may invite or deter certain stakeholders. Specifically, the "end-user" concept is highly likely to discourage SMEs.

15

Standardization and Innovation: a Multipriority Approach

Processes standardization (to be distinguished from product and technology standardization, which deal with specifications for products and technologies; hereinafter, "standardization") is one of the most acceptable practices used to improve performance, including efficiency, quality and the prevention of errors in organization. A process that is standardized is constantly performed following the same sequence of steps. Standardization is achieved by setting formal rules of work in instructions, guidelines, manuals and work procedures to guide employees' activities. Standardization assists in improving performance because it is a repository of organizational memory, expresses past experience and the best available knowledge, improves knowledge transfer among employees, and provides control and coordination (Nissinboim, Naveh, 2018).

The growing complexity, dynamism, and interconnectedness of contemporary business environments compel organizations to cope simultaneously with multiple contradictory and tensional requirements and priorities. In order to succeed, organizations must be innovative and also provide high-quality products and services; they must prevent errors from occurring while dealing with time pressure and other resource limitations. This development resonates with organizational research, but only to a certain extent. Although we have learned much about standardization, we know little about how multifaceted forces, especially when they contradict each other, might affect the pathways of standardization in organizations. Thus, there is a significant opportunity for the development of stronger links between standardization and factors such innovation, entrepreneurship and agility. A multiple-priority situation results in hidden tensions. In many circumstances, findings from the literature on single prioritization do not apply to multiple-priority

Chapter written by Eitan NAVEH.

situations (Lei, Naveh, Novikov, 2016). In this chapter, we discuss the conditions under which organizations can manage and even benefit from these tensions. More specifically, I refer to dual-priority situations involving standardization and innovation and to ways to reach a balance between those factors.

15.1. Mutual existence of standardization and innovation

We will first discuss the standardization and innovative activities that organizations promote by means of the concept of climate. These are defined as the shared perceptions of employees concerning the practices, procedures and kinds of behavior that are rewarded, supported and expected in a workplace setting (Schneider, 1990). Given that multiple climates often exist simultaneously within a single organization or team, climate is best regarded as a specific construct with a referent – that is, a climate is a climate *for* something, such as a climate for innovation. The literature robustly supports the claim that climate is a powerful predictor of organizational performance outcomes (Schneider, White, Paul, 1998; Naveh, Katz-Navon, Stern, 2011).

Standardization creates an organizational climate that emphasizes precision, accuracy and focused-oriented processes. This climate involves adherence to routines and attention to detail through the adoption of standardized best practices (Blank, Naveh, 2014; Naveh, Erez, 2004). An innovation climate refers to the employees' shared perception that they are expected to generate new, useful ideas, and to implement them in new products, processes and procedures (Amabile, 2000; West, Anderson, 1996). Innovation climates are characterized by openness to different ways of thinking, autonomy, breaking existing paradigms, taking risks, experimenting, trial and error, and tolerating mistakes (Brown, Eisenhardt, 1998). Thus, innovation climates exert a positive influence on radical innovative performance (Miron-Spektor, Erez, Naveh, 2011).

Standardization and innovation are mutually permitting and their simultaneous existence is required for organizations to successfully participate in competitive markets. Nevertheless, the relationship between standardization and innovation is also fraught with tension, which makes their simultaneous existence a challenge. The reason for said tension is that innovation climates contradict certain characteristics that are required in order to adhere to standards (Miron-Spektor, Erez, Naveh, 2011). Standardization promotes activities such as the use of existing technology and a focus on well-organized, well-planned and systemic processes (Naveh, Erez, 2004). Innovation climates generate variation, which is something the activities associated with standardization cannot accept. Moreover, an innovation climate encourages employees to explore their ideas, even when these are not necessarily in line with existing standardization. Thus, by emphasizing stable routines and processes, standardization may interrupt the generation of creative ideas, thinking "outside the box", going beyond routines and common assumptions, and taking risks, which are the basis for radical innovative performance (Naveh, 2007).

15.2. Approaches to the balance of standardization and innovation

The literature suggests that organizations should implement different approaches to assist them in attaining balance between innovation and standardization (Smith *et al.*, 2017). We now put forward eight approaches that can help organizations to balance innovation with standardization:

1) Benner and Tushman (2002) and Gupta, Smith and Shalley (2006) suggest the concept of ambidexterity – the capacity to capitalize on an existing set of resources and capabilities while at the same time developing new combinations of resources to meet future market needs. Specifically, in the case of innovation and standardization, one form of implementation of ambidexterity is the geographical separation between research and development activities and manufacturing activities. Placing simultaneous emphasis on both innovation and standardization harms the two processes; thus, the structural separation of units that deal with each of these activities is suggested;

2) Lewis *et al.* (2002) refer to a different aspect of ambidexterity. Instead of a structural separation, they suggest a temporal separation in which innovation and exploration are emphasized in the initial stages of a project, and as it progresses the emphasis is gradually transferred onto standardization;

3) Gibson and Birkinshaw (2004) focus on the individual employee level and suggest contextual ambidexterity, in which the individual engineer or employee decides when to emphasize innovation and when to emphasize standardization;

4) to successfully innovate and deal with the complexity of new technologies and information, organizations increasingly rely on teams whose members have different knowledge, skills and perspectives (Lovelace, Shapiro, Weingart, 2001). The configuration of members' attributes in a team (i.e. the proportion of members with different attributes) may influence the team's tendency toward radical innovation because it affects the knowledge, skills and effort that team members apply to their task (Kozlowski, Klein, 2000). In this respect, following Miron-Spektor, Erez and Naveh (2011), one way of balancing the tension between innovation and standardization is by referring to team configuration. A team configuration in which a few members have creative personalities, but at least one member has an attention-to-detail orientation (which supports standardization), is associated with achieving radical innovation;

5) Naveh and Erez (2004) suggest a simultaneous implementation of contradictory managerial practices that encourage both innovation and standardization. In a longitudinal study, they showed that the implementation of opposing management practices, such as a combination of the ISO 9001 quality management standard (which reduces discretion and increases adherence to procedures) and teamwork (which increases team autonomy), enables both innovation and adherence to standardization;

6) in accordance with Katz-Navon, Naveh and Stern (2009), placing simultaneous emphasis on both innovation and standardization is not necessarily the best combination. Specifically, they examined the relationship between learning and safety in hospitals and showed that climates of learning and priority of safety interact in order to influence the rate of residents' errors. In fact, they generate a U-shaped relationship between priority of safety and number of errors committed by resident physicians when the active learning climate is high. A decrease in the number of errors is evident as the level of priority of safety increases and the active learning climate is low. Thus, these results suggest that encouraging both innovation and standardization at the same time is not optimal, and that organizations should give a higher priority to either innovation or standardization;

7) Blank and Naveh (2014) suggest that there are additional organizational factors that balance quality and innovation; consequently, there may be more than one best way to combine innovation and standardization. The authors showed that within a high information exchange climate (characterized by knowledge exchanges and information sharing), the innovation climate improved quality performance and the quality climate improved radical innovative performance. In practical terms, their findings suggest that managers can improve their organizations' adherence to standardization and innovation simultaneously by nurturing an information exchange climate in their corporate departments;

8) context dependence (Katz-Navon, Naveh, Stern, 2009) suggest that the balance between innovation and quality relates to organizational context. For example, hospitals should emphasize quality more and innovation less because the consequences of low quality may impinge on life and death, while high-tech companies in which low quality does not have such significant consequences should emphasize innovation and, to some extent, compromise on quality. Volume and risk are additional contextual parameters that influence innovation and quality. Thus, organizations may decide on the balance between standardization and innovation in accordance to their specific context.

To summarize, both standardization and innovation are required for organizations to succeed in competitive markets. While standardization and innovation are mutually permitting, their relationship is also marked by tension. The eight approaches we describe in this chapter can help managers to balance innovation and standardization.

15.3. Acknowledgements

This work was supported in part by the European Union's Horizon 2020 Research and Innovation Program under the Marie Sklodowska-Curie Grant Agreement 702285, by the State of Israel, Ministry of Science and Technology (MOST), applied science and engineering science research Grant number 3-12482, and by the Gordon Center for System Engineering at Technion, the Israel Institute of Technology.

15.4. References

AMABILE T.M., *Stimulate Creativity by Fueling Passion*, Blackwell, Boston, 2000.

BENNER M.J., TUSHMAN M., "Process management and technological innovation: A longitudinal study of the photography and paint industries", *Administrative Science Quarterly*, vol. 47, pp. 676–706, 2002.

BROWN S.L., EISENHARDT K.M., *Competing on the Edge: Strategy as Structured Chaos*, Harvard Business School Press, Boston, 1998.

BLANK T.H., NAVEH E., "Do quality and innovation compete against or complement each other? The moderating role of an information exchange climate", *Quality Management Journal*, vol. 21, no. 2, pp. 6–16, 2014.

GIBSON C.B., BIRKINSHAW J., "The antecedents, consequences, and mediating role of organizational ambidexterity", *Academy of Management Journal*, vol. 47, pp. 209–226, 2004.

GUPTA A.K., SMITH K., SHALLEY C.E., "The interplay between exploration and exploitation", *Academy of Management Journal*, vol. 49, p. 693, 2006.

KATZ-NAVON T., NAVEH E., STERN Z., "Active learning: When is more better? The case of resident physicians' medical errors", *Journal of Applied Psychology*, vol. 94, no. 5, p. 1200, 2009.

KOZLOWSKI S.W., KLEIN K.J., "A multilevel approach to theory and research in organizations: Contextual, temporal, and emergent processes", in KLEIN K.J., KOZLOWSKI S.W. (eds), *Multilevel Theory, Research and Methods in Organizations: Foundations, Extensions and New Directions*, Jossey-Bass, San Francisco, 2000.

LEI Z., NAVEH E., NOVIKOV Z., "Errors in organizations: An integrative review via level of analysis, temporal dynamism, and priority lenses", *Journal of Management*, vol. 42, no. 5, pp. 1315–1343, 2016.

Lewis M.W., Welsh M.A., Dehler G.E. *et al.*, "Product development tensions: Exploring contrasting styles of project management", *Academy of Management Journal*, vol. 45, no. 3, pp. 546–564, 2002.

Lovelace K., Shapiro D.L., Weingart L.R., "Maximizing cross-functional new product teams' innovativeness and constraint adherence: A conflict communications perspective", *Academy of Management Journal*, vol. 44, no. 4, pp. 779–793, 2001.

Miron-Spektor E., Erez M., Naveh E.,"The effect of conformist and attentive-to-detatil members on team innovation: Reconciling the innovation paradox", *Academy of Management Journal*, vol. 54, pp. 740–760, 2011.

Naveh E., "Formality and discretion in successful R&D projects", *Journal of Operations Management*, vol. 25, pp. 110–125, 2007.

Naveh E., Erez M., "Innovation and attention to detail in the quality improvement paradigm", *Management Science*, vol. 50, pp. 1576–1586, 2004.

Naveh E., Katz-Navon T., Stern Z., "The effect of safety management systems on continuous improvement of patient safety: The moderating role of safety climate and autonomy", *Quality Management Journal*, vol. 18, no. 1, pp. 54–67, 2011.

Nissinboim N., Naveh E., "Process standardization and error reduction: A revisit from a choice approach", *Safety Science*, vol. 103, pp. 43–50, 2018.

Schneider B., *Organization Climate and Culture*, Jossey-Bass, San Francisco, 1990.

Schneider B., White S.S., Paul M.C., "Linking service climate and customer perceptions of service quality: Test of a causal model", *Journal of Applied Psychology*, vol. 83, pp. 150–163, 1998.

Smith K.W., Erez M., Jarvenpaa S. *et al.*, "Adding complexity to theories of paradox, tensions, and dualities of innovation and change: Introduction to organization studies special issue on paradox, tensions, and dualities of innovation and change", *Organization Studies*, vol. 38, pp. 303–317, 2017.

West M.A., Anderson N.R., "Innovation in top management teams", *Journal of Applied Psychology*, vol. 81, no. 6, p. 680, 1996.

16

Why Should Interoperability R&D Work be Driven by Agile Integration and Message Standards Concerns?

Smart manufacturing assumes agile integration of manufacturing services and applications [IVE 17, KUL 16]. This implies that manufacturing message standards, which are key to services integration, need to be quickly created, used and managed. That is a far cry from the best practices today. The interoperability R&D community should take on the challenge of enabling new message standards lifecycle management (LCM) capabilities needed for rapid integration and reconfiguration of manufacturing systems.

16.1. Vision: rapid integration and reconfiguration of manufacturing systems

Manufacturing is on the cusp of being massively transformed: static and monolithic manufacturing systems are changed into dynamic networks of distributed manufacturing services. This transformation is even more radical now with the application of the Industrial Internet of Things (IIoT) technologies in manufacturing.

In the new state, the required functionalities will be provided by services, which could be much more flexible and cost-effective to use. Manufacturing, however, requires reliable transformation approaches for the new service-based networks, including efficient integration, configuration and re-configuration of services and IIoT solutions. Despite the complexity, visions of agile, re-configurable, service-oriented manufacturing systems continue to drive industry investments.

Chapter written by Nenad IVEZIC and Boonserm KULVATUNYOU.

16.1.1. *Example: smart supply chain scenario*

The manufacturing operations management (MOM) or enterprise resource planning (ERP) services of a manufacturing company will communicate with third-party logistics (3PL) services to set up a temperature monitoring service in containers to carry the manufacturer's sensitive products. The messages necessary for setting up such services may include information about (1) the temperature range that will invoke a notification if there is violation, (2) what and how much data to send, (3) where to send the data and so on. Upon receiving a violation notification from a 3PL service (based on a communicated status of containers equipped with smart sensors) the MOM or ERP services will react to rapidly reconfigure the existing supply-chain network. This will include placing an additional order for the materials; rerouting or recalling the truck; dumping and picking up new lot and so on.

16.2. Key enabler: message standards for services integration

A key to the vision of smart manufacturing systems is that manufacturing services may be efficiently integrated, configured and reconfigured to meet rapidly changing user requirements and market forces. Yet, the service integration and configurations depend on effective and meaningful service communications.

To provide for such services communications, correct message specifications must be developed for each specific use case (i.e. target business process). Message standards are used to develop such specifications in a precise and efficient manner.

A message standard refers to a set of shared rules and constraints, commonly called schemata, that allow correct design and implementation of message exchanges and processing. Well-constructed message standards can enable efficient implementation of communicating services. This is a pre-requisite for efficient integration, configuration and re-configuration of smart manufacturing systems.

16.3. A major problem: simplistic practices for message standards development, use and management

Today, a message standard (as a schema) may be very large with hundreds of thousands of data elements. Also, message standards are typically designed and maintained in an implementation-specific manner (e.g. with specific expression syntax and integration patterns), making it difficult to reuse the standard for a new implementation. Additionally, message standards management is very inefficient, often taking months to bring necessary updates to the user community.

These challenges in the current practice exist because message standards management (i.e. development, use and maintenance) is a very complex affair, yet very poorly supported, leading to simplistic standards management practices. One consequence of these simplistic practices is that message standards are used to represent many use cases. Following such practices, a message schema is incrementally developed in a manner that ignores the intended usage. When the time comes for its use, the message schema is again used in a fashion that ignores any prior usage and it is used for each integration use case independently.

In such simplistic message schema development, the main principle is not to affect backward compatibility. This means that schemas are monotonically growing with all previously added components remaining within the new releases of message schemas. At the same time, the specific usage situation of the message standard additions, which drove the previous incremental change, is discarded. Message standards architects increment message standards with little concern for the previous usage situations. This results in limited reuse of previously added components and extensive additions of new components, giving rise to bloated message standards.

The bloated standards with poor usage documentations extend the problem to the usage phase. The users typically adapt the message standards independently for each specific and isolated use case. Such an approach views a usage situation as a separate, independent episode of a message standard customization. Consequently, there is very limited chance for meaningful reuse of standard components and virtually no chance of quickly achieving interoperable services using the message standards.

These complexities are even more evident for the new generation of dynamic and flexible networks of manufacturing services, which are designed for increased agility. There, the customization of message standards needs to happen very efficiently, as user requirements and market forces rapidly change, while new services are introduced in the ecosystem of providers and users of these services.

16.4. Root cause: lack of support for message standards lifecycle management

If the message standards are to support efficient reconfiguration of networks of manufacturing services, an unprecedented support of message standards lifecycle management (LCM) is required. Such support needs to address concerns not dealt with by the message standards development organizations (SDOs) to any significant extent: traceability, role-based management, collaboration and continuity of LCM.

Traceability of LCM: the message-standards LCM needs to keep track of the customizations to the message standard to an unprecedented degree of precision.

These customizations result in adaptations of message standards for a specific usage situation. That may introduce variability at any level of 1) granularity, 2) aggregation, 3) contextualization and 4) parallel customizations of components of message standards. Granularity- and aggregation-related traceability needs to track changes made on every level – from simple data types to complex message schemas. Contextualization-related traceability needs to track changes made for any usage situation – from general contexts to very specific contexts. A general context is defined by, say, type of manufacturing process and geographic region. A specific context is defined by, say, role, application and event types for the message usages. Parallel customization-related traceability needs to track changes for numerous parallel usages of the standard in an ecosystem of service providers and users.

Role-based LCM: first, there is a need to support concurrent and independent customizations of the message standards by individual companies, which take on specific trading partner roles within various business processes. Second, there is a need for timely, synchronized management of message standard updates and releases by responsible standards development organizations.

Collaboration in LCM: first, as concurrent and independent customizations of a message standard take place in a specific company, multiple participants within the company will collaborate to adapt the message standard to their needs. Second, when management of a message standard release takes place at a standards development organization, the organization will collaborate with companies to manage customizations as well as new integration requirements into the standard.

Continuity of LCM: when the customizations of the message standards take place in companies, they will need to consider both prior customizations as well as prior and current releases of the message standard for its impact on existing and future operations of the company. In addition, when maintenance of a message standard release takes place at a standards development organization (SDO), it will need to consider prior releases, customizations and the current release of the standard from the perspective of impacts on the existing and future users of the standard.

Today, there is a lack of tools that can provide the required traceable, role-based, collaborative and continuous message-standards LCM. This prevents rapid integration and configuration of communicating services and IIoT components.

16.5. Impact of the lacking message-standards LCM

If the message standards LCM is not traceable, role-based, collaborative and supporting continuous processes, there will continue to be many undesirable consequences, preventing the efficient reconfigurability of manufacturing services.

With respect to *traceability* of LCM, while customizations of message standards have been provided at any level of granularity or aggregation, such customizations, in some cases, could not be captured with required precision. For example, differences in the intended usage of data types or elements at multiple places in a message component were not captured precisely, causing integration problems.

The lack of approaches to formally and commonly document contextualized use of a message standard results in limited reuse of message customizations, difficulty in achieving interoperability, and bloated (i.e. very large and with redundant components) message standards. This makes message standards use inefficient. The cost of a message development is much higher then what may be possible if contextualized use were harnessed. Also, the systems integrations are brittle, with small requirements changes leading to unwanted behavior of the integrated system.

The lack of approaches to capture changes in a message standard, as they occur in parallel customizations, results in a failed opportunity to manage message standards in a proactive manner. Since message standards are large, and standards users are concerned only with a specific task of integration, there is a need to capture and act on independent, parallel changes in a proactive and constructive manner. Without such support, the standards will continue to be very hard and costly to use, especially in the open ecosystems of services with large parallel uses of standards.

With respect to *role-based* LCM, there is no distinction between a standards user and developer. A user has no support to manage multiple revisions of a single component type for multiple use cases, while a developer has no support to work on multiple releases that consider various standards customizations and requirements. These limitations result in inefficient standards development and use processes.

Collaborative capabilities, both within companies and between companies and SDOs, are very limited and in the form of out-of-band, free-form messages. That, however, causes limited precision of, and low efficiency in, collaborative activities between various roles in collaborating organizations.

With respect to the *continuity* of LCM, little exists in the way of support. Publishing a new release is largely a manual affair. No explicit relationships between the elements, components and types of the new and prior releases or customizations are kept. This causes limited understanding of the impact of changes. An existing customization of a message standard that needed to be moved to a new standard release needs to be manually analyzed and updated. This, in turn, is very tedious to accomplish on a realistic scale. Lack of such support prevents any automation when implementing the changes in message standards. Ultimately, updates to a message standard used in existing service configurations may be a very costly proposition.

16.6. Conclusion

Today, message standards development, use and management take place over many weeks and months. This prevents efficient standards use for service-oriented, modularized applications integrations at a realistic scale, such as in enterprise-wide rationalizations of application functionalities and in an open marketplace of apps and services. In addition, the maintenance process of message standards typically continues indefinitely, presenting even greater challenges to the best practice processes. To enable reconfigurable services, we need to deliver new message standards lifecycle management capabilities. Development of technologies necessary for these capabilities is a challenge that the interoperability R&D community could take on and use to deliver impactful results to the industry.

16.7. Disclaimer

Any mention of commercial products is for information only; it does not imply recommendation or endorsement by NIST.

16.8. References

[IVE 17] IVEZIC N., KULVATUNYOU B., BRANDL D. *et al.*, Drilling down on Smart Manufacturing–enabling composable apps, US Department of Commerce, National Institute of Standards and Technology, available at: https://doi.org/10.6028/NIST.AMS. 100-8, 2017.

[KUL 16] KULVATUNYOU B., IVEZIC N., MORRIS K.C. *et al.*, "Drilling down on Smart Manufacturing–enabling composable apps", *Manufacturing Letters*, vol. 10, pp. 14–17, 2016.

17

Managing IT Standardization in Government: Towards a Descriptive Reference Model

Government agencies aim to provide seamless services and data flows in order to increase the benefits of information technology (IT) for both citizens and companies. A prerequisite is interoperability at different levels – legal, organizational, semantic and technical – between involved organizational entities based on their jurisdiction. To allow for interoperable exchange of information among functional actors, corresponding standards play is required. Unfortunately, managing IT standardization – development, acceptance, enforcement, diffusion of standards – in government appears to be particularly challenging: uncoordinated efforts due to legal roles, overlapping or conflicting standards, heterogeneity versus vendor lock-in. We propose the mediation of the standardization process by using a descriptive reference model for standardization artifacts. Based on an extensive review of the literature, a current management framework at EU level and a set of IT standardization projects from practice, we develop a reference model described by two dimensions: (1) interoperability level and (2) artifact function. Our model provides a sound framework for analysis that is applicable in theory and practice, which we exemplify using one project from Germany.

17.1. Introduction

With regard to IT management – for example, master data management, software system interoperability and integration, service delivery [1] – standards play an important role in interoperable exchange of information among functional actors [2]. Particularly in governments, standards enhance communication between agencies [3].

Chapter written by Dian Balta, Nina-Mareike Harders and Helmut Krcmar.

For instance, standards are a way to secure and correct information exchanged at the right time with the right people and in the right quality [4] by enabling the interconnectivity of the information systems that underlie the provision of services to citizens [5]. Thus, standards for managing information are a necessity in improving the maturity of digitalized government services [6], and so standardization has gained increased attention in government [7], [8].

Although research on standardization in organizations [9] and information systems management [10] has emphasized measures to counter complexity challenges in IT management (e.g. [11]), the applicability of the provided measures in a government context is limited by differences between private organizations and government bodies [12], [13]. In particular, IT standardization management is challenged by the complexity of government procedures [14], [15], stakeholder dependencies and their benefit expectations [16], [17] and is often ineffective in practice [18], [19]. Hence, while various approaches to IT management that are tailored to the context of government bodies through standardizations – for instance, SAGA [20] with its focus on software specifications and development methods in the context of government bodies, and the European Interoperability Framework [3] – have been developed in response [21], [22], IT standardization management in government is yet to advance its practice.

We address the challenges described above with regard to extant research on mediating the standardization process [23], [24] through reference models [25], [26]: our research objective is to lay the foundation for effective standardization management based on a descriptive reference model for IT standards in government.

17.2. Research background and methodology

We define a standard as "a uniform set of measures, agreements, conditions or specifications between parties" [27]. The process of reaching a standard encompasses stabilizing and solidifying its definition and boundaries [11], [28], that is, standardization represents "the activity of establishing and recording a limited set of solutions to actual or potential matching problems directed at benefits for the party or parties involved balancing their needs and intending and expecting that these solutions will be repeatedly or continuously used during a certain period by a substantial number of the parties for whom they are meant" [29].

The process of standardization can be divided into different stages [24]. We focus on the first stage: defining a reference model [23], [24] which allows for a mutual understanding between public administrations with regard to modeling particular standards. Hence, we aim at applying their descriptive function as "generic conceptual models that formalize recommended practices for a certain domain" [25] and thus showing the communalities between entities. For instance, reference models can take into account the established or best practices of standardization efforts in government, provide reusable structure and ways to bundle interoperable artifacts for effective and efficient management of IT.

To develop the descriptive reference model, we conducted a structured literature review on standardization in government and applied the results to ten cases of government IT standardization projects in Germany. In a first step, we searched in sources of eGovernment literature and categorized artefacts of standardization (e.g. a business process definition or a data format). Second, we grouped all artifacts in categories of interoperability [3] based on different layers of interoperability discussed in literature (e.g. [30], [31]). Consequently, we built a matrix scheme with two dimensions and assigned each artifact. Finally, we selected ten cases according to predefined characteristics, analyzed the cases with our scheme and refined it.

17.3. A descriptive reference model of IT standardization in government

The presented model consists of three interoperability levels (organizational, semantic and technical/syntactical) and five categories that correspond to the function of each type of standardization artifact (administration, modeling, processing, communication and interaction, security and privacy).

	Administration	Modeling	Processing	Communication and Interaction		Security and Privacy Standards
Organizational	Business Process	Business Process Modeling Language				Information Access
	Record					
	Form					
	Law/ Regulation	Process Reference Architecture	Business Process Modeling Tool	Process Model Exchange Format	Web Forms	Document Integrity
	Information Service					
Technical/ Semantic	Business Reporting	Application Architecture	Operating System	Messaging	User-Portal	Authentication
			Logging	Geo-Referencing		
			Archiving	Web Service		
			SDK/API	Protocol		
		Computing Language	Database	Network	Website	Data Encryption
		Design Patterns	Software Application	Directory Service		Communication Security

				Data Format	Barrier-free representation	
		Data Modeling Language	Data Modeling Tool	Message Format	Representation Formats	
				File Format		
				Character Set		
Semantic	Shared Terminology	Ontology	Information Search Service	Metadata Definition	Micro Format	
				Repository		
				Code List		

Table 17.1. *Descriptive reference model*

17.4. Application and conclusion

In this chapter, we present the results of a descriptive reference model for management of IT standardization in government. To exemplify its application, we study the case of the electronic tax return project in Germany called ELSTER. According to our analysis, the project has mainly focused on the technical/syntactic layer of standardization. For instance, it provides APIs for software integration, software applications, web-based user portals, data and file formats. This is an interesting finding, since in practice the project is the *de facto* and the *de jure* standard for tax filing in Germany – without explicitly providing specific artifacts on the organizational or semantic interoperability layers.

We hope that a more detailed version of the reference model will support the IT standardization management in practice to structure and prioritize standardization efforts. Moreover, our reference model can support future research towards studying configurations of successful IT standardization projects.

17.5. References

[1] Krcmar H., *Informationsmanagement*, 6th ed., Springer-Verlag, 2015.

[2] International Organization for Standardization, ISO/IEC 2382:2015 information technology – vocabulary. Fundamental Terms, 2015.

[3] European Commission, European interoperability framework (EIF) for European public services, Brussels, 2010.

[4] Radack S.M., "More effective federal computer systems: The role of nist and standards", *Government Information Quarterly*, vol. 7, pp. 37–49, 1990.

[5] Borras J., "International technical standards for e-government", *Electronic Journal of eGovernment*, vol. 2, pp. 75–80, 2004.

[6] Lam W., "Barriers to e-government integration", *Journal of Enterprise Information Management*, vol. 18, no. 5, pp. 511–530, 2006.

[7] Charalabidis Y., Lampathaki F., Askounis D., "A comparative analysis of national interoperability frameworks", *15th Americas Conference on Information Systems (AMCIS 2009)*, no. 694, pp. 1–10, 2009.

[8] Hellberg A.S., Grönlund Å., "Conflicts in implementing interoperability: Re-operationalizing basic values", *Government Information Quarterly*, vol. 30, no. 2, pp. 54–62, 2013.

[9] Brunsson N., Rasche A., Seidl D., "The dynamics of standardization: Three perspectives on standards in organization studies", *Organization Studies*, vol. 33, pp. 613–632, June 2012.

[10] Lyytinen K., King J.L., "Standard making: A critical research frontier for information systems research", *MIS Quarterly*, vol. 30, pp. 405–411, August 2006.

[11] Hanseth O., Jacucci E., Grisot M. *et al.*, "Reflexive standardization: Side effects and complexity in standard making", *MIS Quarterly*, vol. 30, pp. 563–581, 2006.

[12] Rainey H.G., Ronquillo J.C., Avellaneda C.N., "Decision making in public organizations", *Handbook of Decision Making*, vol. 6, pp. 349–377, 2010.

[13] Jurisch M.C., IT-enabled business process change in private and in public sector organizations, PhD thesis, Technische Universität München, 2014.

[14] Bharosa N., Lee J., Janssen M., "Challenges and obstacles in sharing and coordinating information during multi-agency disaster response: Propositions from field exercises", *Inf. Syst. Front.*, vol. 12, no. 1, pp. 49–65, 2009.

[15] Janssen M., "Sociopolitical aspects of interoperability and enterprise architecture in e-government", *Social Science Computer Review*, vol. 30, no. 1, pp. 24–36, 2011.

[16] Balta D., Greger V., Wolf P. *et al.*, "Why realization mismatches expectations of e-government project benefits? Towards benefit realization planning", in Tambouris E. *et al.* (eds), *Electronic Government*, Springer, Cham, 2015.

[17] Balta D., Greger V., Wolf P. *et al.* (eds), "E-government stakeholder analysis and management based on stakeholder interactions and resource dependencies", *48th Hawaii International Conference on System Sciences (HICSS)*, IEEE, 2015.

[18] Blum U., "Lessons from the past: Public standardization in the spotlight", *International Journal of IT Standards and Standardization Research*, vol. 3, no. 1, pp. 1–20, 2005.

[19] Scholl H.J., Kubicek H., Cimander R. *et al.*, "Process integration, information sharing, and system interoperation in government: A comparative case analysis", *Government Information Quarterly*, vol. 29, no. 3, pp. 313–323, 2012.

[20] Federal Government Commissioner for Information Technology, Saga-modul grundlagen version de.Bund 5.1.0, Berlin, 2011.

[21] Guijarro L., "Interoperability frameworks and enterprise architectures in e-government initiatives in Europe and the United States", *Government Information Quarterly*, vol. 24, no. 1, pp. 89–101, 2007.

[22] Büttner F., Bartels U., Hamann L. *et al.*, "Model-driven standardization of public authority data interchange", *Science of Computer Programming*, vol. 89 (part B), pp. 162–175, 2014.

[23] Cargill C.F., *Information Technology Standardization: Theory, Process, and Organizations*, Digital Press, 1989.

[24] Egyedi T.M., *Shaping Standardization: A Study of Standards Processes and Standards Policies in the Field of Telematic Services*, Delft University Press, 1996.

[25] Rosemann M., "Application reference models and building blocks for management and control", in Bernus P., Nemes L., Schmidt G. (eds), *Handbook on Enterprise Architecture*, Springer-Verlag, 2003.

[26] Janssen M., Snijders B., Herkemij F., "A reference architecture for interoperable and adaptive processes", in Charalabidis Y. (ed.), *Interoperability in Digital Public Services and Administrations: Bridging e-Government and e-Business*, IGI Global, 2011.

[27] Spivak S.M., Brenner F.C., *Standardization Essentials: Principles and Practice*, CRC Press, 2001.

[28] David P.A., Greenstein S., "The economics of compatibility standards: An introduction to recent research", *Economics of Innovation and New Technology*, vol. I, nos 1–2, pp. 3–41, 1990.

[29] De Vries H.J., *Standardization: A Business Approach to the Role of National Standardization Organizations*, Springer Science & Business Media, 2013.

[30] Saekow A., Boonmee C., "A pragmatic approach to interoperability practical implementation support (ipis) for e-government interoperability", *Electronic Journal of e-Government*, vol. 7, no. 4, pp. 403–414, 2009.

[31] Kubicek H., Cimander R., "Three dimensions of organizational interoperability", *European Journal of ePractice*, vol. 6, pp. 3–14, 2009.

18

Review: What are the Strategies for and Benefits of Effective IT Standardization in Government?

Information technology (IT) has led to a transformation in the practices of government agencies, especially regarding the way they exchange information and provide services. Since efficiency is often set as a goal of this transformation, IT standardization and its management play an important role. Unfortunately, there is a lack of understanding of standardization – process dynamics, influencing factors, expected outcomes – in the government context. Moreover, extant studies from a private organization context have only limited applicability due to the differences with public administrations: for instance, legal framework, decision-making, strategic goals and so on. To address this gap, we review pertinent literature and IT standardization projects and derive an analysis framework that comprises: (1) determinants, (2) process stages and strategy types and (3) expected benefits. We exemplify the application of the proposed framework in one project and discuss future research towards a quantified theoretical model of IT standardization management.

18.1. Introduction

IT standards play an important role in effective and efficient service provision in government [1], [2]. For instance, standards are applied to harmonize business processes [3] and to efficiently share information [4]. In consequence, choosing a suitable standardization approach based on the context and expected benefits of a specific project is crucial for its success [1], [5], [6] and the coordination of the standardization effort is crucial [7], [8].

Chapter written by Dian Balta, Florian Feller and Helmut Krcmar.

Unfortunately, the required coordination faces a number of challenges in the government domain [2], [9], [10]. Research on standardization in organizations [11] and information systems management [12] has emphasized measures to counter complexity challenges (e.g. [5], [13]), but these measures' applicability in a government context is limited by differences between private organizations and government bodies [14], [15]. In particular, standardization is challenged by the complexity of government procedures [9], [2] and is often ineffective in practice [16], [17]. Various approaches to information management that are tailored to the context of government bodies through standardization have been developed in response [18], [19]. For example, frameworks like SAGA in Germany [20], with its focus on software specifications and development methods in the context of government bodies, and the European Interoperability Framework [21] have been proposed for management practice.

Our research objective is to review extant research on standardization in government and to encompass approaches to effective coordination in a structured manner based on determinants, process dynamics and strategy types as well as expected benefits in IT standardization projects in government.

18.2. Research background and methodology

We define a standard as "a uniform set of measures, agreements, conditions or specifications between parties" [22]. The process of reaching a standard encompasses stabilizing and solidifying its definition and boundaries [5], [23], that is, standardization represents "the activity of establishing and recording a limited set of solutions to actual or potential matching problems directed at benefits for the party or parties involved balancing their needs and intending and expecting that these solutions will be repeatedly or continuously used during a certain period by a substantial number of the parties for whom they are meant" [24].

The concept of standardization strategies "denotes the strategies or approaches chosen for developing new standards, that is, how the development of new standards are organized and which steps are taken or procedures followed in the definition and implementation of a new standard" [1]. We distinguish three types of strategies [1]:

1) anticipatory standardization: "top-down standard process, worked out as detailed compromises";

2) integrated solutions: "user-driven projects, with standards as part of requirements specifications";

3) flexible generification: "work processes and actual use determine standards, which are adapted pragmatically."

Additionally, we distinguish between three stages of development and use of a standard: (1) development and design, (2) acceptance and enforcement, and (3) choice and diffusion.

We will review extant literature on IT standardization in government based on a list of relevant context-specific outlets [25] as well as information systems outlets [26]. Next, we structure the results based on iteratively developed categories. Finally, we will apply the developed framework on 18 projects of successful standardization in government [4].

18.3. A framework for analysis

The proposed analysis framework encompasses three categories of determinants, three types of strategies and three categories of expected benefits (see Figure 18.1). The organizational determinants (with three subcategories and a total of 26 factors) include factors such as the political or management sponsorship of a standardization project, the identification of salient stakeholders or the visibility of the standard. Environmental determinants (with three subcategories and 18 factors in total) include factors that cannot be influenced by an organization such as market structure or laws and regulations. The technical determinants (with two subcategories and a total of nine factors) include factors such as the complexity of a standard or the heterogeneity of IT systems (e.g. legacy versus newly developed).

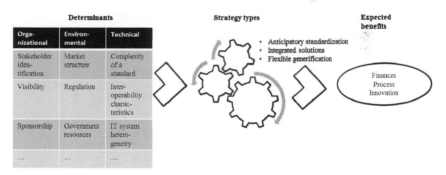

Figure 18.1. *Framework*

The expected benefits (17 in total) are structured in the categories finances, process and innovation. The finances category includes expected benefits such as cost reduction [1]. The process category includes expected benefits such as transparency between actors involved in a standardized IT system [27] or avoiding lock-in [28]. The innovation category includes expected benefits such as support of innovative service provision [1].

The strategy types and the stages of the development in standardization are applied to structure particular strategies found in literature (see Table 18.1). For instance, the FreESBee-SP strategy [29] aimed to improve existing system architecture and further develop IT systems. It is categorized as anticipatory standardization, since it was organized top-down. Still, the strategy was a mixture – it had components of flexible generification, since it allowed reuse of existing standards. Finally, it focused on design and development of a standard as well as on acceptance and enforcement, since it aims at deploying performance tests of the newly developed standard to increase acceptance.

Strategies	Anticipatory standardization	Integrated solutions	Flexible generification
Hybrid recommender		Design & development	Design & development
IPIS	Design & development		Design & development
Metadata model		Design & development	Design & development
FreESBee-SP solution	Design & development, acceptance & enforcement		Design & development, acceptance & enforcement
Internet EDI Model	Design & development		Design & development

Table 18.1. *Strategies assigned to types and stages of standardization*

18.4. Application and conclusion

In this chapter, we first presented the results of an analysis framework for management of IT standardization in government that consists of a set of determinants, strategies and expected benefits. To exemplify its application, we study the case of eID in Estonia [4], [30]. It was one of the first projects that allowed citizens to use an electronic ID card and to consume public services in a more convenient way. Based on the project analysis, we assign eID to anticipatory as well as to flexible generification. Technical determinants such as the complexity of the standard and environmental determinants such as regulations were emphasized. Emphasized expected benefits were part of the process category such as a standardized identification platform for all public and private services.

Our analysis has shown so far that most of the standardization projects implement a mixture of strategy types and focus on design and development. We suggest that future research should focus on analyzing specific patterns based on our framework in order to provide deeper insight for theory and practice of standardization in the government domain.

18.5. References

[1] HANSETH O., BYGSTAD B., "Flexible generification: ICT standardization strategies and service innovation in health care", *European Journal of Information Systems*, vol. 24, no. 6, pp. 645–663, 2015.

[2] JANSSEN M., CHARALABIBIS Y., KUK G. *et al.*, "Guest editors' introduction: E-government interoperability, infrastructure and architecture: State-of-the-art and challenges", *Journal of Theoretical and Applied Electronic Commerce Research*, vol. 6, no. 1, pp. I–VIII, 2011.

[3] BECKER J., ALGERMISSEN L., FALK T., *Modernizing Processes in Public Administrations: Process Management in the Age of e-Government and New Public Management*, Springer-Verlag, 2012.

[4] SCHOLL H.J., KUBICEK H., CIMANDER R. *et al.*, "Process integration, information sharing, and system interoperation in government: A comparative case analysis", *Government Information Quarterly*, vol. 29, no. 3, pp. 313–323, 2012.

[5] HANSETH O., JACUCCI E., GRISOT M. *et al.*, "Reflexive standardization: Side effects and complexity in standard making", *MIS Quarterly*, vol. 30, pp. 563–581, 2006.

[6] HANSETH O., MONTEIRO E., HATLING M. *et al.*, "Developing information infrastructure: The tension between standardization and flexibility", *Science, Technology & Human Values*, vol. 21, no. 4, pp. 407–426, 1996.

[7] CHARALABIDIS Y., LAMPATHAKI F., ASKOUNIS D. *et al.*, "A comparative analysis of national interoperability frameworks", *15th Americas Conference on Information Systems*, no. 694, pp. 1–10, 2009.

[8] GIONIS G.A., SCHROTH C., JANNER T., "Advancing interoperability for agile cross-organisational collaboration: A rule-based approach", in CHARALABIDIS Y. (ed.), *Interoperability in Digital Public Services and Administrations: Bridging e-Government and e-Business*, IGI Global, 2011.

[9] BHAROSA N., LEE J., JANSSEN M., "Challenges and obstacles in sharing and coordinating information during multi-agency disaster response: Propositions from field exercises", *Inf. Syst. Front.*, vol. 12, no. 1, pp. 49–65, 2009.

[10] JANSSEN M., "Sociopolitical aspects of interoperability and enterprise architecture in e-government", *Social Science Computer Review*, vol. 30, no. 1, pp. 24–36, 2011.

[11] BRUNSSON N., RASCHE A., SEIDL D., "The dynamics of standardization: Three perspectives on standards in organization studies", *Organization Studies*, vol. 33, pp. 613–632, June 2012.

[12] LYYTINEN K., KING J.L., "Standard making: A critical research frontier for information systems research", *MIS Quarterly*, vol. 30, pp. 405–411, August 2006.

[13] MARKUS M.L., STEINFIELD C.W., WIGAND R.T., "Industry-wide information systems standardization as collective action: The case of the U.S. Residential mortgage industry", *MIS Quarterly*, vol. 30, pp. 439–465, August 2006.

[14] RAINEY H.G., RONQUILLO J.C., AVELLANEDA C.N., "Decision making in public organizations", *Handbook of Decision Making*, vol. 6, pp. 349–377, 2010.

[15] JURISCH M.C., IT-enabled Business Process Change in Private and in Public Sector Organizations, PhD thesis, Technische Universität München, 2014.

[16] BLUM U., "Lessons from the past: Public standardization in the spotlight", *International Journal of IT Standards and Standardization Research*, vol. 3, no. 1, pp. 1–20, 2005.

[17] SCHOLL H.J., KLISCHEWSKI R., "E-government integration and interoperability: Framing the research agenda", *International Journal of Public Administration*, vol. 30, nos 8–9, pp. 889–920, 2007.

[18] GUIJARRO L., "Interoperability frameworks and enterprise architectures in e-government initiatives in Europe and the United States", *Government Information Quarterly*, vol. 24, no. 1, pp. 89–101, 2007.

[19] BÜTTNER F., BARTELS U., HAMANN L. *et al.*, "Model-driven standardization of public authority data interchange", *Science of Computer Programming*, vol. 89 (part B), pp. 162–175, 2014.

[20] FEDERAL GOVERNMENT COMMISSIONER FOR INFORMATION TECHNOLOGY, Saga-modul grundlagen version de.Bund 5.1.0., Berlin, 2011.

[21] EUROPEAN COMMISSION, European interoperability framework (EIF) for European public services, Brussels, 2010.

[22] SPIVAK S.M., BRENNER F.C., *Standardization Essentials: Principles and Practice*, CRC Press, 2001.

[23] DAVID P.A., GREENSTEIN S., "The economics of compatibility standards: An introduction to recent research", *Economics of Innovation and New Technology*, vol. I, nos 1–2, pp. 3–41, 1990.

[24] DE VRIES H.J., *Standardization: A Business Approach to the Role of National Standardization Organizations*, Springer Science & Business Media, 2013.

[25] SCHOLL H.J., DWIVEDI Y.K., "Forums for electronic government scholars: Insights from a 2012/2013 study", *Government Information Quarterly*, vol. 31, no. 2, pp. 229–242, 2014.

[26] LOWRY P.B., MOODY G., GASKIN J. *et al.*, Evaluating journal quality and the association for information systems (AIS) senior scholars' journal basket via bibliometric measures: Do expert journal assessments add value?, Report no. ID 2186798, Social Science Research Network, Rochester, 2013.

[27] KING N., "Exploring the impact of operating model choice on the governance of inter-organizational workflow: The U.S. E-prescribing network", *European Journal of Information Systems*, vol. 22, no. 5, pp. 548–568, 2013.

[28] GALASSO G., ARESU F., LUPPI M. *et al.*, Study on best practices for ICT procurement based on standards in order to promote efficiency and reduce lock-in, DG Communications Networks, Content & Technology, available at: https://publications.europa.eu/en/publication-detail/-/publication/152a29e9-e10c-11e5-8a50-01aa75ed71a1/ language-en, 2016.

[29] MECCA G., SANTOMAURO M., SANTORO D. *et al.*, "On federated single sign-on in e-government interoperability frameworks", *International Journal of Electronic Governance*, vol. 8, no. 1, p. 6, 2016.

[30] CIMANDER R., AARMA A., JÄRV A., Good Practice Case eID in Estonia, available at: https://www.ifib.de/publikationsdateien/Interoperability_in_eID_in_ Estonia.pdf, 2006.

19

Licensing Terms for IoT Standard Setting: Do We Need "End-User" or "License-for-All" Concepts?

The development of 5G and IoT standards requires the active participation of small and medium-sized companies (SMEs). These SMEs do not always have the resources and expertise to participate in the work of standard development organizations (SDOs). The valuation of the patents in standards can be based on "license-for-all" or "end-user" concepts. A specific choice for use-based licensing terms by an SDO might drive SMEs more towards standard setting in consortia. This chapter will discuss the competition law aspects of both licensing concepts for SMEs and the recent communication in this field by the EU Commission.

19.1. Introduction

The intersection of standard setting, IPRs and competition law has become more and more complex in recent years. This standardization eco-system strongly depends on the willingness of companies (e.g. SMEs) to participate and share their proprietary solutions. The management of standardization and the treatment of intellectual property rights is therefore a crucial factor in the decision-making process of companies. Research shows that the IPR-policies of standardization bodies is a crucial element for the decision of whether to invest and participate in standard-setting activities. At the same time, standard setting facilitates exclusion (a common feature of patent rights) and collusion. As a result, antitrust authorities should identify the circumstances that lead to anticompetitive effects of the use of standards and pay special attention to these circumstances, possibly addressing them through their regulatory frameworks.

Chapter written by Matt HECKMAN.

19.2. The development of 5G and the Internet of Things standards

The development of the 5G standard will see the implementation of a wide range of (consumer) products. The automotive industry, smart city development, new aircraft and household appliances will all incorporate Internet of Things (IoT) technology and standards. Implementers of this new IoT standardized technology will have to pay for the patented technology and traditionally rely on fair, reasonable and non-discriminatory ("FRAND") licensing terms. Since these new entrants to the licensing discussion come from a different industry tradition, experts expect an increase in the volume of disputes evolving on SEPs. Furthermore many of these new entrants/ implementers of the IoT-technology are small and medium-sized companies ("SMEs"). These SMEs usually do not often participate in standards development in SDOs. The development process in SDOs is a lengthy and costly process that does not match the resources and expertise of many SMEs. However, a recent study shows that when SMEs do participate in the work of SDOs the acceptance rate of their technology is almost equal to that of larger companies [GUP 17]. A continuous and structural participation of SMEs in SDOs does not fit with their short-term objective to grow and make profit. This brings us to the heart of the discussion: how do we strike the right balance between innovators and implementers?

19.3. The concept of "use-based" licensing terms

The European Union has expressed its intention to deploy 5G in the EU by 2025, as part of the Digital Single Market [EUR 16]. This objective can only be reached if the balance between innovators and implementers is reached by means of effective standard essential patent (SEP)-licensing. According to the EU Commission, some of the licensing of IoT-technology should be in conjunction with non-EU-based industries, which underlines the necessity to have a balanced and predictable system for SEP-licensing. In its recent communication the Commission identified, three possible challenges: opaque information about SEP-exposure, unclear valuation of patented technologies and risks of uncertainty in enforcement. The EU Commission sees a clear task and role for the European Telecommunication Standards Institute (ETSI) and the European Patent Organization (EPO). At the same time the EU Commission notes that the role of SDOs in this process can only be very limited[1]. The EU Commission wants to give proper guidance on the valuation of SEPs and the practical application of the FRAND-principle. As one of the main reasons, the EU Commission explains that this guidance would encourage SMEs to increase their participation in standard-setting activities. The discussion on SEP-licensing terms has recently been divided into two different camps. The division is centered on the

---

1 It remains unclear why the EU Commission holds ETSI in a higher esteem than other SDOs.

concept of "use-based" or "license-for-all" licensing terms. The "use-based" licensing concept enables licensors to offer licensees different royalty fees that depend on how the technology is being used [HUN 17]. Under this approach licensors may refuse a license if the final use of the technology cannot be identified. Representatives of small and medium-sized companies claim that this approach is undermining innovation inside the EU. The "use-based" concept calculates the value of the license based upon how the technology that uses the SEP is being used in practice[2]. The SEP-holders would be able to charge different royalties depending on the application of the technology and irrespective of the value of the SEP itself. In this scenario SEP-holders would automatically receive some of the value that was created by downstream innovators. Obviously as stated before, SMEs would be in a very delicate position, since they do not have the resources or expertise to engage in patent litigation, but they often do create value on the downstream market.

"License to all" is a concept wherein the implementer can seek a license from the SEP-holder irrespective of the downstream use of the technology. Opponents of this concept claim that this will lead to a stark increase in licensing negotiations, legal fees and delays in standard setting. Some experts think that "license to all" will have a negative effect on innovation and the competitiveness of the EU, and ultimately kill many jobs in Europe[3].

Obviously, the EU Commission is faced with a daunting choice. At first sight, SMEs will suffer the consequences of the adoption of the "use-based" principle. The SMEs will add value to the downstream inventions that consequently have to be shared with the holders of the patented technology. End-user licensing will increase the transaction costs for the implementer and could lead to higher royalty costs; both consequences are detrimental for the participation of SMEs in IoT standard setting. Depending on the interpretation, end-user licensing could also include the value of other technologies that are incorporated in the product[4].

19.4. Competition law aspects of the debate on "end-user device" versus "license for all"

The development of the IoT-standards has put more precise focus on the discussion at which level of the value chain licensing should occur and, more importantly, on which legal basis. Most experts agree that the active participation of SMEs in IoT-standardization is crucial for its success. Economic literature is decisive on the positive impact of standards and SDOs on innovation. Technology

2 See, for more background: http://ipkitten.blogspot.nl/2017/11/who-is-going-to-win-big-eu-commission.html.
3 https://www.iptalks.eu/news/license-to-all-is-a-license-to-kill-innovation-and-jobs-in-europe.
4 At the moment it is relatively unclear how the different values have to be calculated.

firms, including SMEs, may decide to reduce their participation in SDOs and their standard-setting activities. It would be interesting to research the difference in legal treatment between FRAND commitments that are made within the context of an SDO and those commitments made outside the SDO framework. If the latter commitments give firms an advantage, this will encourage the development of *de facto* standards. Experts hold the opinion that *de facto* standards are very important for both innovation and competition. The strategic choice for working in a SDO or standard-setting in consortia could be directly influenced by the choice of licensing concept. If SDOs expressly opt for end-user device licensing, this could drive especially SMEs in the direction of standard setting by consortia. SDOs traditionally require participating companies to commit to FRAND licensing terms. The IPR-policies of the SDOs leave sufficient room for interpretation of this FRAND-commitment. In the heated debate on the licensing base, some experts see "license for all" as a movement towards compulsory licensing. Legally, it is inherent to the patent right that every patent holder has the right to exclude and choose who to license and ultimately who to sue for patent infringement.

In order to make IoT-standardization attractive for SMEs, SDOs must adopt an IPR-policy that fully recognizes the position of SMEs. The lack of resources and expertise of SMEs prevents an effective participation in expensive patent litigation. EU competition law demands: "*Standard setting can, however, in specific circumstances, also give rise to restrictive effects on competition by [...] exclusion of, or discrimination against, certain companies by prevention of effective access to the standard*" [EUR 14]. The participation of SME standard setting can be increased by providing more transparency. One of the key discussions centers on methods for valuing SEPs, which explains the EU Commission's eagerness to reach a consensus. A widely accepted valuing method would assist SMEs in securing early-stage funding for their innovations. Recent case-law on FRAND-licensing does not provide clarity regarding the royalty rate setting or the basis thereof. For SMEs, these discussions are very specialized and difficult to follow. The patent valuation guidelines of the EU Commission bear the risk of provoking SMEs to leave SDO-discussions or even refuse to agree to FRAND commitments. Again this might result in a higher participation of SMEs in consortia standard setting. The position of SMEs in consortia is even more unclear. For standards consortia, this could be a strategic opening to encourage SMEs to join their discussions and standardization.

19.5. Communication of the EU Commission: "Setting out the EU approach to Standard Essential Patents"

In November 2017, the EU Commission published its communication: "Setting out the EU approach to Standard Essential Patents" [EUR 17]. The communication shows that the EU Commission still allows for great flexibility regarding the valuation/establishment of FRAND-rates. The main conclusion is that the value of the SEP should be based on the patented technology and not upon the fact that the technology is included in a standard. The value of individual SEPs should not be considered in isolation. To avoid royalty stacking, parties need to seriously consider a reasonable aggregate rate for the standard based on the overall value of the added value of the technology. Most importantly the EU Commission did not express an explicit mandate for cither use-based licensing or license-for-all concepts. The decision should be related to the individual characteristics of the case and may vary between sectors and business models. The EU Commission stated that *"once a standard is established and the holders of the SEPs have given a commitment to license them on fair, reasonable and non-discriminatory (FRAND) terms, the technology included in the standard should be available to any potential user of the standard"* (i.e. chipset licensing still possible) [EUR 17, p. 8]. Furthermore, there is no one-size-fit-all solution on what FRAND is: what can be considered fair and reasonable can differ from sector to sector and over time. Efficiency considerations, reasonable license fee expectations on both sides and the facilitation of the uptake by implementers to promote wide diffusion of the standard should be taken into account [EUR 17, note 8].

19.6. Conclusion

In its recent communication, the EU Commission takes a holistic approach towards the basis of SEP licensing. There is no specific mandate for either use-based licensing or license-for-all concepts. The EU Commission hopes that sectoral discussions will lead to common licensing practices. If SDOs choose for one specific license valuation base this might have direct consequences for the (necessary) participation of SMEs in the 5G and IoT standard setting. This might drive SMEs towards standard setting in consortia, if they consider a more appropriate SEP-valuation base. For many SMEs, IPR policies are at the heart of the matter of the standardization management discussion. Given the importance of the participation of SMEs in standardization for the Digital Single Market, the EU Commission and consequently the European Court of Justice could give more guidance on their preferences regarding the bases of SEP licensing.

19.7. References

[EUR 14] EUROPEAN COMMISSION, Guidelines on the application of Article 101 of the Treaty on the Functioning of the European Union to technology transfer agreements, Commission of the European Union, Brussels, 2014.

[EUR 16] EUROPEAN COMMISSION, State of the Union address 2016: Towards a better Europe – A Europe that protects, empowers and defends Strasbourg, Speech, September 14, available at: http://europa.eu/rapid/press-release_SPEECH-16-3043_en.htm, 2016.

[EUR 17] EUROPEAN COMMISSION, Setting out the EU approach to Standard Essential Patents, no. 712, 2017.

[GUP 17] GUPTA K., The role of SMEs and startups in standards development, available at: https://papers.ssrn.com/sol3/papers.cfm?abstract_id=3001513, 2017.

[HUN 17] HUNT M, Patent licensing: 5G and the Internet of Things, available at: https://www.bristows.com/news-and-publications/articles/patent-licensing-5g-and-the-internet-of-things/, 2017.

Industrial Big Data and Platforms

Part 5 Summary: Industrial Big Data Platforms Enabling Enterprise Interoperability for Smart Services

This is a short report stemming from the BD4EI workshop that was held in conjunction with the I-ESA conference on March 20, 2018 in Berlin, Germany. The objective of this workshop was to bring together researchers and practitioners working on big data platforms, smart enterprise services and enterprise interoperability, and to identify and discuss achievements, challenges and visions within and across various application domains.

Introduction

The availability of new online data sources, such as sensors, loggers and social media, provides opportunities as well as challenges to improve products and services. Opportunities arise because the data can be analyzed to learn more about the context and the specific situations in which products and services are being used. This in turn opens the possibility to adapt the products and services, such that they become more usable and useful. In the case of software services, adaption can be dynamic and performed in real-time. Challenges arise because the collection and analysis of data can be complex and subject to time and storage constraints. Specialized hardware and software solutions are then needed, which has led to the introduction of big data platforms. Big data platforms aim to offer a cohesive solution with ease of use for developing, deploying, operating and managing big data, and aim to reduce the interoperability problems that are inherent in using heterogeneous data sources and data applications.

Chapter written by Marten VAN SINDEREN and Sergio GUSMEROLI.

Contributions and discussion

At the workshop, 11 papers were presented, the results of which are included in this book as subsequent chapters, with the following titles:

Chapter 20: Semantic Interoperability for the IoT: Analysis of JSON for Linked Data
Chapter 21: FIWARE for INDUSTRY: A Data-driven Reference Architecture
Chapter 22: European Big Data Value Association Position Paper on Smart Manufacturing Industry
Chapter 23: SmTIP: A Big Data Integration Platform for Synchromodal Transport
Chapter 24: Fault Prediction in Aerospace Product Manufacturing: Development of a Model-based Big Data Analytics Service
Chapter 25: A SAREF Extension for Semantic Interoperability in the Industry and Manufacturing Domain
Chapter 26: A Building Information Model-centered Big Data Platform to Support Digital Transformation in the Construction Industry
Chapter 27: ISBM: A Data Integration Infrastructure for IoT Applications
Chapter 28: RS4IoT – A Recommender System for IoT

The workshop opened with a number of questions, asking about the challenges, solutions, influencers, and gaps in this field. We briefly summarize how these questions were discussed during the workshop, and are now covered in the following chapters.

Challenges for the smart manufacturing industry are comprehensively covered in Chapter 22, which reports on the efforts of the Big Data Value Association (BDVA) to define research challenges for the smart manufacturing industry. Among these are the data integration and data analytics challenges. These challenges are not unique for the logistics domain, but also exist for, for example, logistics and building, as described in Chapters 23 and 26. Another important challenge is the development of suitable reference ontologies to enable semantic interoperability, as argued in Chapter 25.

Solutions that address these challenges exist at different levels, from reference architectures to implementations. Reference architectures that help to position and relate big data technologies in the IT stack include Industrial Internet Reference Architecture (IIRA), Reference Architecture for Manufacturing Industry 4.0 (RAMI 4.0), and Industry Value Chain Reference Architecture (IVCA). Chapter 21 describes the FIWARE open source standard platform to ease development of smart applications. Other chapters cover solutions for specific challenges and for specific domains: data integration is addressed in Chapter 27, selection of data sources in Chapter 28, data analytics in Chapter 25, and semantic operability using ontologies in Chapters 20 and 25.

Influencers are organizations that draft research agendas, define reference architectures, develop standards, and provide reference implementations. Chapters 21, 22, and 25 mention several such organizations, including BVDA, EFFRA, Platform Industry 4.0, IVCI, IIC JTG2, ISO JTC1 WG9, ETSI STF 513 and FIWARE Open Initiative. The projects mentioned by several papers are also potential influencers in this field. In terms of adoption and exploitation, the manufacturing sector has played a pioneering role.

Gaps between current solutions and the needs of industry are revealed by current research agendas and by the future work identified in many of the following chapters. Chapter 22 lists the research priorities identified by BDVA towards a smart manufacturing industry. Chapter 21 describes the FIWARE for Industry initiative aiming at a federation of data-driven architectures and platforms for data management in industrial scenarios, and building on a convergence of RAMI and IIRA as developed by IIC JTG2. Chapter 25 mentions further work on a reference ontology for industry and manufacturing, executed by ETSI STF 513. Chapters 23 and 26 call for attention to non-manufacturing domains, namely logistics and construction, where existing reference architectures and platforms have been less successful.

The discussion during the workshop mainly focused on the overwhelming number of solutions and the complexity of picking the right one for the specific situation of an enterprise. SMEs especially do not have the resources to investigate and try out different options to realize their digital transformation. Moreover, in a connected society, data integration crosses organizational and even domain boundaries, which contributes to the problem. A guideline on selecting and implementing solutions for specific scenarios would be useful. The FIWARE Technologies and FIWARE for Industry specifically aim to lower existing barriers in the adoption of new big data technologies and platforms for smart application, and therefore provide a good starting point.

20

Semantic Interoperability for the IoT: Analysis of JSON for Linked Data

Recently a number of IoT platforms have been developed to cope with the big data generated and consumed by sensors and actuators. Some IoT platforms achieve syntactic interoperability by adopting JavaScript Object Notation (JSON) to represent the message payload produced by devices. Usually, semantic interoperability of IoT solutions is also required. JSON for Linked Data (JSON-LD) is a syntax to serialize RDF and, therefore, can provide semantic interoperability to IoT solutions. Although JSON-LD is designed to be lightweight, it causes an increase of the size of messages if compared to native JSON, due to the additional metadata. This paper presents an empirical performance analysis of JSON-LD compared to JSON in common IoT scenarios. Event data produced by a sensor are serialized as JSON and JSON-LD and the total transaction time is compared in request/reply and publish/subscribe architectures. The results indicate that JSON-LD is adequate.

20.1. Introduction

Current IoT solutions follow the event-driven architecture for data exchange among IoT devices, networks and applications through RESTful web services with JSON as a data exchange format [DIA 16]. JSON for Linked Data (JSON-LD) is a lightweight syntax to serialize RDF as a structured JSON, representing a way to semantically enrich conventional JSON messages [JAN 16]. JSON-LD is a W3C standard [W3C 18] recommended by schema.org and Google. To the best of our knowledge, no empirical performance analysis has so far been performed to evaluate the impact of applying JSON-LD instead of native JSON to similar IoT messages.

Chapter written by João Luiz REBELO MOREIRA, Luís FERREIRA PIRES and Marten VAN SINDEREN.

The payload of a JSON-LD message varies according to the ontologies chosen and how they are used. Although JSON-LD is built to be lightweight, this choice can affect the time to transfer and process sensor data, and, therefore needs to be investigated. In this paper we present our empirical analysis for the overhead of JSON-LD using the European standard for IoT semantic interoperability – the Smart Appliances REFerence (SAREF) ontology – compared to similar data represented as JSON in IoT scenarios, following the Experimentation in Software Engineering methodology [WOH 12]. Section 20.2 presents the background, section 20.3 presents the study design, section 20.4 presents the results and section 20.5 summarizes contributions and future work.

20.2. Related work

The REpresentational State Transfer (REST) is a design pattern for interaction with resources. It relies on stateless, cacheable client–server communication, mapped onto HTTP methods. JSON is a lightweight data-interchange format that is intuitive for humans to read/write and adequate for machines to parse and generate. JSON is programming language independent, supports high scalability and is faster, uses fewer resources and yields more compact models than XML [AFS 17]. Because of these benefits, JSON is often used as payload notation for IoT solutions [RIZ 16].

```
"@id" : "example1TESS005-UCM",
"@type" : [ "s4envi:TESS", "owl:NamedIndividual" ],
...,
"location" : "example1LocationTESS005-UCM",
"hasManufacturer" : "Universidad Complutense de Madrid",
"hasName" : "stars5",
"exposes" : "example1PowerProfileTESS005-UCM",
"hasFrequencyMeasurement" : "example1FequencyMeasurementTESS005-UCM",
"hasTransmissionPeriod" : "example1TransmissionPeriodTESS005-UCM",
"hasVersion" : "v1",
"makesMeasurement" : [
    {
      "@id" : "example1Measurement2016-10-05T08:15:30TESS005-UCM",
      "@type" : [ "owl:NamedIndividual", "s4envi:Measurement" ],
      "label" : {
        "@language" : "en",
        "@value" : "Measurement 2016-10-05T08:15:30 TESS005-UCM"
      },
      "hasValue" : "0.1",
      "isMeasuredIn" : "example1mgPerarcsec2",
      "hasTimestamp" : "2016-10-05T08:15:30",
      "relatesToProperty" : "s4envi:LightMagnitude"
    }
],
"measuresProperty" : "s4envi:LightMagnitude",
"usesCommunicationInterface": [ "example1Bluetoothv2-1",
"example1Wi-Fiv802-11ah",
"example1RS232v24" ],
"usesCommunicationProtocol" : "example1MQTT-Broker",
"@context" : ...
```

Figure 20.1. *JSON-LD message from the SAREF4Envi extension.*
For a color version of this figure, see www.iste.co.uk/zelm/enterprise.zip

Numerous ontology-based IoT approaches have been proposed [PAL 16, LI 16] and the SAREF umbrella includes extensions for vertical markets [EC 17], e.g. smart energy, environment (SAREF4Envi) and buildings [ETS 17]. SAREF4Envi enables the representation of data about light pollution which is collected with a photometer device that monitors light magnitude, and which sends the measurements to a server.

JSON-LD is a lightweight syntax to serialize RDF, providing semantics to JSON data at web-scale, conceived to introduce linked data in web-based programming environments. JSON-LD is gaining popularity and is recommended by the W3C to semantically enrich data embedded in HTML pages by adding the script type tag *application/ld+json*, which enables search engines to understand these data. JSON-LD introduces features as the Internationalized Resource Identifier (IRI), annotations with different languages and graphs expression. The core part of JSON-LD is the set of syntax tokens that are prefixed with "@", for example @context, @id, @value, @type, @graph, among others. An example of a JSON-LD message is shown in Figure 20.1, which represents an instance of a photometer device (from SAREF4Envi), providing measured data and other information. The measurements, linked through the *makesMeasurement* property, represent the data underlining continuous monitoring.

The migration of JSON-based approaches to JSON-LD may cause additional message overhead because of these tokens. Moreover, it is necessary to analyze the impact on processing performance of JSON-LD (de)serialization by existing libraries, such as the JSON-LD processor and API implementation in JavaScript [DIG 11].

20.3. Case study design

This performance analysis followed the Experimentation in Software Engineering methodology [WOH 12] and considered two common event-driven architectures [DOU 18]: request/response (scenario 1) and publish/subscribe message broker (scenario 2). The metric considered when formulating the hypotheses was the adequacy of JSON-LD for IoT solutions, which is a metric that balances the benefits of semantics and performance. Performance is measured in terms of total transaction time of a sensor data producer interacting with a consumer. Total transaction time includes data transfer and processing at both sides. The null hypothesis is: (H0) JSON-LD is not adequate to be used in IoT solutions; the performance loss is too high compared to the semantics benefit. The alternative hypothesis is: (H1) JSON-LD provides an equivalent performance compared to JSON. The first variable is the payload, that is the message size in bytes. The assumption is that small messages containing, for example, only one device measurement (e.g. Figure 20.1), yields a bigger delay in the difference of the total transaction time average between JSON and JSON-LD. The @context property does not grow linearly with the message size. @context only increases when new ontologies are used and/or when new classes and properties are used. Since this evaluation targets the performance of real time observations described with SAREF, the message sizes were classified according to the number of measurements within a message: small (1 measurement), medium (10) and large (100). The file sizes (in bytes) are: for JSON, small 309, medium 4880 and large 42211. For JSON-LD the file sizes are: small 3389 bytes, medium 7567 and large 45264 bytes. Besides the message size, simple processing was added by comparing a measurement with a constant, logging the result in the terminal (a simple I/O command). The second variable is the type of scenario: (S1) asynchronous request/reply; and (S2) publish/subscribe (Figure 20.2).

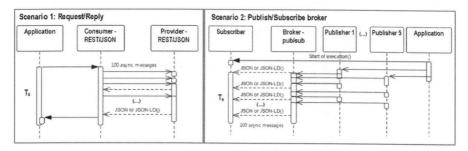

Figure 20.2. *IoT scenarios used in our experiments*

S1 includes two sensor data providers following the RESTful pattern, where one provides data as JSON while the other provides the same data as JSON-LD. The consumer sends 100 asynchronous requests to the provider in each transaction. An application computes the average of the total transaction time by executing (synchronously) the consumer for 1000 times. So, in total 1000 x 100 requests are forwarded to the provider. S2 includes a lightweight message broker, where five topics are created in the broker to simulate five devices publishing event data. One subscriber that listens to all topics is also created. An application sends a synchronous request to the subscriber informing the beginning of the execution, so the subscriber is able to identify the first message and computes the total time on the arrival of the 100th message. The application simulates 20 asynchronous events for each topic.

Each scenario was executed 1000 times, according to the configuration of the variables. They were implemented with NodeJS, commonly used in IoT solutions [DIA 16], which allows the implementation of REST/JSON services with a few lines of code (https://github.com/jonimoreira/JSON-LD). In S1, the total transaction time is collected from the application for each request to the customer to avoid noise in both sides. Anomalous values were discarded, that is values greater than the mean plus the standard deviation. In S2, a popular open source broker (Mosquitto) was used. An application executed five publishers in parallel, so the subscriber computes 5 x 100 messages of each size (1, 2, 3). Both scenarios were deployed in the cloud (AWS EC2); the provider/publisher was deployed in a server in Brazil and the consumer/subscriber in a server in Australia. For S2, the MQTT broker was deployed in a third server in Australia, simulating a broker gateway near the device (provider/publisher). Brazil and Australia were chosen because they have the slowest link for data transfer within AWS regions. Our intention was to perform the analysis in an environment that presents a large difference in terms of data propagation, thus where the message size can affect the performance of the total transaction time.

20.4. Results

Scenario S1 presented a difference among the executions with different message sizes, where JSON is on average 0.15% faster than JSON-LD. For size 1, the difference of total time average was very small (less than 1 second): JSON is 0.17% (without processing) and 0.19% (with processing) faster than JSON-LD. For size 2, JSON is 0.11% (without processing) and 0.12% (with processing) faster than JSON-LD. For size 3, JSON is 0.05% (without processing) and 0.07% (with processing) faster than JSON-LD. Figure 20.3 shows this comparison: the different experiments are on the horizontal axis, while the vertical axis represents the message size (left) and the percentage difference between JSON and JSON-LD (right).

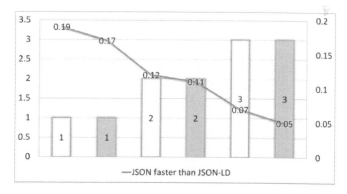

Figure 20.3. *Result analysis comparing performance of JSON vs JSON-LD. For a color version of this figure, see www.iste.co.uk/zelm/enterprise.zip*

White and grayed bars represent executions with and without processing, respectively. As the messages get larger, the difference between JSON and JSON-

LD decreases. This behavior was expected because the message growth, in terms of number of measurements, is not linear to the size in bytes. The size 1 message in JSON is 11 times smaller than in JSON-LD (in bytes), whereas the size 3 message in JSON is 1.08 times smaller than in JSON-LD (in bytes). We conclude that if the number of measurements transmitted by the device is greater than 100, then JSON and JSON-LD perform almost identically. S2 confirmed our findings from S1, providing similar results. The only difference observed compared to S1 is a small increase on the total transaction time (less than 0.01%), which was expected because of the broker. This indicates that the choice for Mosquitto as a lightweight broker was appropriate, causing minimal impact with a few publishers sending data to a topic.

20.5. Conclusion

Although JSON-LD was built as a lightweight syntax, an analysis must be performed to empirically demonstrate that the impact on performance is minimal when migrating from IoT applications using JSON. We compared JSON and JSON-LD in terms of the total transaction time for IoT applications. Messages that contained measurements of an IoT device (a photometer) were used. The variables included the message size with three variations of measurements per message, and consumer (subscriber) side data processing, i.e. deserialization of the JSON-LD message with an API. The results show that a small message (with one measurement) has the biggest impact when porting from JSON to JSON-LD: 0.19% of the total transaction time.

This is the worst-case scenario, meaning that migrating from JSON to JSON-LD is feasible for most IoT solutions. Developers of applications that have strict time response constraints (critical systems) and use JSON must consider this result. This paper also introduced an approach for comparing ontologies in terms of verbosity. By using the analysis methodology and implementation, one can compare ontologies that represent the same domain, such as, for example SAREF and W3C SSN.

Future work includes inspecting high scale volume of traffic and the impact of libraries in different programming languages with messages using our extension of SAREF for healthcare (SAREF4health, under construction). Moreover, we plan to investigate the impact of storing JSON-LD messages in a NoSQL database.

20.6. References

[AFS 17] Afsari K. *et al.*, "JavaScript Object Notation (JSON) data serialization for IFC schema in web-based BIM data exchange", *Automation in Construction*, vol. 77, pp. 24–51, 2017.

[DÍA 16] Díaz M., Martín C., Rubio B., "State-of-the-art, challenges, and open issues in the integration of IoT and cloud computing", *Journal of Network and Computer Applications*, vol. 67, pp. 99–117, 2016.

[DIG 11] digitalbazaar, A JSON-LD processor and API implementation in JavaScript, Github code, available at: https://github.com/digitalbazaar/jsonld.js, 2011.

[DOU 18] Douzis K., Sotiriadis S., Petrakis E.G.M. *et al.*, "Modular and generic IoT management on the cloud", *Future Generation Computer Systems*, vol. 78-1, pp. 369–378, 2018.

[EC 17] European Commission, "Rolling plan on ICT standardisation", available at: http://joinup.ec.europa.eu/collection/rolling-plan-ict-standardisation, 2017.

[ETS 17] ETSI, "New version of the M2M Standard for Smart Appliances", available at: http://www.etsi.org/technologies-clusters/technologies/smart-appliances, 2017.

[JAN 16] Janes D.P., "Semantic metastandards will unlock IoT interoperability", *Internet of Things. IoT Infrastructures: Second International Summit, IoT 360°, Rome, Italy, October 27–29, 2015, Revised Selected Papers, Part II*, Springer, Cham, 2016.

[LI 16]   Li H. *et al.*, "Enabling Semantics in an M2M/IoT Service Delivery Platform", *IEEE 10th International Conference on Semantic Computing (ICSC)*, Laguna Hills, 4–6 October, 2016.

[PAL 16] Palavalli A., Karri D., Pasupuleti S., "Semantic Internet of Things", *IEEE Tenth International Conference on Semantic Computing (ICSC)*, Laguna Hills, 4–6 October, 2016.

[RIZ 16] Rizzardi A. *et al.*, "AUPS: An Open Source AUthenticated Publish/Subscribe system for the Internet of Things", *Information Systems*, vol. 62, pp. 29–41, 2016.

[W3C 18] W3C, "JSON for Linked Data (JSON-LD) latest version (1.1)", available at: https://json-ld.org/spec/latest/json-ld/, 2018.

[WOH 12] Wohlin C. *et al.*, *Experimentation in Software Engineering*, Springer, Heidelberg, 2012.

21

FIWARE for Industry: A Data-driven Reference Architecture

This paper describes an approach for "smart industries" that goes well beyond the current reference architectures (RA) for Industry 4.0 such as RAMI, IVRI and IIRA. We are emphasizing the data sharing aspect between different businesses, as well as reaching out to other established eco-systems (e.g. smart cities). In a hyper connected society, the integration of many different data sets into a single application can improve efficiency and speed up production processes. For instance, in an urban manufacturing environment, optimizing the goods inbound and outbound logistics is closely dependent on non-manufacturing data sources, such as traffic, mobility, meteorological or other typical "smart city" applications. Manufacturing-oriented reference architectures and implementations in many cases need to be integrated in a seamless way with processes not following the same rules and standards. In this sense, digital manufacturing platforms need to be open and secure, thus data exchange and sharing interoperability processes need to be specified and implemented.

21.1. Introduction

The final report of the Digitising EU Industry Working Group about Digital Industrial Platforms [EU 17] concludes that the "digitisation of the industrial sector, which constitutes one of the main pillars of the European economy, has an impact on innovation, growth and prosperity in Europe that significantly exceeds the size of the sector itself".

Chapter written by Stefano DE PANFILIS, Sergio GUSMEROLI, Jorge RODRIGUEZ and Jesús BENEDICTO.

The main aim of this paper is to demonstrate how FIWARE architecture and open source platforms could be extended with additional enablers relevant for the Industry sector, in order to implement data-driven smart industry-integrated applications. One element of this strategy is the establishment of industrial data platforms enabling a secure data exchange between stakeholders. The advantage of a data-driven approach is a decoupling of the industrial processes while securing the important element, the data. Furthermore, we can control the data flow better, while still reaching the fast integration of many industrial and business processes. This emphasizes the digitalization of the smart Industry as identified in the above mentioned report. Such industrial data platforms are enabling not just Industry 4.0 production plant or smart product–service systems, but also new digital business models in the so-called global data economy. Those business models can reach to end-customers and enable traditional business to tap into new revenue models based on generated data.

In the following sections, this paper discusses an overview of FIWARE, the ecosystem for building smart services born in Europe, but nowadays globally adopted, together with the FIWARE for Industry initiative, which aims to make FIWARE compliant with existing manufacturing reference architectures following a data-driven approach. As a matter of fact, a comprehensive data-driven approach applied also to smart industry will dramatically improve the decoupling of processes and the re-use of data. The main challenges when transforming a component-driven RA, such as FIWARE, into a data-driven one is the difference between data-in-motion and data-at-rest and how this reflects in the RA. To implement such transformation we need specific enablers developing the concepts of data-driven smart factory and smart products. "FIWARE for Industry" is defining these new enablers and creating the first reference implementations. These reference implementations use the existing generic enablers from FIWARE such as context broker, historical storage, big data analytics, and many others, but also introduce new enablers for the industrial case. The paper concludes with an outlook that data-driven architectures supported by respective runtime systems will enable a better control over the processes as well the data ownership as data can be traced and controlled across many different data processing applications.

21.2. Industrial reference architectures

Nowadays, several consortia have been working to provide different reference models from various perspectives and viewpoints. The Industrial Internet Consortium (IIC), the Industrial Value Chain Initiative and the Working Group for Industry 4.0 have all provided recommendations and guidelines in the form of the Industrial Internet Reference Architecture (IIRA) [IIC 17a], the Industry Value

Chain Reference Architecture (IVRA) [NIS 17] and the Reference Architecture Model for Industry 4.0 (RAMI 4.0) [HAN 15], respectively. All of them articulate the creation of industrial Internet systems and cyber physical systems as fundamental building blocks for the industrial internet. Having as a starting point these existing industrial Internet reference architectures, the objective of this paper is to provide an approach of a data-driven reference architecture capable of driving the industrial sector transformation into a networked, data driven environment in order to optimize production systems and value chains, and radically improve sustainability, productivity, innovation and customer service using the value of the data.

21.3. FIWARE and the FIWARE for Industry initiative

FIWARE (https://www.fiware.org/) is an open initiative targeted to create a sustainable ecosystem able to capture the opportunities that will emerge with the new wave of digitalization brought by combining context information management, fed by the Internet of Things, with big data services on the cloud.

FIWARE technologies combine an open source standard platform integrating a number of components making it easier to develop smart applications. For this, the FIWARE platform provides a rather simple yet powerful set of APIs (application programming interfaces) that ease the development of smart applications in multiple vertical sectors. The specifications of these APIs are public and royalty-free. Additionally, an open source reference implementation of each of the FIWARE components is publicly available so that multiple FIWARE providers can emerge faster in the market with a low-cost proposition. FIWARE also provides a non-commercial sandbox environment called FIWARE Lab, where innovation and experimentation based on FIWARE technologies take place, and where entrepreneurs and individuals can test the technology as well as their applications on FIWARE Lab.

On the other hand, FIWARE for Industry (http://www.fiwareforindustry.eu/) develops and extends FIWARE Technologies towards the implementation of Smart–Digital–Virtual Factories of the Future through open source components and a hub of reference architectures and digital platforms. This initiative originates from the FP7 FI PPP Phase II FITMAN project and is now brought forward by an ecosystem of several H2020 projects, sharing the same vision and mission.

Currently this ecosystem has more than 30 specific software components including those coming from FIWARE, such as those developed in FIWARE for Industry, and some brand new components needed for implementing a real data-driven approach which are being developed. All in all, such assets implement access to shop floor data sources, data brokerage and complex event processing, advanced HCI at the shop floor, data integration and interoperability with legacy systems, data descriptive and predictive analytics and finally data presentation, advanced visualization, business intelligence and decisional support.

21.4. A data-driven reference architecture for Industry 4.0

One of the most accepted reference architecture for Industry 4.0 is the Industry Value Chain Reference Architecture (IVRA). IVRA provides three perspectives to understand manufacturing industry as a whole: the knowledge-engineering flow, the demand-supply flow and hierarchical levels from the device level to the enterprise level. A key element is the introduction of smart manufacturing units in a way that allows to smoothly integrate human beings as elements with their autonomous nature.

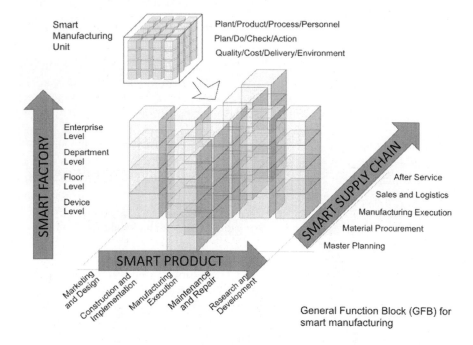

Figure 21.1. *Industry Value Chain Reference Architecture. For a color version of this figure, see www.iste.co.uk/zelm/enterprise.zip*

Starting from this overall holistic picture we can rename the three IVRA dimensions as Smart Factory, Smart Product and Smart Supply Chain scenarios, in agreement with FITMAN categorization of manufacturing industry scenarios smart–digital–virtual platforms.

In order to depict a data-driven architecture for FIWARE for Industry, we took as a reference the convergence between RAMI and IIRA, recently developed by an IIC working group called JTG2, as presented in the white paper "Architecture Alignment and Interoperability: An Industrial Internet Consortium and Platform Industrie 4.0 Joint Whitepaper" [IIC 17b].

If we take the IIRA data-driven reference architecture as a paradigm, we can therefore easily map any development versus RAMI and therefore achieve a full alignment and compatibility with Platform Industrie 4.0 and the overall network of Industry 4.0 National and Regional initiatives. More in particular, the data-driven implementation of the IIRA foresees four main databus layers (Figure 21.2) where data exchange/sharing processes are taking place. The Machine Databus is the real-world databus, to be implemented in a factory shopfloor, in the operations of a product or in transportation-logistics scenarios. The Unit Databus is usually implemented by dedicated edge-fog data gateways as a bridge between the real and digital worlds. The Site Databus implements the databus of a single administrative domain, being it a company, an IT department, a plant, a fleet of logistics vehicles. On top of that, the Inter-site Databus materializes B2B data exchange/sharing business processes across at least two different administrative domains.

The implementation of the reference architectures in the three scenarios mentioned above shows that the smart factory and smart product scenarios are implemented by the first three databus layers, while the supply chain scenario is implemented by the top Intersite Databus.

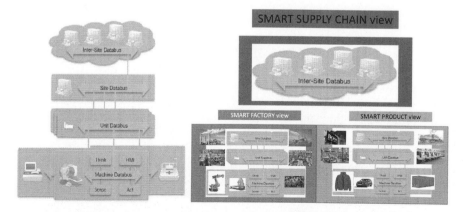

Figure 21.2. *Data-driven implementation of the IIRA and their mapping to the smart factory and smart product scenarios. For a color version of this figure, see www.iste.co.uk/zelm/enterprise.zip*

Particularly, the Unit Databus could be materialized by an open edge/fog computing architecture such as FogFlow.

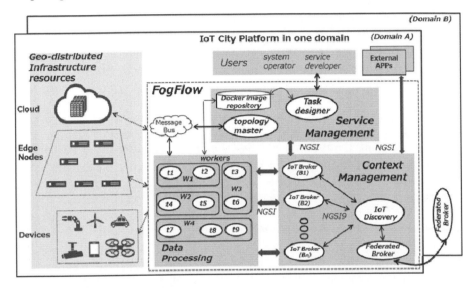

Figure 21.3. *System architecture of FogFlow and its major components. For a color version of this figure, see www.iste.co.uk/zelm/enterprise.zip*

FogFlow [CHE 17] is a cloud–edge programming system that implements the data stream programming model. Different data can be inserted into a flow, for example data from sensors, status information from machineries (e.g. using OPC-UA), aggregated information from other flows, events from cloud applications and elsewhere.

FogFlow uses the FIWAREs NGSI data model as a container architecture into which many different data can be placed, and enables the allocation of FogFlow components to either cloud or edge servers. During runtime, the FogFlow architecture supervises (1) the available data sources and adds newly discovered sources to the flow, and (2) adapts the data stream to changes in resource situations, for example when components with a higher priority need to be allocated to edges [PAP 15]. Due to its dynamic resource allocation as well as the ability to dynamically extend existing flows, FogFlow can realize a very intelligent Unit Databus.

The Site Databus is instead to be implemented by the FIWARE Orion Context Broker, which is the aggregation point of the FIWARE IoT architecture (data in Motion) and the major publish/subscribe broker for FIWARE Analytics applications (data at Rest).

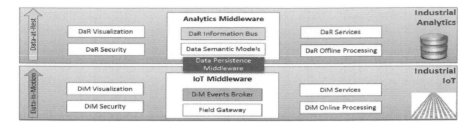

Figure 21.4. *Implementation of the Site Databus. For a color version of this figure, see www.iste.co.uk/zelm/enterprise.zip*

The MIDIH project (www.midih.eu) is the Factories of the Future project where these scenarios will be implemented by a collaboration of four main platforms and experimented in a network of industrial facilities located all around Europe. The Arrowhead distributed automation platform, the FIWARE Data in Motion and Data at Rest platforms and the IDS RA open source implementation via Blockchain Smart Contracts will be integrated into a unique modular architecture for Smart factory, Smart Products and Smart Supply Chains industrial scenarios.

21.5. Conclusion

This paper introduces the FIWARE for Industry reference architecture and implementation, an innovative alliance of data-driven architectures and platforms for data management in industrial scenarios. Based on the FIWARE Industrial IoT and Industrial Analytics platforms, this new collaboration encompasses edge/fog computing as well as distributed ledger technologies to implement any industrial scenario in the smart factory, smart product and smart supply chain domains. Architecture, reference implementations and experimentations for their validation are being conducted in several European (but also national and regional) projects, but especially in the MIDIH I4MS Innovation Action.

The main goal of this reference architecture and the implementation of FIWARE Specific Enablers covering manufacturing needs is to help industrial companies in their digital transformation, trying to eliminate existing barriers in the adoption of new technologies and platforms mainly present in SMEs.

21.6. References

[CHE 17] Cheng B., Solmaz G., Cirillo F. *et al.*, "FogFlow: easy programming of IoT services over cloud and edges for smart cities", *IEEE Internet of Things Journal*, vol. 5, no. 2, pp. 696–707, 2017.

[EU 17] European Union, Digitising European Industry: Working Group 2 – Digital Industrial Platforms, Report, available at https://ec.europa.eu/futurium/en/implementing-digitising-european-industry-actions/report-wg2-digital-industrial-platforms-final, 2017.

[HEN 15] Hankel M., Rexroth B., The Reference Architectural Model Industrie 4.0 (RAMI 4.0), Report, ZVEI, available at https://www.zvei.org/en/press-media/publications/the-reference-architectural-model-industrie-40-rami-40/?, 2015.

[IIC 17a] Industrial Internet Consortium, Industrial Internet Reference Architecture V1.8, Standard, available at: https://www.iiconsortium.org/IIRA.htm, 2017.

[IIC 17b] Industrial Internet Consortium, Architecture Alignment and Interoperability, Report, available at: https://www.iiconsortium.org/pdf/JTG2_Whitepaper_final_20171205.pdf, 2017.

[NIS 17] Nishioka Y., "Industrial value chain reference architecture", Forum Industrie 4.0 meets the Industrial Internet, Hannover Messe, Hannover, Germany, 24–28 April, 2017.

[PAP 15] Papageorgiou A., Cheng B., Kovacs E., "Real-time data reduction at the network edge of Internet of Things systems," *11th International Conference on Network and Service Management (CNSM)*, Barcelona, Spain, 9–13 November, pp. 284–291, 2015.

22

European Big Data Value Association Position Paper on the Smart Manufacturing Industry

In this chapter we introduce and summarize the European Big Data Value Association's (BDVA) research in the context of the smart manufacturing industry domain. Gathering the knowledge of its members on state of the art in technologies and research projects results in manufacturing, BDVA have created a first version of their Smart Manufacturing Industry position paper that proposes upcoming research challenges on Big Data for Manufacturing.

22.1. Introduction

The BDVA Strategic Research and Innovation Agenda [BDV 17] (SRIA) defines overall goals, technical and non-technical priorities, and research and innovation challenges for this European Public Private Partnership (PPP) on big data. The current expectations of the data market in Europe is around €60 billion and manufacturing was also at the front in 2016 with €12 billion the 2020 projections project €17.3 billion. These figures reveal the major role of manufacturing in the overall data economy market. With the aim to find an agreed synthesis, the BDVA adopted the "Smart Manufacturing Industry" (SMI) concept definition, including the whole value chain gravitating around goods production.

Starting from data market and manufacturing industry relevance in Europe and in following the European initiative of Digitation of Industry [EC 16], several experts

Chapter written by Anibal REÑONES, Davide DALLE CARBONARE and Sergio GUSMEROLI.

from BDVA have started a collective effort to define a position paper that proposes research challenges for the manufacturing industry with a Big Data point of view.

22.2. BDVA technical priorities in relation to the smart manufacturing industry

The BDVA has defined a BDV Reference Model or framework that shows Big Data technologies in the IT stack. This model is compatible with reference architectures, like ISO JTC1 WG9 Big Data Reference Architecture. With this reference model in mind, the BDVA community identified five technical priority areas for research and innovation that serve as the main classification for research challenges in manufacturing:

– *Data management and lifecycle* generated by the data explosion, where current practices for its storage and management are able to resist the evolution of size and speed of data delivered,

– *Data processing architectures* created by fast development of the Internet of Things (IoT) and the need to process immense amounts of generated sensor data;

– *Data analytics* that aims to progress technologies and develop abilities to transform Big Data into value, but also to make those abilities understandable to bigger audiences;

– *Data protection* addressing the need to ensure the correct use of information whilst guaranteeing user privacy. It includes advanced data protection, privacy and anonymization technologies;

– *Data visualization and user interaction* means capable of handling the increasing complexity and size of generated data that support the user in the effective exploration and understanding of Big Data.

During a series of workshop activities that began at the 2016 EBDVF Valencia Summit 2016 until the 2017 EBDVF Versailles Summit, BDVA experts from different fields (industry and IT) distilled a set of research challenges for the three grand scenarios of smart manufacturing. Based on the expert panel technical expertise, these research challenges were filtered, prioritized and mapped to the five technical priority areas of the Big Data reference model.

22.3. Smart manufacturing industry grand scenarios

The smart manufacturing industry task force of the BDVA adopted a "smart manufacturing industry" (SMI) definition. This includes whole value chain of goods production, and then identified three scenarios to represent all the distinct characteristics of a SMI in Europe.

– *Smart Factory scenario*: in this one, data appears inside production lines and expected analytics has three main objectives: safety, optimization and diagnosis of the plant as well as for the workers. There are several key topics in the smart factory scenario: cyber physical production systems, machinery and robots, factory automation, internal logistics and smart workplaces. In this scenario, analytics could support advanced applications such as, production lines design and ramp-up, production scheduling, modeling and simulation of CPS, production monitoring and control, energy/waste consumption optimization, maintenance, zero-defect manufacturing, diagnosis and prediction, workplace human–machine interaction, workers training and augmented reality.

– *Smart Supply Chain scenario*: data is generated here by suppliers, distributors, providers and retailers. Analytics are needed for integration of value chain and collaboration of management and executives. The main topics in this scenario are: analysis of trends and sentiment, supply and distribution chain optimization, inbound and outbound logistics optimization, open innovation and Living Labs, synchronization of closed-loop manufacturing, industrial symbiosis, co-operative working environments for engineers and managers, retail and consumer experience monitoring and ecosystems of product-service cross-domain.

– *Smart Product Lifecycle*: grand scenario, where data is generated by the product-service itself along its lifecycle in a circular economy perspective and analytics is needed for product operations monitoring and control. Key topics in this scenario are: new product-service ideation and design, closed- loop engineering, product operations monitoring, product preventive and predictive maintenance, de- and re-Manufacturing and re-cycling, as-designed, as-built, as-maintained models, sharing and service economy and business models for product service systems.

22.4. Relation with other initiatives

The efforts to define research priorities for Big Data into the manufacturing environment were synchronized with ongoing initiatives. Associations like the European EFFRA identified in its 2020 roadmap [EFF 13] several domains related with manufacturing like "Adaptive and smart manufacturing systems", "Digital, virtual and resource efficient factories" or "Collaborative and mobile enterprises". The research projects originating from this roadmap have been a valuable source of inspiration for the current BDVA SMI position paper. Among them, a recent CSA known as ConnectedFactories [EFF 16], formed by a cluster of 10 projects, has created a 2030 roadmap that defines three main types of connected factories, which have been labeled with different personas: (1) Hyperconnected Factories, (2) Autonomous Factories, and (3) Collaborative Product-Service Factories. Members both from BDVA and from the ConnectedFactories project have shared their mutual views to ensure that a stronger and coherent vision is created. Both the Industrial Internet Consortium and Plattform Industrie 4.0 have developed IT reference architectures in the manufacturing domain: Plattform Industrie 4.0's Reference Architecture Model for Industrie 4.0 (RAMI 4.0) [PLA 15] and the Industrial Internet Reference Architecture (IIRA) [IIC 17a]. The shared goal of both architectures is to make manufacturing operations more intelligent, orchestrating and optimizing its processes in a digital fashion. Ongoing efforts to ensure interoperability of these architectures [IIC 17b], is focused on mapping the so-called IIRA functional domains/crosscutting functions and RAMI 4.0 architecture layers. The SMI position paper carefully analysed the interoperability aspects of both architectures to take them into account in the BDVA technical priorities and corresponding research challenges addressing specific interoperability aspects, were added for the three SMI scenarios.

22.5. Research challenges of Big Data in smart factory scenarios

The current paper shows the list of such research challenges within the three SMI scenarios. The readers are encouraged to analyze the full set of challenges in the first version of the SMI white paper [BDV 18]. The following three tables gather the headings for the challenges identified and discussed by the BDVA.

Data Management	*Data Visualization*
- CPS data sources integration automation systems semantic interoperability - Smart factory data annotation - Smart factory unstructured, semi-structured and missing data - Industrial IOT data availability	- Context-aware visualization in smart workplaces - Visual analytics for smart factory decision makers - Smart factory natural language interaction interfaces - Cross-domain and data exploration - Simulation and training environments
Data Processing Architectures	*Data Analytics*
- On-premise vs. cloud smart factory architectures - Hybrid clouds and edge automation architectures - Smart factory data in motion, data at rest integration	- Prescriptive analytics in industrial plants - Machine and deep learning in smart factory - Analytics for data–human interaction of factory models - Analytics-based decision support in manufacturing operations management - Embedded analytics
Data Protection and Security Challenges	
- Sensitive data privacy in future workspaces	

- Protection against cyber-attacks in smart factories - Access control and data integrity in smart factory critical infrastructures - Selective anonymization in smart workspaces	- Analytics-oriented manufacturing simulation model - Digital twin for analytics

Table 22.1. *Smart Factory scenario research challenges*

Data Management - Product design interoperability - Product operations data cleaning and curation - Product lifecycle data management - Provider–user product data integration *Data Processing Architectures* - Data at rest smart product pre-production - Data in motion for smart product post-production *Data Protection and Security Challenges* - Data confidentiality and IPR in smart products pre-production - Privacy preservation in smart products post-production and operations	*Data Visualization* - 3D visualization of complex smart products - VR/AR in maintenance and operations of complex smart products - Update smart products visualization at runtime - Highly configurable smart products visualization for the user - Product data visualization by the user *Data Analytics* - Pre-processing product data and deep learning - Real time analytics in smart products operations - Complex products digital twins alignment - Product-service systems modeling

Table 22.2. *Smart Product Lifecycle scenario research challenges*

Data Management - Heterogeneous data in business ecosystems - Cross-enterprise data value chain management - Data traceability in value networks - Supply chain collaboration for component, machine and plant providers - Adaptive and flexible supply chain data management	*Data Visualization* - VR/AR technologies in supply chain integration - Customized user interface in business ecosystems *Data Analytics* - Data analytics for supply chain optimization - Supply chain condition and risk analysis

Data Processing Architectures - Vertical supply chain data integration - Real-time supply chain data processing *Data Protection and Security Challenges* - Cybersecurity and trust in agile value networks	- Analytics-based decision support in business ecosystems - Data analytics for supply chain workforce management - Prescriptive maintenance in production chains

Table 22.3. *Smart Supply Chain scenario research challenges*

22.6 Conclusion

The challenges set initially in first version of the SMI position paper establish the state of upcoming research needs in different Big Data areas related to manufacturing. In particular, the Smart Factory scenario focuses on integration of multiples sources of data coming from the shop floor and the offices, traditionally separated in Industry 3.0 paradigm. Interoperability of existing IT systems and the challenge of integrating disruptive IIoT technologies are major challenges in the data management area. Analytics challenges are focused on prescriptive analytics as tools for an optimal decision-making process at the manufacturing operations management site including the optimization through the evolved concept of the digital twin.

22.7 References

[BDV 18] Big Data Value Association, Big Data Challenges in Smart Manufacturing v1, Report, available online at http://www.bdva.eu/node/1002, 2018.

[BDV 17] Big Data Value Association, Strategic Research and Innovation Agenda v4.0, Report, available online at http://www.bdva.eu, 2017.

[EC 16] European Commission, *Digitising European Industry: Reaping the Full Benefits of a Digital Single Market*, COM(2016), 2016.

[EFF 16] Effra, ConnectedFactories H2020 project, available at http://www.effra.eu/connected factories, 2016.

[EFF 13] Effra, Multi-annual roadmap for the contractual PPP under Horizon 2020, available online at https://www.effra.eu/factories-future-roadmap, 2013.

[IIC 17a] Industrial Internet Consortium, *Industrial Internet Reference Architecture v1.8*, available online at http://www.iiconsortium.org/IIC_PUB_G1_V1.80_2017-01-31.pdf, 2017.

[IIC 17b] Industrial Internet Consortium and Plattform Industrie 4.0, Architecture Alignment and Interoperability, Whitepaper, IIC:WHT:IN3:V1.0:PB:20171205, 2017.

[PLA 15] Plattform Industrie 4.0, Reference Architecture Model Industrie 4.0 (RAMI 4.0), available online at https://goo.gl/6MA64H, 2015.

23

SmTIP: A Big Data Integration Platform for Synchromodal Transport

This chapter reports on the design of an integration platform that supports the collection and analysis of third-party, real-time data for the dynamic planning of cargo transportation. Especially, flexible allocation of cargo to transportation modes and routes is targeted, also known as synchromodal transportation. A prototype of the integration platform was developed, including a user interface for planners, to support them in decision-making by providing information about potential disruptions of planned or ongoing shipments. Potential disruptions are detected by analysis of data received from one or more live data sources.

23.1. Introduction

Cargo transportation is an important part of logistics, which in turn is a major enabler of trade and commerce in economy. Innovation, and therefore adoption of new technology, plays an important role in the transportation business where margins are low and competition is fierce. A current wave of innovation is driven by the availability of big data technology and analytics [MIK 15]. Transport companies wants access to third-party real-time data about traffic conditions, weather conditions, road conditions and so on. This contextual data allows for dynamic planning and better information (e.g. track and trace) services. Dynamic planning can improve performance and reduce costs. Specifically, performance improvement relates to efficient use of resources (high utilization), less waiting time for customers (low lead time), shorter transportation times, less fuel consumption, and lower

---

Chapter written by Prince M. Singh, Marten van Sinderen and Roel Wieringa.

transportation costs. Customers profit from performance improvement and lower costs. Governments also profit from performance improvement, since it supports their goal of efficient use of transport infrastructure (rail, road, water) and pollution reduction. An important challenge faced by transport companies is the creation of an integration platform that facilitates the collection of contextual data, such that the data can be shared, combined with proprietary logistics data and processed for the realization of dynamic planning and information services [SIN 16b]. This paper reports on the design of an integration platform that supports the collection and analysis of contextual data for dynamic planning of cargo transportation. Especially flexible allocation of cargo to transportation modes and routes is targeted, also known as synchromodal transport (SmT) [SIN 16a]. The proposed platform is called Synchromodal Transportation Integration Platform – SmTIP. We followed the design science methodology to develop the SmTIP platform.

The rest of this paper is organized as follows: section 23.2 presents a domain model of synchromodal transport resulting from our problem investigation, section 23.3 presents the design of our SmTIP platform to improve dynamic planning and information services for synchromodal transport, section 23.4 presents the development of a prototype for the validation of the SmTIP design and section 23.5 presents our conclusions and future work.

23.2. Domain model of synchromodal transport

During our problem investigation, we interviewed stakeholders to understand their goals, what is happening in their business, why and how is this happening, and the impact on their business. As a result we formulated the main research question (the design problem): "How can we design an integration platform for synchromodal transport that provides access to third-party real-time contextual data and supports dynamic planning and information services? Our focus is on synchromodal transport, which targets the flexible allocation of cargo to transport modes and routes in order to achieve a better balance of cost, performance and service levels [SIN 16b]. We explicitly consider the role of 4PL (4th party logistic service provider): an integrator that accumulates resources, capabilities and technologies to run complete supply chain solutions. The first step we did in the design of an integration platform was to create a domain model. Figure 23.1 shows the domain model which was derived from the stakeholder interviews and a literature review. Some relevant works consulted for deriving the domain model include [IAC 13, GET 15, IFR 17, SIN 16b, GS1 17].

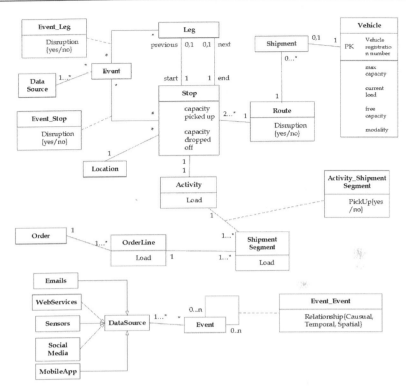

Figure 23.1. *Conceptual domain model for synchromodal transport*

The domain model represents the main concepts from the synchromodal transport domain and their relationships. It shows, for example, that a customer *order* is divided into one or more order lines. Each *order line* is concerned with a load that has to be picked up at some location and dropped off at another location. These locations are *stops* along a *route*, which belongs to a *shipment* that has been assigned to one or more *vehicles* of the same modality (truck, sea vessel, barge, or train). A shipment combines order lines from one or more orders, such that the capacity of the vehicle is optimized. If the load of an order line does not fit the capacity of a single vehicle, the shipment is divided into multiple *shipment segments*, each with its own vehicle. The objective of a planning algorithm is to find a mapping between orders and shipments, such that a balanced optimization of possibly conflicting objectives, like minimum lead time (high customer satisfaction) and maximum utilization of resources (low operational costs), is achieved. Contextual events may affect the planning. A traffic accident, for example, can prevent a vehicle from using the originally planned route, and therefore a re-planning is necessary. The domain model shows that contextual *events* are derived from one or more *data sources*. An event is only relevant if it can impact a shipment, and it can only impact a shipment if its space and time coverage overlaps with the route and time plan of a shipment. Hence, an event is related to zero or more routes, or more precisely, to the stops and *legs* that make up a route. If a relation to a stop or leg exists, it has to be decided whether it can disrupt any of the shipments that use the stop or leg. For this, the properties of the event have to be evaluated in relation to properties of the shipments, including the possible time overlap. This may be done semi-automatically, and in case it is decided that an event is disruptive with respect to a shipment, the shipment has to be re-planned.

23.3. SmTIP design

During the SmTIP design, we first performed a systematic literature study to identify the state-of-the-art of integration platforms (IPs) and define a generic integration platform.

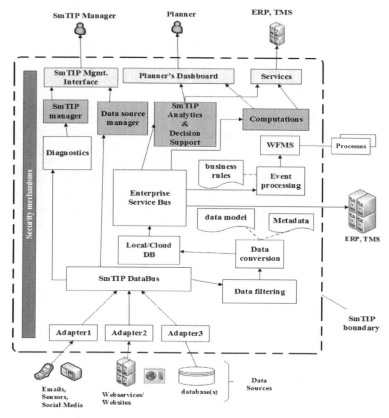

Figure 23.2. *SmTIP architecture. For a color version of this figure, see www.iste.co.uk/zelm/enterprise.zip*

Next, we used the interview results to extract requirements for an integration platform for synchromodal transport and specialize the generic IP towards an SmTIP. The SmTIP architecture, as shown in Figure 23.2, consists of: an enterprise architecture (presents main components at business, application and technology level with their mutual relationships), a data-driven architecture (presents the structure of data in stages from multiple data sources via aggregation, analysis and detection to multiple data sinks), and middleware and application architecture (presents the data processing applications and how they are able to interact in a distributed and decentralized environment via service decoupling).

23.4. Prototype development and validation

During SmTIP validation, we developed a prototype of the SmTIP using Mendix© [MEN 17]. The prototype provides a user interface to planners who are responsible for transport planning by dividing orders into orderlines which are then assigned to shipments with a certain modality and route. The prototype can accept customer orders as input and can be connected to live data sources providing data or events of interest to the planning process. The planner can define conditions on events and data values that make up situations of interest. One particular situation of interest is a disruption precondition. A disruption precondition is a situation in which shipments might be delayed (i.e. cannot be realized according to planning). For example consider the following shipment and a disruption situation:

– a shipment is planned (and potentially is in process) from A to B between t1 and t2;

– a disruption situation that satisfies conditions on planned construction work, expected extreme weather conditions, and current traffic densities, with a location on the route from A to B and a time between t1 and t2. Concretely: "A1 Amersfoort to Amsterdam, at Eembrugge. Driveway closed. From 26 February 2018 to 1 March 2018 daily between 22:00 and 05:00" (source: ANWB), or "Published/issued on 27 February 2018, 20:29 hrs, valid on 27 Feb 2018: Locally slippery due to snow, after midnight temperature below -15 degrees. Across the country, with the exception of the south, it can be locally slippery due to snow or snowfall" (source: KNMI) or perhaps an XML message validated against DATEX II XSD about traffic data at a specific measurement site in near real-time (e.g. traffic flow) (source: NDW).

The platform connects to the live sources, collects the data, performs preprocessing to make the data suitable for further use, detects situations of interest, identifies potentially affected entities, decides on an action, executes the action (e.g., inform planner or change plan, i.e. issue a warning or run an automated response). The developed prototype is demonstrated to various experts in the field, and small experiments in which experts perform a predefined planning tasks using the prototype are conducted. Opinions and experiences are collected and analyzed.

23.5. Conclusion

We discussed our initial results in the design and development of SmTIP, a big data integration platform for synchromodal transport. The conceptual domain model helps future researchers to understand important concepts of the synchromodal transport domain, which plays a role in data analysis. Using Figure 23.1 we described the concepts used in synchromodal transport planning and related them to events and data sources. Our major contribution is the design of a SmTIP platform, which collects, transforms, analyzes and stores contextual data from diverse data sources. A SmTIP prototype was developed for validation purposes and has been applied in iterative cycles to improve the design. Further validation cycles are planned which involving stakeholders to test the contribution of SmTIP to stakeholder goals.

23.6. References

[BRE 17] Breivold. H.P., "A survey and analysis of reference architectures for the Internet of Things", *12th International Conference on Software Engineering (ICSEA 2017), IARIA*, pp. 132–138, 2017.

[GET 15] Dijkman R., "Data model for project service platform for Green European Transport (GET Service)", Public Document No. D1.2.1., 2015.

[GS1 17] GS1, Global Standards One, available at http://www.gs1.org. 2017.

[ITR 17] Itria M.L., Kocsis-Magyar M., Ceccarelli A. *et al.*, "Identification of critical situations via event processing and event trust analysis", *Knowledge and Information Systems*, vol. 52, no. 1, pp 147–178, 2017.

[IAC 13] Iacob M.E., van Sinderen M.J., Steenwijk P. *et al.*, "Towards a reference architecture for fuel-based carbon management system in logistic industry", *Information System Frontiers*, vol. 15, no. 5, pp 725–745, 2013.

[MEN 17] Mendix, Website, available at http://www.mendix.com, 2017.

[MIK 15] Mikavica B., Kostić-Ljubisavljević A. Radonjić V., "Big data: challenges and opportunities in logistics systems", *2nd Logistics International Conference*, Belgrade, Serbia, 21–23 May, 2015.

[SIN 16a] Singh P.M, van Sinderen M.J., Wieringa R.J., "Synchromodal transport: pre-requisites, activities and effects", *6th International Conference on Information Systems Logistics and Supply Chain*, Bordeaux, France, 1–4 June, 2016.

[SIN 16b] Singh P. M., van Sinderen M.J., "Big data interoperability challenges for logistics", in Zelm M., Doumeingts G. and Mendonça J.P. (eds), *Enterprise Interoperability in the Digitized and Networked Factory of the Future*, pp. 325–335, ISTE Ltd, London, 2016.

24

Fault Prediction in Aerospace Product Manufacturing: A Model-based Big Data Analytics Service

The aeronautical sector is an intricate net of industrial relationships and data emerging in different phases of product development that needs to be managed and integrated. Based in this context, this chapter's aim is to describe the contribution given to the development of the Model-based Big Data Analytics as-a-Service (MBDAaaS) framework, proposed by the Toreador project, within an aerospace manufacturing context. In particular, the development of the fault prediction service, able to detect manufacturing machine faults before the quality of the product is jeopardized, is described in detail.

24.1. Introduction

A huge volume and variety of data is currently associated with an internet-worked aeronautical enterprise supply chain [SCH 17]. Although the volume of data is growing exponentially, aeronautical companies currently leverage only a small part of it; still, in many cases, real-time data processing and analysis are not conducted yet. In such a data-driven industrial context, Big Data analytics promises significant performance improvements along the entire supply chain [TIW 18].

Following the principles of the Digital Agenda for Europe [EC 10], an important Italian aerospace company, which designs, manufactures and maintains components and systems for civil and military aviation, has committed to the smart use of technology with the aim to better leverage manufacturing data. Today, in the

Chapter written by Anna Maria CRESPINO, Carla DI BICCARI, Mariangela LAZOI and Marianna LEZZI.

majority of the company's manufacturing cells, computer numerical control (CNC) machines record a large amount of sensor data. The challenge is to aggregate and analyze such data in order to obtain useful insights for improving performance of the manufacturing lines.

The paper aims to describe an application of the Model-based Big Data Analytics as-a-Service (MBDAaaS) framework [ARD 17], proposed by the Toreador project for developing a set of big data analytics services, within the above mentioned aerospace company (representing one of the four pilot cases in the Project).

24.2. Related works

Predictive maintenance (PdM) is currently enabled by smart technologies, usually embedded in physical assets. In particular, by leveraging the massive amount of data produced by these technologies and applying the right Big Data analytics, machine failures can be predicted, with evident benefits in terms of parts' efficiency and in minimizing unnecessary downtime. Furthermore, early failure detection is well accepted in the industry, since it can potentially eliminate catastrophic machine failures [AMR 18]. Many anomaly detection techniques have already been developed in machine learning and statistical domains by applying supervised, semi-supervised and unsupervised techniques [CHA 09]. Although the majority of them were designed for generic application domains, recent research has also focused on techniques developed for specific ones. In particular, the problem of detecting manufacturing anomalies has received little attention [HAR 06]. Several algorithms are widely used today to identify the abnormal behavior of a subsystem, such as: Principle Component Analysis (PCA), K-Means, C-Means, Hierarchical clustering, neural networks, Gaussian Mixture Model (GMM), and Modified Rank Order Clustering (MROC) [AMR 18]. The main challenge remains in choosing the most fitting algorithm in relation to the industrial context and the business goals, as well as the appropriate approach to implement it considering the pre-existing technological infrastructure.

Recent studies estimate that unplanned downtime costs for the manufacturing industry are $50 billion per year [COL 17]. The use of predictive maintenance and failure detection can support the sector in reducing its costs.

24.3. Research design

After an assessment of the state of the art on analytics approaches for fault detection in manufacturing, the study has been based on the Toreador approach application. The Toreador MBDAaaS framework fosters modularity, reusability, and automation of design and implementation tasks. The contents of the Toreador platform have been developed using model-driven architecture (MDA), a methodology supported by the Object Management Group (OMG) that consists of three fundamental layers: (1) the CIM (computational independent model or declarative model), (2) the PIM (platform-independent model) or Procedural Model, and (3) the PSM (platform-specific model). A set of CIMs (in the form of a .json file) expresses the use cases in terms of goals to be satisfied. Goals and associated indicators and objectives have been (manually) translated into their corresponding PIMs, in the form of an OWL-S workflow. The last step is mapping PIMs into PSMs. To this end, each pilot case produced its platform-dependent workflow (PSM), as an Oozie workflow implementing the OWL-S workflow.

The Toreador project has four pilot cases which each develop and test all the methodological and technological solutions of the project. One of this is the aerospace pilot, managed by DTA (Apulian District of Aerospace) together with Università del Salento and Avio Aero; the core of this research. For the aerospace pilot, a fault prediction use case has been selected since it is the most promising for collecting and analyzing data in streaming, with a higher level of reliability. This use case aims at preventing anomalies on workpieces correlated with machine faults, in particular with the health status of three CNC lathes. The main problems to be handled involve identifying a correct definition of faults, choosing an approach for the data classification model between a statistical and an artificial intelligence one, and determining a suitable model for prediction. It has been chosen to follow a machine learning approach for the detection of peculiar failure statuses that were not pre-determined by CNC manufacturers.

24.4 Results: tailoring the MBDAaaS framework

Following the MDA for developing the MBDAaaS framework, the three models (i.e. CIM, PIM and PSD), representing the fault prediction use case are provided.

The first step produced the .json file (Figure 24.1) containing the specifications for the CIM model (the declarative model) in terms of goals with indicators and objectives. For example, the analytics for the discovery of the behavioral model of machines (an unsupervised, machine learning clustering) has been defined by three Goals: G1 (task, clustering), G2 (models, descriptive), G3 (learning approach, unsupervised).

The second step concerned the PIM (or procedural model) definition, describing in the OWL-S workflow how analytics should be executed and parallelized following the requirements and constraints specified in the declarative model. Figure 24.2 shows the composition result of the Fault Prediction service for streaming data analytics execution. According to protocols and timing of the machines' manufacturing specifications, real-time measurements are streamed by the sensors of the lathes. These properties have been harmonized through an OPC-UA server and client that play the role of a Kafka producer as well. Kafka pushes the data stream towards HBase for data storage. The data stream is also pushed towards the real-time prediction module implemented with Spark Streaming service. Finally, to display the results information the Fault Visualization service is called.

```
"@type": "tdm:Area",
    "tdm:label": "Data Analytics",
    "tdm:incorporates": [
        {
        "@type": "tdm:Goal",
        "tdm:label": "Analytics Aim",
        "tdm:constraint": "{ \"percentage\": {\"value\":23}}",
        "tdm:incorporates": [
            {
            "@type": "tdm:Indicator",
            "tdm:label": "Task",
            "tdm:visualisationType": "Checkbox",
            "tdm:constraint": "{}",
            "tdm:incorporates": [
                {
                "@type": "tdm:Objective",
                "tdm:label": "Flat Clustering"
                }
            ]
```

Figure 24.1. *Part of the json file related to Goal: Analytics Aim*

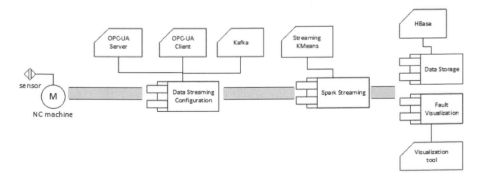

Figure 24.2. *Fault Prediction Service composition*

```
<process:CompositeProcess rdf:about="FaultDetectionProcess">
  <process:composedOf>
    <process:Sequence>
      <process:components>
        <process:ControlConstructBag>
          <list:first>
            <process:Perform rdf:about="Perform0"/>
          </list:first>
          <list:rest>
            <process:ControlConstructBag>
              <list:first>
              <process:Perform rdf:about="Perform1"/>
              </list:first>
              <list:rest>
                <process:ControlConstructBag>
                  <list:first>
                    <process:Perform rdf:about="Perform2"/>
                  </list:first>
                  <list:rest>
                    <process:ControlConstructBag>
                      <list:first>
                        <process:Perform rdf:about="Perform3"/>
                      </list:first>
                      <list:rest
rdf:resource="http://www.daml.org/services/owl-s/1.2/generic/ObjectList.owl#nil"/>
                    </process:ControlConstructBag>
                  </list:rest>
                </process:ControlConstructBag>
              </list:rest>
            </process:ControlConstructBag>
          </list:rest>
        </process:ControlConstructBag>
      </process:components>
    </process:Sequence>
  </process:composedOf>
  <service:describes rdf:resource="#FaultDetectionService"/>
</process:CompositeProcess>
```

Figure 24.3. *Part of the OWL-S workflow file.*

The third step produced the PSM, that is the deployment model, which maps each operation and tool to specific services. The deployment model has been designed starting from the company on-premises infrastructure for data processing, orchestration, analytics and visualization. The transformation from procedural model to deployment model is based on the compiler that takes as input the OWL-S workflow file (Figure 24.3) and information on the target platform and produces as output a technology dependent workflow (Box 24.1). Figure 24.4 shows the target-dependent platform corresponding to the workflow previously described. The infrastructure hosting a Toreador instance automatically injects some Spark deployment properties to fine tune the run-time behavior. To execute the Fault Prediction service from the Toreador platform instance, the following atomic services have been selected: Data Streaming Configuration service to open a secure channel from sensors to Kafka cluster; Spark Streaming service to stream processing of live data streams; Data Storage service to store and retrieve data; Fault Visualization service to display the analytics results.

```
<workflow-app name='FaultDetectionProcess'
xmlns='uri:oozie:workflow:0.1'>
    <start to='DataStreamConfigurationProcess0' />
    <action name='DataStreamConfigurationProcess0'>
        <spark xmlns="uri:oozie:spark-action:0.1">
            <job-tracker>${jobTracker}</job-tracker>
            <name-node>${nameNode}</name-node>
            <prepare>
                    <delete path='${outputDir}' />
            </prepare>
            <master>${master}</master>
            <name>${name}</name>
            <class>${MainClass}</class>
            <jar>${jar}</jar>
            <spark-opts>--num-executors 4 --queue
default</spark-opts>
            <arg>--hostname</arg>
            <arg>${hostname}</arg>
            <arg>--hostport</arg>
            <arg>${hostport}</arg>
            <arg>--username</arg>
            <arg>${username}</arg>
            <arg>--password</arg>
            <arg>${password}</arg>
        </spark>
        <ok to='SparkStreamingProcess1' />
        <error to='kill' />
    </action>
    <action name='SparkStreamingProcess1'>
        <spark xmlns="uri:oozie:spark-action:0.1">
            <job-tracker>${jobTracker}</job-tracker>
            <name-node>${nameNode}</name-node>
            <prepare>
                    <delete path='${outputDir}' />
            </prepare>
            <master>${master}</master>
            <name>${name}</name>
            <class>${MainClass}</class>
            <jar>${jar}</jar>
            <spark-opts>--num-executors 4 --queue
default</spark-opts>
            <arg>--dataStream</arg>
            <arg>${dataStream}</arg>
        </spark>
        <ok to='DataPersistenceProcess2' />
        <error to='kill' />
    </action>
    <action name='DataPersistenceProcess2'>
        <spark xmlns="uri:oozie:spark-action:0.1">
            <job-tracker>${jobTracker}</job-tracker>
            <name-node>${nameNode}</name-node>
            <prepare>
                    <delete path='${outputDir}' />
            </prepare>
            <master>${master}</master>
            <name>${name}</name>
            <class>${MainClass}</class>
            <jar>${jar}</jar>
            <spark-opts>--num-executors 4 --queue
default</spark-opts>
```

```
                <arg>--dataProcessed</arg>
                <arg>${dataProcessed}</arg>
        </spark>
        <ok to='FaultVisualizationProcess3' />
        <error to='kill' />
    </action>
    <action name='FaultVisualizationProcess3'>
        <spark xmlns="uri:oozie:spark-action:0.1">
                <job-tracker>${jobTracker}</job-tracker>
                <name-node>${nameNode}</name-node>
                <prepare>
                        <delete path='${outputDir}' />
                </prepare>
                <master>${master}</master>
                <name>${name}</name>
                <class>${MainClass}</class>
                <jar>${jar}</jar>
                <spark-opts>--num-executors 4 --queue
default</spark-opts>
                <arg>--faultDetected</arg>
                <arg>${faultDetected}</arg>
        </spark>
        <ok to='end' />
        <error to='kill' />
    </action>
        <kill name="kill">
                <message>Task failed, error
message[${wf:errorMessage()}]</message>
        </kill>
        <end name='end'/>
    </workflow-app>
```

Box 24.1. *Technology-dependent workflow*

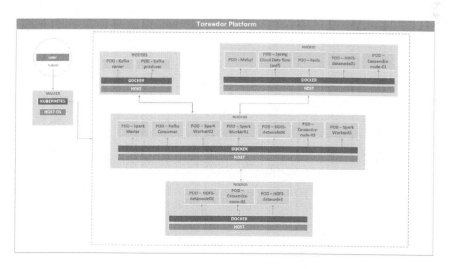

Figure 24.4. *Toreador platform instance. For a color version*
of this figure, see www.iste.co.uk/zelm/enterprise.zip

24.5. Conclusion

Based on the Toreador project, the MBDaaS approach enables setting models reusable and customizable by other industries and companies with similar use cases in order to produce a fault prediction service. Following MBDaaS as a methodology, Big Data exploitation can be made possible even for SMEs (due to lower implementation costs compared to a full solution deployment); on the other hand, the customization of the service still requires a techie user to be correctly adopted in a different environment. The results described in the paper demonstrate the applicability of MDA to the development of a generalizable Big Data pipeline in the context of an aerospace company. The three levels of the framework are applied for a fault prediction use case. Future researches will investigate the usability of the solution among different roles involved in the engineering units of the company both at managerial but also technical levels. Thus, data will be aggregated and analyzed to satisfy the different needs of knowledge within the company, with the aim of predicting pre-determined and new faults.

24.6. Acknowledgements

This work has received funding from the EU H2020 research and innovation program under the TOREADOR project, grant agreement no. 688797.

24.7. References

[AMR 18] AMRUTHNATH N., GUPTA T., "A research study on unsupervised machine learning algorithms for early fault detection in predictive maintenance", *15th International Conference on Industrial Engineering and Applications*, DOI: 10.13140/RG.2.2.28822.24648, 2018.

[ARD 17] ARDAGNA *et al.*, "A model-driven methodology for big data analytics-as-a-service", *BigData Congress, 2017 IEEE International Congress*, pp. 105–112, 2017.

[CHA 09] CHANDOLA V., BANERJEE A., KUMAR V., "Anomaly detection: a survey", *ACM Computing Surveys*, vol. 41, no. 3, i.d. 15, 2009.

[COL 17] COLEMA C. *et al.*, Making maintenance smarter: predictive maintenance and the digital supply network, Report, Deloitte, 2017.

[EC 10] EUROPEAN COMMISSION, A digital agenda for Europe, Communication, 2010.

[HAR 06] HARDING J.A., SHAHBAZ SRINIVAS M., KUSIAK A., "Data mining in manufacturing: a review", *Journal of Manufacturing Science and Engineering*, vol. 128, pp. 969–976, 2006.

[SCH 17] SCHMIDT B., WANG L., GALAR D., "Semantic framework for predictive maintenance in a cloud environment", *Procedia CIRP*, vol. 62, pp. 583–588, 2017.

[TIW 18] TIWARI S. *et al.*, "Big data analytics in supply chain management between 2010 and 2016: insights to industries", *Computer & Industrial Engineering*, vol. 115, pp. 319–330, 2018.

25

A SAREF Extension for Semantic Interoperability in the Industry and Manufacturing Domain

This chapter builds on the success achieved in the past years with SAREF, a reference ontology for IoT created in close interaction with the industry during a study requested by the European Commission in 2015. SAREF is published as an ETSI Technical Specification series that also includes dedicated extensions to specific domains. A proof-of-concept solution based on SAREF and implemented on existing commercial products has been demonstrated in 2017. This chapter introduces a specialists task force that was recently requested by ETSI and the European Commission to further extend SAREF to the industry and manufacturing domain.

25.1. Introduction

SAREF (https://w3id.org/saref) is a reference ontology developed in close interaction with industry during a study requested by the European Commission in 2015 (https://sites.google.com/site/smartappliancesproject/home). The motivation behind this study was that the market would continue to be too fragmented and powerless without a (protocol-independent) semantic layer that could enable interoperability among the various smart appliances from different manufacturers that co-exist in our homes, from lamps and consumer electronics to white goods, such as washing machines and ovens. To that end, SAREF was created with the intention to interconnect data from different protocols and platforms, for instance

Chapter written by Laura M. DANIELE, Matthijs PUNTER, Christopher BREWSTER, Raúl GARCÍA CASTRO, María POVEDA and Alba FERNÁNDEZ.

ZigBee (http://www.zigbee.org), UPnP (now OCF, https://openconnectivity.org/) and Z-Wave (http://www.z-wave.com), enabling the communication between in-home devices that use different protocols and standards. SAREF is not about the actual communication with devices and has not been set up to replace existing communication protocols, but it lays the base for enabling the translation of information coming from existing (and future) protocols to and from all other protocols that are referenced to SAREF. As confirmed in the EC's "Rolling Plan for ICT standardization 2017", SAREF is the first ontology standard in the Internet of Things (IoT) ecosystem, and sets a template and a base for the development of similar standards for the other verticals to unlock the full potential of IoT.

Following the momentum gained during the smart appliances study, SAREF was published by the European Telecommunication Standards Institute (ETSI, http://www.etsi.org/) as a Technical Specification (TS 103 264 V1.1.1). In 2016, ETSI further requested a Specialists Task Force (STF) to provide input on the management of SAREF and create dedicated extensions for specific domains. The STF 513 was consequently established and developed extensions of SAREF in the energy, environment and building domains (TS 103 410-1, TS 103 410-2 and TS 103 410-3, respectively). The STF 513 additionally developed an updated, more modular and flexible SAREF specification (TS 103 264 V2.1.1), using the feedback received from the industrial stakeholders since the first release of SAREF in 2015.

Over time, the SAREF initiative has been welcomed by smart appliances manufactures and IoT industry, which clearly indicated the intention to adopt SAREF and its related communication framework. Other standards organizations and initiatives, such as CEN/CENELEC (https://www.cencenelec.eu), AIOTI (https://aioti.eu) and IERC (http://www.internet-of-things-research.eu), have also acknowledged SAREF and its position in the current IoT landscape [VER 17]. Moreover, a proof-of-concept solution has been recently demonstrated in a follow up study on SAREF for the European Commission [DAN 18] that shows how to integrate different standards for demand response [CLC 17, IEC 17] and the oneM2M standard for machine-to-machine communication (http://onem2m.org/), using SAREF and its extension to the energy domain (SAREF4ENER) as basis for interoperability. This proof-of-concept demonstrates how commercial appliances from different manufacturers (such as washing machines, dish washers, smart meters, electric vehicle charging stations and photovoltaic inverter for solar panels) can communicate their capabilities and needs (e.g. who they are, what model, from which maker, if they are already running or ready to run, how much they are consuming, when they will finish their current activity, and more) with a Consumer Energy Manager (CEM). The CEM is a logical function that aggregates and process information from several devices, and can indicate to the individual appliances when to start, stop, pause, decrease or increase their consumption and so on, according to user preferences, production forecasts (e.g. by solar panels available in the home), smart grid conditions and price incentives at different times during the day. The CEM can be implemented in a component that physically resides in the home or runs remotely in the cloud.

25.2. SAREF extension to industry and manufacturing

A number of industrial sectors expressed their interest to extend SAREF into their domains in order to fill the gaps of the semantics not yet covered by their communication protocols nor by the existing SAREF extensions. To that end, the STF 534 (https://portal.etsi.org/STF/STFs/STFHomePages/STF534.aspx) has been recently launched by ETSI with the goal to create SAREF extensions to the domains of smart cities, smart industry and manufacturing, and smart agri-food, turning SAREF into the umbrella that enables better integration of semantic data from and across various vertical domains in the IoT. The STF 534 consists of two main tasks: (1) gather requirements, collect use cases and identify existing sources (e.g. standards, data models, ontologies, etc.) from the domains of interest (i.e. smart cities, smart industry and manufacturing, and smart agri-food); and (2) produce extensions of SAREF for each domain based on these requirements. This paper focuses on the extension of SAREF to the smart industry and manufacturing domain, which will result in a new ontology, called SAREF4INMA, to be published as part of the SAREF series in a new ETSI Technical Specification. The paper describes our approach and presents some initial requirements for the SAREF4INMA ontology.

SAREF contains core concepts that are common to several domains. To be able to handle specific data elements for a certain domain, dedicated extensions of SAREF can be created. Each domain can have one or more extensions, depending on the complexity of the domain. As a reference ontology, SAREF serves as the means to connect the extensions in different domains. Domain specific extensions should reuse and specialize core concepts from SAREF, and can also reuse concepts from other extensions. Extensions can be created by any interested stakeholder, but for an extension to be standardized, it needs to be submitted, discussed and approved by the SmartM2M Technical Committee in ETSI. Extensions have to be created following some best practices, such as: (1) be designed according to the criteria for ontology development specified by [GRU 95], that is clarity, coherence, extendibility, minimal encoding bias and minimal ontological commitment; (2) relevant stakeholders in the domain of interest should be involved in the creation process; (3) the group/community that creates the extension should be committed to contribute to its maintenance; (4) SAREF should be properly re-used and the extension should not add concepts that are already present in SAREF or other extensions; (5) the extension needs to be properly documented and published. More details on the extension and maintenance guidelines can be found in the corresponding ETSI Technical Report (TR 103 411 V1.1.1).

In order to create the SAREF4INMA extension, we follow an interactive and iterative approach, based on the experience gained in the past years with SAREF, which was created in a very transparent manner to allow all stakeholders to provide input and follow the evolution of the work [DAN 15]. The first step of the approach consists of collecting the requirements that can guide the implementation and validation of the ontology. To that end, we need to acquire the necessary information (i.e. specifications, datasets, standards, API specifications, data formats, etc.) from domain experts and existing initiatives in the industry and manufacturing domain. The second step is to collect the use cases for which the ontology has to be used. We specify these use cases in natural language. The third step is to define the purpose and scope of the ontology for the identified use cases. Based on the information acquired from the domain experts, the related initiatives, the use cases and the identified purpose and scope, it is then possible to generate a first version of the requirements. We write these requirements in the form of Competency Questions [GRU 95]. An interactive validation with domain experts and stakeholders should follow, in order to assess whether the requirements are correct and complete. The requirements are then finalized and used to guide the creation of the SAREF4INMA ontology, which should also be iteratively validated with the stakeholders and domain experts in an interactive manner.

25.3. Related initiatives, standards and use cases

There are various member states initiatives aimed to support the digitization of European industry and manufacturing [DEI 17], such as platform Industrie 4.0 in Germany, Industria 4.0 in Italy, Industrie du futur in France and the Smart Industry initiative in the Netherlands. These initiatives focus on aspects such as: (1) cyberphysical systems, that is the usage of robots and advanced IT-capabilities (sensors, data analytics) in a production environment; (2) digital manufacturing technologies, i.e., new manufacturing technologies, such as 3D printing, requiring a high level of digital input; and (3) new business models and propositions, that is lot size one-manufacturing, servitization of manufacturing, maintenance, and other new business propositions leading to changes in the way businesses and their networks are structured. The various Industry 4.0 initiatives are used to provide input to the SAREF4INMA extension in terms of key use cases and standards. In particular, we have collected 24 relevant standards from these initiatives and grouped them based on their scope (e.g. digitization, communication, engineering, life cycle, etc.) and the topic they cover (i.e. factory, product, process). We have further distinguished the standards in the scope of the SAREF4INMA extension from those that are out of scope. These standards in scope include **IEC 62794**, which is a reference model for automation assets and structural and operational relationships; **IEC 62832**, which identifies the general principles of the Digital Factory framework (i.e. a set of model elements and rules for modeling production systems); **IEC 62264**, which describes the manufacturing operations management domain and its activities; **IEC 61512 Batch control**, which is a reference model for batch control as used in the process industries; **IEC 62541 OPC UA**, which describes the OPC-UA architecture, machine to machine communication protocol for industrial automation; **IEC 62890**, which describes the lifecycle management for systems and products used in industrial process measurement, control and automation; **IEC 61360/ ISO 13584**, which specifies a general purpose dictionary covering the field of electro technology, electronics and related domains; **IEC 62424 Topology**, which specifies procedures and specifications for the exchange of process control engineering relevant data provided by the Piping and Instrumentation Diagram (P&ID) tool; and **IEC 62714 AutomationML**, which defines a data exchange solution based on an XML schema for the domain of automation engineering and integrates **IEC 61131**, **IEC 62424** and **ISO/PAS 17506**.

Concerning the use cases, we have selected the **zero-defect manufacturing** use case as basis for the SAREF4INMA ontology. The competitiveness of a manufacturing process is often defined by its ability to be flexible (i.e. quickly change from one product to the other) and have a manufacturing process with as little yield loss as possible. Zero-defect manufacturing focuses on reducing the yield loss to zero, often combined with an increase in flexibility. To that end, a combination of precision manufacturing technology, data collection and process control is needed. Two cycles are especially needed in the zero defect manufacturing use case: (1) the first cycle is a **real-time loop** that focuses on the immediate collection of data from sensors in or around a production equipment (e.g. a stamping machine that takes a metal sheet as raw material and produces a certain metal object as a result). This data consists of the machine settings and states, its measurements (e.g. temperature, pressure, force measured by the machine during production) and units of measure, but also characteristics of the resulting product (e.g. properties of the metal object produced by the machine). Based on this data, a controller component can decide to change the settings of the production equipment in real-time to avoid errors that could possibly lead to defects in the final product; (2) the second cycle is a **data collection and analysis loop** needed to achieve a continuous process analysis and improvement. This loop also includes smart sensors, but it has a longer time span compared to the real-time loop. It can measure the characteristics of the incoming (raw) material to update the production settings accordingly in a later moment. Similarly, it can detect feedback parameters to predict the quality of the end-product and provide feedback to the production process. Over a longer period of time, these parameters are fed to a self-learning framework which can be used to detect patterns leading to errors and/or areas for further improvement. In the zero-defect manufacturing use case, interoperability is especially required between sensors, production equipment and the data collection environment for the data collection and analysis loop (second cycle). The Productive 4.0 innovation and lighthouse program (https://productive40.eu/) provides us with several concrete examples of this use case relating to the stamping of metal objects and chatter control in milling. Competency questions that we have extracted from this use case as basis to create SAREF4INMA include the following: (1) What type of production equipment is used in the factory? (2) What is the incoming (raw) material to the production process? (3) What is the resulting product? (4) What parts is this product made from? (5) Which sensors are used in the production process? (6) Which actuators are used in the production process? (7) Which properties need to be observed and/or controlled by the production equipment? (8) What are the properties of the final product? (9) Which units of measure are these properties measured in?

25.4. Conclusions

This paper introduced the initial work carried out in a dedicated ETSI specialists task force to extend SAREF to the industry and manufacturing domain. This work is done in close collaboration with industry experts, who expect to adopt this extension in specific applications. The paper presented our approach, related initiatives and standards. The paper further described the zero defect manufacturing use case chosen as basis to create SAREF4INMA, formulating some initial requirements extracted from this use case. Future work is focused on finalizing the formalization of these requirements and align them with the semantics extracted from the standards in section 25.3. The final version of these requirements is expected for June 2018. These requirements will be subsequently validated with stakeholders and used to create the SAREF4INMA ontology. A stable version of the SAREF4INMA is expected in November 2018, while the final version is planned for February 2019.

25.5. References

[CLC 17] CENELEC, "B5 50631-1 Household appliances network and grid connectivity – Part 1: General requirements, generic data modelling and neutral messages", available at https://standards.globalspec.com/standards/detail/?docid=10196921, 2017.

[DAN 18] DANIELE L., STRABBING W. et al., "Study on ensuring interoperability for enabling Demand Side Flexibility", European Commission, 2018 (forthcoming).

[DAN 15] DANIELE L., DEN HARTOG F., ROES J., "Created in close interaction with the industry: the Smart Appliances REFerence (SAREF) ontology", in CUEL R., YOUNG R. (eds), *Proceedings of Formal Ontologies Meet Industry*, Springer, pp. 100–112, 2015.

[DEI 17] DG GROW, DG CONNECT, Standardisation to Support Digitisation – Report from the Workshop on Standardisation to Support Digitising European Industry, Report, available at https://ec.europa.eu/digital-single-market/en/news/workshop-standardisation-support-digitising-european-industry, 2017.

[GRU 95] GRUBER T., "Toward principles for the design of ontologies used for knowledge sharing", *International Journal of Human-Computer Studies*, vol. 43, nos 5–6, pp. 907–928, 1995.

[IEC 17] IEC, "62056-6-2 Electricity metering data exchange - The DLMS/COSEM suite - Part 6-2: COSEM interface classes", International Standard, available at https://webstore.iec.ch/publication/34317, 2017.

[VER 17] VERMESAN O., BACQUET J. (eds)., *Cognitive Hyperconnected Digital Transformation: Internet of Things Intelligence Evolution*, River Publishers, Gistrup, Denmark, 2017.

26

A Building Information Model-centered Big Data Platform to Support Digital Transformation in the Construction Industry

This chapter reports on a case study that has been performed at a medium-sized Dutch construction company. We propose a reference architecture and data platform to help overcome the barriers of building information modeling (BIM) adoption by the architecture, engineering, and construction (AEC) industry and to support digital transformation and transition to smart industry.

26.1. Background

Traditionally, the architecture, engineering, and construction (AEC) industry relies heavily on the use of paper-based communication. This is a major source of errors resulting in extra costs, delay, friction and even lawsuits in the construction process, since AEC projects typically involve complex communication-intensive processes across multiple organizations. For example, Hendrickson and Au [HEN 08] describe a large-scale project ($10M+) comprising 420 companies, 50 different types of documents, spanning 56,000 pages. It is therefore not surprising that the AEC industry has long searched for techniques to decrease communication errors, project costs, increase productivity and quality, and reduce project delivery time [AZH 11]. The concept of building information modeling (BIM) has the potential to help achieve these goals [AZH 08].

Chapter written by Yvar BOSDRIESZ, Marten VAN SINDEREN, Maria IACOB and Pieter VERKROOST.

In the first version of the National BIM Standard – United States ([NIB 07], p.21), BIM is characterized as "a digital representation of physical and functional characteristics of a facility. As such, it serves as a shared knowledge resource for information about the facility forming a reliable basis for decisions during its life cycle from inception onward. A basic premise of BIM is the contribution of different stakeholders at different phases of the facility's lifecycle to insert, extract, update, or modify information in the BIM to support and reflect the roles of that stakeholder".

26.2. Problem

Many construction and civil engineering companies already use BIM in their building projects. However, there are mixed perceptions and opinions of the benefits of BIM, leading to a general misunderstanding of its expected outcomes [BAR 12]. Yan and Demian [YAN 08] found that the most important barrier to BIM adoption is the effort and costs of BIM training. This seems in line with a more recent study of BIM adoption in the Dutch construction industry [BOU 15]. This study also concluded that the required training for and knowledge of BIM is the number one concern regarding BIM adoption. A close second is "difference in BIM usage between parties". One of the major benefits of BIM is the potential it offers for facilitating digital collaboration between the many stakeholders in a construction project. This benefit is however complicated by both technical (lack of interoperability between BIM software vendors) and organizational factors (fear of collaborating with competitors, ownership of data, cost sharing, etc.). In the AEC industry, the level of detail (LOD) denotes how detailed a model is in describing a construction project. The LOD ranges from 100 (sketch) to 500 (as-built with the real specifications for all elements). Song *et al.* [SON 17] discovered that only a low percentage of daily work orders from the construction site had corresponding elements in BIM with a medium level of detail, and that higher levels of detail (which are supported by BIM) are therefore critical.

26.3. Goal

As mentioned, the most notable technical reason AEC companies are not yet reaping the full benefits of adopting BIM is the lack of interoperability between BIM implementations, organizational barriers for collaboration, and different maturity levels of using BIM across but also within organizations. In view of this, we argue that a *reference architecture* and a *data platform* are useful artifacts to help overcome these barriers. A reference architecture could embed generic AEC processes and link them to BIM elements, and a data platform could support the flexible delivery of data from BIM compliant applications to business processes. AEC companies can assess their maturity level by referring to this reference architecture. The reference architecture may be complemented with a roadmap that provides guidelines on how to migrate from their current level to a higher level, while mentioning the relative benefits of the higher maturity levels. AEC companies can use the data platform to overcome the technical interoperability problems, but also as a means to achieve more "intelligent" delivery of data or data-driven services. The goal of this paper is therefore to support the digital transformation and transition to smart AEC industry by using a BIM-centered reference architecture and data platform.

26.4. Approach

After completing a literature study on the state-of-art of BIM adoption by the AEC industry, we investigated the use of BIM in a medium sized Dutch construction company. We explored typical intra- and inter-organizational processes and identified the input/output data requirements of these processes. Our idea is to compare the data requirements with the elements of the BIM standard, and analyze whether the current use of BIM can be improved. More precisely, we want to (1) understand the extent to which BIM elements are correctly and consistently used for the data requirements of processes, (2) identify processes that cannot be linked to BIM elements and their data requirements, and (3) find opportunities to adapt processes such that they can become more effective/efficient in making use of available BIM data. This way, we obtain insights in the shortcomings of current processes and how they can be improved. We propose a roadmap for the AEC industry (especially medium-sized companies) to improve BIM integration. The roadmap is supported by a reference architecture, which models processes and their relation to BIM. The roadmap and the architecture can be seen as conceptual support tools for the digital transformation of medium-sized companies. An important component in the reference architecture is a data platform for BIM integration. We consider this to be a *big data* platform because of the volume and variety of BIM data elements. The ultimate goal of our research is to validate the platform with a prototype. In this paper, we discuss its main functional features and we give an account of the current prototype status. The platform supports the interaction between a BIM-compliant storage layer and a data-dependent process layer. The platform separates the process layer from the various existing BIM software packages/vendors, and makes the storage layer independent of specific input/output data formats of process implementations. Moreover, the platform enables processes to subscribe to certain events that result in BIM data updates, and be informed about such events when they occur. The platform can be extended with a knowledge layer that interprets data events as a representation of the status of a project in progress, compares the status with the expected or desired status, and takes appropriate actions (send reminders, etc.) in case of threshold-exceeding deviations.

26.5. Solution design

While investigating the medium-sized Dutch construction company, it became clear that a gap exists between the possibilities of BIM described in the extant literature, and the actual usage of so-called BIM models in practice. We found that BIM is currently used extensively in the planning and design phase of a construction project; mainly for collision testing and collaboration with subcontractors. An initial design is shared with subcontractors using an industry standard file format called Industrial Foundation Classes (IFC), and subsequently finalized through collaboration with subcontractors. However, it seems that the BIM model and data are rarely used later during the construction process, despite the benefits of BIM claimed in existing literature. Data from the model is sometimes used in further processes, but always manually and in an ad hoc fashion. Our findings are corroborated by earlier research at another medium sized construction company in the Netherlands [BER 15]. The same data is stored in multiple locations, requiring manual actions to extract and use, despite being available in the BIM model as well. This leads to extra work and possible data inconsistencies. The ideal situation would be to have BIM as a single data source, allowing each of the processes/departments to interact with it, and enrich the same source data (see Figure 26.1). To achieve this BIM-centric approach, it is imperative to have integrations between applications used by these processes, and the BIM platform. This also relieves users of the need to fully learn BIM tooling, which is one of the major impediments of BIM adoption.

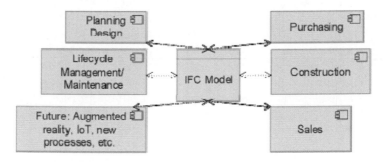

Figure 26.1. *Desired BIM-centric situation. For a color version of this figure, see www.iste.co.uk/zelm/enterprise.zip*

For the prototype we connect one process, namely the purchasing process, with a central BIM storage solution, which makes use of the IFC standard for the models. As storage solution, we use BIMServer. BIMServer is an open source model server allowing stakeholders to collaborate on central repositories of BIM models [BEE 10].

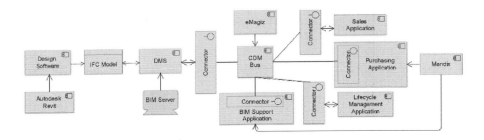

Figure 26.2. *BIM-centered solution architecture. For a color version of this figure, see www.iste.co.uk/zelm/enterprise.zip*

We hope to ease the shift towards an inter-organizational collaborative platform, by providing an example of successfully integrated intra-organizational processes and developing a Common Data Model (CDM). For the integration, we use a message bus architecture, implemented in the eMagiz Integration Platform as a Service (IPaaS). The CDM will be based on the messages in the BIM Service interface exchange (BIMSie)[1]. For the Purchasing Portal a simple demo application developed in Mendix is sufficient. This leads to the architecture shown in Figure 26.2.

An extra Mendix application, referenced in Figure 26.2 as BIMSupport, is used to store the IFC data required to enrich IFC data in the external applications. It enables the purchasing application to use its own terminology rather than having to store IFC terminology in all connected applications. See Table 26.1 for an example.

	BIMServer/ BIMSupport Object	Related Purchasing Object
Type	IfcDoor	Door
GUID	22erBPISX01uqcwczID30V	
ObjectID	600492430	
ArticleNr		
Name	swedex_draaideur_SL01	swedex_draaideur_SL01

Table 26.1. *Purchasing data object in relation to BIMSupport object*

Figure 26.3 shows the eMagiz architecture of the bus component of the architecture. The bus, using the CDM, is used as common ground between the

1 https://www.nibs.org/?page=bsa_bimsie.

connectors used to connect the BIMServer with the purchasing portal (and other similar applications).

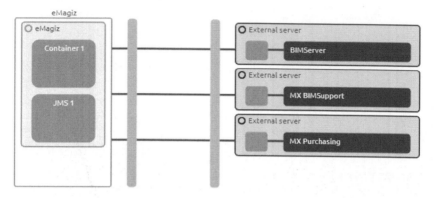

Figure 26.3. *eMagiz architecture. For a color version of this figure, see www.iste.co.uk/zelm/enterprise.zip*

eMagiz translates all incoming and outgoing messages to the CDM. The internal transformations are handled in the main container, while a JMS server takes care of all messaging operations. All messaging services on both sides of the bus use the SOAP protocol and are in XML format. This architecture allows other applications and subcontractors to easily connect to the existing system in the future. The prototype is capable of retrieving all IfcTypes from the model, selecting the ones relevant for the purchasing application, and translating object information to the correct purchasing terms. These objects can then be enriched in the purchasing application with manufacturer information, which is then stored back into the original model.

26.6. Conclusion

BIM is the future for the construction industry. While existing research has determined it to be useful for many different tasks and processes, in practice we found extensive use during planning and design, but limited use during other steps of the construction process. In order to allow other processes to also profit from the data stored in BIM, we propose a BIM-centered platform, which we prototyped for the purchasing process of a medium-sized Dutch construction company. We believe this platform provides a good foundation for BIM-centered integration. The prototype provides AEC companies with a clear example of how BIM data can be used and integrated into their processes. It is extendable for further process integration, as well as inter-organizational integration. The goal is to further validate and improve this prototype, extending the scope to other processes and opportunities for integration.

26.7 References

[AZH 11] Azhar S., "Building information modeling (BIM): trends, benefits, risks, and challenges for the AEC industry", *Leadership and Management in Engineering*, vol. 11, no. 3, pp. 241–252, 2011.

[AZH 08] Azhar S., Nadeem A., Mok J. *et al.*, "Building information modeling (BIM): a new paradigm for visual interactive modeling and simulation for construction projects", *First International Conference on Construction in Developing Countries*, pp. 435–446, Karachi, Pakistan, 4–5 August, 2008.

[BAR 12] Barlish K., Sullivan K., "How to measure the benefits of BIM – A case study approach", *Automation in Construction*, vol. 24, pp. 149–159, 2012.

[BEE 10] Beetz J., van Berlo L., de Laat R. *et al.*, "BIMserver.org – an open source IFC model server", *27th International CIB W78 Conference*, Cairo, Egypt, 16–19 November, 2010.

[BER 15] van Berlo L., Derks G., Pennavaire C. *et al.*, "Collaborative engineering with IFC: common practice in the Netherlands", *32nd International CIB W78 Conference*, Eindhoven, The Netherlands, 27–29 October, 2015.

[BOU 15] Bouwkenn is, "BIM & Ketensamenwerking in Kaart", Factsheet, available at https://www.bouwkennis.nl/product/bim-in-kaart, 2015.

[HEN 08] Hendrickson C., Au T., "Project management for construction. Fundamental concepts for owners, engineers, architects and builders", Version 2.2, available at: http://pmbook.ce.cmu.edu/, 2008.

[NIB 07] National Institute of Building Sciences, "NBIMS version 1.0. 2007", available at: 5http://www.1stpricing.com/pdf/NBIMSv1_ConsolidatedBody_Mar07.pdf, 2007.

[SON 17] Song M.H., Fischer M., Theis P., "Field study on the connection between BIM and daily work orders", *Journal Construction Engineering and Management*, vol. 143, no. 5, 2017.

[YAN 08] Yan H., Demian P., "Benefits and barriers of building information modeling", *Twelfth International Conference on Computing in Civil and Building Engineering*, Beijing, China, 16–18 October, 2008.

27

ISBM: a Data Integration Infrastructure for IoT Applications

Literature on the Internet of Things (IoT) has reported a large gap in platforms for people with little programming experience to easily for an easy way to develop IoT applications for IoT devices, sensor networks, and embedded systems. Research indicates that domain-specific languages (DSL) can contribute to tackle this challenge. This paper presents the programming infrastructure of IoT Service-Based Machine (ISBM), which aims to simplify the access and integration of data from different sources, e.g., sensor networks, regular web pages, and social media. ISBM incorporates a virtual machine capable of interpreting the ISBM code on different software platforms, including desktop, web and mobile applications. The visual editor of ISBM supports editing and connecting to IoT services, as well as associating different data sources and the editing of rules in visual form.

27.1. Introduction

One of the hallmarks of Internet of Things (IoT) applications is the use of data from many different sources [GIU 10] – from sensors to regular databases, from social networks to generic web pages – which will feed different information systems and support various business processes. Therefore, the integration of heterogeneous data is an important requirement for systems supporting IoT applications. However, as reported in the literature [MIN 16], there is a research gap in programming infrastructures and access to IoT services. Particularly, there is a lack of programming infrastructures that facilitate the development of query-based

Chapter written by Helder Oliveira GOMES FILHO, José Gonçalves PEREIRA FILHO and João Luiz REBELO MOREIRA.

IoT applications, which would be especially useful for people with low programming skills. In this sense, domain-specific languages (DSL) and their development environments can contribute to reduce this gap by offering programming facilities, access to services and integration of the various data sources collected by the application.

This paper presents the programming infrastructure of IoT Service-based Machine (ISBM), which provides features for accessing and integrating data in IoT application scenarios. ISBM promotes the interaction between different data sources, which happens transparently to the developer, who does not have to worry about the task of connection to services and the transfer of data. Included in the ISBM proposal is a virtual machine capable of interpreting the ISBM code on different platforms, including desktop (Windows, Linux and OSX), web and mobile devices (Android and iOS). To facilitate the use of the language and allow users with low programming skills to describe rules using the ISBM language primitives, a visual editor of the ISBM language is also provided.

The remainder of this chapter is as follows. Section 27.2 presents the ISBM architecture, section 27.3 describes the ISBM language and services, section 27.4 introduces the ISBM Visual Editor, section 1.5 presents a small case study highlighting the advantages of using ISBM facilities in an IoT scenario, and finally section 27.6 concludes the paper, pointing out future research on the ISBM project.

27.2. ISBM architecture

The ISBM architecture is divided into four major modules and their respective sub-modules, as shown in Figure 27.1. The modules in yellow are part of the ISBM infrastructure and were all implemented in the project's source code. The gray (lower) modules are IoT services and databases external to ISBM which are created and managed by third parties. The purple (top left) modules are external systems or agents that can instantiate an ISBM virtual machine and execute ISBM code via programming libraries or simply access the shared memory area via HTTP/TCP (JSON). In blue (top center) are programs written in ISBM, and in green (top right) are the possible graphical interfaces generated by these programs. The four major ISBM modules (in large center box, yellow) are described in briefly in the following paragraphs.

The ISBM Language module is responsible for analyzing the incoming ISBM program and for verifying its compliance with the lexical and syntactic specifications of the ISBM Language as well as performing its interpretation throughout the execution of the program in the virtual machine. Besides allowing integration between different databases, ISBM also allows a program to be written only once and executed in several existing environments. For this to be done in a user-friendly way, the ISBM Language relies on the concept of abstract graphic interfaces. Graphical interface sections can be defined in an ISBM program and, at runtime, these sections can be rendered in different ways, allowing the same program to have different views for each environment in which it runs. There are currently five rendering modes in ISBM: pipe, command line, desktop, web, and Android. For example, the pipe renderer was created for the purpose of making graphical interface sections passable via pipe to be interpreted by external programs in the same Linux environment, and the web renderer is able to display the sections defined in the ISBM program on a web page. Layout can be customized via HTML/CSS and can be accessed by any device with HTTP connection support.

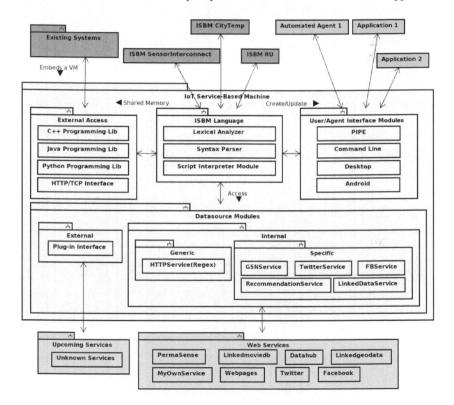

Figure 27.1. *ISBM architecture. For a color version of this figure, see www.iste.co.uk/zelm/enterprise.zip*

The datasource modules are responsible for interpreting each data source in which there is a wrapper in the ISBM, extracting the data in real time, and converting them to a format understandable by the virtual machine. The datasource

Modules are divided into internal and external. The internal services were provided during the development of ISBM and a wrapper for each of them was created directly in the source code of the project. Each wrapper is responsible for connecting to the specific service and converting the data in real time to a format in which the ISBM machine understands. Specific services in the current version of ISBM are as follows: (1) GSN service; (2) Twitter service; (3) Facebook service; (4) Linked data service; (5) recommendation service.

The generic services wrapper (GSN) allows data to be extracted from arbitrary websites using regular expression specifications [THO 68]. For new services manipulating new data source it is enough for an ISBM developer to deploy a wrapper plugin. Existing ISBM programs may remain unchanged.

An ISBM program can generate conclusions from the data collected and cross-referenced between different databases. The conclusions are stored in an area of shared memory that can be accessed by external processes or even external devices. It is possible to access, for example in Java, an object containing all the conclusions of the ISBM machine instantiated by the external process. External devices can access the shared memory area of the ISBM via HTTP interface using JSON as a method of transferring the conclusions. In this way, ISBM can act as a service that generates conclusions based on complex rules and makes them available to any agent to consume the data.

27.3. The ISBM Language and services

The ISBM Language defines a set of objects, commands and functions. The objects can be accessed at any time, with the exception of the *Entity* object, which can only be accessed within a DatasetLoop. Some objects have different behavior depending on where the virtual machine runs (desktop, mobile devices), such as the *Device* object. Five objects are provided: *Vars, Calendar, Clock, Device,* and *Entity*. A Vars object, for example, accepts writing and reading of global variables in the virtual machine, a Device object contains information about the device on which the ISBM machine is running, and Entity objects contain information of the current entity at each iteration of a DatasetLoop. A detailed description of the objects, commands and functions of the ISBM language can be found in the project site (http://1sec.com.br/ISBM).

To connect to existing services wrappers were created directly in the ISBM code. For example, HttpService connects to an arbitrary data source via HTTP. GSNService connects to GSN sensor middleware database [ABE 06], and LinkedDataService connects to linked data endpoints. The project site provides details of all existing ISBM wrappers along with several examples.

27.4. Results

The visual editor was created to allow non-expert users to create an IoT application with low programming skills. The editor is organized in three simple tabs: services, entities and rules.

To design a program, the user must follow the editor tabs, and at the end of all steps the user can export a complete ISBM program. The Services tab provides an interface to connect to datasets. The Entities tab provides a visual interface to get entities from datasets selected. The Rules tab provides an interface for simple rules design, allowing the link with the entities selected.

The editor comes with some pre-registered datasets. New services can be added by the editor user, which will serve as data sources in the Services tab. In addition, services can be added to the Service Manager by the recommender service component. In the Services tab the user can select which services registered in the Service Manager that their ISBM program will connect to. In the Entities tab the user can decide which entities are relevant through a visual rule editor.

The interface is organized by datasets. For each entity selected, the user can execute an ISBM code, such as saving the value of each entity of interest in the Vars object. Upon completion of these steps, the user can execute the ISBM program by launching a virtual machine directly from the editor interface, or exporting the ISBM code to run on any platform that owns the ISBM Virtual Machine. Some of the main screens of the ISBM Editor are shown in Figure 27.2.

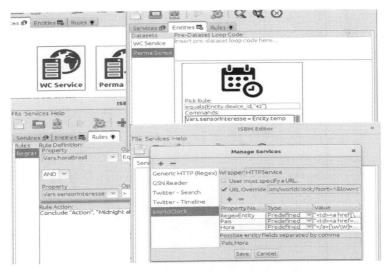

Figure 27.2. *The ISBM Visual Editor. For a color version of this figure, see www.iste.co.uk/zelm/enterprise.zip*

27.5. Proof of concept scenario

In the context of coffee production, luminosity, humidity and temperature are key factors for grain quality. Approaches based on wireless sensor networks (WSN) have been used to monitor these variables, leveraged by the low cost of deployment, sensing capabilities and wireless communication. Open data, such as weather forecasting and grain price values, integrated with crop production data provided by WSNs can contribute to decision to increase profitability. In this scenario, the WSN collects temperature, humidity and luminosity information from a particular coffee growing region and sends it to a base station that makes it available in accordance with the standards for syntactic interoperability on the web. The base station has an application that collects information from the serial interface and persists in the relational database. The business process environment, in turn, consumes endpoint data for decision making. Since coffee quotation data is available on a raw and unstructured basis, ISBM was used to obtain the unstructured coffee quotation data and make them available in a structured way via JSON to the business process environment. HttpService was used to extract the data.

27.6. Conclusion

This paper presented the ISBM data integration infrastructure to support the development of IoT applications. Unlike related work [BER 14, NOD 16, OPE 16], a program written in ISBM Language can be rendered in several different ways because the display interface is fully decoupled through the abstract graphics interface concept. This same program can also run on devices that do not have local rendering capability through the web renderer. In addition, the ISBM application can generate conclusions that can easily be available in a JSON interface, so that other services or systems can take advantage of the conclusions infrastructure as if they were a new JSON data source. The visual language editor, in turn, provides a user-friendly interface to non-expert users. Future work includes the development of a virtual machine for iOS and a PDF data wrapper.

27.7 References

[ABE 06] ABERER K., HAUSWIRTH M., SALEHI, A., "A middleware for fast and flexible sensor network deployment", *Proceedings of the 32nd International Conference on Very Large Databases*, Seoul, Korea, 12–15 September, pp. 1199–1202, 2006.

[ATZ 10] ATZORY L., IERA A., MORABITO G., "The Internet of Things: a survey:, *Computer Networks*, vol. 54, no. 2010, pp. 2787–2805, 2010.

[BER 14] BERTRAN B. *et al.*, "DiaSuite: a tool suite to develop sense/compute/control applications", *Science of Computer Programming*, vol. 79, no. 2014, pp. 39–51, 2014.

[MIN 16] MINERAUD J. *et al.*, "A gap analysis of Internet-of-Things platforms", *Computer Communications*, vols 89–90, pp. 5–16, 2016.

[NOD 16] NODE-RED, http://nodered.org/, accessed on 25 September, 2016.

[OPE 16] OpenHAB, http://www.openhab.org, accessed on 25 September, 2016.

[THO 68] THOMPSON K., "Programming techniques: regular expression search algorithm", *Communications of the ACM*, vol. 11, no. 6, pp. 419–422, 1968.

28

RS4IoT: a Recommender System for IoT

This paper presents RS4IoT, a recommendation web service for smart devices. RS4IoT provides an API to perform multi-attribute sensor recommendation tasks, in which client applications can inform which features the sensors to be recommended should contain. In addition, RS4IoT interacts with social networks to identify how certain sensors and actuators are evaluated by users and to gauge their importance in the recommendation. RS4IoT provides interoperability through an information model based on the W3C Semantic Sensor Network (SSN) standard.

28.1. Introduction

Market forecasts estimate a population of over 50 billion IoT smart objects by 2020 [MAC 15]. In such an environment, excessive data production can create more misinformation than information. Moreover, finding the correct resources among the myriad of objects with different types of hardware, software, processing, storage, communication and sensing capabilities is a great challenge. In this scenario, it is important to provide customers (e.g. developers and applications) with a way to find and identify sensors that best meet the expectations of users and applications.

Several researchers investigate ways to facilitate the consumption of information from the IoT environment. Recommender systems (RS) [VAL 14, CHU 14, CHO 15], for example, could bring to the IoT domain the benefit of identifying the best services for a particular user and application, according to their preferences. Integrating RS with IoT using social networks (SN) as a complementary source of

Chapter written by Caio Martins BARBOSA, Roberta Lima GOMES, José Gonçalves PEREIRA FILHO and João Luiz REBELO MOREIRA.

information is a relatively new concept, which is explored as a way to facilitate the identification of the best objects and sensors for a given user and application.

This paper presents RS4IoT, a web service for recommendation of smart devices. We propose the creation of a content-based RS that relies on sensors' metadata collected from different open interface platforms, such as IoT hubs (message brokers) [MIN 16]. RS4IoT provides an API to perform multi-attribute sensor recommendation tasks, in which client applications can inform which features the sensors to be recommended should contain. Interoperability is a key requirement to RS4IoT as it needs to properly represent different kinds of sensors' information that are collected from completely unrelated IoT hubs. Not to mention the inherent heterogeneity of IoT resources per se. In order to tackle this matter, RS4IoT is based on the W3C Semantic Sensor Network (SSN) standard [LEF 11]. The SSN based data model proposed by RS4IoT provides a uniform representation of the relevant devices' features and their related services. This is of utmost importance for allowing RS4IoT to achieve the best recommendations according to the criteria specified a priori.

The remainder of this paper is as follows. Section 28.2 details the components of RS4IoT architecture and briefly discusses related works for comparison purposes. Section 28.3 presents the implementation issues and the plan for functional validation in a case study. Finally, some conclusions are presented in section 28.4.

28.2. RS4IoT: recommender system for the Internet-of-Things

Current RS for IoT do not really focus on the sensors, but on the services that have been developed based on those sensors. For example, Valtolina *et al.* [VAL 14] developed a RS capable of suggesting gastronomy services (e.g. dishes recipes) according to the user profile, context and other available data from IoT devices. Mul-SWoT [CHU 14] is another solution providing recommendations of IoT-based services considering the IoT devices belonging to the users. Choi *et al.* [CHO 15] proposes that IoT service recommendations will be mainly based on the information gathered from IoT devices present in different environments, for example home, roads, school, where these devices collect information related to users preferences.

RS4IoT, on the other hand, focuses on the recommendation of sensors and actuators in IoT devices, that is its main objective is to find which devices are the most appropriate according to the informed criteria. RS4IoT provides a web service to perform multi-attribute sensor recommendation tasks, where client applications can inform which features the sensors to be recommended should be present. The recommendation algorithm is content-based, that is, the recommendation is determined by comparing the metadata (sensor type, location, measured physical property, etc.) that represent the items. The similarity calculation is performed by the cosine metric, which computes the angle between two vectors, and the smaller the angle, the more similar the item will be in relation to that term. The mathematical formalization of cosine similarity is represented in [28.1] [OLI 05].

$$\text{similarity} = \cos(\theta) = \frac{A.B}{||A||.||B||} = \frac{\sum_{i=1}^{n} A_i.B_i}{\sqrt{\sum_{i=1}^{n} A_i^2} \cdot \sqrt{\sum_{i=1}^{n} B_i^2}} \qquad [28.1]$$

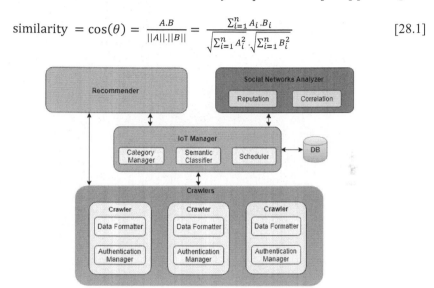

Figure 28.1. *R4IoT conceptual architecture. For a color version of this figure, see www.iste.co.uk/zelm/enterprise.zip*

The similarity score between two items is calculated by first computing the similarity between item data for each column and then taking a weighted average of column similarities to obtain the final similarity. Recommendations are generated according to the average similarity of a candidate item to all items in the item set.

Besides the similarity analysis, RS4IoT interacts with SN to identify how certain sensors and actuators are evaluated by users and to gauge the importance of such sensors/actuators in the recommendation.

The RS4IoT is structured based on a conceptual architecture, as depicted in Figure 28.1. The "crawler" is the responsible for discovering the sensors published on the IoT platforms, translating the information from the sensors to the recommender system data model and mediating the retrieval of sensor measurements. The IoT Manager performs the activities of coordination and management of the general context of the RS4IoT, interacting with the other components. It is also responsible for classifying the sensors according to their types. The Social Networks Analyzer captures information about sensors (e.g. reputation) from SN such as Facebook and

Twitter, in order to be used to refine the recommendations. The Recommender is the main module since it is the place where sensor recommendations occur.

Interoperability is a fundamental requirement for RS4IoT. In order to accurately represent different types of sensor information that are collected from completely independent IoT hubs, RS4IoT relies on an information model based on SSN. Besides SSN concepts, this model also combines some concepts from the DUL[1] e PROV[2] ontologies. Thus, the Data Formatter, one of the Crawler sub-modules, is in charge of translating all the data gathered from its associated IoT hub according to the information model defined for RS4IoT.

28.3. Implementation and case study

Scalability and performance are important requirements for RS4IoT. Such a recommendation system must be able to handle a number of users and application requests in reasonable time, while having to deal with a myriad of IoT metadata. Aiming to achieve better scalability while ensuring the expected performance, being able to handle multiple user requests in a timely manner, the RS4IoT was designed using the microservice architecture. The distributed nature of the microservice facilitates modular growth and the distribution task execution, while removing any single failure point (at the cost of greater implementation complexity).

The scalability provided by the microservice architecture was in fact reached using resource virtualization techniques that allow the creation of isolated execution contexts, also known as containers. In the construction of the RS4IoT architecture, a cluster of Docker[3] containers was created, with one manager node, responsible for managing the cluster, and three worker-type nodes, responsible for performing specific recommendation service tasks. The use of Docker technologies allows the distribution of services, which use REST interfaces and TCP sockets, between the virtual machines and the load balancing of requests between them, improving the services' availability.

To demonstrate the use of our IoT recommender system, we use RS4IoT as a data source for an IoT-based Early Warning System (EWS) being developed by Moreira *et al.* [MOR 18], the INTER-IoT-EWS, which is being carried out as a scenario of the INTER-IoT project [LLO 16]. Basically the function of an EWS is to monitor the physical world and issue alerts if abnormal situations are detected. Moreira's work focuses on interoperability of IoT-based emergency systems based

---

1 http://ontologydesignpatterns.org/wiki/Ontology:DOLCE+DnS_Ultralite.
2 https://www.w3.org/ns/prov#.
3 https://www.docker.com/.

on the SEMIoTICS framework that guides the application of distributed software components, as RS4IoT. The goal of INTER-IoT-EWS is to reduce the risk of fatal accidents in the Port of Valencia, improving health prevention and enabling rapid reaction by reducing the response times [LLO 16]. INTER-IoT-EWS monitors the health of truck drivers by means of electrocardiography (ECG) sensors and truck location using GPS information from the drivers' cell phones. However, with this information, INTER-IoT EWS effectively fulfills only part of the role of preventing the occurrence of accidents, since it is limited to use ECG, GPS and acceleration sensors. This can be improved by adopting information provided by other sensors for richer early warning notifications. For example, in case of accidents involving explosive material, temperature sensors could be used to inform the temperature in the emergency location, which would support first responders to be prepared with specialized safety equipment for high temperatures.

In our case study, RS4IoT is integrated to INTER-IoT-EWS to provide information about temperature and sound (noise), as well as information collected from SN, so the EWS can combine this information with other available sensor data to estimate the extension of the accident and, if so, calculate the degree of danger the support team will be exposed to. To achieve this goal, RS4IoT captures temperature and sound information (noise) from sensors placed in the Port of Valencia area. Unlike INTER-IoT controlled scenario, the sensors provided by the R4IoT may be published in any IoT platform, for example ThingSpeak.

An example of joint operation scheme between INTER-IoT-EWS and RS4IoT is shown in Figure 28.2. In (1), when an accident is detected in the Port of Valencia, the EWS sends a request to RS4IoT (via REST) for the temperature, the sound and the SN information. For example, the EWS could consume the service by passing the parameters: temperature (type of sensor), sound (type of sensor), social network = true, latitude = 39.4463113, longitude = -0.3204029, number of sensors = 50, and total of registers per sensor = 100. In (2) and (3) the Recommender module requests IoT Manager to obtain a list of sensors. In (4) Recommender executes the recommendation algorithm to find which sensors meet the reported criteria. In (5) and (6) Recommender asks the Crawler for the measurements of the recommended sensors and responds to INTER-IoT-EWS with the recommended data and sensors. Finally, in (7), the INTER-IoT EWS combines temperature and sound information, together with information coming from SN and other existing sensor data, to measure the urgency and severity of the accident, and correctly notify the support team about which equipment should be used to treat the accident, according to existing emergency procedures.

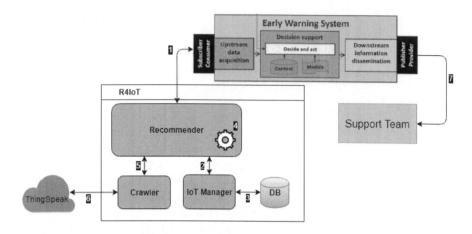

Figure 28.2. *Interaction of RS4IoT with the INTER-IoT-EWS. For a color version of this figure, see www.iste.co.uk/zelm/enterprise.zip*

28.4. Conclusion

Due to the intrinsic dynamicity and heterogeneity of IoT resources, discovering the most relevant or suitable ones among a myriad of devices connected to the Internet is a major challenge. Accordingly, it is really important to provide effective mechanisms supporting application developers and final users to find and identify the most appropriate devices to meet their requirements.

In order to address this matter, our work proposes a recommendation service for sensors of IoT devices, called RS4IoT. The recommendation is performed based on multiple attributes such as location, measured property and so on, combined with additional information about the researched services retrieved from SN. Besides, RS4IoT uses an information model based on the SSN ontology to describe sensors.

The RS4IoT distributed architecture and the technologies used on its prototype have been designed to promote scalability, fault tolerance and high availability. The application scenario chosen as case study illustrates the relevance and benefits of such a recommendation system, highlighting its potential use and the adoption as a tool to facilitate the development of IoT services and applications.

28.5. References

[CHO 15] CHOI S.M., LEE H., HAN Y.S. *et al.*, "A recommendation model using the bandwagon effect for e-marketing purposes in IoT", *International Journal of Distributed Sensor Networks*, vol. 11, no. 7, p. 475163, 2015.

[CHU 14] CHUNG *et al.*, "MUL-SWoT: a social Web of Things platform for Internet of Things application development", *2014 IEEE International Conference on Internet of Things (i Things), and IEEE Green Computing and Communications (GreenCom) and IEEE Cyber, Physical and Social Computing (CPSCom),* Taipei, Taiwan, 1–3 September, pp. 296–299, 2014.

[LEF 11] LEFORT L. *et al.*, Semantic sensor network XG final report, W3C Semantic Sensor Network Incubator Group, available at https://www.w3.org/2005/Incubator/ssn/XGR-ssn-20110628/, 2011.

[LLO 16] LLOP M. *et al.*, INTER-IoT deliverable: D2.4. Use cases manual, available at http://www.inter-iot-project.eu/deliverables, 2016.

[MAC 15] MACAULAY J., BUCKALEW L., CHUNG, G., Internet of things in logistics. A collaborative report by DHL and Cisco on implications and use cases for the logistics industry, Report, DHL Customer Solutions & Innovation, Troisdorf, 2015.

[MIN 16] MINERAUD J., MAZHELIS O., SU X. *et al.*, "A gap analysis of Internet-of-Things platforms", *Computer Communications*, vol. 89, pp. 5–16, 2016.

[MOR 18] MOREIRA J., PIRES L.F., VAN SINDEREN M. *et al.*, "Improving the semantic interoperability of IoT Early Warning Systems: the Port of Valencia use case", *I-ESA Conference*, Berlin, Germany, 2018.

[OLI 05] OLIVEIRA E. *et al.*, Assigning Subject Titles to Automatic Document Categorization, XXI CBBD – 2005, Curitiba, PR, Brazil, 2005.

[VAL 14] VALTOLINA S. *et al.*, "User-centered recommendation services in Internet of Things era", *Cultures of Participation in the Digital Age (CoPDA), Workshop*, Como, Italy, 27 May, 2014.

Predictive Maintenance

Part 6 Summary: Predictive Maintenance in Industry 4.0 – Methodologies, Tools and Interoperable Applications

Maintenance is a key business function within manufacturing enterprises related to all of their processes and focuses not only on avoiding the equipment breakdown but also on improving business performance. In recent years, due to the evolution of technology, products and machines have become more and more complex. Consequently, the costs of time-based (planned) maintenance have increased and predictive maintenance has evolved as a novel lever for maintenance management. To this end, the emergence of the Internet of Things (IoT) can enhance the condition monitoring capabilities by paving the way for extensive use of physical and virtual sensors generating a multitude of data. In this way, predictive maintenance can significantly evolve in the framework of Industry 4.0. Industry 4.0 indicates the flexibility that exists in value-creating networks which enables machines and plants to adapt their behavior to changing orders and operating conditions through self-optimization and reconfiguration with the aim of implementing distributed and interconnected production facilities in future smart factories.

The workshop in which these chapters were conceived was organized and supported by the H2020 FoF-09-2017 projects UPTIME and Z-BRE4K, which have received funding from the European Union's Horizon 2020 research and innovation programme. The workshop aimed to promote and encourage research and industrial efforts in order to cover a number of topics related to methodologies, concepts, architectures, tools and interoperable applications for predictive maintenance in the frame of Industry 4.0. The main goal of this workshop was to provide a forum for

Chapter written by Gregoris MENTZAS, Karl HRIBERNIK, Klaus-Dieter THOBEN, Dimitris KIRITSIS and Ali MOUSAVI.

researchers and practitioners with diverse backgrounds to meet, exchange research and implementation ideas, and share experience and results regarding predictive maintenance within the Industry 4.0 paradigm.

A brief overview of the nine chapters and their contributions is given below.

The first chapter, entitled "Using Sensor Data for Predictive Maintenance of a Complex Transportation Asset", presents the H2020 European project UPTIME which aims to develop an innovative maintenance platform, based on the latest technologies – such as IoT or big data analytics. The paper focuses on one industrial use case from the project, the maintenance of a complex transportation asset from the aviation sector.

The second chapter, entitled "The ProaSense Platform for Predictive Maintenance in Automotive Lighting Equipment Industry", presents the ProaSense platform and how it can facilitate predictive maintenance. The paper also presents the results and the lessons learned from its deployment in HELLA Saturnus Slovenija, an automotive lighting equipment company. The ProaSense platform was developed and evaluated in the context of the FP7 European project ProaSense.

The third chapter, entitled "Predictive Maintenance Framework: Implementation of Local and Cloud Processing for Multi-stage Prediction of CNC Machines Health", presents a predictive maintenance framework for CNC machines focusing on a multi-stage prediction of machines' health status. The paper presents the proposed approach and describes and discusses its benefits. The proposed predictive maintenance framework will be implemented in the H2020 European PROGRAMS project.

The fourth chapter, entitled "An Onboard Model-Of-Signals Approach for Condition Monitoring in Automatic Machines", presents the realization of a prototype infrastructure aiming at providing a useful framework to collect and elaborate information in a big data and IoT environment. The paper presents a novel approach related to predictive maintenance for automatic packaging machines, dealing with condition monitoring of mechanical components.

The fifth chapter, entitled "Maintenance Planning Support Tool Based on Condition Monitoring with Semantic Modeling of Systems", provides an approach to developing a maintenance planning support tool based on condition monitoring with semantic modeling of systems. The approach is based on the H2020 European project Z-Bre4k concerning strategies and predictive maintenance models wrapped around physical systems for zero-unexpected-breakdowns and increased operating life of factories.

The sixth chapter, entitled "SERENA: Versatile Plug and Play Platform Enabling Remote Predictive Maintenance", presents a conceptual framework of a predictive maintenance approach based on equipment condition-based modeling and evaluation through modern technologies (sensors and embedded systems, data analytics and advanced networking), as a step towards reducing breakdowns as well as the overall maintenance costs, through a more efficient time scheduling of the maintenance operations.

The seventh chapter, entitled "DRIFT: data-driven Failure Mode, Effects, and Criticality Analysis Tool", presents a tool that, on the basis of maintenance related information gathered for a target equipment, performs FMECA, that is, identifies what the failure modes, effects and criticalities of components and systems are in a data-driven way. The paper presents DRIFT in the context of the H2020 European UPTIME project and its potential to three industrial use cases.

The eighth chapter, entitled "Real-time Predictive Maintenance Based on Complex Event Processing", presents the concept of complex event processing in the field of predictive maintenance. This concept enables a surveillance of the system state in real-time using complex event processing technology, identifies fault causes and evaluates the condition of the technical components. On the basis of this information, various maintenance measures can be initiated. In doing so, the paper proposes a method for identifying the relevant amount of states to be monitored.

The ninth chapter, entitled "The Standards as Critical Means of Integration of Advanced Maintenance Approaches to Production Systems", presents a state of the art regarding standardization for integration of advanced maintenance approaches as predictive maintenance in production and logistics system with an application in the H2020 European UPTIME project. It positions the different levels of predictive maintenance regarding a larger context of industrial standards recently developed or in the making.

29

Using Sensor Data for Predictive Maintenance of a Complex Transportation Asset

In this chapter one of the three industrial use cases will be presented of those which are going to be developed to evaluate the results achieved by the European project UPTIME (Unified Predictive Maintenance System). The main objective of the project is the development of an innovative maintenance platform, based on the latest technologies – such as IoT or big data analytics. The paper focuses on the application of future UPTIME results in the aviation sector.

29.1. Introduction

The UPTIME project develops an integrated predictive maintenance system for the manufacturing industry. The motivation comes from the increasing demand for product quality and reliability of production. Predictive maintenance can have a considerable influence, for example on the availability of production equipment, by carrying out maintenance and repair measures not statically but on the basis of permanently measured condition data.

The UPTIME maintenance system will be able to process heterogeneous data from different sources (e.g. sensors, machine and production control data, field reports). Based on this, smart analytics and tailored visualizations will allow

Chapter written by Bernd BREDEHORST, Olaf PETERS, Jeroen VERSTEEG, Markus NEUHAUS, Carl HANS and Moritz VON STIETENCRON.

the identification of impending machine failures and suggest countermeasures. UPTIME will thus expand and standardize new digital maintenance services and tools to unlock the full potential of predictive maintenance management by sensor-generated big data processing, e-maintenance support, proactive data processing and the four levels of data analytics maturity [KAR 13].

The system is validated by three end users providing three completely different business cases: the production of tumble dryer drums, cold-rolled steel, and the operation of large transportation assets for shipping aircraft parts between different production sites distributed all over Europe. The latter is the subject of this paper and different from the other business cases as it is a static asset and not a production line. Nonetheless, it requires lots of maintenance activities and challenges comprising planned maintenance (different kinds of check routines) and unplanned repair activities. Reliability and availability of these assets are an important aspect to ensure the overall performance of the underlying distributed manufacturing system.

29.2. Use case: maintenance of a complex transportation asset

The transportation asset (see Figure 29.1) consists of a steel structure (the so-called main jig) and an associated light-weight roof component (Top Weather Protection) made from aluminum profiles. The asset is 40 m long with an empty weight of around 2,350 kg and was designed to transport wing covers of a commercial aircraft between plants of a transnational manufacturer in Germany and the United Kingdom. During its journey, the asset is moved by different means of transportation on land, water and air. All these environments impose different kinds of stress on the asset.

Concerning their specific environments each of these transportation modes comes along with individual requirements and impacts with respect to health monitoring of the asset. While live monitoring through mobile connectivity is possible on land and water, any transmissions functions must be disabled when the asset is aboard the cargo plane to comply with airworthiness regulations. Other issues to be considered during operation of the transportation asset (or transportation jig) cover the loading/unloading of aircraft parts as well as the assembly/disassembly of the asset after loading or prior to unloading of aircraft parts (attaching/detaching the top weather protection on the main jig). Furthermore, load/unload procedures between the different legs of the journey should be observed with respect to potential damages of the asset.

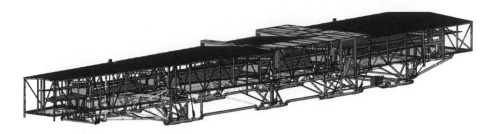

Figure 29.1. *Transportation asset ("jig") with inserted payload. For a color version of this figure, see www.iste.co.uk/zelm/enterprise.zip*

Indeed, there are many situations where damages can occur – often such damages will remain undetected and have to be addressed by urgent repair activities in order to keep the transportation in operation – particularly with respect to its airworthiness. Unfortunately, the manufacturer of the transportation asset, who is in this case also responsible for its maintenance, will see the assets only at the beginning as well as end of a transportation cycle on the German site and can neither anticipate the needed measures to prepare the asset for the next cycle nor is any information available which indicates any kind of damages – such as mishandling of the asset during the loading and unloading between different transportation modes.

29.3. UPTIME support for the aviation use case

Although the maintenance approach foresees a number of maintenance activities which are done either regularly after each transportation cycle or periodically, there are many unplanned repair activities which have to be done on short notice. Particularly, such unplanned activities are targeted by the analysis of data which have been measured before and uploaded to the UPTIME system. Data of interest for the analysis are provided by sensors directly attached to the asset – such as strain gauges, location sensing devices, noise detectors, shock detectors as well as sensors for temperature and humidity.

These data will then be used to get information about special events during the multiple transport and loading processes (truck, ship and airplane). A large part of maintenance efforts is assumed to be caused by such events. Except for obvious damages during loading/unloading processes, it is difficult to detect and exactly refer to the source of damage later. Particularly cracks in the lightweight structure of the transport asset can lead to non-availability of the asset due to strict regulations concerning the airworthiness of a transportation jig. Consequently, this will cause product delivery delays and airplane assembly delays and thus affects a complete value chain.

29.4. Stakeholders in the transport chain

In addition to the constant data monitoring and analysis, the system also has to consider and address the individual information needs of the different stakeholders in the value chain. To provide usable results for the different use cases each end user's business case has been carefully analyzed during the first phase of the project. In general, three groups of stakeholders have been identified:

– the manufacturer of the transportation assets who is also responsible for their maintenance;

– the customer who is shipping aircraft parts between its European plants using the asset;

– additional service providers who are involved, for example in the road transportation phase of the asset's journey.

Related to these stakeholder groups several roles have been identified to be the most relevant users of the UPTIME system:

– the manufacturer's **designers** are very much interested in identifying problem hot-spots to derive design modifications for the current fleet as well as the design of future assets;

– the manufacturer's **maintenance coordinator** plans and coordinates scheduled as well as unscheduled maintenance events, and is also responsible for spare part logistics and communication with the customer. This role is interested in getting information about possible damages as soon as possible. Furthermore, the coordinator gathers information about damages and repairs which occur frequently, for example in order to propose continuous improvements which are usually expected by the customer as part of the maintenance contracts;

– the manufacturer's **maintenance technician** is responsible for the actual inspection and on-time repair measures. When the asset has returned from a cycle, the technician will carry out a so-called pre-load check. All issues found during this inspection are recorded and fixed immediately – if possible, before the asset is flagged as "ready for flight" again. If repair of an issue affecting airworthiness is not possible, the asset has to be grounded until the repair is completed and accepted;

– the **customer's coordinators** take care of the logistics planning and all loading/unloading processes of the assets during a transportation cycle. They also coordinate the logistic chain including the costly scheduling of the cargo flights between Germany and the United Kingdom. While doing this the coordinators need reliable information about the availability of transportation jigs;

– several logistics processes are performed by external **logistic services providers** which are responsible for road as well as water transportation during the cycle from the manufacturing site in Germany to the production site in the UK and back again to Germany.

29.5. Monitoring the asset

There are various events which may occur during the journey of the transportation asset all of which may cause considerable damages, endangering the availability of the asset and thus have to be considered with respect to transportation safety. The most relevant ones are briefly described in the following:

– weather conditions like rain and snowfall: water may collect on either the payload or the tarpaulin covering the asset. It must be removed before loading the asset into the aircraft: as the cargo hold is not pressurized nor air-conditioned, it would freeze and become a threat for flight safety;

– road and flight conditions like potholes or air turbulences may cause vibrations and impacts which lead to deformations and cracks of the asset's light-weight frame construction;

– mishandling, like unintended contact of the asset or its components with the surrounding environment during transportation or loading, unloading causing structural deformations. Such situations may arise during attachment/detachment of the top weather protection if a wrong or not properly adjusted hoisting tool is used. Another reason concerns accidents which may happen while maneuvering the assets in a narrow space. Such situations are not always reported which induces tremendous efforts to restore their operational readiness.

29.6. Benefits of the UPTIME system

Coming along with the UPTIME platform various benefits are expected each of which will help to increase the transparency and efficiency of the logistics processes through preventive maintenance. Among of those are the following aspects:

– flexible process planning and integration: through the availability of information related to the condition of assets, planning can be improved considerably, for example by ensuring the availability of resources (equipment, spare parts, materials, etc.);

– continuous information management: relevant information of the transportation assets can be shared among all stakeholders. All maintenance activities can be documented at a centralized knowledge base. Thus, configuration management becomes much more integrated;

– continuous improvement: smart analytics of condition information helps to indicate weaknesses (such as potential sources of damages) and to propose improvements to the customer.

29.7. UPTIME architecture

In order to realize the UPTIME platform for the aviation use case the following architecture is proposed. It comprises functional modules for optimisation, reporting or planning all of which are connected to a private (cloud-based) data archive. Different interfaces are provided for the involved stakeholders – each providing specific views and variety of functions.

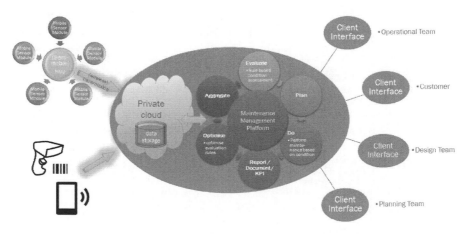

Figure 29.2. *UPTIME architecture. For a color version of this figure, see www.iste.co.uk/zelm/enterprise.zip*

29.8. Conclusion and outlook

Based on a unified platform supporting predictive maintenance by providing tailored views supporting all stakeholders of a given value chain as well as new innovative service offers current challenges in the manufacturing sector are addressed. Automatic anomaly detection for anticipation of needed maintenance activities, monitoring of asset condition and health or the provision of interactive dashboards for fault analysis are just a few examples out of many on how maintenance – as an important aspect in the manufacturing value chain – can be improved to ensure the competitiveness of the European manufacturing industry. The given use case provide much room for such improvements. Thus, the stakeholders of the use case depicted here pursue the results of UPTIME with the highest interest.

29.9. Acknowledgements

The UPTIME project has received funding from the European Union's Horizon 2020 research and innovation programme under grant agreement No. 768634.

29.10. References

[KAR 13] KART L., LINDEN A., SCHULTE W.R., *Extend Your Portfolio of Analytics Capabilities*, Gartner, 2013.

30

The ProaSense Platform for Predictive Maintenance in the Automotive Lighting Equipment Industry

The emergence of the Internet of Things enhances the monitoring capabilities of enterprises by means of extensive use of sensors generating a multitude of data. To this end, proactive decision making can provide meaningful insights about potential problems before they occur. In this paper, we present the ProaSense platform that facilitates proactive decision making in predictive maintenance, as well as the results and the lessons learned from its deployment in HELLA Saturnus Slovenija, an automotive lighting equipment industry.

30.1. Introduction

The emergence of the Internet of Things paves the way for enhancing the monitoring capabilities of enterprises by means of extensive use of physical and virtual sensors generating a multitude of data (big data). This fact leads to a strong demand for real-time data efficient processing in order to get meaningful insights about potential problems before they occur [SEJ 16]. To this end, proactive event processing, that is, the ability to decide and act ahead of time based on event stream processing technologies, is facilitated [ENG 12]. Proactivity can be seen in the context of the "Observe-Orient-Decide-Act" (OODA) loop of situational awareness [MAG 14]. The ProaSense (Proactive Sensing enterprise) platform implements the OODA model for facilitating predictive maintenance in the frame of Industry 4.0.

Chapter written by Alexandros BOUSDEKIS, Babis MAGOUTAS, Dimitris APOSTOLOU, Gregoris MENTZAS and Primoz PUHAR.

In this paper, we present the ProaSense deployment in HELLA Saturnus Slovenija, an automotive lighting equipment company, along with the results and lessons learned.

30.2. The HELLA use case

HELLA is a manufacturing company that produces and delivers large quantities of automotive lighting technology (e.g. headlamps) in batches. Its aim is to turn from a reactive into a proactive sensing enterprise and to apply predictive maintenance in this context in order to support their key performance indicator (e.g. reduce downtime, maintain running stock, improve products' quality) and to achieve "zero defects" and reduced downtime. Defects in HELLA's use case consist of downtimes and scrap rate. The production process includes different process steps from supplier deliveries, warehousing, plastics injection molding, surface treatment, metalizing, preassembly of groups and finished goods assembly. Table 30.1 presents the SWOT analysis of HELLA in the context of predictive maintenance.

Strengths	Weaknesses
HELLA Saturnus Slovenia is a producer of high quality and high volume automotive lighting equipment in a very competitive market segment. Hella has always been innovative and is therefore still a key player. Hella has operators that are experts in molding and lens production.	Part of the scrap production and downtime is due to the fact that customers demand high quality functionality and appearance. Downtime appears during maintenance of complex production processes, which results in a lower OEE. Customers demand more complex products that will increase the scrap rate and downtime. HELLA is not able to analyze the machines that are offline in the production process. It has only aggregated data on the scrap rate.
Opportunities	Threats
Automotive lighting equipment is more and more advanced and new technologies are being introduced (i.e. LED, OLED, LASER, etc.). With an innovative approach, it could be one step in front of competitors putting the machines online and offer customers cutting-edge products. HELLA has the opportunity to reduce cost and downtime in order to deliver even better performance and keep competitive advantage.	Introducing new technologies into automotive lighting equipment means the headlamp production process becomes even more complex. In the future, HELLA might not be able to master the process with reasonable OEE. Other competitors that can produce more precise products, for lower costs.

Table 30.1. SWOT analysis of HELLA

The sensor data related to the production line's effectiveness are derived from its various stages, for example molding machine, lacquering stations and ovens, as well as from ambient information, material structure information, personnel working at the line and so on. There are several parts of equipment on the production line that could lead to a damaged product leading to scrap (e.g. incorrect parameters on molding machines). Predictive maintenance using sensors placed on the molding machines could provide input to identify the cause of a problem that could help to mitigate scrapped parts (e.g. the pressure and temperature of the mould or oil, or injection speed). Some values could be obtained through sensors placed on the equipment, while others could be processed by other data sources (e.g. from the production plan or running stock). Until now, the installed monitoring functionality mainly shows the current status of the tool wear and machine configuration. To achieve proactivity in equipment maintenance, there is a need to anticipate which parameters need to be adapted and when a parameter may deviate from the acceptable set based on the available data sources and the detected patterns potentially leading to undesirable situations. Table 30.2 presents the elements of the strategy derived from the analysis of the strengths and weaknesses with respect to opportunities and threats from the implementation of the ProaSense platform.

	Opportunities	Threats
Strengths	Considering HELLA's innovative approach, the knowledge that is available on offline analysis of the molding machine prepares ProaSense as the logical next step.	With the use of the experts on molding in combination with the new feedback ProaSense can give, HELLA will be able to deliver higher quality products with less scrap produced and less downtime.
Weaknesses	ProaSense will enable HELLA to master even more complex production processes and improve OEE. Also ProaSense will enable more feedback that is not possible today. Even before a breakdown/downtime or scrap occurs.	ProaSense will enable HELLA to at least maintain current OEE value with the introduction of even more complex products and production processes.

Table 30.2. *Strategy derived from SWOT analysis*

30.3. The ProaSense platform and deployment in HELLA

The ProaSense platform provides early notifications about equipment problems and proactive recommendations about optimal decisions on the basis of sensor-generated data. ProaSense uses smart sensing systems able to cope with a huge amount of heterogeneous (big) data in real-time. It is based on the OODA loop of situational awareness and consists of the components shown in Table 30.3. The deployment of the ProaSense platform in HELLA and its integration into the data sources is shown in Figure 30.1. Sensors monitor and gather data on the relevant parameters of the machines in order to detect anomalies through *StreamPipes* [RIE 15]. Sensor data, historical data and contextual information are further used in order to derive predictions about defects (e.g. black dots on cover lens) through *StreamStory* [STO 15]. *PANDDA* [BOU 17] recommends proactive actions for eliminating the scrap rate based on the predictions as well as the business context derived from the enterprise context model (e.g. production plan, running stock, customer, complexity of the product vs. the production cost). Finally, the *Business Analyzer* enables the company to set its business requirements.

Observe	Orient	Decide	Act
StreamPipes	StreamStory	PANDDA	Business Analyzer
Complex Event Processing (CEP)	Predictive Analytics	Proactive Decision Making	KPI Modeling
Flexible modeling toolkit for data processing pipelines for business users	Advanced data exploration platform producing online outputs	Tool for proactive recommendations with an adaptation mechanism	Modeling tool to define and visualize KPIs and target values
ProaSense Adapter Library & Storage			

Table 30.3. *The ProaSense components*

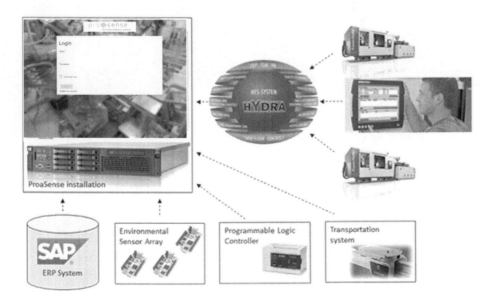

Figure 30.1. *Deployment of the ProaSense platform in HELLA*

30.4. Results and lessons learned

The deployment of the ProaSense platform in HELLA allows the company to gain a strong competitive advantage based on reduced downtimes and optimized performance. The results, conclusions and lessons learned are outlined below:

30.4.1. *Technical implications*

– HELLA started to prove correlations between scrap rate and: different molding machines, injection molding parameters, different molding materials, material properties, shop floor shifts, air temperature, air humidity, cover lens temperature and automated transportation line delays. They allowed the avoidance of defect-causing combinations and adaptation to the process to avoid predicted defects;

– since the system enabled the solution of various pilot's use cases, it is perceived as both flexible and robust enough to handle a wide range of applications;

– data-driven approaches to optimization become only as good as the input data provided and the assumptions made during system configuration;

– hosting modern ICT solutions within an existing operating IT environment has proven a considerable undertaking throughout the development and testing. The fact that the infrastructure is Linux based and build on open-source components have challenged the company's corporate privacy and security policies considerably. Security of corporate data is an important requirement;

– outlining use cases across the layers of the OODA cycle has matured the organization establishing new requirements for the collection of context data to be used in maintenance optimization;

– full exploitation of ProaSense assumes a large amount of real-time data for processing as well as high quality contextual information for documenting the results of reducing equipment downtime economically in business KPIs. Getting hold of such kinds of information has proven highly challenging.

30.4.2. *Managerial implications*

– The system development process revealed a new understanding of the challenge in cooperating across business domains. Adopting key competency within both production processes and computer science is critical to succeed in big data analytics. Through ProaSense, HELLA has acquired increased understanding of the complexity in system architecture and revealed the needs of dedicated system users with both business optimization competency and technical equipment understanding. The involved costs need to be considered and approved. Hence, the need of organizational development in the field of business analytics is provided as input to the company's business development strategy;

– there are different kinds of corporate governments, which can lead subsidiary companies from headquarter (centrally) or leave the subsidiary company to be guided by the local management. HELLA is becoming more and more centrally guided. Consequently, HELLA Saturnus Slovenija d.o.o., a subsidiary of HELLA KGaA Hueck & Co., has limitations due to central management decisions, but also through technology and new system implementations. HELLA headquarters is preparing guidelines on which system the rest of the companies over the world will use for ERP, MES or SCADA. Therefore, HELLA was urged to use MES Hydra system for gathering production data;

– with the new perspective of Industry 4.0 and the Internet of Things, there is a need for integration of new sensing equipment. Considering the legacy equipment, investment is significant and has to be approved by the headquarters;

– for the deployment of ProaSense, HELLA had to stop the fully automated production process running on a four-shift model and to fully book capacity on injection molding machines. This fact was a great challenge and such aspects are some of the key reasons why large enterprises are slowly adopting new technologies.

30.5. Conclusions and future work

We presented the use of the ProaSense platform for predictive maintenance of an automotive lighting equipment company. We described the HELLA use case and we presented the ProaSense platform along with results and the lessons learned. Regarding future work, HELLA will extend the use of ProaSense to final headlamp production in order to increase the quality of the final product (average light intensity in photometric points reserve over legal values) and reduce its price. Moreover, the concept of the proactive enterprise in predictive maintenance will be further extended and validated in the context of the H2020 UPTIME project.

30.6. Acknowledgements

This work is partly funded by the European Commission projects: FP7 ProaSense "The Proactive Sensing Enterprise" (612329) (http://www.proasense.eu/) and H2020 UPTIME "Unified Predictive Maintenance System" (768634) (https://www.uptime-h2020.eu/).

30.7. References

[BOU 17] BOUSDEKIS A., PAPAGEORGIOU N., MAGOUTAS B. *et al.*, "An Information System for Deciding and Acting ahead of Time in Sensing Enterprises", *Information, Intelligence, Systems & Applications (IISA), 8th International Conference*, IEEE, 2017.

[ENG 12] ENGEL Y., ETZION O., FELDMAN Z., "A Basic Model for Proactive Event-driven Computing", *6th ACM International Conference on DEBS 2012*, ACM, pp. 107–118, 2012.

[MAG 14] MAGOUTAS B., STOJANOVIC N., BOUSDEKIS A. *et al.*, "Anticipation-driven Architecture for Proactive Enterprise Decision Making", *CAiSE (Forum/Doctoral Consortium) 2014*, pp. 121–128, 2014.

[RIE 15] RIEMER D., KAULFERSCH F., HUTMACHER R. *et al.*, "StreamPipes: Solving the Challenge with Semantic Stream Processing Pipelines", *Proceedings of the 9th ACM International Conference on Distributed Event-Based Systems 2015*, ACM, pp. 330–331, 2015.

[SEJ 16] SEJDOVIC S., KLEINER N., "Proactive and Dynamic Event-driven Disruption Management in the Manufacturing Domain", *Industrial Informatics (INDIN), 2016 IEEE 14th International Conference*, IEEE, pp. 1320–1325, 2016.

[STO 15] STOPAR L., GROBELNIK M., MLADENIC D., "Multi-scale Methodology for Explaining Data Streams", *International Multi Conference on Information Society IS-2015*, 2015.

31

Predictive Maintenance Framework: Implementation of Local and Cloud Processing for Multi-stage Prediction of CNC Machines' Health

This paper presents a predictive maintenance framework for CNC machines focusing on a multi-stage prediction of machines' health status. For the implementation of such a multi-stage prediction, the proposed approach includes two prediction layers: the cloud prediction layer and the local prediction layer. Each layer provides a prediction of machine health status in different timescale. The local prediction layer, based on data analysis techniques, is responsible for predicting the health status of the machine for a short time period. Thus, this prediction can be used as an alarm aiming to prevent unexpected breakdowns. The cloud prediction layer, based on digital physical-based models, is responsible for providing a more general overview of machine health status using Prognostics and Health Management (PHM) techniques, useful for long timespan strategies definition. This paper presents the proposed approach and its benefits are described and discussed. The proposed approach will be implemented in the PROGRAMS project.

31.1. Introduction

Maintenance and its related costs continue, over the years, to draw the attention of production management since the unplanned failures decrease the reliability of the system, and also the return on investments [MOU 15]. Taking under consideration that the maintenance accounts for as much as 60% to 70% of the production lifecycle total costs, it is a core activity of most industrial sectors [DHI 06]. More specifically,

Chapter written by Panagiotis AIVALIOTIS, Konstantinos GEORGOULIAS, Raffaele RICATTO and Michele SURICO.

industrial studies have revealed that the cost of replacing worn-out components may be as high as 70% of the total maintenance cost [VEN 10].

Nowadays, the high complexity is an important characteristic of the CNC machines which are used for industrial applications. Several hundreds of components are required to allow the CNC machine functionality. For example, the implementation of a maintenance strategy requires continuous monitoring of each piece of equipment to be aware of its real deterioration status. Due to the high complexity of the CNC machines, a multi-stage predictive maintenance framework is needed to enable the prediction of machine health status over different timescales, aiming to ensure the prediction over both long and short time periods of operation.

One the one hand, a long-time period prediction of the CNC machines' health status is useful for the precise selection and scheduling of the best moment for maintenance, right before a component breaks down. However, prediction like this requires a long time period simulation and, accordingly, huge computational time. On the other hand, a short time period prediction is required to prevent unexpected breakdowns in the near future. Such predictions are based on the use of historical data and comparison techniques, which require small computational time.

31.2. Method

This paper presents an approach which implements this integration of long and short term prediction in a multi-stage predictive maintenance framework with two different layers: the cloud prediction layer and the local prediction layer. The cloud prediction layer is responsible for providing a more general overview of machine health status using Prognostics and Health Management (PHM) techniques over a long time period. The local prediction layer is responsible for predicting the health status of the machine using data driven models over a short time period.

The main pillar of a PHM system is the prediction of the Remaining Useful Life (RUL) that depicts the time after which a system or a machine's component no longer performs its intended function [AIV 17]. According to previous research, a maintenance action should be executed taking under consideration both health assessment information (such as RUL) as well as additional information from multi-criteria mechanisms [PAP 07]. The RUL is the most important parameter to be taken under consideration for the creation and execution of a maintenance plan [OKO 04]. Thus, a number of predictive maintenance platforms are based on RUL prediction to fulfill the needs of the data analysis and knowledge management [MYC 10]. These platforms are based on three main stages: the first stage is responsible for data extraction and processing; the second one focuses on the maintenance knowledge modeling and calculation of RUL; and the third stage provides advisory capabilities for maintenance planning [EFT 12].

In the proposed research, machine component physical-based models will be used for the calculation of the RUL for each machines' components. The proposed method will be used in the PROGRAMS project. More specifically, some data will be gathered by the machines' controllers and external sensors, which will be structured and uploaded to a cloud database. Some of this data will be used for the simulation of the digital models, while some will be used to update the simulation models, aiming to ensure that the simulated functionalities of the machines will be the same as the real one. Therefore, a digital twin of the real production equipment will be created. Finally, the upcoming process plan of the machine will make up the input for the simulation model. The output of the simulation, in combination with the reliability parameters of the machines and the real time monitored data, will be used for the final RUL calculation. The above procedure is depicted in Figure 31.1.

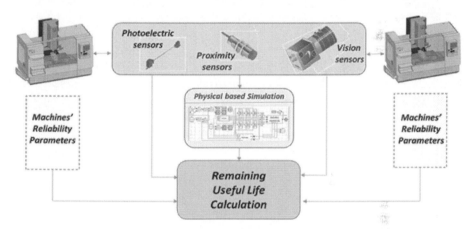

Figure 31.1. *RUL calculation main concept [AIV 17]. For a color version of this figure, see www.iste.co.uk/zelm/enterprise.zip*

For the local prediction layer and its prediction techniques, the proposed approach is based on algorithms that use the data-driven approach to prognosis learn models directly from the data, rather than using a hand-built model based on human expertise [SCH 05]. Considering that data batches collected from a repetitive operation are generally similar unless in the presence of an abnormality, a condition change can be inferred by comparing the monitored data against an available nominal batch [BIT 14]. Other researches attempt to address this problem with intelligence-oriented techniques, such as dynamic wavelet neural networks (DWNNs). DWNNs incorporate temporal information and storage capacity into their functionality so that they can predict the future, carrying out fault prognostic tasks [WAN 01].

In this research, an already existing data-driven prediction methodology based on Artificial Neural Networks will be used for the local prediction. This proposed data-driven method is not a part of the PROGRAMS project. Available historical data will be used for the training of the neural network and the real time gathered data will be compared with the historical data aiming to identify potential upcoming failures.

The strong point of the presented approach is the integration of the physically-based and data-driven methodologies for the prediction of the machines' health status in a multi-dimensional time frame. The benefits of this approach when applied to CNC-driven industrial equipment are presented in detail in the following section.

31.3. Approach

Two main factors have limited the diffusion of predictive maintenance so far: on the one hand, the huge amount of data that must be preventively collected in order to train and validate the health status prediction algorithms; on the other hand, the somewhat limited choice left to the monitored production equipment owner (replace the worn component or live with it). This scenario however changes drastically when machine tools equipped with CNCs are considered. In fact, the latest generation of smart CNCs allow the recording of internal signals with sample rates near or equal to the CNC cycle time (usually 1–2 ms), to internally analyze real time data to detect if an equipment component is working and under which stress conditions, and to exploit knowledge of equipment's health status to adjust the processing performance.

The data produced can successively be moved to a remote cloud storage (for example a factory-wide database) for applications that go beyond the straight process management. The added value of implementing these features directly inside the CNC, as opposed to using external Programmable Logic Controllers (PLCs) and Programmable Automation Controllers (PACs), is that the bulk of machine tool data and the capability for process parameters management are already available and ready to be exploited. In addition, only a limited set of CNCs allow one to relinquish the control of process parameters to third party applications, both for quality management and for security/safety reasons. It then becomes clear that a new maintenance paradigm can be originated, by combining these functionalities with an advanced tool capable of using smart (data-driven or model-based) algorithms, to understand the equipment's current status and to predict the time when it will become irreversibly worn out. With this objective in mind, a smart CNC producer (like FIDIA) can decide to interface its controllers with a new maintenance platform, in order to offer a whole new set of functionalities to its customers.

The health status of production equipment can be computed by data-driven algorithms. The main advantage of these tools is that they do not rely on complicated system modeling and can be thus applied directly to the historical CNC records (for training) or even to real time data (for fast evaluation of the current equipment's status). Once the health status of the main equipment's components is available, the CNC must then correlate it with the impact it could have on the process. In fact, a worn component is usually not an important enough reason to stop the production and request a maintenance activity. In most cases, when the equipment's status deviates from the nominal one, the operator evaluates the deviation and, based on it, decides whether the machine is still fit for its purpose. In most cases (like for mass-produced parts), the operator limits itself to warning the operators that will use the machine in the next shift to monitor it closely. Only in the presence of drastic deviations does the operator decide to request a maintenance activity but even in those cases the production is not stopped. Instead the processing parameters are modified (usually by lowering speeds and loop gains) to continue to safely produce (albeit at a slower rate) while waiting for a replacement/repair intervention.

By implementing such a functionality directly inside the machine's CNC, it would be possible to directly exploit smart CNC customization features. This functionality (such as FIDIA's *Look ahead*) allows modifying large sets of parameters with a single command. If specific sets of parameters are created for specific machine tools' health status and process conditions, it then becomes a trivial task to correlate the output of the status evaluation platform with an automatic process parameter adaption feature. However, the limits of data driven analysis should be taken into account while using such a method for health status evaluation. The most important one is that these algorithms are able only to detect when the machine performs out of nominal boundaries, but cannot provide any information on which is the cause of such behavior. On the contrary, a model-based approach would allow one to actually correlate the deviation from nominal conditions to a specific restricted set of responsible components. This approach has several benefits, since it would allow: (1) the adaptation of only those parameters directly related to the component's behavior, thus reducing the impact on the whole process; (2) storing of information about both the signals and the components that have failed, for components' models improvement; (3) restriction of the set of components that could be malfunctioning, making the duration of the maintenance intervention easier and shorter; (4) a wider time span between the prediction of the incoming failure and insurgence, granting a better maintenance scheduling. It is worth noting that a model-based health detection status would greatly benefit from a cloud deployment. On the one side, this would allow using data coming from whole families of identical but widely spread similar machine tools (thus supporting also the machine tool design phase). On the other side, this would limit the computational burden at the factory level, relieving resources that could be better exploited for different objectives. In order to allow a cloud-based approach however, the CNC should allow functionalities that go beyond the simple process management. These functionalities include the availability of web based services for sending information to the cloud (relevant sensor data for health status computation), retrieving data from the cloud (the computed components' status) and the writing of information on a database (for successive analysis and model training). In the framework of the PROGRAMS project, FIDIA will integrate its CNCs with the project's platform and test the new functionalities on the pilot line of one of the end users.

31.4. Acknowledgments

Part of the work reported in this paper makes reference to the EC research project "PROGRAMS – PROGnostics based Reliability Analysis for Maintenance Scheduling" (www.programs-project.eu), which received funding from the European Union's Horizon 2020 research and innovation programme under the Grant Agreement No. 767287.

31.5. References

[AIV 17] AIVALIOTIS P., GEORGOULIAS K., CHRYSSOLOURIS G., "A RUL calculation approach based on physical-based simulation models for predictive maintenance", *International Conference on Engineering Technology and Innovation (ICE IEEE)*, 2017.

[BIT 14] BITTENCOURT A.C., SAARINEN K., SANDER-TAVALLAEY S. *et al.*, "A data-driven approach to diagnostics of repetitive processes in the distribution domain – Applications to gearbox diagnostics in industrial robots and rotating machines", *Mechatronics*, vol. 24, no. 8, pp. 1032–1104, 2014.

[DHI 06] DHILON B.S., *Maintainability, Maintenance, and Reliability for Engineers*, Taylor and Francis, 2006.

[EFT 12] EFTHYMIOU K., PAPAKOSTAS N., MOURTZIS D. *et al.*, "On a Predictive Maintenance Platform for Production Systems", *Procedia CIRP*, vol. 3, pp. 221–226, 2012.

[MOU 15] MOURTZIS D., VLACHOU E., MILAS N. *et al.*, "A cloud-based approach for maintenance of machine tools and equipment based on shop-floor monitoring", *Procedia CIRP, 48th CIRP Conference on Manufacturing Systems*, vol. 41, pp. 655–660, 2015.

[MYC 10] MYCAR, Deliverable D2.3.1 – D3.3.1 – D4.3.1 – D5.3.1 – Refinement and Industrial Implementation, 2010.

[OKO 14] OKOH C., ROY R., MEHNEN J. *et al.*, "Overview of Remaining Useful Life Prediction Techniques in Through-Life Engineering Services, Product Services Systems and Value Creation", *Proceedings of the 6th CIRP Conference on Industrial Product-Service Systems*, pp. 158–163, 2014.

[PAP 07] PAPACHATZAKIS P., PAPAKOSTAS N., CHRYSSOLOURIS G., "Condition based operational risk assessment an innovative approach to improve fleet and aircraft operability: Maintenance planning", *1st European Air and Space Conference*, Germany, pp. 121–126, 2007.

[SCH 05] SCHWABACHER M., "A Survey of Data-Driven Prognostics", *Infotech@Aerospace Conferences*, 2005.

[VEN 10] VENKATARAMAN V., *Maintenance Engineering and Management*, PHI Learning Private Limited, 2010.

[WAN 01] WANG P., VACHTSEVANOS G., "Fault prognostics using dynamic wavelet neural networks", *Artificial Intelligence for Engineering Design and Manufacturing*, vol. 15, pp. 349–365, 2001.

32

An Onboard Model-of-signals Approach for Condition Monitoring in Automatic Machines

In this chapter we present the realization of a prototype infrastructure aiming at providing a useful framework to collect and elaborate information in a big data and IoT environment. The work presents a novel approach related to predictive maintenance for automatic packaging machines, dealing with condition monitoring of mechanical components. The knowledge of the state of machinery parts is crucial to trigger dynamic scheduling of their servicing before they are worn out or get corrupted, saving time and money. In this fashion, condition monitoring, also known as incipient fault diagnosis, has a key role in the estimation of components' condition and their remaining working time.

32.1. Introduction

This project is within the Industry 4.0 framework. It refers to the need to perform predictive maintenance on machinery working with heavy-duty cycles. This is a major request from machinery vendors and their customers: let the machine inform the user (and its seller) about its components state. Diagnosis of faulty or corrupted components have become complex due to growing machinery complexity. In this fashion, the University of Bologna and its industrial partners are developing predictive maintenance and diagnosis techniques by exploiting the Internet of Things and big data concepts of Industry 4.0.

Chapter written by Matteo BARBIERI, Alessandro BOSSO, Christian CONFICONI, Roberto DIVERSI, Matteo SARTINI and Andrea TILLI.

Rules and models are needed to achieve effective incipient fault diagnosis especially if they are to be capable of both detecting and isolating harmful machine states so as to trigger a predictive maintenance process.

Two main kinds of approaches can be found to address this purpose: model-based and signal-based fault detection and isolation. In the former, physical laws are exploited to derive dynamical models but, in this case, machinery model definition must struggle with its various non-linearities as well as the identification of its uncertainties, resulting in a time-consuming approach, which may not successfully address the complexity of the machine. On the other hand, regarding signal-based methods, techniques like FFT or limit checking can be directly applied to the signals sampled from the machine, thus inferring upcoming faults from them. Although this approach looks easier than the previous one, it fails in representing the inherent dynamical behaviour of mechanical systems.

In this scenario, our proposal is to apply a model-of-signals technique based on system identification algorithms to address components' states embodying features of both previous approaches. Conditions are obtained by dynamic models of the signals measured on the machine, resulting in "physics-free" state descriptions. The drawback in performing this approach is that it requires many elaborations and data to be sampled during machinery working in many different conditions: from healthy to faulty passing through going-to-fail ones.

In the packaging field, many signal sources may be exploited to derive machinery conditions. The quantities measured to perform models' computations are both the ones already available on-board the machines as well as others in addition. The former is, for example, the drives' currents and torques as well as load cells and pressure gauges, while the latter are accelerometers and microphones, useful in gathering information on mechanical components' condition.

The amount of data and elaborations requested to perform the depicted approach may lead to a "Huge Data" problem instead of a "Big Data" one. To avoid this condition, in this paper, we present an architecture in which the models-of-signals approach is performed on board the machinery. The modeling of the sensors' signals is done by means of system identification algorithms running in the machine controller. The computed model parameters are then transferred to a remote storage and elaboration facility by means of Industry 4.0 communication standards, such as OPC, OPC-UA, MQTT. Data are arranged to potentially feed machine learning algorithms and predictive maintenance procedures.

In this way, computational loads are distributed amongst the PLCs and their supervising servers, and the data stream, collected from the large number of sensor signals, is reduced to a set of models.

Taking the cue from the above-mentioned framework, in this paper we present a prototype seamless infrastructure for local data collection and elaboration and transmission to remote servers. In the local side, an accelerometer has been placed on board of the machine and its data collected via an acquisition module. At this point, a system identification library has been designed to develop diagnosis algorithms to process sensor collected data. On the other hand, an infrastructure via OPC protocol has been designed to let the industrial PC send and receive information about its diagnosis work from and to a remote computing system, in this case a remote MATLAB instance within the PLC LAN. An illustration of the whole information workflow is depicted in Figure 32.1.

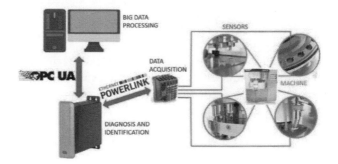

Figure 32.1. *Schematic of the framework. For a color version of this figure, see www.iste.co.uk/zelm/enterprise.zip*

32.2. Hardware setup

The hardware set up composed to fulfil the project task is composed by the following components:

– Accelerometer PCB 356B21;

– B&R modules X20 BC0083, X20 PS9400, X20CM4810-C01;

– Powerlink cabling;

– B&R CPU X20 CP1586;

– PC with MATLAB and Simulink.

32.3. System identification tools

In line with the model-of-signals approach, the machine vibrations are represented by autoregressive (AR) models and the identification tool for estimating the AR parameters is the recursive least squares (RLS) algorithm.

The main reasons behind the choice of this algorithm are the following:

– it is optimal and consistent for AR estimation;

– in its recursive form it is computationally efficient enough to be implemented on a PLC.

32.3.1. *Recursive least squares*

The recursive least squares algorithm for AR models identification [GUI 03] will be depicted in SISO form, starting from its difference equations representation:

$$y(t) = \alpha_1 y(t-1) + \cdots + \alpha_n y(t-n) + e(t) \qquad [32.1]$$

where $e(\cdot)$ is a stochastic white process with null expected value and $\mathbf{n}$ denotes the order of the model and the parameter vector results to be the following:

$$\theta = [\alpha_1 \alpha_2 \ldots \alpha_{n-1} \alpha_n]^T \qquad [32.2]$$

Then, the least squares expression is, as is widely known:

$$\theta = (H^T H)^{-1} H^T Y \qquad [32.3]$$

where the Hankel matrix of order $\mathbf{n}$ of the output $H(y)$ is defined as such:

$$H(y) = \begin{pmatrix} y(n) & \cdots & y(1) \\ \vdots & \ddots & \vdots \\ y(L-1) & \cdots & y(L-n) \end{pmatrix} \qquad [32.4]$$

While the vector $\mathbf{Y}$ is defined as:

$$Y = [y(n+1) \ldots y(L)]^T \qquad [32.5]$$

Notice that the whole calculations are done by samples of the output signal $\mathbf{y}(\cdot)$ within the time interval $[1, L]$ and the predictor uses $\mathbf{N} = \mathbf{L} - \mathbf{n}$ of them for computations.

The recursive least squares implementation starts from the estimate of θ obtained at time $\mathbf{t} = \mathbf{L}$ by means of the whole set of estimates:

$$\theta(t) = S(t)^{-1} H^T(t) Y(t) \text{ with: } S(t)^{-1} = (H^T H)^{-1} \qquad [32.6]$$

Then it is possible to write the analogous at time $t-1$ as such:

$$\theta(t) = S(t-1)^{-1}H^T(t-1)Y(t-1) \qquad [32.7]$$

Then, the final recursive form is given by

$$\theta(t) = \theta(t-1) + K(t)\epsilon(t) \qquad [32.8]$$

where:

$$K(t) = S(t)^{-1}h^T(t) \quad \text{and} \quad \epsilon(t) = y(t) - h(t)\theta(t-1) \qquad [32.9]$$

that is the update of the parameter vector θ at time t starting from the estimate obtained at the previous instant $\theta(t-1)$, where:

$$h(t) = [y(t-1) \dots y(t-n)] \qquad [32.10]$$

depicts the last row of $H(t)$ that is nothing but the update of $H(t)$. At this point, to avoid numerical problems, since the use of $S(t)$ may lead to instability of the estimate, the algorithm may rely on the update of

$$R(t) = \frac{S(t)}{N} \qquad [32.11]$$

and so the definition of the matrix gain $K(t)$ becomes

$$K(t) = \frac{R(t)^{-1}h^T(t)}{N} \qquad [32.12]$$

Finally, to solve the matrix inversion issue it is possible to exploit the matrix inversion lemma.

In the end, the computation for $R(t)^{-1}$ within [32.12] turns out to be:

$$R(t)^{-1} = \frac{NR(t-1)^{-1}}{N-1}\left[I - \frac{h^T(t)h(t)R(t-1)^{-1}}{N-1+h(t)R(t-1)^{-1}h^T(t)}\right] \qquad [32.13]$$

The algorithm needs to be initialized with parameter vector θ_0 as well as a R_0 and H_0. Those variables may be both previously computed off-line or on-line during the initialization phase of the algorithm. In the problem here depicted it is advisable to perform those calculations off-line, maybe with other systems, that is, with a PC application.

32.3.2. *NRMSE index*

The NRMSE (Normalized Root Mean Square Error) index is used in condition monitoring to address differences between models. In condition monitoring it is used to detect when the machine is starting to diverge from its nominal behaviour due to an incipient fault. The definition is the following:

$$NRMSE = \sqrt{\frac{||\theta - \theta_{Nom}||}{||\theta_{Nom}||}}$$ [32.14]

32.4. System identification Library

In order to implement on the PLC the system identification algorithm depicted previously, some operations must be performed, starting from the definition of a software library, *LL_Sys_ID*, containing:

– Matrix types and operations;

– RLS implementation;

– NRMSE index computing function.

32.5. OPC interface

The configuration of the OPC framework on the PLC side needs variables (e.g. θ identified) to be published on a node on its OPC server which in turn must be activated. Once done, with the help of the OPC toolbox it is possible to access those data from a MATLAB OPC client. To do so, a script has been developed which connects to the input PLC OPC server and samples data from it. After the collection, one can perform further computations such as, in the simplest case, the mean value. Those data have been defined as:

– actual RLS parameter estimation;

– actual NRMSE value related to those parameters;

– time stamp of the measurement.

32.6. Framework experimental evaluation

The setup is attached to a test bed with three bearings, one working normally and the others two with increased level of wear. The goal of this test is to simulate an incipient fault on the bearing by firstly putting the accelerometer over the healthy one and then the sensor above the faulty ones and letting the machine detect the faults by looking at the NRMSE value. Everything was done while a MATLAB script via OPC was sampling RLS computed parameter values and related NRMSE, returning per each measurement the mean of the identified parameter set, the mean NRMSE and their timestamp.

The nominal healthy model has been obtained in advance via an off-line procedure (courtesy of LIAM Lab) and provided to the machine:

$$\theta_N = [\alpha_1\ \alpha_2\ \alpha_3\ \alpha_4\ \alpha_5]^T = [0.48\ 0.07\ 0.44\ -0.44\ 0.49]^T \qquad [32.15]$$

32.7. Results

Table 32.1 presents the results obtained during the above-mentioned trials.

Attempt	α_0	α_1	α_2	α_3	α_4	NMRSE	Timestamp
1st H	0.48	0.04	0.40	−0.40	0.46	0.06	10:12:35
2nd H	0.43	0.12	0.36	−0.47	0.54	0.11	10:19:58
1st F1	0.35	0.22	0.18	0.03	0.10	0.74	10:25:14
1st F2	0.07	0.29	0.10	−0.74	−1.42	2.17	10:34:31
3rd H	0.52	−0.01	0.47	−0.52	0.53	0.14	10:42:23
2nd F1	0.33	0.22	0.16	0.04	0.14	0.73	10:48:45
2nd F1	0.10	0.24	−0.04	−0.87	−1.44	2.23	10:54:30
4th H	0.52	−0.01	0.46	−0.52	0.53	0.14	11:06:48

Table 32.1. *Summary of results*

The depicted framework can gather an on-line model-of-signals from the sensors and compute simple condition monitoring indexes above them. Moreover, it prepares them to be deployed for further and more involved elaborations on remote computing systems.

32.8. Acknowledgments

This work was supported by the Department of Electrical, Electronic and Information Engineering (DEI) of the University of Bologna and the LIAM Lab industrial automation laboratory within the European project POR FESR PATTERN, CUP E42F16000180007.

32.9. References

[GUI 03] GUIDORZI R., *Multivariable System Identification: From Observations to Models*, Bononia University Press, Bologna, 2003.

[LIU 99] LIUNG L., *System Identification: Theory for the User*, Prentice Hall, 1999.

33

Maintenance Planning Support Tool Based on Condition Monitoring with Semantic Modeling of Systems

A traditional maintenance policy is translated into ineffectiveness during the whole operative lifetime of the production plant, in particular for those systems often subjected to overloads to enhance productivity, resulting not only in high maintenance costs, but compromising the overall duration of the equipment. The well-consolidated preventive maintenance strategies implemented to avoid critical failures are suitable for traditional highly repetitive mass production processes, but show some limitations in the novel production context, where more adaptive and responsive maintenance strategies are needed. Guided by this challenge, the study provides an approach to develop a maintenance planning support tool based on condition monitoring with semantic modeling of systems. The approach is based on the implementation in a large collaborative EU-funded H2020 research project entitled Z-Bre4k, that is, strategies and predictive maintenance models wrapped around physical systems for zero-unexpected-breakdowns and increased operating life of factories.

33.1. Introduction

In today's competitive marketplace, the requirement for high quality manufactured products, which often entails complex production assets and equipment, is combined with the current trend of mass customization and individualization, which implies a continuous changing of manufacturing configuration needs and consequently, a complexity in planning and control of production. The shift toward Industry 4.0 requires the development and

Chapter written by Alice REINA, Sang-Je CHO, Gökan MAY, Eva COSCIA, Jacopo CASSINA and Dimitris KIRITSIS.

implementation of new multidisciplinary methods and tools for intelligent predictive maintenance, aligned with the main design principles for Industry 4.0 scenarios [HER 16], especially with respect to interoperability, virtualization and real-time capability, these being the most relevant among others for intelligent predictive maintenance scenarios [MON 14]. In that regard, the role of big data and analytics are of major importance for achieving these smart factories of Industry 4.0 [ZHO 15, LEE 14]. In that vein, this paper provides an approach to developing a maintenance planning support tool based on condition monitoring with semantic modeling of systems and their healthy/deteriorated signatures.

A large collaborative EU-funded H2020 research project entitled Z-Bre4k [ZBR 17) has been the main driver of the described approach and is designed for its validation. The project comprises of 17 partners from nine European countries, as well as from different areas of interest including the manufacturing industry, academic research and system development. Accordingly, a Condition Monitoring module is proposed in order to support different actors of the company to evaluate machines and production systems conditions in order to avoid critical and potential failures. The industrial machine module in fact will support production managers during the daily production monitor and assessments but the module will be also used by workers to detect the main machine issues in order to act in short time. The innovation of the proposed method lies in the development of an approach to lift various types of data (component, machine, production, quality, product and business data) and develop an integrated digital representation based on semantic knowledge representation formalisms.

In this context, reference models are created using ontologies and annotations to describe the optimal conditions of assets and products as well as reference to the context and processes where they operate. The ontology describes the basic entities of Z-Bre4k and models relevant structures of manufacturing systems and processes, establishing a methodological framework for modeling not only the actors and procedures at the shop floor, but also machinery and their critical components, their failure modes and their criticality, their signatures of healthy and deteriorated conditions and so on. Moreover, innovation lies in the application of quality control data as an enrichment information for the implementation of more robust predictions of future equipment and process condition. Asset/product/process signatures are also supported as a collection of reference structures and several conditions snapshots representing optimal and deteriorated conditions can be detected through the production operations. In that regard, the Knowledge Base (KB) used for data analysis is the central module of the system, and includes context-aware ontology and algorithms to support predictive maintenance and extended operating lives of assets in production facilities and the relevant decision support system that endows wisdom to the Z-Bre4k approach by making use of historical data and the acquired knowledge for all the operations occurred.

33.2. I-LiKe machines framework

The overall structure of the maintenance planning support tool will be based on Holonix I-LiKe machines, a web based platform aimed at the monitoring of industrial machines and production lines. It offers the possibility of retrieving, organizing and visualizing, almost in real time, all the data that are relevant to know the history and the current status of a machine/system in order to monitor the status of the production machine, alerting them in case of problems. Within the Z-Bre4K project, the condition monitoring will be integrated with a semantic description of machines and systems, in order to develop a Knowledge Base System (KBS) including simple rules and degradation models to support maintenance planning/scheduling. The core of I-LiKe machines consists of a cloud platform, a set of gateways to read data from the field and a set of web and mobile apps to present the data to the users. The cloud platform is in charge of storing relevant information collected during the machines' operating life, maintaining a complete representation, at any moment, of the machines' current status and keeping track of the machines' status history. Anomalous conditions can be identified, and notifications to the users and maintainers about them can be sent. In the current configuration, no prediction related to the status of a machine and/or its components can be done in order to set up a predictive maintenance plan based on the actual conditions of a component.

In order to feed the cloud platform, data must be collected from the machines and production lines. This is achieved by implementing a software component (gateway) that talks to the machines, does the basic computations that are easy to be performed with low latency access to the machine and sends the data in a secure way to the cloud platform adhering to its API. This part is often customized to the specific machine, as protocols might change across various machine types and might be proprietary. It can reside on hardware already present on the machines or on embedded systems added on purpose. On top of the cloud platform, domain-specific web and mobile apps can be built. In the Z-Bre4K framework, a specific monitoring mobile app for the end users will be developed, showing in a user friendly interface the current status of the machines/components, its recent history (alarms, stops, maintenance operations) and the approaching critical conditions, sending notifications and triggering alarms.

33.3. Semantic model

The main approach of Z-Bre4k is based upon exploitation of various data sources (component, machine, production, quality, product and business data) and access to different aspects of machinery and process-related data and knowledge. Its innovation lies in the incorporation of various domains of knowledge in the way of semantic knowledge representation formalisms. In the main architecture of Z-Bre4k, the semantic model plays the role of the backbone of the entire platform in the middleware and will be implemented in the form of ontology. Ontology is defined as "an explicit, formal specification of a shared conceptualization of a domain of interest" [GRU 93]. An ontology serves to enable machines to understand context in the way of interoperability and description of a meta-model. Establishing a methodological framework, the Z-Bre4k ontology delivers the meta-model describing not only the actors and procedures at the shop floor, but also machinery and their critical components, their failure modes and their criticality, their signature of healthy and deteriorated conditions and so on. The Knowledge Base System (KBS) which stores data with the fundamental principles of the Z-Bre4k ontology, provides semantic features and context for each individual data. In addition, it facilitates semantic enrichment (e.g. annotations, tagging), active exploration of the linked data sets, and implicit knowledge discovery.

To recognize the semantic context of data brings values as follows: (1) end users can easily recognize and identify the meaning of data individuals and search meaningful data; (2) SW developers can harmonize data from various sources and request required data for each system component, and facilitate the design of machine-understandable components in an intelligent engine; and (3) requirements of end users can be satisfied since knowledge representation acts as a bridge between end users of an SW platform and platform developers for design to meet the requirements of end users. In addition, a semantic model as domain knowledge representation has features of (1) information extraction, (2) reasoning or inference, (3) correct information placement, (4) explicitness and disambiguating context, (5) power of inheritance, and (6) reuse of domain knowledge. To encourage the semantic achievement, the Z-Bre4k platform requires a special data storage to deal with triplex collections. One of the common frameworks for implementation of triple store is the Resource Description Framework (RDF), which is a standard model for data interchange on the web. In the Z-Bre4k semantic Framework, the RDF repository is in the form of Triplestore, which is designed to store and retrieve identities conducted from triplex collections representing a subject-predicate-object relationship [RUS 01]. The Triplestore database will be integrated in the I-LiKe machines cloud structure. All the semantic data from the Z-Bre4k main repository will be stored in the RDF repository, referring to Z-Bre4k ontology.

Following the structure of Z-Bre4k ontology, semantic data individuals will be stored with a subject-predicate-object relationship. Semantic Web Service components will support management of the RDF repository in the way of search, authentication, dataset, revision, and SPARQL. To follow this approach, the Z-Bre4k platform will achieve semantic enrichment. In the Z-Bre4k Semantic Framework, the Z-Bre4k ontology 1) provides the main structure of triplex as a reference model and 2) provides semantic parameters and enables querying to satisfy the requirements of the maintenance planning support tool. The Z-Bre4k Ontology consists of three kinds of entities: Information Entities, Physical Entities and Failure Mechanism Entities (see Figure 33.1). Information Entities consider condition monitoring, managing sensor data, its history and key performance parameters, whereas Physical Entities will manage the information of a physical structure of the target product to achieve semantic enrichments of 3D measurement. In addition, Failure Mechanism entities represent effects and symptoms of each failure mode following the IEC 60812 which is the international standard of Failure Mode, Effects, and Criticality Analysis (FMECA) published by International Electrotechnical Commission. This logical diagram will be specialized and customized in the context of different business cases in Z-Bre4k.

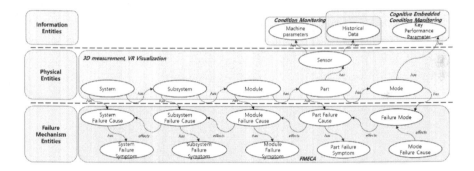

Figure 33.1. *Logical diagram of Z-Bre4k semantic model. For a color version of this figure, see www.iste.co.uk/zelm/enterprise.zip*

33.4. Demonstration scenario

The approach for predictive maintenance proposed in this study will be demonstrated on a Continuous Compression Molding (CCM) machine produced by SACMI, an international group manufacturing machines and complete plants for the ceramics, packaging, and food industries. This kind of machine is used to produce bottle caps with a productivity up to 2000 caps/min. It is quite clear, with such a high productivity, how the correct execution and timing of maintenance activities are crucial to minimize downtimes and maximize the useful life of components. Thermoplastic pellets are first mixed, prepared and melted. The compound passing through the extruder, where it is plasticized, is then cut into suitable size pellets and inserted into cavities. A hydraulic system clamps the moulds: clamping pressure can also be adjusted during the production cycle.

After an identification of the most common failure modes, data will be acquired from the machines and complementary sensors to monitor failure related parameters, that is, vibrations, absorbed energy and so on. All this information will be stored in the novel condition monitoring module, used to establish rules according to the developed knowledge base system, and relevant indicators will be visualized in the properly developed application.

33.5. Conclusion

In this study, a methodology is proposed to address the need for predictive maintenance, which is becoming more and more relevant in the current framework of flexible and non-repetitive manufacturing. The approach developed in the framework of the EU H2020 Z-Bre4k project is based on condition monitoring of machines/components, acquiring machine/sensor data and sending them to the cloud where they will be stored and represented in an ontological framework. Ontology will be used also to represent failure modes and criticalities. This will enable the development of a knowledge-based system to identify healthy as well as deteriorated conditions, supporting the design of a proper condition-based maintenance plan.

33.6. Acknowledgments

This work has been carried out in the framework of the Z-Bre4k Project, which has received funding from the European Union's Horizon 2020 research and innovation programme under grant agreement no. 768869.

33.7. References

[GRU 93] GRUBER T.R., "A translation approach to portable ontology specifications", *Knowledge Acquisition*, vol. 5, no. 2, pp. 199–220, 1993.

[HER 16] HERMANN M., PENTEK T., OTTO B., "Design Principles for Industry 4.0 Scenarios", *49th Hawaii International Conference on System Sciences (HICSS)*, 2016.

[LEE 14] LEE J., KAO H.A., YANG S., "Service Innovation and Smart Analytics for Industry 4.0 and Big Data Environment", *Procedia CIRP*, vol. 16, pp. 3–8, 2014.

[MON 14] MONOSTORI L., "Cyber-physical production systems: roots, expectations and R&D challenges", *Procedia CIRP*, vol. 17, pp. 9–13, 2014.

[RUS 01] RUSHER J., Triple Store, World Wide Web Consortium, http://www.w3. org/2001/sw/Europe/events/20031113-storage/positions/rusher.html, 2001.

[ZHO 15] ZHOU K., LIU T., ZHOU L., "Industry 4.0: Towards future industrial opportunities and challenges", *12th International Conference on Fuzzy Systems and Knowledge Discovery*, August, 2015.

[ZBR 17] Z-Bre4k, https://www.z-bre4k.eu/, 2017.

34

SERENA: Versatile Plug-and-Play Platform Enabling Remote Predictive Maintenance

The increasing complexity of modern engineering systems and manufacturing processes remains a challenge to operating production systems at high levels of reliability. The maintenance of manufacturing assets remains a critical function of every production system since the related cost often reaches 60–70% of its overall lifecycle cost.

Machinery maintenance can cause costly disruptions in the manufacturing process. With predictive analytics, however, repairs and maintenance tasks can be prioritized and allocated to pre-planned outages based on real-time probabilities of various future failures. The strategy of predictive maintenance saves time and money and helps minimize costly production downtimes.

Modern technology in the context of Industry 4.0, including sensors and embedded systems, data analytics and advanced networking, are key enabling technologies towards minimizing downtime of the production system. Empowered by the aforementioned, this study discusses a conceptual framework of a predictive maintenance approach based on equipment condition-based modeling and evaluation, as a step towards reducing breakdowns as well as the overall maintenance costs, through a more efficient time scheduling of the maintenance operations.

Chapter written by Sotirios MAKRIS, Nikolaos NIKOLAKIS, Konstantinos DIMOULAS, Apostolos PAPAVASILEIOU and Massimo IPPOLITO.

34.1. Introduction

The growing complexity of modern engineering systems and manufacturing processes [CHR 06] is an obstacle to conceptualizing and implementing Intelligent Manufacturing Systems (IMS) and thus keeping these systems operating at high levels of reliability. Additionally, the number of sensors and the amount of data gathered on the factory floor constantly increases [SIP 16], while there are also hidden resources: 85% of data and information are unstructured and 42% of all transactions (sending and receiving information) are still based on paper [THE 15]. This opens the vision of truly connected production processes where all machinery data are accessible, allowing easier maintenance of them in case of unexpected events. SERENA will build upon these needs to save time and money, minimizing the costly production downtimes.

34.2. State of the art and progress beyond

In the literature, several approaches on predictive maintenance platforms have been introduced (e.g. [SPE 17, LIN 17]) but they fail to adequately address the fundamental tension between the flexibility to host many applications, the need of security privacy, data transmission and the user's limited control and management. Condition-based predictive maintenance represent the maintenance approach supported by sensor measurements [COL 14]. The collaboration between IT tools can be enabled and facilitated through mobile technology and communication [MOU 14].

Advantages of cloud computing include the virtualization of resources, parallel processing, security of data and service integration, thus minimizing the cost and restriction for automation and maintenance infrastructure [CHI 13]. An integrated predictive maintenance platform is proposed in [EFT 12], consisting of three main pillars: (1) data acquisition, extraction and analysis; (2) maintenance modeling, knowledge modeling and representation; and (3) advisory capabilities on maintenance planning with emphasis on environmental and energy performance indicators. A semantic framework for predictive maintenance in a cloud environment is introduced in [SCH 17]. The proposed framework is focused on improving decision support in maintenance operations and enabling prediction-as-a-service through data collection, analysis and knowledge sharing. In a similar approach, a condition-based maintenance policy is discussed in [SHI 15] that makes a diagnosis of the asset status using monitored data to predict the asset's abnormalities and executing suitable maintenance actions before serious problems occur. A dynamic predictive maintenance framework is presented in [HOR 13] that deals with decision making and optimization in multi-component systems taking into account the degradation as well as the dependencies of each subcomponent of the multi-component system.

Moving beyond the existing state of the art, the proposed solutions with SERENA cover the requirements for versatility, transferability, remote monitoring and control by: 1) a plug-and-play cloud-based communication platform for managing the data and data processing remotely; 2) an advanced IoT system and smart devices for data collection and monitoring of machinery conditions; 3) artificial intelligent methods for predictive maintenance (data analytics, machine learning) and planning of maintenance and production activities; and 4) AR-based technologies for supporting the human operator for maintenance activities and monitoring of the production machinery status (Figure 34.1).

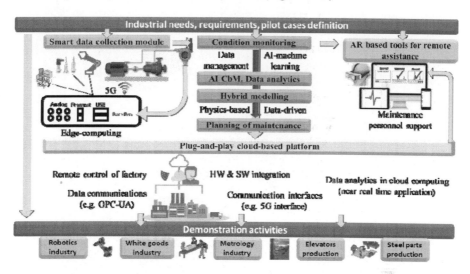

Figure 34.1. *SERENA technologies overview. For a color version of this figure, see www.iste.co.uk/zelm/enterprise.zip*

34.3. Pilot case description

The SERENA solutions, enabling the predictive maintenance concept, will be tested and evaluated in different industrial sectors. The following section will describe the application in the robotics and white goods industry.

34.3.1. Robotics industry use case

Currently, the maintenance plan of industrial robots tends to follow mostly the preventive maintenance concept leading to over-maintained machines and thus increased maintenance costs and downtime. The purpose of SERENA is to predict the possible failures of an industrial robot which is executing repeatedly a pick-and-place operation in advance of the actual event. This will be achieved by creating normal operation and failure profiles based on sensor data. Physical models (Figure 34.2) will be created in order to digitally simulate the whole process. The correlation between the two data types, real-world and simulation-driven, will provide a basis for estimating the degradation of the machine as well as its condition.

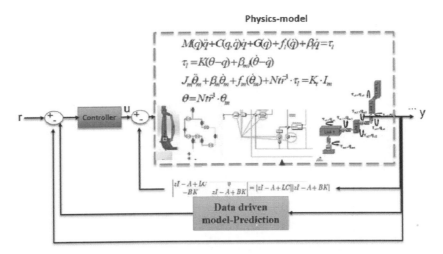

Figure 34.2. *Proposed hybrid approach for predictive maintenance.*
For a color version of this figure, see www.iste.co.uk/zelm/enterprise.zip

The use of AR technologies ([MIC 15, MAK 16]) can support the operators during a maintenance activity. By using smart AR glasses the employees' hands remain always free and all information is displayed right in front of them. Through the same software system and with different authorization levels, equipment providers may provide remote assistance to factory personnel, while field operators, running client side applications on mobile devices, will be provided by an overview of the machine and equipment condition, as well as maintenance-related instructions if needed (Figure 34.3).

Experts can directly connect to the ego-perspective of the employees and guide them through maintenance tasks. The operators will be supported with instructions regarding maintenance/repairing activities *in situ*, reducing thus the time and cost for maintenance service from the machine provider. The SERENA solutions provide a first approach to prognostics on specific machines, enabling the condition-based and the predictive maintenance approach.

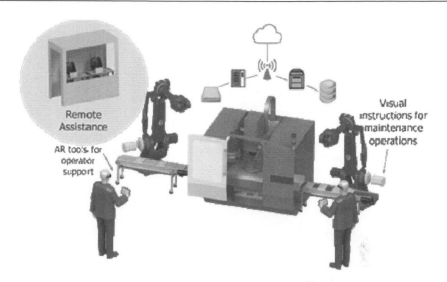

Figure 34.3. *AR-based technologies for remote assistance and human operator support . For a color version of this figure, see www.iste.co.uk/zelm/enterprise.zip*

34.3.2. *White goods industry use case*

The white goods use case will focus on the refrigerator cabinet polyurethane foaming, the core process in fabricating refrigerators and one of the most complex processes in the white goods industry. Computational Intelligence (CI) and Data Mining Technologies (DMT) are required in order to cope with this changing complexity and simplify the decision-making processes with regards to machine maintenance (Figure 34.4).

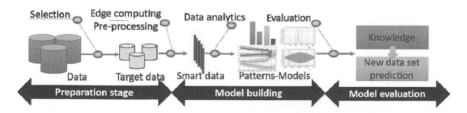

Figure 34.4. *AI condition-based maintenance and planning techniques. For a color version of this figure, see www.iste.co.uk/zelm/enterprise.zip*

Hybrid models consisting of a combination of physics-based and data driven approaches are to be considered in this pilot for increased prediction accuracy. The corrective maintenance activities shall cope with the production activities and thus an intelligent decision making framework is proposed for scheduling and planning the maintenance activities to take place with respect to the existing production orders.

34.4. Acknowledgments

This research has been supported by the project "SERENA – VerSatilE plug and play platform enabling REmote predictive mainteNAnce" (Grand Agreement: 767561) (http://serena-project.eu/) funded by the European Commission. The authors would also like to express their gratitude to the SERENA consortium for the valuable information and assistance they have provided.

34.5. References

[CHI 13] CHIH-WEI L., CHIH-MING H., CHIH-HUNG C. *et al.*, "An Improvement to Data Service in Cloud Computing with Content Sensitive Transaction Analysis and Adaption", *IEEE 37th Annual, Computer Software and Applications Conference Workshops (COMPSACW)*, pp. 463–468, 2013.

[CHR 06] CHRYSSOLOURIS G., *Manufacturing Systems: Theory and Practice*, 2nd ed., Springer-Verlag, New York, 2006.

[COL 14] COLLEDANI M., TOLIO T., FISCHER A. *et al.*, "Design and management of manufacturing systems for production quality", *CIRP ANNALS – Manufacturing Technology*, vol. 63, pp. 773–796, 2014.

[EFT 12] EFTHYMIOU K., PAPAKOSTAS N., MOURTZIS D. *et al.*, "On a Predictive Maintenance Platform for Production Systems", *Procedia CIRP*, vol. 3, pp. 221–226, 2012.

[HOR 13] HORENBEEK A., VAN L., PINTELON L., "A dynamic predictive maintenance policy for complex multi-component systems", *Reliability Engineering and System Safety*, vol. 120, pp. 39–50, 2013.

[LIN 17] LINDSTROM J., LARSOON H., JOHNSSON M. *et al.*, "Towards intelligent and sustainable production: combining and integrating online predictive maintenance and continuous quality control", *Procedia CIRP*, vol. 63, pp. 443–448, 2017.

[MAK 16] MAKRIS S., KARAGIANNIS P., KOUKAS S. *et al.*, "Augmented reality system for operator support in human-robot collaborative assembly", *CIRP Annals – Manufacturing Technology*, vol. 65, pp. 61–64, 2016.

[MIC 15] MICHALOS G., KARAGIANNIS P., MAKRIS S. *et al.*, "Augmented Reality (AR) Applications for Supporting Human-Robot Interactive Cooperation", *CIRP Conference on Manufacturing Systems (CMS)*, vol. 41, pp. 370–375, 2015.

[MOU 14] MOURTZIS D., DOUKAS M., VANDERA C., "Mobile applications for product customization and design of manufacturing networks", *ELSEVIER Manufacturing Letters*, vol. 2, pp. 30–34, 2014.

[SCH 17] SCHMIDT B., WANG L., GALAR D., "Semantic framework for predictive maintenance in a cloud environment", *Procedia CIRP*, vol. 62, pp. 583–588, 2017.

[SHI 15] SHIN J., JUN H., "On condition based maintenance policy", *Journal of Computational Design and Engineering*, vol. 2, pp. 119–127, 2015.

[SIP 16] SIPSAS K., ALEXOPOULOS K., XANTHAKIS V. *et al.*, "Collaborative maintenance in flow-line manufacturing environments: An Industry 4.0 approach", *Procedia CIRP*, vol. 55, pp. 236–241, 2016.

[SPE 17] SPENDLA L., KEBISEK M., TANUSKA P. *et al.*, "Concept of Predictive Maintenance of Production Systems in Accordance with Industry 4.0", *IEEE 15th International Symposium on Applied Machine Intelligence and Informatics (SAMI)*, pp. 405–410, 2017.

[THE 15] THEORIN A., BENGTSSON K., PROVOST J. *et al.*, "An Event-Driven Manufacturing Information System Architecture", *IFAC-PapersOnLine*, vol. 48, pp. 547–554, 2015.

DRIFT: A Data-driven Failure Mode, Effects and Criticality Analysis Tool

DRIFT is a tool that, on the basis of maintenance related information gathered for a target equipment, performs a FMECA, that is, it identifies what are the Failure Modes, Effects and Criticalities of components and systems.

35.1. Introduction

FMEA (Failure Modes and Effects Analysis) and FMECA (Failure Modes Effects and Criticality Analysis) are bottom-up analytical approaches to system design that are used to assess failure impacts. To do so, such analysis methods define and estimate the occurrence probability of each failure mode providing an evaluation of its consequences.

This approach was formally developed in the 1940s by the U.S. military forces and become famous because it was used by NASA for the Apollo program. Nowadays it is widely used, mostly in avionic and automotive industries.

FMEA and FMECA start from the identification of the failure modes (i.e. how something can break down or fail) associated with each component of an equipment and analyze the impact of such failures on the whole system according to its physical and logical design; failure occurrence probability is then estimated on the basis of simulations or historical records. The combination of these elements gives feedback on the reliability of the chosen design identifying weak elements for which improvements are needed[1]. The target of this analysis is to reduce the consequences

---

Chapter written by Davide Zanardi, Manuele Barbieri and Giovanni Uguccioni.
1 To be held typically at Preliminary Design Review (PDR) phase.

of critical failures; this is not only applicable to physical systems but also to processes as well.

35.1.1. *Existing approaches and tools*

There are different standards that deal with FMEA and FMECA issued by the major associations or authorities. The most popular are:

– MIL-STD-1629A issued by the U.S. Department of Defense in 1980 which is an evolution of the first standardization dated 1949;

– AIAG FMEA-4 issued in 2008 by the Automotive Industry Action Group (AIAG); next issue expected in Q2 2018;

– SAE J-1739 and ARP5580 issued by the Society of Automotive Engineers (SAE): J-1739 is specific for surface vehicles, ARP5580 is a collection of recommended best practices for non-automobile applications;

– IEC 60812 issued in 2006 by the International Electro-technical Commission (IEC).

The operative approach to FMECA is almost the same for all the standards and consists, as already introduced above, in identifying and collecting all the equipment failure modes to be organized in a working table. Rankings are given to quantify the severity of their occurrence with respect to different aspects that go from safety issues to operative/economical aspects; the consequence on the system are tracked having in mind both its physical and logical block diagrams; probability of occurrence and probability of detection are evaluated and ranked as well. The result is to provide an evaluation of the risk associated with each failure mode that is then calculated as the simple product of the severity, occurrence and detection ratings in the so-called Risk Priority Number (RPN):

$$RPN = Severity * Occurrence * Detection \qquad [35.1]$$

There are many tools available for FMEA and FMECA that guide the user in the compilation of the tables according to the different standards available but – since the mathematical approach is quite simple – many industries have developed their own software typically tailored to their own needs and business.

35.2. The DRIFT tool

DRIFT is a complex database that contains a collection of items and related reliability data (failure rate, active repair time and downtime) obtained from reliability databases internationally recognized (i.e. OREDA DB). So far, it has been used for classical FMECA analysis in different projects especially for the Oil and Gas industry.

The analysis is performed considering the most relevant failure modes associated with the project's equipment (e.g. static equipment and/or rotating machineries) through a precompiled fit-to-purpose worksheet. DRIFT provides two main capabilities:

– *Library Capability* that allows the FMECA engineers to collect and characterize information from several sources; a specific configuration section allows the engineer to customize frequencies of occurrence, severity and Risk Matrix creating a FMECA Evaluation Model to be deployed in a project;

– *Project Capability* that allows the user to conduct a FMECA project by instantiating one or more item characterized in the Library, inheriting in this way associated failure modes and rates. When starting a new project the list of items and relative associated failure modes has to be selected; each equipment under analysis is therefore linked to a reference item thus automatically charging the rows associated to it.

The current version of DRIFT implements the FMECA methodology and algorithms described in the document 158844-SA-3J00-HS-001 – FAILURE MODE, EFFECT AND CRITICALITY ANALYSIS (FMECA); this Methodology is compliant to the following standards: MIL-STD-1629A an IEC 60812. The tool is actually thought as a stand-alone software.

35.2.1. *The UPTIME project*

UPTIME project is a Horizon 2020 European project started in Autumn 2017 that aims to build a complete framework for the definition of predictive maintenance strategies. This framework will include the definition of sets of sensors to be deployed on target systems for real-time strategic data acquisition and storage; such strategic information will support that collected by PLC systems – that drive and supervise process execution – in order to build a pool of data where big data analysis techniques could be used for monitoring and detecting early warning signals that machines or systems are degrading or are in danger of breakdown.

UPTIME will enable manufacturing companies to reach Gartner's level 4 of data analytics maturity ("optimized decision-making") in order to improve physically-based models and to synchronize maintenance with quality management, production planning and logistics options. In this way, it will optimize in-service efficiency through reduced failure rates and downtime due to repair, unplanned plant/production system outages and extension of component life. Moreover, it will contribute to increased accident mitigation capability since it will be able to avoid crucial breakdowns with significant consequences.

35.3. DRIFT value within the UPTIME project

Within the UPTIME project, DRIFT will contribute to the project goals (i.e. to provide maintenance recommendations along with appropriate logistics, production and quality-related advices) by interacting with the Diagnosis and Prognosis service and providing a continuous improvement mechanism through its data-driven FMECA approach. Typically FMECA activities start in the early design stage of the system and should continue throughout the whole life cycle but this is rarely done. For complex systems, FMECA results are given as input to the logistic support studies that define the needed maintenance procedures (both corrective and preventive) and that will size the spare part supplies and warehouse.

Currently, there is not any FMECA software tool integrated in a unified maintenance information system under a complete predictive maintenance framework as the UPTIME project is proposing. Therefore, the integration of the tool in the loop is an innovation per se: DRIFT is fed with data from action-related information collected from the industrial operation management phases (design, logistics and production info); it provides inputs to the Diagnosis and Prognosis, thus linking e-maintenance services and e-operations using the incorporated algorithms for the identification of potentially relevant and critical failures modes. The algorithms per se are not innovative: they are based on almost state of the art and literature available. What is new is the capability to use them "live" in an automatized way and the capability to work with huge amounts of data that will be generated in the process.

DRIFT tool will interface the other UPTIME components according to the functions/interfaces schema shown in Figure 35.1.

The DRIFT Local DB component imports relevant data from the UPTIME Data Storage and Times Series DBs: out-of-threshold parameter list, asynchronous external events and configuration parameters. The main functions have been allocated to two components:

– The Active Functions Manager that provides FMECA Analysis capability through periodic evaluation of current and evolving risk;

– The Passive Functions Manager that provides FMECA feedback capability interfacing with other system functionalities (i.e. product-tree, RBD (Reliability Block Diagrams) schema, parameter-threshold, downtime and prevention and mitigation analysis).

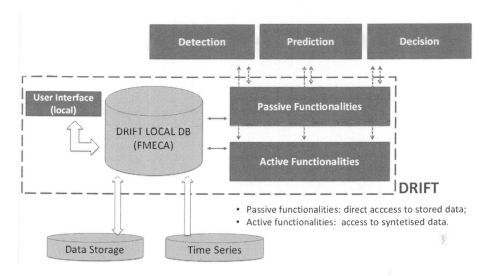

Figure 35.1. *DRIFT functionalities within UPTIME Project. For a color version of this figure, see www.iste.co.uk/zelm/enterprise.zip*

35.4. Predictive maintenance scenarios

DRIFT as part of the UPTIME tool will be validated on three different business cases each with different conditions and with different data, thus allowing to some extent the demonstration of its scalability and replication:

– complex automatic production line to produce drums for dryers;

– cold rolling mill stands for the production of rolling products;

– hoisting and lifting equipment for maintenance in the avionic sector.

In highly mechanized assembly lines, PLCs control every step of the production process: the controls are punctual and practically every movement of the apparatus can be brought under control. This means that any deviations from the expected nominal behavior result in a stop in the chain: the process will hardly interrupt because something has broken; most likely human errors or product defects will create issues. For such systems, qualitative measures of the different phases of the production could also be used as input parameters to understand how the whole system is working; a way to detect and manage the human factor should be assessed as well.

The challenge in the next years of the project is to define and validate models that could link the measures – both physical and qualitative – to the failure rate of components in a way that goes beyond the simple definition of thresholds that could lead to generic warnings or alarms; such models should also take into account that local measures could affect distributed areas according to the product tree and RDB schemas.

For that purpose, DRIFT models will define – at a first approach – simplified equipment models that could be as general as possible in order to be used for different equipment/lines for each business case foreseen in UPTIME project, that is:

– press and handling system;

– rolling mill system;

– hoisting system.

35.5. Conclusion

FMECA analysis has been used so far as a powerful instrument to design resilient equipment. However, once put in real life conditions, such equipment doesn't match the expected performance in terms of overall failure rates. DRIFT tool aims to take FMECA in-line – within a predictive maintenance approach – using a simplified set of (mechanical) models to evaluate the operational environment effects on the equipment life span.

35.6. References

MIL-STD-1629A, Military Standard: Procedures for Performing a Failure Mode, Effects, and Criticality Analysis (1980)

AIAG FMEA-4, Potential Failure Mode & Effects Analysis FMEA Reference Manual (4th Edition) (2008)

SAE J-1739, Potential Failure Mode and Effects Analysis in Design (Design FMEA), Potential Failure Mode and Effects Analysis in Manufacturing and Assembly Processes (Process FMEA) (2009)

ARP5580, Recommended Failure Modes and Effects Analysis (FMEA) Practices for Non-Automobile Applications (2001)

IEC 60812, Analysis techniques for system reliability – Procedure for failure mode and effects analysis (FMEA) (2006)

UPRIME PROJECT, https://www.uptime-h2020.eu/ (2017)

36

Real-time Predictive Maintenance Based on Complex Event Processing

With the progress in the computation technologies, new information and communications technologies (ICT) have emerged in the last decade. These new technologies open and offer the opportunities to deal with complex technical systems and hence to implement real-time predictive maintenance. Indeed, the purpose of real-time predictive maintenance is the fast identification and classification of possible incipient faults and their locations. In this context, we introduce the concept of complex event processing in the field of predictive maintenance. This concept enables a surveillance of the system state in real-time using complex event processing technology, identifies fault causes and evaluates the condition of the technical components. On the basis of this information, various maintenance measures can be initiated within the framework of maintenance planning. In doing so, the presented approach proposes a method for identifying the relevant amount of states to be monitored.

36.1. Introduction

Maintenance management has changed from being a pure cost driver to a cross-company business process. It is actively involved in the value creation of a company; both in the interest of the producer as well as of the operator. To be able to compete economically against global competition, a high reliability of machines and plants with concomitant reduction of machine downtime is an absolute must for today's production. The development of a Maintenance Management System is, however, a challenging and complicated task, due to a high degree of system complexity in

Chapter written by Klaus-Dieter Thoben, Abderrahim Ait-Alla, Marco Franke, Karl Hribernik, Michael Lütjen and Michael Freitag.

combination with dynamic processes and probabilistic disturbances like machine failure. This complicates the creation of a holistic system model and thus also the optimization of decision making in the maintenance management system. Furthermore, the failures of individual components can have an effect on other components, subsystems and even on the entire system. In these cases, a decision has to be made in real time concerning which measures have to be taken to avoid this or to repair the affected resource. To this end, Condition-Based Maintenance (CBM) is a conceptual approach that aims at surveying the dynamic behavior of a system or of individual components by means of online monitoring, thus deducing the system state or the corresponding degree of wear and tear. Subsequently, the planning of the maintenance measures can be undertaken within the framework of condition-based maintenance and under consideration of the priorities, maintenance and work volume as well as the existing resources. So far, this is already a good solution for individual components where various methodological approaches are being used (e.g. Signal Processing and Dynamic Scheduling).

When looking at complex systems, however, the consideration of all interdependencies between subsystems represent a significant criterion. Furthermore, the amount of state-driven data of a complex system is so high that existing predictive maintenance approaches cannot handle it in real time. Therefore, the batch processing approach that uses data storage and a subsequent processing must be exchanged through an approach, which works on data streams and generates only a subset of data describing the relevant information. To this end, there is a significant need for the development of formal methods and concepts that consider the entire system and systematically combine individual streams of information to derive further information. In this context, Complex Event Processing (CEP) operates on events instead of state information. It creates a new approach, which puts the arising events in relation with each other based on event patterns using predictive analytics and data mining methods. Furthermore, it analyzes these newly created complex events in real time. The objective of this paper is the introduction of the concept of complex event processing in the field of predictive maintenance. This concept enables a surveillance of the system state in real-time using CEP technology, identifies fault causes and evaluates the condition of the technical components. Based on this information, various maintenance measures can be initiated within the framework of maintenance planning. In general, CEP was initially used in the finance sector, but it can also be applied to other areas (especially in Business Activity Monitoring, and sensor networks). The use of CEP technology requires the development of new information landscapes that are based on event-driven architecture.

In the following, we present the basics of data stream processing in CEP. Based on the general motivation and the presented data stream processing, the problem statement is defined. To solve the challenge, a method for identifying the relevant amount of events for real-time CEP is presented. Subsequently, the possible implementation is shown on available frameworks. Finally, a conclusion and outlook are given.

36.2. CEP approach

Nowadays, real-time data mining processes including data acquisition, classification, assimilation and correlation can be almost completely automated at reasonable cost with modern computing technologies [NYA 13]. However, the most important challenge in dealing with real-time decision-making systems is the processing of huge amounts of multivariate, nonlinear and often sub-optimally structured data. Today, the majority of complex systems like wind turbines are equipped with various sensors that measure different components to detect their condition so that the system may react to and prevent undesired behavior. This has been empowered by the shift of maintenance strategies from cyclic and corrective policies where maintenance activities are carried out after the occurrence of failures, towards condition-based maintenance (CBM) which uses condition monitoring systems to observe different indicators that can describe the health condition of the system [OEL 16]. Processing the data collected in this way can help both identify unexpected states as well as consequent faulty behaviors that can lead to problems in the systems. These unexpected states can be defined as complex events that describe the change in the systems and which can be detected through the processing of different basic events. Luckham [LUC 08] basically defines the notion of the event as an object representing a record of an activity. In the CEP context, an event is therefore a discrete occurrence of an activity. In this context, each data occurrence can be considered as a basic or simple event, which alone doesn't contain meaningful information. In order to feed the CEP system with basic events, an event adapter transforms the emitted data from different data source to basic events, which have a common format for further processing. These basic events create a so-called event cloud. By applying methods of stream processing, the event cloud can be monitored in real-time and analyzed to extract features in form of high level or complex events, which can indicate some undesired system changes [LUC 08]. In this context, complex events reflect any relevant possible change in the system's behavior. Most conventional processing methods cannot manage the huge amount of condition data continuously generated by the sensors in real time, but stream processing allows processing data in real-time. Event-driven architectures are designed to process events. A novel approach for the dynamic processing of complex events (CEP) was developed on that basis. The main task of CEP is the extraction of patterns from events to identify which events indicate a change in a system or the malfunction of a machine. To realize real-time predictive maintenance based on an event-driven architecture using CEP (Figure 36.1), data from different sensors in a complex system is streamed into the event processing engine.

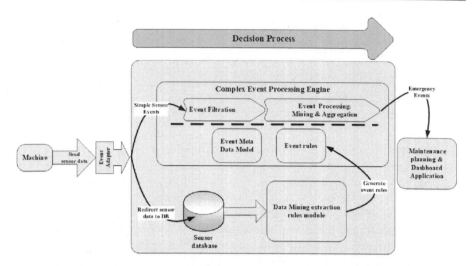

Figure 36.1. *Process flow of a complex event processing system*

This data is then transformed into events based on the event adapter that feeds an event stream or cloud. The sensor data is simultaneously stored in a persistent database via batch processing. The CEP engine detects events by extracting event patterns from the event cloud which indicate a change in a system or the malfunction of a machine. The events have to be filtered for redundancy and sensor errors, since the sensors can themselves be subject to malfunction. An event model is used to describe abstract definitions of events. Event rules describe the causal, temporal, and spatial relationship between different levels of event abstraction. In this case, the complex events represent a high level of abstraction and the basic events a low level of abstraction. A processing engine with an SQL-like language is used to detect complex events by aggregation and correlation of events (Figure 36.1). An offline data mining extraction rules module (batch processing module) is used to generate the event rules. Typically, the deployment of the data mining extraction rules module alone is sufficient to detect system behavior. However, the processing of incoming data from sensors in real-time is not adequate for a timely response to emergencies, because data is first stored in a database and then queried, which is a relatively time-consuming operation. For that reason, real-time processing is guaranteed by applying the module as a rule extraction tool, and afterwards, using those rules in event processing.

36.3. Approach for deriving relevant events

The objective of this approach is to achieve the applicability of existing data streaming capabilities into the CEP, in cases where a huge amount of data have to be processed. In doing so, the requirements with respect to scalability and guaranteed real-time capabilities have to be met. To achieve both requirements, the proposed approach focuses only on the analysis of the relevant subset of incoming data. The data relevant to CEP must be defined to understand which incoming data are relevant and which data can be skipped during stream analysis. The chosen subset must allow the identification of states which define a fault state, a sequence of states which will result definitely in a fault state as well as a sequence of states which will result with a specific presumption into a fault state. The last two identification capabilities are necessary to enable predictive maintenance methods on top of CEP. The proposed approach doesn't use general anomaly detection or classification algorithms which detect differences from usual data streams on the initial run but rather explicitly defines the relevant amount of parameters, relevant parameter values and thresholds for usage scenarios. The corresponding method is presented in Figure. 36.2. Data is acquired from both a file system as well as data streams. The file system is used for log data, test models, simulation models and inspection data. All mentioned data sources define the current behaviour (expected or faulty) of a single system on different abstraction levels.

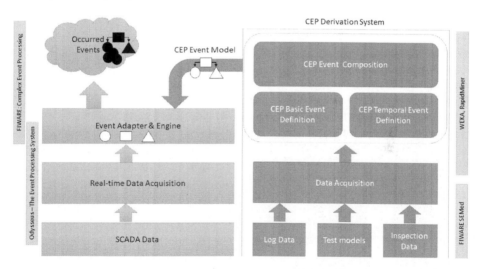

Figure 36.2. *Technologies for method and application of the CEP Derivation System. For a color version of this figure, see www.iste.co.uk/zelm/enterprise.zip*

The content of the data sources is extracted using graph-based methods for each of the information type's relevant parameters, relevant parameters' values, relevant structural relations between parameters and relevant temporal relations. Finally, the common set of events and event compositions including spatial, temporal, and causal relationships, are derived as an event model. Subsequently, the event model is provided to the event adapter and engine to know which events and therefore data must be detectable. As an outcome, the event adapter and engine would know which subset of incoming data have to be analyzed and which subset can be skipped. Moreover, this initial set of events describes which sequences of events will occur until a fault state arises and could be used by an on-top predictive maintenance module.

The proposed approach describes the derivation of an event model without considering specific framework details. Therefore, the integration into a specific framework can cause additional effort with respect to the specific event model. A corresponding demonstrator could be used to evaluate whether the derivation of events are sufficient for a subsequent real-time predictive maintenance, which uses a CEP implementation internally. Examples are given of which frameworks are applicable for the specific CEP implementation.

36.4. Conclusion and outlook

The chapter was motivated by predictive maintenance, which is based on a real-time CEP. To enable a real-time event adapter and engine, the chosen amount and complexity of detectable events needs to be considered. To identify an initial selection of relevant events, the paper proposed a method for event derivation. It is based on static files like log files, test models and so on. Moreover, the paper indicated how the method can be implemented exemplarily for future evaluation. Future work will include setting up and integrating the frameworks as a demonstrator. The derivation of events will be carried out in the exemplary use case of a wind energy turbine. Finally, SCADA data will feed the demonstrator to enable a predictive maintenance.

36.5. References

[LUC 08] LUCKHAM D.C., *The Power of Events: An Introduction to Complex Event Processing in Distributed Enterprise Systems*, Addison-Wesley, Boston, 2008.

[NYA 13] NYANTEH Y., EDRINGTON C., SRIVASTAVA S. *et al.*, "Application of artificial intelligence to real-time fault detection in permanent-magnet synchronous machines", *Industry Applications*, IEEE Transactions, vol. 49, no. 3, pp. 1205–1214, 2013.

[OEL 16] OELKER S., LEWANDOWSKI M., AIT ALLA A. *et al.*, "Preactive Maintenance – A modernized approach for efficient operation of offshore wind turbines", KOTZAB H., THOBEN K.-D. (eds), *Conference Proceedings of the 4th International Conference on Dynamics in Logistics (LDIC 2014)*, Spinger Verlag, Berlin/Heidelberg, 2016.

37

The Standards as Critical Means of Integration of Advanced Maintenance Approaches to Production Systems

This paper focuses on a state of the art regarding standardization for integration of advanced maintenance approaches as predictive maintenance in production and logistics system with an application in the UPTIME project. It positions the different levels of predictive maintenance regarding a larger context of industrial standards recently developed or in the making. A discussion gives a first exploration of the standardization issues at stake to offer the best guarantees of success of deployment of new predictive maintenance platforms on the market.

37.1. Introduction

Predictive maintenance is an additional means to improve the performance and the safety of complex production systems. Maintenance activities being planned and scheduled more accurately, the predictive maintenance process will bring substantial benefits. A set of standards has been recently developed and implementation means compliant with the standards are available. Beyond the impact of standards on the internal components of a predictive maintenance platform, the integration of these means in an overall production information system is the goal of the UPTIME [1] project in order to leverage the outcome of predictive maintenance methods and tools.

Section 37.2 gives a big picture of the standards of interest regarding industrial data for predictive maintenance.

Chapter written by Yves KERARON.

Section 37.3 presents the results of a questionnaire on the standards answered by the members of the UPTIME consortium.

Before our conclusion, Section 37.4 briefly discusses different organizational, methodological and technological issues to be addressed.

37.2. The standardization landscape to be considered

37.2.1. *Predictive maintenance and standardization*

Joël Levitt [2] defines predictive maintenance as "any inspection carried out with high technology tools that use advanced technology to detect when failures occur. Such tools can increase your return and give you some time to intervene before failure". He also writes that "predictive maintenance is how you use the data".

R. Keith Mobley [3] insists on cultural change to benefit from the full potential of predictive maintenance: "predictive technologies should be used as a plant or process optimization tool. In this broader scope, they are used to detect, isolate and provide solutions for all deviations from acceptable performance that result in lost capacity, poor quality, abnormal costs or a threat to employee safety".

Predictive maintenance is all about data, data from different sources which need to be combined to exploit the full potential of the available techniques.

Standardization plays a critical role in enabling this combination of predictive maintenance techniques and fulfiling the promise of an overall improvement of a production system in terms of capacity, safety and environment protection thanks to these advanced techniques.

37.2.2. *Main relevant standards*

Many relevant standards have been published, some quite recently as we can see in the tables below. Table 37.1 gives the generic standards for condition monitoring and diagnostics of machines.

Norm	Topic	Title
ISO 13372: 2012	Vocabulary	
ISO 13374-1: 2003	Data processing, communication and presentation	Part 1: General guidelines
ISO 13374-2: 2007	Data processing, communication and presentation	Part 2: Data Processing

ISO 13374-3: 2012	Data processing, communication and presentation	Part 3: Communication
ISO 13374-4: 2015	Data processing, communication and presentation	Part 4: Presentation
MIMOSA [4] OSA-CBM and OSA-EAI	OSA-CBM Compliant with ISO 13374	
ISO 13379-1: 2012	Data interpretation and diagnostics techniques	Part 1: General guidelines
ISO 13379-2: 2015	Data interpretation and diagnostics techniques	Part 2: Data-driven applications
ISO 13379-3: 2015	Data interpretation and diagnostics techniques	Part 3: Knowledge-based applications
ISO 17359	General guidelines	
ISO 13381-1: 2016	Prognostics	
ISO 13381-2, -3 and -4 (Planned)	Performance changes (trending) approaches (ISO 13381-2), cyclic-driven life usage techniques (ISO 13381-3), and useful-life-remaining models (ISO 13381-4).	
ISO 18129: 2015	Approaches for performance diagnosis	
ISO 18436-1 (-2, -3, -4, -5, -6, -7): 2004	Requirements for qualification and assessment of personnel	Part 1: Requirements for assessment bodies and the assessment process

Table 37.1. *General standards for condition monitoring and diagnostics of machines*

Table 37.2 gives standards specific to vibration condition monitoring.

Vibration monitoring is the most common technique used in predictive maintenance; other techniques are also standardized. As we have seen, the predictive maintenance approach is to combine detection techniques, including operation data and other sources of data for production optimization.

Norm	Topic	Title
ISO 13373-1: 2002	Vibration condition monitoring	Part 1: General procedures
ISO 13373-2: 2016 Published	Vibration condition monitoring	Part 2: Processing, analysis and presentation of vibration data

ISO 13373-3: 2015 Published	Vibration condition monitoring	Part 3: Guidelines for vibration diagnosis
ISO 13373-7: 2015 Published	Vibration condition monitoring	Part 7: Diagnostic techniques for machine sets in hydraulic power generating and pump-storage plants
ISO 10816 (6 parts)	Evaluation of machine vibration by measurements on non-rotating parts	
ISO 7919 -3, -4, -5	Evaluation of machine vibration by measurements on rotating shafts	For different types of machines (Coupled industrial machines,…)

Table 37.2. *Specific standards for vibration condition monitoring*

Table 37.3 gives application integration standards.

ISO 18435-1 defines an integration modeling method and its use to integrate diagnostics, capability assessment, prognostics and maintenance applications with production and control applications. Other parts of ISO 18435 will define the activity domain matrix elements and the detailed integration methods between applications in the application domain integration diagram.

These parts can be helpful to fulfill the ambition of UPTIME in supporting integration with production and logistics Information Systems.

We need also to consider maintenance terminology standards such as EN 13306: 2010 or maintenance vocabulary such as ISO 13372 for a common language of the stakeholders for a successful predictive maintenance approach.

Beyond these standards, attention needs to be given to other initiatives like Industry 4.0 [5], Smart Industry, The Industrial Internet Consortium [6], Usine du futur, or China 2025.

The impact on industry of Internet standards is also critical in this perspective for implementation of predictive maintenance solutions.

Norm	Topic	Title
ISO 18435-1: 200909	Diagnostics, capability assessment and maintenance applications integration	Part 1: Overview and general requirements
ISO 18435-2: 2012	Diagnostics, capability assessment and maintenance applications integration	Part 2: Descriptions and definitions of application domain matrix elements
ISO 18435-3: 2015	Diagnostics, capability assessment and maintenance applications integration	Part 3: Applications integration description method

Table 37.3. *Application integration standards*

37.3. First approach of standardization in UPTIME

37.3.1. *Objectives of the UPTIME project*

UPTIME, Unified Predictive Maintenance system, will enable manufacturing companies, having installed sensors, to fully exploit the availability of huge amounts of data with respect to the implementation of a predictive maintenance strategy. Moreover, production, quality and logistics operations driven by predictive maintenance will benefit from UPTIME. It will optimize in-service efficiency through reduced failure rates and downtime due to repair, unplanned plant/production system outages and extension of component life. Moreover, it will contribute to increased accident mitigation capability since it will be able to avoid crucial breakdown with significant consequences.

UPTIME will exploit the full potential of predictive maintenance management and its interactions with other industrial operations by investigating a unified methodology and by implementing a unified information system addressing the predictive maintenance strategy.

Standardization will clearly play a key role in achieving the unification of processes, methods and tools to aggregate data from different sources and realize the full potential of predictive maintenance techniques.

37.3.2. *Questionnaire on the important standards for the project*

In order to assess the level of knowledge of the UPTIME partners of the standards listed in section 37.2, to get their feedback on the importance according to the stakeholders and to possibly complete this first list of standards, we made a questionnaire and received eight answers from various actors of the partners of the UPTIME project.

The first lessons we can draw at the beginning of the project are the following:

– the level of knowledge of the standards at the beginning of the project is not homogeneous and globally low;

– the stakeholders are aware of the importance of standards for the success of the project:

    - the generic condition monitoring and diagnostics standards and the MIMOSA implementation schema are considered as important;

    - the usage of vocabulary and terminology standards is also identified as particularly important for optimum communication;

    - the broader integration and interoperability standards are perceived as less important.

37.4. Discussion

The number of quite complex standards in the field of maintenance and of industrial data makes it difficult to have a big picture, able to support a vision of a "world class maintenance" [3], and realize the full potential of a predictive maintenance vision as a production systems optimization.

Standardization is also a part of a larger strategic business model approach for platforms developers and for industrial companies.

Communication between and with cyber-physical systems, and semantics for interoperability of the components of the information management system, could be the two most important areas where standardization is necessary to make concrete a vision of the factory of the future where predictive maintenance will fully play its expected role in terms of business benefit.

As we have seen, semantics is perceived by stakeholders as a critical point in order to share a common language and to make automatically interoperable various applications. The ontology-based approach is also an active domain of interest for researchers. For example, El Kadiri and Kiristsis [7] have made a state of the art on ontologies in the context of product lifecycle management and Karray [8] proposed a semantic maintenance architecture based on an ontology.

In a top-down approach, BFO, Basic Formal Ontology, could be used as a top-level ontology with a related maintenance domain ontology, as for instance IMAMO [9].

A bottom-up and rigorous approach, starting from the existing norms, standards and models, using advanced mathematics, will also be needed possibly in the near future to tame the inevitable diversity of the involved models in system engineering in general [10].

W3C standards are already being used, like XML for the MIMOSA CBM schema.

More expressive W3C standards like RDF, RDF-S, OWL 2DL, SPARQL are being used to deal with semantics aspects, to aggregate data from different sources databases and to compute them, as is the case for example in advanced industries like the oil and gas industry in Norway for various information hubs. These standards have also been used for implementation of data integration standards for process industries as developed in the European project OPTIQUE [11] with use cases in energy and oil and gas domains.

37.5. Conclusion

Predictive maintenance is a new promising area where standards will play a major role to draw the full benefit of the approach and to build modular platforms, able to be plugged into various and changing industrial data environments.

One obstacle could be the poor initial knowledge in industry of the new architecture and standards of advanced information management systems but the first feedback from initial industrial experiences is rather positive.

Technically, solutions will soon be available and support the combination of various data for optimized and continuously improved production capacities.

The major obstacle is obviously a cultural one. The capabilities offered by a predictive maintenance approach on one hand and by the advanced information technologies for implementation on the other first need organizational changes, new management approaches and new relationships between stakeholders.

37.6. References

[1] UPTIME PROJECT, https://www.uptime-h2020.eu/, 27 July 2018.

[2] LEVITT J., *Complete guide to preventive and predictive maintenance*, Industrial Press, New York, 2003.

[3] KEITH MOBLEY R., *An introduction to preventive maintenance*, Elsevier Science, Oxford, 2002.

[4] MIMOSA OSA CBM, http://www.mimosa.org/mimosa-osa-cbm, 27 July 2018.

[5] INDUSTRY 4.0 STANDARDS, http://i40.semantic-interoperability.org/, 27 July 2018.

[6] INDUSTRIAL INTERNET CONSORTIUM, http://www.iiconsortium.org/, 2018.

[7] EL KADIRI S., KIRITSIS D., "Ontologies in the context of product lifecycle management: state of the art literature review", *International journal of production research*, vol. 53, no. 18, pp. 5657–5668, 2015.

[8] KARRAY M.H., MORELLO B.C., ZERHOUNI N., "Towards A Maintenance Semantic Architecture", *Proceedings of the 4th World Congress on Engineering Asset Management*, Athens, Greece, 28–30 September 2009.

[9] INDUSTRIAL MAINTENANCE MANAGEMENT ONTOLOGY, http://ieportal.ncor.buffalo.edu/ontologies/IMAMO, 27 July 2018.

[10] BREINER S., SUBRAHMANIANA E., JONES A., "Categorical foundations for system engineering", *15th Annual Conference on Systems Engineering Research Disciplinary Convergence: Implications for Systems Engineering Research*, 2017.

[11] OPTIQUE PROJECT, http://optique-project.eu/about-optique/about-optique, 27 July 2018.

PART 7

Industry 4.0 Qualification

Part 7 Summary:
Industry 4.0 Qualification: Education for the Era of Industry 4.0

The I-ESA2018 workshop on "Industry 4.0 Qualification – Education for the Era of Industry 4.0" aimed to foster the academic and industrial discussion about the future of education in the Industry 4.0 era. It was initiated by the EC-funded projects SPRINT4.0 and LINCOLN as well as the project "Innovativ Kraft", funded by the Research Council of Norway and invited the presentation of research and industrial efforts related to methodologies, concepts, architectures, tools and interoperable applications in the area of Industry 4.0 qualification. The main goal of this workshop was to provide a forum for researchers and practitioners with diverse backgrounds to meet, exchange research and implementation ideas, and share experience and results regarding higher education and qualification of professionals for the Industry 4.0 paradigm. Three papers were presented at the workshop, which – while highlighting individual aspects of the Industry 4.0 paradigm – presented numerous links between them and provided a fruitful basis for discussions. The following chapters draw on the papers presented at this workshop.

The first chapter of this part, Chapter 38, "Evaluation of Industry 4.0 Technology – Applications", written by Moritz von Stietencron, Bjørnar Henriksen, Carl Christian Røstad, Karl Hribernik and Klaus-Dieter Thoben presents a simple approach for the selection of Industry 4.0 technologies for given use cases built around the method of set-based concurrent engineering.

The second chapter, Chapter 39, "Improving the Efficiency of Industrial Processes with a Plug and Play IOT Data Acquisition Platform", written by Daniele Mazzei,

Chapter written by Moritz VON STIETENCRON.

Gabriele Montelisciani, Giacomo Baldi, Andrea Baù, Matteo Cipriani and Gualtiero Fantoni presents a practical discussion of industrial problems and how they have been addressed using Industry 4.0 methods built on a innovative Internet of Things solution.

The final chapter of this part, Chapter 40, "Knowledge Transfer from Students to Companies: Understanding Industry 4.0 Maturity Levels", written by Leonello Trivelli, Simona Pira, Gualtiero Fantoni and Andrea Bonaccorsi presents a methodology for assessing the maturity of companies regarding the topic of Industry 4.0 as well as recommended opportunities for increasing the benefits of Industry 4.0 in a company.

Evaluation of Industry 4.0 Technology – Applications

38.1. Introduction

Traditionally, a significant period of time passes before new technologies go from the phase of fundamental technology research and development to the phase of experimentation and focus on technology application research. The evolution of radio frequency identification (RFID), as documented for example through the Gartner Hype Cycle editions of the years 2002 [LIN 02] to 2009 [FEN 09], serves as a good example for the delay in wide industrial applications. With the successive realisation of the Industry 4.0 paradigm, the readiness of many companies for the adoption of technologies which have far surpassed the prime of fundamental research – like RFID – is growing.

However, this does not only produce a multitude of ideas and well-proven possibilities but also brings the tightly linked questions of applicability, effectiveness and process security. The selection of appropriate technologies for any given process potential is thus an increasingly relevant challenge. While not all technologies are novel and, in some cases extensive experience has been collected, the application and process specific evaluation is essential before important investment decisions are taken. To be able to offer reliable decision support in the selection of process supporting technologies, a systematic evaluation of Industry 4.0 technologies and their applicability for individual industrial use case is necessary [HEN 17].

Chapter written by Moritz VON STIETENCRON, Bjørnar HENRIKSEN, Carl Christian RØSTAD, Karl HRIBERNIK and Klaus-Dieter THOBEN.

38.2. Background and approach

Requirements and approaches for decision support in technology selection has been extensively modelled and discussed in the past. However, they mainly focus on specific cost-value calculations [HO 10], require the creation of complex mathematical procedures and notions [CHA 00] or are limited to a specific technology [COO 01]. Thomassen, Sjobakk and Alfnes [THO 14] arrive at the same conclusion; they propose their own strategy for decision-making in automation technology selection, which consists of five parts: technology strategy decision, process analysis, technology analysis, technology/process ranking, and consideration on investment and implementation. Some other examples are the lead user-method, relying on the quantification of qualitative data for improving lead customer satisfaction [TOR 02], and the multiple-criteria decision-making (MCDM) approach, aiming at a decision without sacrificing any of the crucial criteria and using a specialized decision-making software [KAR 08].

Which is why we have aimed at developing what is missing for the swift and broad adoption of these technologies – an easy-to-use decision support process, which allows for the technological development to be concluded and focuses on the assessment of the applicability of the respective technology in the intended application scenario. To achieve this goal, the concept of set-based concurrent engineering is adopted from the field of product development and combined with proof of concepts in order to create a practical decision support process.

Set-based concurrent engineering (SBCE) combines the more traditional point-based concurrent engineering, amongst others with the Lean Product Design principles [LIK 96; KER 14; SOB 99] and with the paradigm of considering a solution as the intersection of a number of feasible options. This approach is used rather than the one focusing on the iteration over a number of individual "point-based" solutions [HEN 17].

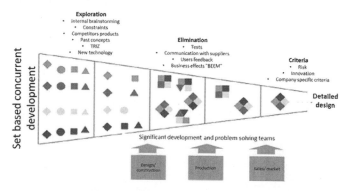

Figure 38.1. *SBCE "Solution Tunnel" [HEN 17]*

One element which is provided by SBCE can be named a "solution tunnel". This describes the impact that information has on the total amount of available solutions. Figure 38.1 gives a schematic overview of how the influence of different stakeholders can have an effect on the process of detailing a product design.

38.3. Evaluation process

The process for the evaluation of Industry 4.0 technologies follows three main consecutive steps, which are summarised in Figure 38.2. The initial step of problem and requirements elucidation is a critical necessity to create the solution tunnel, adopted from SBCE and introduced in the previous section.

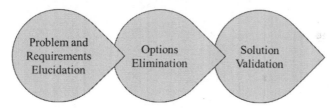

Figure 38.2. *Process steps for technology evaluation*

It is not only important to document the requirements, but also to weight them, so that they can be prioritized if not all can be met either due to technical feasibility or cost constraints. The following figure presents a typical scheme of the options elimination process, which evaluates six technologies (1–6) as options against a set of 10 requirements (A–J) that have been weighted and ordered by their magnitude of relevance.

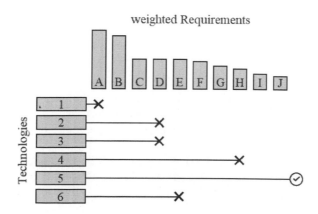

Figure 38.3. *Technology elimination process with weighted and sorted requirements*

This set of requirements is then processed and, in iterative loops, each of the available options is evaluated for the respective requirement under consideration. From the magnitude of relevance (in the figure above, indicated by the height of the requirements' bar) the requirements A and B of the example can be considered as a "set", which thus eliminates technology 1 from the options. For requirements of minor or comparable (if not equal) relevance, it might be necessary to perform the evaluation concurrently to allow for a re-ordering amongst this sub group. For the evaluation of the individual technology options different approaches can be used, which should be decided based on the individual technology concerned. To allow for an efficient evaluation process, this evaluation is usually done in a lab environment.

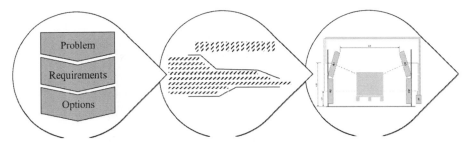

Figure 38.4. *Schematic example of a technology selection and evaluation process*

The final step of the options selection is a comparison of the remaining options, also under cost considerations. Based on the outcome of this, a final proof of concept is built in the process environment of the intended application, delivering the final validation of the technology application concept. The above figure shows the schematic process of the evaluation of RFID as a technology for an incoming goods registration process.

38.4. Discussion

Through the well-balanced combination of scientific methodology and agile and problem-related concept validation, a successful model for applied technology consulting has been developed. This procedure has already been successfully applied in a number of technology consulting contracts with industrial partners from various domains, such as electronics production [HEG 14], automotive parts [WER 14] or logistics and warehousing processes, as well as in the context of collaborative research on projects in the domains of pre-fabricated buildings, white goods, marine auxiliaries, and power boats.

38.5. Acknowledgements

The research leading to these results has received funding from the Research Council of Norway within the projects "Innovativ Kraft" (project no. 235708) and "Live Innovation Performance" (project no. 25666).

38.6. References

[COO 01] COOPER K., *Rapid Prototyping Technology: Selection and Application*, CRC Press, 2001.

[CHA 00] CHAN F.T.S., CHAN M.H., TANG N.K H., "Evaluation methodologies for technology selection", *Journal of Materials Processing Technology*, vol. 107, nos 1–3, pp. 330–337, 2000.

[FEN 09] FENN J., RASKINO M., GAMMAGE B., Gartner's Hype Cycle Special Report for 2009, Report, Gartner, 2009.

[HEG 14] HENGST T., SCHNATMEYER M., LEWANDOWSKI M. *et al.*, "RFID speichert digitalen Produktlebenslauf", *RFID im Blick - Industrie 4.0 und Logistik 4.0 aus Bremen*, pp. 42–43, 2014.

[HEN 17] HENRIKSEN B., RØSTAD C.C., VON STIETENCRON M., "Development projects in SMEs", in Lödding H. *et al.* (eds), *IFIP International Conference on Advances in Production Management Systems*, Springer, Cham, pp. 193–201, 2017.

[HO 10] HO W., XU X., DEY P.K., "Multi-criteria decision making approaches for supplier evaluation and selection: a literature review", *European Journal of Operational Research*, vol. 202, no. 1, pp. 16–24, 2010.

[KAR 08] KARSAK E.E., AHISKA S.S., "Improved common weight MCDM model for technology selection", vol. 46, no. 24, pp. 6933–6944, 2008.

[KER 14] KERGA E. *et al.*, "Teaching set-based concurrent engineering to practitioners through gaming", *International Journal of Product Development*, vol. 19, nos 5–6, pp. 348–365, 2014.

[LIK 96] LIKER J.K. *et al.*, "Involving suppliers in product development in the United States and Japan: evidence for set-based concurrent engineering", *IEEE Transactions on Engineering Management*, vol. 43, no. 2, pp. 165–178, 1996.

[LIN 02] LINDEN A., FENN J., Emerging Technologies Hype Cycle: Trigger to Peak, Report, Gartner, 2002.

[SOB 99] SOBEK D.K., WARD A.C., LIKER J.K., "Toyota's principles of set-based concurrent engineering", *Sloan Management Review*, vol. 40, no. 2, p. 67, 1999.

[THO 14] THOMASSEN M., SJØBACK B., ALFNES E., "A Strategic Approach to Automation Technology Initiatives Selection", in GRABOT B. *et al.* (eds), *Advances in Production Management Systems: Innovative and Knowledge-Based Production Management in a Global-Local World: IFIP WG 5.7 International Conference*, APMS 2014, Proceedings, Teil 3; Band 440 von IFIP Advances in Information and Communication Technology, Springer, Ajaccio, France, September 20–24, 2014.

[TOR 02] TORKKELI M., Technology selection and group decision support systems: case studies on supporting strategic technology selection processes, Doctoral dissertation, Lappeenranta University of Technology, Industrial Engineering, 2002.

[WER 14] WERTHMANN D., LEWANDOWSKI M., Herausfordernde Verkehrsszenarien: RFID-Kennzeichen im Praxistest, RFID im Blick – Industrie 4.0 und Logistik 4.0 aus Bremen, 2014.

39

Improving the Efficiency of Industrial Processes with a Plug and Play IOT Data Acquisition Platform

Manufacturing companies, warehouses and industrial machines producers have all the same need: make their processes more efficient. The lack of full business processes visibility makes it hard to measure the performances and implement corrective actions. Scarce visibility is mainly due to the absence of a continuous data flow to be analysed in order to identify processes' inefficiencies. TOI (Things On Internet), an Italian tech company, have developed the "4Zero Platform", an industrial IOT (IIOT) data acquisition and analysis stack for the improvement of production efficiency. The 4Zero Platform is based on the 4ZeroBox, a plug and play industrial data acquisition unit that can be connected to PLC-equipped machines but also to old apparatuses through the use of industrial analog and digital sensors. Data gathered by the 4ZeroBox can be sent to different cloud services and also processed locally for the extraction of machine's KPI. In this paper the use of the 4ZeroBox for the real-time calculation of machine's OEE (overall equipment efficiency) KPI is presented. This chapter describes how the OEE is calculated, analyzing data gathered from the machine and merging it with data acquired from the company ERP server. The chapter concludes with the description of an industrial use case where the technology presented here has been tested for the monitoring of a cutting tools production line based on a series of legacy CNC machines.

Chapter written by Daniele MAZZEI, Gabriele MONTELISCIANI, Giacomo BALDI, Andrea BAÙ, Matteo CIPRIANI and Gualtiero FANTONI.

39.1. Production efficiency

One of the most frequent questions that manufacturers have while looking at the IIoT (industrial Internet of Things) is: *can it help to address one of my primary challenges: unscheduled downtime? This is often the number one issue for my plants!* (See also [RES 17]).

Often, one of the causes of a portion of this unscheduled downtime is that a significant percentage of today's global installed base of automation systems are at least 20 years old and becoming increasingly difficult and costly to maintain properly. The average impact of unscheduled downtime in the process industries alone is around $20 billion. This makes unscheduled downtime minimization one of the best ways for industrial organizations to improve their efficiency. Unscheduled downtime reduces the asset's availability but also causes ripple effects throughout the organization, such as an estimated 5 to 10% increase in inventories and labor costs and delayed delivery of finished goods, all resulting in reduced profitability.

This lack of assets' efficiency can result in equipment damage, lower key performance indicators (KPIs), environmental harm, and most importantly worker endangerment. Lower KPIs include reduced overall equipment effectiveness (OEE), decreased efficiency, and reduced profitability. However, manufacturers are often not aware of the magnitude of unscheduled downtime in their own plants [RON 05].

Since industry will not be doing a complete "rip and replace" of all of these legacy automation assets simultaneously, the best way that industry has to minimize unscheduled downtime is to deploy IIoT technology to better detect the health of these legacy machines while optimizing operation scheduling and maintenance activities.

In Figure 39.1, the six possible states in which a machine can be are reported together with the related production time frames. Knowing these time frames it is possible to calculate the OEE in realtime. OEE is a KPI percentage calculation that summarizes *how well a piece of equipment or production line is operating* [MUC 80].

In [RON 05], the following definition of overall equipment efficiency OEE is given:

$$OEE = \frac{theoretical\ production\ time\ for\ effective\ units}{total\ time}$$

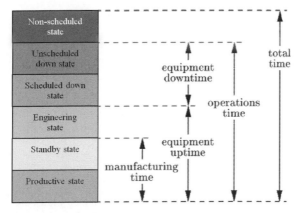

Figure 39.1. *Equipment states in OEE calculation. For a color version of this figure,
see www.iste.co.uk/zelm/enterprise.zip*

39.2. OEE realtime calculation

The Internet of Things brings new capabilities to help manufacturers identify and remedy areas negatively impacting OEE. Detailed understanding of equipment performance through instrumentation and analytics can help identify and remedy problems in three ways:

1) monitoring the production line KPIs in realtime;

2) providing advanced warning of impending equipment degradation or failure to avoid unplanned downtime;

3) analyzing historic process and performance data to optimize maintenance planning, schedules, and resources, leading to lower maintenance costs, reduced material and supplies, and greater equipment availability.

In order to enable this new industrial process management paradigm it is necessary to add connectivity to productive assets. However, wherever an appropriate business case has yet to be made, this creates a big challenge for manufacturers to find a way to not only provide interoperability between the plant floor and enterprise, but also to provide a link between multiple generations of legacy automation assets. Adding and retrofitting IIoT technology to those legacy automation assets can be a quick and justifiable way to help reduce unscheduled downtime and leverage the full potential of all the assets on the plant floor.

4ZeroBox (www.4zerobox.com) is a plug and play data gathering and processing unit that can be plugged to modern and old machines in order to easily extract processes' data and calculate KPIs in realtime. The 4zeroBox has been designed in order to allow different installation paradigms:

– **Data Gathering:** acquire digital data from RS232, RS485 (Modbus, Profibus), CAN (CAN Open, NMEA 2000), Ethernet (OPC UA, Siemens S7, Profinet) and other digital port of the PLC (Figure 39.2);

– **Retrofitting:** acquire data from legacy machines by plugging the 4ZeroBox in parallel to the PLC using the available sensors or installing new probes;

– **Hybrid:** merge the two paradigms to extract data available on the machines integrating them with data from other sensors in order to allow KPI calculation that are not achievable by using the PLC data only. The 4ZeroBox is endowed with a set of libraries that enable a connection with all the most used cloud services (Microsoft Azure, Google IOT, Amazon Web Services and IBM Bluemix). Data gathered from machines and/or sensors can be used to calculate various KPIs locally and in particular the real-time OEE. In order to do this the 4ZeroBox is interfaced with a remote server or database where the machine schedule is exposed.

FEATURES

- DIN-rail mountable (9 slots)
- 24V Supply voltage
- Connectivity: WiFi, BLE, Ethernet, RS-485, RS-232, CAN
- 4 analog input channels configurable as: 4-20mA single-ended; 4-20mA differential; 0-10V
- 3 non-invasive current sensor channels
- 4 analog channels configurable for RTD or contact/proximity sensors
- 2 opto-isolated digital inputs with configurable input voltage (24V to 5V)
- 2 sink digital output (60A @ 30V)
- 1 Digital I/O + 2 Digital Input (3.3V)
- 2 NO/NC Relay (10A @ 250V AC)
- 2 on-board mikroBUS expansion sockets
- MicroSD card slot
- LiPo battery support with on board charging unit
- JTAG connector
- RGB status led
- Power led
- ESP32 32bit Microcontroller (240MHz clock, 4Mb of Flash, 312Kb SRAM)

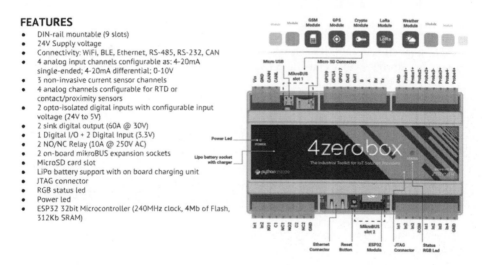

Figure 39.2. *The 4zerobox unit with reference to the various onboard available features. For a color version of this figure, see www.iste.co.uk/zelm/enterprise.zip*

39.3. Use case: OEE real-time calculation of a legacy CNC machine

Cutting tools production includes various steps mostly executed with legacy CNC machines. In order to optimize a cutting tools production line the producer needs to optimize the machine operation scheduling taking into consideration the state of each machine involved in the process. The company analyzed here is characterized by a large number of orders of few pieces each. For this reason, machine scheduling needs to be very flexible and adaptable to inline changes. In this context, unscheduled downtime or unscheduled maintenance have strong consequences on the business efficiency.

Here is reported how the 4ZeroBox has been used for the OEE real-time calculation of a set of cutting tools production machines. The installation here reported has been based on the retrofitting setup above described and it did not require any intervention in the machine PLC or changes to the electrical schema of the machines.

The 4ZeroBox has been installed on the machine electric cabinet and interfaced with the wires connected to the security window position switch and with the wires connected to the lamp of the machine status semaphore. Moreover, a non-invasive current sensor has been plugged to the main motor power cable thus allowing the detection of the main motor state.

Thanks to the data extracted in realtime by these sensors the 4ZeroBox has been programmed in order to estimate the various production time frames required for the calculation of the machine OEE. Moreover, the 4ZeroBox has been also connected to the company ERP (enterprise resource planning) server via Ethernet connection in order to gather the machine scheduling. The 4ZeroBox to ERP connection has been based on an MQTT protocol over a secure SSL connection.

The various machine states have been detected on the basis of the following simplified truth table.

	Data from the machine					Data from the company ERP server		
State	Semaphore Red lamp	Semaphore Yellow lamp	Semaphore Green lamp	Main Motor	Machine Window	Scheduled Maintenance	Scheduled Engineering	Scheduled Production
Nonscheduled	Off	Off	Off	Off	–	No	No	No
Unscheduled down	On (failure)	–	–	Off	–	No	No	Yes
Scheduled down	–	–	–	–	–	Yes	No	No
Engineering	–	–	–	–	–	No	Yes	No
Standby	Off	On (Waiting)	Off	–	Open	No	No	Yes
Productive	Off	Off	On (work in progress)	On	Closed	No	No	Yes

Table 39.1. *4ZeroBox CNC machine state detection truth table*

In order to calculate the machine OEE in realtime, the manufacturing time is required, but this information is not available on the companies' ERP because it is influenced by the real operations like: machine setup, cleaning, parts and material provisioning, etc. Thanks to the 4ZeroBox, this data has been available directly on the machine side and in real-time allowing the calculation of a real operation-influenced machine OEE. This KPI is no longer based on scheduled operation but reflects in real-time the real use and functionalities of the machines.

39.4. Conclusions

Industrial processes have been engineered for many years using well-defined and tested designing and optimization methods. Optimization methods are limited only by the information availability and by the factual knowledge of industrial processes. Industrial IOT has the potential to boost industrial process optimization, pushing toward new levels of efficiency that were possible only in theory due to the lack of real and continuous information.

To enable this scenario a shift of paradigm is mandatory. Typical industrial control design paradigms are unable to modernize the current industrial panorama. It is necessary to take inspiration from the "smart" world where simple technological elements are used in a pervasive way to gather data from everything, everyone and everywhere, creating a ubiquitous network of information providers.

Lastly, it must be said that Industry 4.0 paradigms are being extended to broader industrial ecosystems that include logistics, services and transport. One of the most promising sectors is surely the nautical one, where the number of involved actors and critical processes to manage and optimize is very high. For this reason the presented methodology is being implemented in the LINCOLN project (http://www.lincolnproject.eu) for the monitoring, management and optimization of operational processes in the nautical sector. An NMEA2000-connected Marine Gateway based on 32-bit microcontrollers and embedded sensors is being designed to be installed on special vessels. The gateway will be able to acquire navigation data (position, acceleration, velocity, etc.) and elaborate information that will be streamed to different cloud services in order to implement operational optimizations as well as generate new services for the stakeholders of the system.

39.5. Acknowledgements

The financial support of the following projects is kindly acknowledged: SPRINT 4.0 (Erasmus+ Strategic Partnership for Higher Education N. 2017-1-IT02-KA203-036980) that is currently under development; LINCOLN project (European Union

Horizon 2020 Innovative Action N. 727982) that is currently under development (www.lincolnproject.eu).

39.6. References

[MUC 80] Muchiri P., Pintelon L., "Performance measurement using overall equipment effectiveness (OEE): literature review and practical application discussion", *International Journal of Production Research*, vol. 46, no. 13, pp. 3517–3535, 2008.

[RES 17] Resnick C., "Add IIoT to legacy automation assets to reduce unscheduled downtime", available at https://industrial-iot.com/2017/05/iiot-legacy-automation-downtime/, May 2017.

[RON 05] de Ron A.J., Rooda J.E., "Equipment effectiveness: OEE revisited", *IEEE Transactions on Semiconductor Manufacturing*, vol. 18, no. 1, pp. 190–196, 2005.

40

Knowledge Transfer from Students to Companies: Understanding Industry 4.0 Maturity Levels

Facing the challenges coming from the fourth industrial revolution means dealing with new difficulties to implement and exploit digital technologies. This chapter discusses an initiative undertaken at the University of Pisa to provide its students with valuable skills to address Industry 4.0. In particular, the research shows the training program on the assessment model and its practical application conducted by students in one company from the region of Tuscany.

40.1. Introduction

In last decades, the advent of ICT has been changing our society and the continuous development of the digital economy has led to the inexorable decline of consolidated business models in many industries. In fact, giants such as Polaroid, Nokia and Blockbuster have gradually lost their markets, and new players such as Netflix or AirBnB have risen thanks to their ability to exploit new technologies. This continuous innovation and the increasing adoption of digital technologies within business processes has seen its sublimation in the Industry 4.0 paradigm, which is considered, by policy makers and companies, as the best way to bring Western countries' economies to growth again. However, entrepreneurs often fail to fully understand how new technologies can contribute to the improvement of their companies' processes and therefore the implementation of the underlying principles of the new paradigm remains a difficult goal. To this regard, providing companies with reliable measurements about their maturity level and the possible improvements is

Chapter written by Leonello TRIVELLI, Simona PIRA, Gualtiero FANTONI and Andrea BONACCORSI.

the key to enable them to act. To address such an issue, new competencies and skills might be provided to the managers of tomorrow to allow them to analyze, design and test new solutions which can contribute to the renewal of both industrial processes and business models. The paper describes an evaluation model to assess companies' Industry 4.0 maturity level, and to identify and prioritize new opportunities generated by the implementation of the new paradigm. The research shows a case study concerning the training and the implementation of the proposed model. In particular, the focus is on an initiative undertaken by the University of Pisa to provide its students with valuable skills to address Industry 4.0 implementation, and to transfer these skills to companies through internships aiming at assessing the maturity level of hosting companies from Tuscany Region.

40.2. Context

Industry 4.0 is acquiring an increasingly central role in the discussions of entrepreneurs, experts, scholars and policy makers about the future of industrial production systems and is considered by many to be a fundamental change in economic and production systems on a global scale. The new paradigm is based on the digitization of factories, the use of internet in industrial processes, and the diffusion of ICT technologies to create intelligent devices, machines and systems [LAS 14]. According to Boston Consulting Group [RÜß 15], the fourth industrial revolution is based on the implementation of nine enabling technologies that allow companies to renew their business models. The following list shows these technologies: the cloud; additive manufacturing; simulation; augmented reality; Big Data and analytics; autonomous robots; industrial Internet of Things; vertical and horizontal integration; cybersecurity. The implementation of these technologies is expected to raise the competitiveness of companies by increasing flexibility, speed and productivity of processes, and the quality of products [WEE 15]. Moreover, Kagermann et al. [KAG 13] identify additional drivers such as the ability of companies to meet customized clients requests, the optimization of decision-making processes, and the creation of new value thanks to innovative services.

Such a huge innovation impact is based on the integration of existing technologies and their adoption within production systems. Therefore, instigating such a huge innovation impact means to support companies in raising their awareness on how the 4.0 paradigm can be integrated within their strategy through the identification of what Ganzarain and Errasti [GAN 16] call Vision 4.0. Indeed, Industry 4.0-enabling technologies contribute to generating new business models and increasing companies' revenues thanks to the development of new products and services [GEI 14, KÖL 17]. At the same time, the development, diffusion and implementation of existing technologies under an Industry 4.0-based perspective generates critical issues that companies have to address [LIE 17]. In particular, organizational issues linked to different factors ranging from the lack of standards for Industry 4.0, to the uncertainty about the return on investments in Industry 4.0 technologies, to the critical issues related to the integration of business functions and between companies belonging to the same value chain [UHL 17]. Instead, as far as the technological aspects are concerned, most companies are not sufficiently ready to adhere to the underlying concepts of Industry 4.0 and thus so-called "smart retrofitting" is a good option to start integrating Industry 4.0-enabling technologies in dated machinery [GUE 18].

The need to promote the understanding of the fundamental elements of Industry 4.0 and to facilitate its implementation has led to the creation of the DIN SPEC 91345:2016 standard which is today the first standard developed in this field. However, the identification of preconditions necessary to implement Industry 4.0 principles and technologies remains a key issue to address. These conditions depend on the current situation of companies aspiring to adhere to the Industry 4.0 paradigm [CRN 17]. Identifying such preconditions is a challenge that many researchers and scholars have tried to address by designing models able to deepen the maturity level of companies, and by supporting them in the transition towards 4.0 [GÖK 17].

In some cases, the focus is on specific aspects that characterize companies. For example, the SIMMI 4.0 model [LEY 16] analyzes the development level of company's IT systems with respect to the requirements of the Industry 4.0 paradigm. Instead, many models provide an analysis of the entire organization by identifying specific dimensions to be investigated through a measurement scale. De Carolis et al. [DEC 17] have developed the DREAMY model that measures the digital maturity of companies standing on the principles of the Capability Maturity Model Integration (CMMI) framework. A similar model is proposed by Gökalp et al. [GÖK 17] which evaluate the maturity level by integrating the CMMI and the SPICE model (developed in the automotive sector to conduct process assessment and to understand possible improvements). In particular, the process dimensions of the SPICE model are reviewed as "aspects" of Industry 4.0. The maturity level of these aspects is assessed according to the CMMI framework. The Acatech study [SCH 17] describes a model which analyzes four structural areas (information systems, resources, organizational structure and culture) and identifies six levels of a firm's maturity that enable the clear identification of the transition between Industry 3.0 and Industry 4.0. The IMPULS model [LIC 15] studies companies operating in the mechanical and manufacturing sector according to six dimensions (strategy and organization, smart factory, smart operations, smart products, data-driven services and employees) to which a readiness level (on a scale of six that goes from "outsider" to "top performer") is assigned. However, the abovementioned approaches are mainly used by researchers or by big consulting firms and their adoption in other companies is not obvious. Indeed, companies often lack the knowledge to perform such an analysis and need to refer to external consultants to better understand their real situation regarding the Industry 4.0 paradigm.

40.3. Methodology

The present research stands on the application of a three-step evaluation model [FAN 17a, FAN 17b] that was developed by the University of Pisa and the University of Siena in collaboration with the region of Tuscany to assess the maturity level of local companies concerning the Industry 4.0 paradigm. Such a model was based on existing approaches and standards already used by researchers and practitioners to analyze other dimensions of companies such as processes and management systems. In particular the three-step evaluation model was inspired by the following:

– ISO 9001:2015 – Quality management systems;

– ISO 19011:2012 – Guidelines for management systems audit;

– DIN SPEC 911345:2016;

– acatech STUDY; and

– European Foundation for Quality Management Model.

40.3.1. *Three-step evaluation model*

The proposed evaluation model has been developed by integrating the most convincing characteristics of the reference models described in previous section. The approach aimed at creating a path that favours the increase of entrepreneurs' awareness concerning Industry 4.0 maturity levels of their companies. At the same time, it attempted to support companies in implementing the most suitable solutions according to their current situation. The proposed evaluation model encompasses three successive steps: (1) preliminary evaluation; (2) assessment; (3) audit.

40.3.1.1. *Preliminary evaluation*

The first step consists of an online questionnaire that addresses the main issues related to Industry 4.0. The questionnaire aims to help companies to increase their awareness of the new paradigm and to have an initial understanding of their digital maturity level. The preliminary evaluation questionnaire is filled by the entrepreneur or by a company manager and provides the company with a brief assessment of the company's digital maturity level according to a scale from 1 to 6 that is based on the pattern proposed by IMPULS [LIC 15]. This assessment is accompanied by a short report containing an overview for the company about the main drivers of Industry 4.0.

40.3.1.2. *The assessment*

The second step is an assessment model which provides the company with a detailed picture of its digitalization level by investigating all its different business areas. The assessment is conducted by an external auditor (who has the basic skills to understand the Industry 4.0 technologies and to evaluate the organizational structure and the corporate culture) through a visit to the company lasting at least one day. The first part of the visit takes place through an interview with some managers of the company including the quality manager (who is the person who best knows the business processes). Then, the second part of the visit takes place in the operational unit of the company (for example in the factory) so that the consultant conducting the assessment can see with their own eyes the company's reality and can avoid any bias that may mitigate or exaggerate any perceptions of the company representatives involved in the evaluation. The visit has the purpose of filling out a checklist that represents the starting point for the preparation of the assessment report. The assessment model reflects some of the sources taken as reference for the construction of the model. The execution approach is typical of management systems audits as described in ISO 19011. Moreover, the assessment questionnaire combines the central elements of the DIN SPEC 91345 standard and the Acatech study. In fact, the assessment focuses on all the company assets by analyzing the characteristics that an asset must possess to comply with the DIN standard. Finally, the structure of the survey to submit is a checklist inspired by the ISO 9001 standard.

40.3.1.3. *The audit*

The third step aims to provide a more dynamic and prospective vision of the company through the completion of an audit. The audit is conducted by an external consultant during a one-day visit to the company, and it is divided into two parts according to the following scheme:

– Part 1: interview with company managers;

– Part 2: visit to the company's operating area.

Unlike what happens during the assessment, the audit does not refer to a checklist, but is carried out following the typical form of the European Foundation for Quality Management (EFQM) model, which provides for each dimension an evaluation based on a score from 0 to 100. The description of five levels of maturity helps the consultant in understanding the actual maturity level of each dimension under analysis. The results of step 2 are the starting point for the audit, and focuses on the business area that is the most interesting according to the assessment results. Thus, the audit investigates business and technology strategies and provides a development plan that allows the company to improve performance by implementing Industry 4.0 solutions.

40.3.2. *The university–business collaboration*

With the aim to increase entrepreneurs and companies awareness on Industry 4.0, the University of Pisa has piloted the proposed three-step evaluation model into local companies. To reach this goal, after the implementation of a web platform where companies could complete the preliminary assessment, a dedicated initiative was put in place by University of Pisa to perform assessment in local companies thanks to a collaboration between the Engineering Management course and the companies themselves. Thanks to such an initiative, 30 undergraduate students brought their knowledge into local companies to support them in understanding Industry 4.0 basic concepts and analyzing their maturity level. The companies participating in such an initiative came from different sectors and were of different dimensions so that each student experienced different contexts and businesss approaches.

40.4. Case study – Industry 4.0 knowledge transfer from students to companies at University of Pisa

40.4.1. *The approach*

To undertake such a knowledge transfer process, the University of Pisa have designed a two-phase approach. The first phase was a training on the assessment model to be used. This training activity addressed undergraduate students from the Engineering Management course to provide them with the guidelines, the methodology and the tools for performing the assessment according to the UNI EN ISO 19011 which describes how to conduct audits for analyzing quality and environmental management systems. The second phase was an internship that students completed in local companies to support them in assessing their maturity level according to the assessment model described in section 40.3.1.2. The internship lasted 150 hours and students had the possibility to experience the company environment in a safe way by putting in practice the notions they had learned in the subjects of mechanics, logistics, computer science and management.

40.4.2. *Knowledge transfer in Industry 4.0. from students to companies*

The activities carried out during the internship were mainly focused on conducting the assessment on Industry 4.0 maturity level. Students were responsible for the assessment and they directly referred to a tutor assigned by the hosting company. Moreover, the students provided feedback and insights on the technologies that the company already adopted and about the possible connections between them under an Industry 4.0 perspective. The case of two students hosted by a corporation operating in Tuscany was one of the most interesting ones. The students were selected to investigate two different business units of the company in order to analyze their Industry 4.0 maturity levels. They worked in an innovative and challenging environment thanks to which they had the chance to consolidate their own background. In particular the students performed the assessment model and discussed the results they have collected with the plant manager in weekly meetings. In these meetings the students were able to bring innovative approaches, methods and knowledge in the heart of the company, and provided insights and feedback coming from outside the company. At the same time they experienced the criticalities to manage units based in different countries when completing the assessment. The results of the assessment cannot be shared (as well as the name of the company) for privacy reasons, but the students were able to identify both the strengths and the possible improvement areas of the analyzed business units. Moreover, they provided the company with an overview of new links that could be created by different technologies already adopted in the production processes.

40.5. Final remarks

The knowledge transfer process to support companies in understanding their Industry 4.0 maturity level can be one way through which higher education institutions can support the business environment. Indeed students, can be the ambassadors of innovative approaches that can be valuable for companies regardless of their sector of activity and their dimensions. In particular, students can bring innovative approaches and an overall understanding of the Industry 4.0 concepts that can be provided by university courses. On the other hand, companies can support students in translating such knowledge in best practices and concrete solutions that can be valuable for growing the professional profile of the students themselves, and for developing the company's processes and business models.

40.6. References

[CRN 17] CRNJAC M., VEŽA I., BANDUKA N., "From concept to the introduction of Industry 4.0", *International Journal of Industrial Engineering and Management*, vol. 8, pp. 21–30, 2017.

[DEC 17] DE CAROLIS A., MACCHI M., NEGRI E. *et al.*, "A Maturity Model for Assessing the Digital Readiness of Manufacturing Companies", in LÖDDING H. *et al.*, *IFIP International Conference on Advances in Production Management Systems*, Springer, Cham, pp. 13–20, 2017.

[DIN 16] DIN SPEC 91345:2016-04, Reference Architecture Model Industrie 4.0 (RAMI 4.0), 2016.

[FAN 17a] FANTONI G., CERVELLI G., MOCENNI C. *et al.*, *Impresa 4.0: siamo pronti alla quarta rivoluzione industriale?*, Towel Publishing, Pisa, 2017.

[FAN 17b] FANTONI G., CERVELLI G., PIRA S. *et al.*, *Industria 4.0 senza slogan*, Towel Publishing, Pisa, 2017.

[GAN 16] GANZARAIN J., ERRASTI N., "Three-stage maturity model in SMEs towards Industry 4.0", *Journal of Industrial Engineering and Management*, vol. 9, no. 5, pp. 1119–1128, 2016.

[GEI 16] GEISSBAUER R., SHRAUF S., KOCH V. *et al.*, Industry 4.0: building the digital enterprise – global industry 4.0 survey, Report, PricewaterhouseCoopers, 2016.

[GÖK 17] GÖKALP E., ŞENER U., EREN P.E., "Development of an assessment model for Industry 4.0: Industry 4.0-MM", in MAS A. *et al.* (eds), *Software Process Improvement and Capability Determination*, Palma de Mallorca, Spain, 4–5 October, Springer, Cham, pp. 128–142, 2017.

[GUE 18] GUERREIRO B.V., LINS R.G., SUN J. *et al.*, "Definition of smart retrofitting: first steps for a company to deploy aspects of Industry 4.0", in HAMROL A. *et al.* (eds), *Advances in Manufacturing*, Springer, Cham, pp. 161–170, 2018.

[KAG 13] KAGERMANN H., HELBIG J., HELLINGER A. *et al.*, Recommendations for implementing the strategic initiative INDUSTRIE 4.0: securing the future of German manufacturing industry, final report of the Industrie 4.0 Working Group, Forschungsunion, 2013.

[LAS 14] LASI H., FETTKE P., KEMPER H.G. *et al.*, "Industry 4.0", *Business & Information Systems Engineering*, vol. 6, no. 2, pp. 239–242, 2014.

[LEY 16] LEYH C., BLEY K., SCHÄFFER T. *et al.*, "SIMMI 4.0 – a maturity model for classifying the enterprise-wide IT and software landscape focusing on Industry 4.0", *Computer Science and Information Systems (FedCSIS), 2016 Federated Conference*, Gdansk, Poland, 11–14 September, IEEE, pp. 1297–1302, 2016.

[LIC 15] LICHTBLAU K., STICH V., BERTENRATH R. *et al.*, *Industrie 4.0-Readiness, Impuls-Stiftung*, IMPULS, Frankfurt, 2015.

[RÜß 15] RÜßMANN M., LORENZ M., GERBERT P. *et al.*, *Industry 4.0: The Future of Productivity and Growth in Manufacturing Industries*, Boston Consulting Group, p. 9, 2015.

[SCH 17] SCHUH G., ANDERL R., GAUSEMEIER J. *et al.*, *Industrie 4.0 Maturity Index: Managing the Digital Transformation of Companies*, utz Verlag GmbH, Munich, 2017.

[UHL 17] UHLEMANN T.H.J., LEHMANN C., STEINHILPER R., "The digital twin: realizing the cyber-physical production system for Industry 4.0", *Procedia CIRP*, vol. 61, pp. 335–340.

PART 8

Enterprise Modeling and Simulation

Part 8 Summary: Modeling and Simulation in Designing Advanced Manufacturing Systems

The objective of this workshop was to discuss Modeling and Simulation Methods and Tools (M&SMT) supporting the design of Advanced Manufacturing Systems (AMS). M&SMT can be applied to improve not only the performances of AMS but also for the elaboration and validation of Business Requirements as well as the determination of Technological Requirements, not only in the IT domain but also in the domains of Organization, Human aspects and Physical means.

Chen's chapter highlights the role of enterprise modeling in enterprise engineering to improve the performance of industrial organizations and to develop networked business opportunities. Since the 1970s, many enterprise modeling languages and methods were built using different syntaxes and semantics, creating obstacles, particularly for various interactions between the models or their use. This chapter proposes an alternative approach to develop an Enterprise Modeling Ontology (EMO). It aims to set up a generally agreed understanding of enterprise modeling concepts, to support enterprise models' interpretation and interoperation. A bottom-up approach is used to first build an ontology of individual enterprise modeling language using OWL (Web Ontology Language). Then the set of individual ontologies is compared and merged to the Enterprise Modeling Ontology. The PROTÉGÉ tool is used to represent and publish the EMO on the web so that a continuous refinement/improvement process can be established worldwide to look for consensus. It is believed that the continuous participation and involvement of all

Chapter written by Guy DOUMEINGTS, Amir PIRAYESH, Carlos AGOSTINHO, Gregory ZACHAREWICZ and Yves DUCQ.

enterprise modeling language developers and users is a key factor in reaching a generally agreed and accepted EMO.

In Poler *et al's*. chapter, the authors underline the challenges of decisional modeling and simulation due to the involvement of human aspects. There is a plethora of enterprise modeling languages but few of them are able to model the decisional aspect. The GRAI model, which is the kernel of GRAI modeling, is one of them. GRAI modeling is supported by several software mainly for the modeling of the business processes. A software tool called DGRAI© has been developed based on the concepts of the GRAI decisional model. The DGRAI© model has been implemented in the DGRAI© software tool by the Research Centre on Production Management and Engineering of the Universitat Politecnica de Valencia. It has been transferred to Spin-off UPV EXOS Solutions which use it for the analysis and redesign of Decision Systems in private companies and public administrations. DGRAI© has been used in industrial companies of different sectors (automotive, textile, ceramic, etc.) for simulating companies and supply chains.

The other two chapters (by Pirayesh *et al.* and Agostinho *et al.*), positioned in the context of Cyber Physical Production Systems (CPPS) present the recent industrial application of MDSEA (Model Driven System Engineering Architecture) and MSTB (Manufacturing System Tool Box) which belongs to M&SMT. MDSEA/MSTB was developed in MSEE (Manufacturing SErvice Ecosystem) European project. In the first chapter, this architecture and tool have been applied for the elicitation of business requirements for CPPS development (in its design phase) through the provision of structured and graphical views adapted to the business level. Following these requirements, in the second chapter, a specific IT architecture is proposed for the integration of M&SMT in CPPS design, development and execution phases. The contributions are illustrated through a case study which is a manufacturing system in the cutlery industry adopting a CPPSisation strategy in the frame of a European Research project (BEinCPPS).

In this workshop, the usage of M&STM solutions as a preliminary support, for developing a new enterprise system or improving an existing one was discussed. The workshop covered the conceptual aspect of M&SMT (e.g. elaboration of ontologies), decisional and human dimensions, the methodological usage of M&SMT solutions, and examples of industrial applications. First of all, the necessity of developing unified M&SMT languages and ontologies to improve interoperability in the modeling process was highlighted (see Chen *et al.*). In addition, M&SMT should also focus on decisional and human aspects. Finally, besides the confirmed advantages of M&SMT for the development of traditional manufacturing systems, their adaptability for development AMS was discussed through examples in the CPPS context.

41

Developing an Enterprise Modeling Ontology

Enterprise modeling plays an important role in enterprise engineering to improve the performance of industrial organizations and develop networked business opportunities. Since the 1970s, many enterprise modeling languages and methods have been elaborated for different purposes and with different focuses. However, it is generally agreed Enterprise Modeling Ontology is still missing. This chapter presents some preliminary work done to develop an Enterprise Modeling Ontology (EMO). First the research methodology is explained. Then the ontological OWL models of several known enterprise modeling languages are presented. The comparison and mapping of the OWL ontology models are done and the first version of EMO represented both by OWL and Protégé is outlined. Discussion and conclusion are given at the end of the chapter.

41.1. Introduction

Developing advance manufacturing systems in the context of the factory of the future (Industry 4.0 and Cyber physical systems) will require that enterprises themselves be modeled, analyzed and simulated using enterprise modeling techniques. Since the 1970s, many enterprise modeling languages and methods have been elaborated for different purposes and with different focuses. It has been considered that existing enterprise modeling approaches were built using different syntaxes and semantics, creating obstacles for enterprise models' correct interpretation and interoperation. Several initiatives in the past have tentatively developed UEML (Unified Enterprise Modeling Language) under the European UEML schematic network [6] and INTEROP NoE [3] as well as POP* model in ATHENA IP [2].

Chapter written by David CHEN.

These initiatives were good starting points but they are not further developed to a sound enterprise modeling ontology.

This chapter proposes an alternative approach to develop an Enterprise Modeling Ontology (EMO). It aims at setting up a generally agreed understanding of enterprise modeling concepts, thus to support an enterprise model's interpretation and interoperation. A bottom-up approach is used to first build an ontology of individual enterprise modeling language using OWL. Then the set of individual ontologies are compared and merged to the Enterprise Modeling Ontology. The Protégé tool is used to represent and publish the EMO on the web so that a continuous refinement/ improvement process can be established worldwide to look for consensus. It is believed that the continuous participation and involvement of all enterprise modeling language developers and users are a key factor to reach a generally agreed and accepted EMO.

This chapter reports some preliminary work developed today. At first the research methodology will be explained. Then the ontological OWL representations of several known enterprise modeling languages are presented (IDEF0, IDEF1, IDEF3, GRAI grid and nets, MoGo, BPMN, CIMOSA and ISO 19440). The comparison and mapping of individual modeling language ontologies is performed. The first version of EMO represented both by OWL and Protégé is outlined. It is to note that this initiative can be seen as a journey to develop an enterprise modeling ontology rather than a project limited in time. The work presented in the chapter is tentative and will evolve in the future.

41.2. Related work

Several initiatives to develop ontology in the area of enterprise modeling can be found in the literature. These works have been performed in USA and in Europe since the 1990s. The most known are TOVE, EEO, PSL but also the lesser-known UEEO and IDEF5.

TOVE (TOronto Virtual Enterprise) is a project to develop an ontological framework for enterprise integration (EI) based on and suited for enterprise modeling [5]. It was initiated by Mark S. Fox and others at the University of Toronto at the beginning of the 1990s. The TOVE ontologies are axiomatized using KIF and implemented using Prolog. TOVE ontologies are used to analyze enterprise models and to reason about alternative enterprise designs [5].

Another well-known approach is the Edinburgh Enterprise Ontology (EEO) that has five top-level classes for integrating the various aspects of an enterprise (Activities and Processes, Time, Organization, Strategy and Marketing). The EEO is semi-formal, it provides a glossary of terms expressed in a restricted and structured form of natural language supplemented with a few formal axioms using KIF and Ontolingua [7].

A process ontology has also been developed known as PSL (the Process Specification Language) [10]. PSL defines a set of logic terms used to describe processes. The logic terms are specified in an ontology that provides a formal description of the components and their relationships that make up a process. The ontology was developed at the National Institute of Standards and Technology (NIST), and has been approved as an international standard known as ISO 18629.

We would also like to mention the UEEO (Unified Enterprise Modeling Ontology) [1] which is elaborated on the basis of the work done in the INTEROP NoE (Network of Excellence) to develop UEML (Unified Enterprise Modeling Language). UEML is seen as an enterprise modeling metamodel to support the interoperability of enterprise models [3].

IDEF5 is an ontology description capture method developed under the IDEF initiative [9]. The method provides a structured technique and languages, by which a domain expert can develop and maintain usable domain ontologies. However, IDEF5 ontology does not have an explicit link to IDEF0, IDEF1 and IDEF3 modeling languages, it is a general-purpose ontology for enterprise engineering.

The existing enterprise ontologies were elaborated in different contexts for different purposes. They don't aim to define the enterprise modeling domain by identifying concepts and relationships between the concepts in the domain.

41.3. Research methodology

The present research was carried out in two phases. First, the ontology of individual enterprise modeling languages was elaborated using the OWL ontology tool: IDEF0, IDEF1, IDEF3, MoGo, GRAI grid and GRAI net, BPMN and ISO 19440. Then, individual ontologies are compared and mapped to finally develop a unified Enterprise Modeling ontology modeled using the Protégé tool.

In this research, the UPON Lite methodology for rapid ontology engineering proposed by De Nicolas & Missikoff [4] has been adopted and used. UPON stands for "Unified Process for ONtology building". It is organized as a sequence of steps, where the outcome of each one is enriched and refined in the succeeding step; the steps produce the following outcomes:

1) Lexicon – to identify all the terms belonging to the domain;

2) Glossary – with the list of terms produced as lexicon, each of the terms are then to be given a description;

3) Meronymy – to connect terms with each other in a "PartOf" relationship: one is a component of another;

4) Attribution – to connect terms with each other in a "HasA" relationship, that is, one term is an attribute of another;

5) Taxonomy – to connect terms with each other in an "ISA" relationship, that is, one term is a subclass of another;

6) Ontology – to introduce the domain relations, integrating all the above and represent the ontology in a diagram.

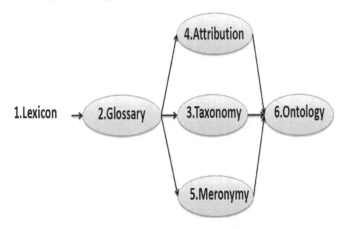

Figure 41.1. *UPON Lite methodology [4]*

41.4. Preliminary result

The ontology of individual enterprise modeling language is elaborated following the UPON Lite methodology. At this stage of the research, steps 4 and 5 are not considered. At first the concepts of an individual enterprise modeling language were identified by decomposing the language into basic elements. Then relationships between the elements are identified. The three basic relationships provided by OWL are used (IS_A, HAS, PART_OF). Figure 41.2 shows the OWL representation of IDEF modeling language ontology (IDEF0, IDEF1 and IDEF3). It is concerned with IDEF modeling concepts to describe functions, information and processes.

A specific enterprise modeling language may use some specific concepts and semantics that are not used in other similar modeling languages. One example is the concept of the 'Unit of Behavior' used in IDEF3 that does not exist in other process modeling languages such as BPMN or MoGo. We have decided to keep this concept in the IDEF modeling ontology. However, it is not selected in the unified Enterprise Modeling Ontology to avoid redundancy and overlapping with process concept.

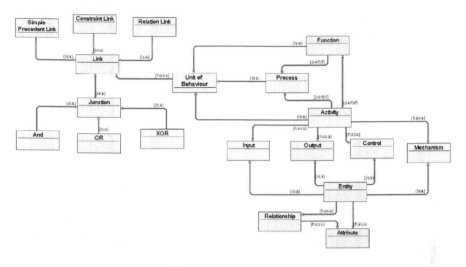

Figure 41.2. *IDEF (0, 1 and 3) ontology representation using OWL [8].*
For a color version of this figure, see www.iste.co.uk/zelm/enterprise.zip

Figure 41.3 presents the GRAI grid and the GRAI net modeling language ontology. GRAI grid aims at modeling a decision system structure with the decision center concept and links between decision centers. GRAI net aims at modeling decision and execution activities inside a decision center.

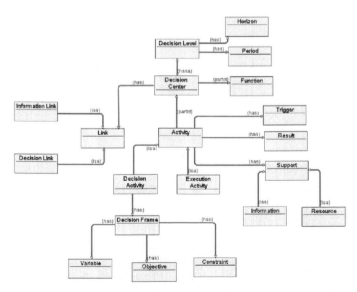

Figure 41.3. *GRAI grid and GRAI net modeling language ontology.*
For a color version of this figure, see www.iste.co.uk/zelm/enterprise.zip

It is to note that at this stage, only concepts and basic OWL relationships are defined without identifying attributes. Besides IDEF and GRAI, other ontology representations were also elaborated for BPMN, MoGo, ISO 19440 modeling constructs. Finally, the unified Enterprise Modeling Ontology is built using both OWL and Protégé tools. Figure 41.4 shows the Protégé representation of the ontology.

This version is obtained using the GRAI grid and net ontology and IDEF (0,1,3) ontology as a basis. Other ontologies (BPMN, MoGo and ISO 19440) are mapped to the GRAI and IDEF ones. Besides the "Unit of behavior" concept, Pool and Lane concepts in BPMN are not considered in the current version because it is too specific. Not all concepts in 19440 are selected (e.g. Role) as they need some further investigations.

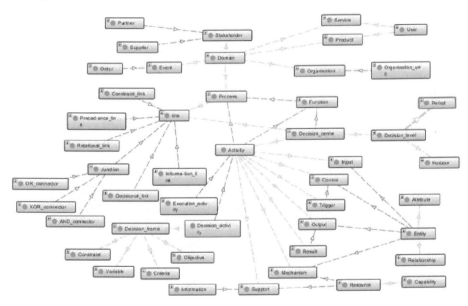

Figure 41.4. *Enterprise Modeling Ontology (version 1.0). For a color version of this figure, see www.iste.co.uk/zelm/enterprise.zip*

41.5. Discussion

– An Enterprise Modeling Ontology is different from an enterprise modeling language metamodel. The first one aims to define the domain of enterprise modeling by identifying the concepts in the domain and relationship between those concepts. The second one's purpose is to define the concepts/constructs used in an enterprise modeling language in order to build an enterprise model.

– An Enterprise Modeling Ontology is not an enterprise ontology although they may share a common set of concepts. Some of the enterprise modeling concepts are artifacts created to represent some aspects of an enterprise, they don't exist in an enterprise.

– The identification of concepts was done based on some selected known enterprise modeling languages. Main issues were to better define the semantics of those concepts. The semantics are defined mainly with the help of the attributes and relationships between concepts.

– It has been found that the basic relationship types provided by OWL (such as IS_A, PART_OF, HAS_A) are quite limited and not expressive enough to represent all important relationships in the domain of enterprise modeling. However, adding specific (personalized) relationships might create additional semantic ambiguity in the ontology which is contrary to the purpose of ontology.

41.6. Conclusion

This chapter has tentatively presented a proposal to develop an Enterprise Modeling Ontology. It focused on explicitly defining the enterprise modeling domain through the identification of a set of concepts and relationships in the domain. Such an ontology should allow enterprise modeling developers and practitioners to better understand the meaning of the modeling concepts used in heterogeneous enterprise modeling languages, to facilitate models exchange and improve their interoperability.

The approach adopted is bottom-up, starting from existing concepts used in enterprise modeling languages. The version 1.0 of the enterprise modeling ontology has been outlined in the chapter. It should be considered as a preliminary result that must be refined and extended to cover other enterprise modeling languages that are not considered in the present version. Another important issue is the ontology validation. An ontology cannot be considered as such if it is not generally agreed and accepted. This would be a rather long and iterative process. To achieve this, it is envisaged to publish the ontology online to collect comments and look for consensus.

41.7. Acknowledgements

This chapter is based on an International Master project on Enterprise Engineering at the University of Bordeaux. The author thanks M.H. Nguyen, S.A. Mamun, Zhang Yue, Wang Yao, J. Wilson and Liu Yuli for their contribution to this research action.

41.8. References

[1] OPDAHL A., "Anatomy of the Unified Enterprise Modelling Ontology", *3rd IFIP Working Conference on Enterprise Interoperability*, Stockholm, Sweden, Springer, pp.163–176, 2011.

[2] ATHENA, ATHENA WDA1.8 - POP* Revised framework, Version 1.0, May 24th, 2006.

[3] BERIO G. *et al.*, UEML 2.0. Deliverable 5.1. INTEROP project UE-IST-508011, available at: www.interop-noe.org, 2005.

[4] DE NICOLAS A., MISSIKOFF M., "A lightweight methodology for rapid ontology engineering", *ACM*, vol. 59, no. 3, pp. 79–86, 2016.

[5] FOX M.S., "The TOVE Project: Towards a Common-sense Model of the Enterprise", *Enterprise Integration Laboratory Technical Report*, 1992.

[6] KNOTHE T., BUSSELT C., BOLL D., Deliverable D23 – Report on UEML (Needs and Requirements), UEML, Thematic Network, 2003.

[7] USCHOLD M., KING M., MORALEE S. *et al.*, "The Enterprise Ontology", *Knowl. Eng. Rev.*, vol. 13, pp. 31–89, Specia, 1997.

[8] NGUYEN M. H., MAMUN S.A., WILSON J. *et al.*, Ontology for enterprise modelling, Master project report, University of Bordeaux, January 2018.

[9] BENJAMIN P.C. *et al.,* IDEF5 Method Report, Armstrong Laboratory AL/HRGA, Wright-Patterson Air Force Base, Ohio, September 21st 1994.

[10] NIST, "PSL Ontology – Current Theories and Extensions", National Institute of Standards and Technology, January 15th 2007.

42

Model-driven Requirements Elicitation for Manufacturing System Development

For a long time, complexity has been mentioned as a real challenge in the development of manufacturing systems. Today, considering new technological trends contributing to the creation of Cyber Physical Production Systems (CPPS), the degree of complexity might even increase. Facing this challenge, enterprise modeling techniques can be applied to simplify the representation and analysis of the systems. This chapter highlights the usage of such techniques for the requirements elicitation phase. The contributions are illustrated through a case study which is a manufacturing system in the cutlery industry adopting a CPPSization strategy in the frame of a European research project. The modeling work was globally guided by Model-driven Service Engineering Architecture (MDSEA). With the support of this architecture and its devoted modeling tool, including modeling languages adapted to the business level, the requirements were identified and validated for the use-case.

42.1. Introduction

One of the current evolution axes for manufacturing systems is to become Cyber-Physical Production Systems (CPPS), based on the prevailing information and communication technological trends towards the fourth industrial revolution (I4.0) [MON 14]. To develop manufacturing systems, and by extension CPPPS, management requires a proper understanding of the processes to rapidly and precisely define the requirements [ROW 97] for the development of the manufacturing system. For this purpose, enterprise modeling techniques can be applied as preliminary support for management by simplifying the representation of

Chapter written by Amir Pirayesh, Guy Doumeingts, João Sousa, Carlos Agostinho, Sudeep Ghimire and Cristiano Fertuzinhos.

the processes [SAV 96, DOU 01, ZAC 17]. Considering the plethora of existing modeling solutions [KET 97], the choice of the adapted language might be challenging. Besides the subject of modeling as a criterion for this choice, the modeling level and profile of the modeler/user should be considered [DOU 98]. This chapter underlines the usage of Model-driven Service Engineering Architecture (MDSEA) [DUC 14], initially proposed based on model-driven engineering and interoperability [SCH 06]. This architecture, its associated methodology and modeling languages, on the one hand, guide the modeling work for requirements elicitation by covering different points of view (e.g. business or technical, static or dynamic); on the other hand, consider the different layers of enterprise management and decision-making (e.g. from machine control to factory management in a manufacturing system). The propositions are illustrated through a case study; an experiment in the frame of a European research project.

42.2. Methodology

To guide the requirements elicitation process and to select the adapted modeling solutions (from business to technical levels), MDSEA [DUC 14], can be followed (see Figure 42.1). This architecture takes into account the various aspects of the manufacturing system from the real world to the technical and human worlds but also along the life cycle of the system, product and services: *Business System Model (BSM)*: models at this level represent the real world (user point of view). BSM describes the running of the manufacturing system at a conceptual level, independent of any specifications concerning human or technical resources; *Technology Independent Model (TIM)*: This level is obtained by extracting and then transforming the concepts identified at the previous level (BSM) in three domains: IT (IT components/artifacts), physical means (machines or tools development) and human/organization (competences/skills and departments); *Technology Specific Model (TSM)*: the TSM is the last and detailed level of modeling. Detailed specifications should be defined here depending on the specific technologies in order to develop or provide software, recruit or train personnel or to purchase machines or means of production.

MDSEA is supported by a modeling tool called the Manufacturing System Tool Box (MSTB) (initially developed in the frame of an MSEE European project [DUC 14]). The tool can be used by enterprises willing to develop a new service/system or wanting to improve an existing one, within a single enterprise or in a supply chain. MSTB is considered as an intuitive tool which could be used by the end-user after an initial training and it does not require the permanent support of a consultant. Model transformation is not completely developed. It should be noted that the focus of this paper is mainly on the BSM level (resulting in the identification of business requirements) and the beginning of the TIM level for IT domain (resulting in the identification of IT requirements and the design of ICT architecture).

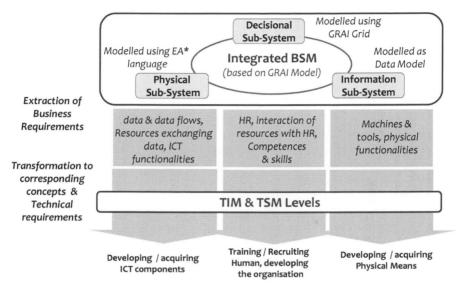

Figure 42.1. *Modeling at BSM level of MDSEA for requirement elicitation*

42.3. Case study

The case study is focused on the management of the production system in a manufacturing company; a young SME in the cutlery industry. This specific sector had a quite linear technological progress, where the production lines were basically human work based in the mid-80s and 90s but has undergone a bold transformation in labor-intensive tasks through the automation and robotization of their production lines. More recently, the in-house machines and tools development has made a great contribution in production scenarios, enabling some flexibility of the production process, a quality increase of final products and the diversification of their catalogue. Furthermore, the cutlery industry has been paying attention to recent Industrial 4.0 initiatives, IoT and CPS developments to remain competitive and updated with modern production lines and an efficiency of their process in terms of time and cost. In the experimentation, the enterprise management team has seen a great opportunity in CPS-ization through increasing the communicational capacity of their PLC and robot-based production process and linking the shop-floor to the higher decisional levels. This evolution is very much in line with recent company business strategy and investments.

42.3.1. *Elaboration of models*

Following the adopted development methodology (i.e. MDSEA), we performed the "requirements elicitation" at the first step, called [integrated] BSM, using enterprise modeling techniques. In order to elaborate the as-is and to-be models at BSM, the GRAI model (Graph with Results and Activities Interrelated) is applied [DOU 84, CHE 96]. In this model, a system or particularly a [manufacturing] enterprise system is decomposed into three sub-systems (see Figure 42.3): *Physical (controlled) Sub-system* transforms the inputs (e.g. materials and information) into outputs (e.g. information, products or services) to be mainly delivered to the customers. At the business level, this sub-system can be modeled as actigrams using Extended Actigram start (EA*) language [CHE 96]; *Decisional (control) Sub-system* manages the physical Sub-system based on the objectives of the global system (i.e. enterprise system) and feedback information in order to deliver actions or adjustments. At the business level, this sub-system can be modeled as a decisional structure using GRAI Grid formalism [CHE 96]; *Information Sub-system* (also called ICT sub-system) mainly includes information from the physical sub-system and the customers, suppliers and other stakeholders (external environment). It also allows exchanging information (e.g. feedbacks) between the other Sub-systems. At the business level, this sub-system can be modeled as a data model based on the notion of class diagrams. It is only an initial model in order to identify the main data/information.

The to-be model was developed based on the as-is model in order to answer to the weaknesses and points to improve those detected in the latter. The comparison between these models allows the elicitation of the business requirements: which part of the model requires improvement?, what are the new functionalities and solutions that should be introduced to the manufacturing system to improve its performance? The business requirements potentially respond to these questions.

42.3.2. *Definition or Business Requirements*

Business Requirements (BU_RQs) were identified by comparing the as-is and to-be models and their elements (e.g. a decision centre in the model of the decisional sub-system) while considering the business objectives (see Figure 42.2.). Such requirements are indeed deduced from the potential high-level solutions required for realizing the to-be model. The identified BU_RQs are presented in this chapter.

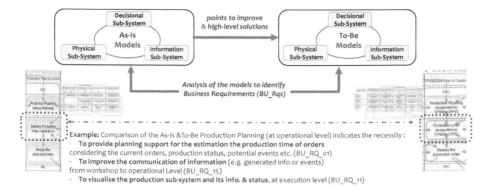

Figure 42.2. *Requirements elicitation through analysis of as-is and to-be models. For a color version of this figure, see www.iste.co.uk/zelm/enterprise.zip*

42.4. Conclusions and discussions

This chapter showcases the application of a model-driven methodology for requirements elicitation in manufacturing system development, where the requirements are defined based on the analysis of system models elaborated at the business level. This methodology is founded on MDSEA and it is illustrated through an industrial use-case in this chapter. At the business level, using adapted modeling languages, it was possible to elaborate a shared vision of the system to be developed for its stakeholders. First, the use-case weaknesses in the business processes were highlighted in an as-is model while identifying the potential cause of the problems. Considering the business objectives and the points to improve, a to-be model was elaborated.

The proposed methodology also facilitates the transformation of the requirements into specifications and supports the implementation of ICT solutions. In the use-case, following the identified requirement, a prototype is currently under development to improve the production planning and control functionality and to enhance workshop bilateral communication with the management, by increasing CPS capacities in the production (CPS-ization) (mainly through improved data generation and communication). Regarding the future research work, the authors intend to investigate the human/organizational domain of MDSEA and its relation with other domains (i.e. ICT and physical means). For instance, it might be necessary to modify the functional structure of the company following new IT implementations or vice versa. The transformation of static models into simulation models in also considered to be a research perspective [ZAC 17].

42.5. Acknowledgments

This work has been partly funded by the European Commission through the BEinCPPS project (H2020-FoF-2015, no. 680633); CPMSinCPPS (Cutting-edge Process Modeling & Simulation in CPPS) experiment.

42.6. References

[CHE 96] CHEN D., DOUMEINGTS, G., "The GRAI-GIM reference model, architecture and methodology", in BERNUS P., NEMES L., WILLIAMS T.J. (eds), *Architectures for Enterprise Integration*, IFIP Advances in Information and Communication Technology, 1996.

[DOU 84] DOUMEINGTS G., Méthode GRAI : méthode de conception des systèmes en productique, PhD Thesis, University of Bordeaux 1, 13 November 1984.

[DOU 98] DOUMEINGTS G., VALLESPIR B., CHEN D., "Decisional modeling GRAI Grid" in BERNUS P., MERTINS K., SCHMIDT G. (eds), *International Handbook on Information Systems*, Springer, Berlin, 1998.

[DOU 01] DOUMEINGTS G., DUCQ Y., "Enterprise Modeling techniques to improve efficiency of enterprises", *International Journal of Production Planning & Control*, vol. 12, no. 2, pp. 146–163, 2001.

[DUC 14] DUCQ Y., AGOSTINHO C., CHEN D. *et al.*, "Generic Methodology for Service Engineering based on Service Modeling and Model Transformation State of the art in model driven approaches and model transformation", *Manufacturing Service Ecosystem: Achievements of the European 7th Framework Programme*, Verlag-Mainz, Aachen, pp. 41–49, 2014.

[KET 97] KETTINGER W. J., TENG J. T. C., GUHA S., "Business process change: a study of methodologies, techniques, and tools", *MIS Quarterly*, vol. 21, no. 1, pp. 55–80, 1997.

[MON 14] MONOSTORIA L., "Cyber-physical production systems: roots, expectations and R&D challenges, Variety Management in Manufacturing", *Proceedings of the 47th CIRP Conference on Manufacturing Systems*, vol. 17, pp. 9–13, 2014.

[ROW 97] ROWEL R., ALFECHE K., *Requirements Engineering: a Good Practice Guide*, John Wiley and Sons, 1997.

[SAV 96] SAVAGE C. M., *Fifth Generation Management: Co-creating Through Virtual Enterprising, Dynamic Teaming, and Knowledge Networking*, Elsevier, 1996.

[SCH 06] SCHMIDT D. C., "Model-Driven Engineering", *IEEE Computer*, vol. 39, no. 2, pp. 25–31, February 2006.

[ZAC 17] ZACHAREWICZ G., PIRAYESH, A., SEREGNI M. *et al.*, "Simulation-based Enterprise Management", in MITTAL S., DURAK U., ÖREN T. (eds), *Guide to Simulation-based Disciplines*, Springer, 2017.

43

A Comprehensive Architecture to Integrate Modeling and Simulation Solutions in CPPS

Concepts such as CPPS (Cyber-Physical Production Systems), and IIoT (Industrial Internet of Things) have emerged to answer the requirements of a continuously changing manufacturing environment. Recent advances on smart sensors together with the consistent decrease of technology costs have contributed for the rapid development of industrially oriented IoT. In parallel, modeling and simulation technologies have proven to be an extremely useful analysis tool that can work with conjunction with IIoT data to contribute to better decisions at the business level. This chapter presents a comprehensive architecture to integrate such technologies in a CPPS solution for SMEs that complement physical production systems with data collection and feedback mechanisms.

43.1. Introduction

Industry 4.0 is recognized as the future of industrial production systems, in which concepts such as the Smart Factory are fundamental. Research and development in manufacturing tend to, traditionally, target the acceleration and mass-replication of more or less static production processes and controller software. However, the last decade has demonstrated that industry cannot proceed with such practice [MAR 17]. With the introduction of the Cyber-Physical System (CPS), all the factory resources will eventually become context aware and will be involved in cooperation and communication activities, monitoring the surrounding

Chapter written by Carlos Agostinho, José Ferreira, Sudeep Ghimire, Gregory Zacharewicz, Amir Pirayesh and Guy Doumeingts.

environment, using sensors and actuators as a support to provide feedback into production, and modifying the physical and digital assets [ZAN 15]. The implementation of CPS technology in production systems leads to Cyber-Physical Production Systems (CPPS) [THI 16].

To implement CPPS and avoid developing yet another framework, it is necessary to choose and adapt the most adequate one. Hence, aiming to improve the adoption of CPPSs all over Europe by means of CPS-driven regional innovation ecosystems, the BEinCPPS project (www.beincpps.eu) analyzed different service platforms and innovative business models ready to be adopted. It is integrating and testing future internet technology in SME environments to improve the performance of industrial processes and to increase their dynamicity [MOL 17]. This chapter addresses and presents the results of the BEinCPPS sub-project CPMSinCPPS, where an architecture has been customized to integrate modeling and simulation solutions. The architecture is being validated in a real use-case scenario, involving a Portuguese SME focused on the production of cutlery. The authors are experimenting with the architecture and its components: (1) to improve the production performance with a better planning and estimation of the lead time; (2) to propose corrective and preventive actions to gain agility; and (3) to improve the awareness of planners about the production status.

43.2. Literature review

CPPS consists of different elements and autonomous systems connected to each other, covering all levels of production, from processes to machines. By modeling its operation and predicting its possible behavior, a new level of control is obtained, creating a series of application-oriented tasks that facilitate the control of the overall production. With the ultimate objective of exploring the relationships of autonomy, cooperation, optimization, and awareness, one possible CPPS approach is to apply analytical and simulation-based methods. Other challenges include dealing with large amounts of data, the retrieval of lost data, representation and interpretation of information and security [MON 14]. The network of sensors allows the company to be able to cross-reference internal information, such as orders and schedules, with information gathered in real time through different types of sensors and middleware such as the FIWARE Orion [CAR 17]. This will become an integral part of the company as object information that enhances enterprise resources with a sense of awareness about the environment, enabling one to know, in real-time, what is happening across the enterprise and enterprise networks [SAN 12]. In such line of work, the OSMOSE Project (FP7 610905) developed a reference architecture, a middleware and some prototypal applications for the sensing enterprise, by interconnecting real, digital, and virtual worlds [AGO 15]. It supports the organization of the entire manufacturing enterprise, bringing them closer to the Industry 4.0 paradigm.

Process Modeling: Enterprise Modeling (EM) is of the many techniques available to take advantage of the cyber worlds. It is intended "to design, control and improve the business processes in order to adapt to the changing business environment and cope with innovations, mutations of customers' expectations and increasing competition" [BUR 01]. As part of EM, a process modeling technique usually provides simplified representations of complex processes and clarifies the key elements [ZAC 17]. Indeed, the use of modeling solutions must be followed by a structural architecture and a methodology that covers different points of view (for example, business or technical, static or dynamic), while being able to consider end users in different layers of the company. To support companies in modeling their processes, some well-know notations are available (e.g. BPMN, UML Activity Diagrams or Actigram) and implemented by different tools (e.g. JBPN (www.jbpm.org), ACTIVITI (www.activiti.org), Modelio (www.modelio.org)).

Process modeling notations are appropriate to separate the business details from the technical details of a system [MOZ 17]. Usually, business details are defined by domain experts to identify requirements, while the technical details consist of specific information about the implementation of a system. Different notations support different levels of detail. Hence, to support this transition, model-driven methodologies such as OMG's MDA or MDSEA have been applied with some degree of success, reusing abstract models in more technical models closer to the real implementation [DUC 14, WHI 14]. The SLM Toolbox[1] is one of the tools supporting such separation, enabling one to perform business modeling using Actigram notation and enabling the transformation to a more technical BPMN language that is used to define service calls ready to be deployed and executed in workflow engines such as the KIE workbench provided by the JBPM.

Process Simulation: simulation has been a widely used tool for manufacturing system design and analysis [ZAC 17]. It has proven to be an extremely useful analysis tool, and many hundreds of articles have focused directly on the topic. Since 1976, Zeigler has proposed the Discrete EVent Specification (DEVS) [ZEI 00] as an integrated formalism which enhances the model designing efficiency with unambiguous specification formalism and provides a methodology for execution by means of an executable semantics. We have chosen DEVS as the simulation language for the previously discussed reasons in order to remove ambiguity and to unify the Modeling and Simulation (M&S) concepts.

There are numerous software products in the simulation field. Many were reported on the use of several relevant application papers from the last decade of Winter Simulation Conference proceedings. Arena and Automod/Autosched were used most frequently, followed by Quest, ProModel, Sigma, and Extend [SEM 06].

---

1 http://interop-vlab.eu/service-lifecycle-manufacturing-tool-box-slmtb/.

Also, simulation tools are developed in the academic and/or open source context (NetLogo, MS4ME, VLE, etc.). The DEVS group standardization maintains on its website the updated list of the most used DEVS tools known by the DEVS community [WAI 13]. In [HAM 12], the authors present a brief description and comparison of popular tools. Mentioning some, ADEVS was the first DEVS tool developed; CD++ Builder is a DEVS modeling and simulation environment that integrates interesting features and facilities for the user; JDEVS is the Java implementation of a DEVS formal framework supporting multi-modeling paradigms based on DEVS and ensuring interoperability among the reused components; SIMSTUDIO for DEVS non Expert and so on. The authors also investigate LSIS_DME which is focused on a graphical interface and code source generation in order to complete the model by complex Java functions.

43.3. Business experiments in CPPS architecture

Following the analysis of the industrial use-case and considering the business and technical requirements identified [CPM 17], a comprehensive architecture is proposed to achieve the objectives of implementing and validating CPPS in a real SME (see Figure 43.1). Its instantiation with specific tools has been supported by the literature review. Illustrated in blue (with the dark background) are the components elected directly from the BEinCPPS reference framework [UM 17], and in orange (with the light background) are the components that complement the architecture, tailored to meet the business objective of the SME. In addition, the architecture is defined considering its application in two complementary phases.

Design Phase: with a selection of components to support the company in the modeling and configuration (engineering) of the CPPS environment. This part of the architecture is composed by the functional components responsible for "business & process modeling" and "CPPS design & simulation". The engineering layer is therefore used for modeling the productions system (i.e. physical and decisional sub-systems), defining the business processes that are comprised of human tasks, machine operations, service calls and so on. Within the engineering layer and connected to the modeling components using an MDA-like approach, are the simulation components. As represented in the figure, there are different tools elected from the state of the art (section 43.2), that is the SLM Toolbox to begin modeling at a higher abstraction level in Actigram, Activiti BPM taking as input the BPMN models created in the Toolbox and enriching them with workflow execution details, Modelio to complement such models with the necessary information about the physical system and enabling a simulation of the resources, and finally SimStudio for the DEVS simulation.

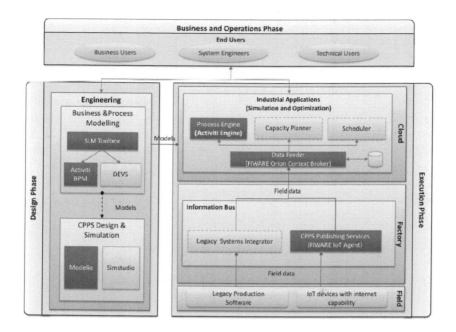

Figure 43.1. *CPMSinCPPS architecture. For a color version of this figure, see www.iste.co.uk/zelm/enterprise.zip*

Execution Phase: with a selection of components to support the execution of the CPPS. It is composed of the Cloud, Field and Factory Layers, which in turn are instantiated by functional components for industrial application (planning and scheduling) and the information "collection" bus. The latter is the broker, responsible for the registration, connection, acquisition, filtering and storage of the data from the shop floor IIoT devices and from the legacy production software, which requires a specific adapter to be developed. The industrial applications include the process engine which deploys and executes the process models defined at the design phase; the capacity planner that compares the working capacities of the machine resources with workload estimated in the production planning (handled at legacy software); and the scheduler to optimize the calendarization of the work in a specific machine resource, accounting for set-up time and maintenance (estimated from IIoT input). As in the design phase, different tools are foreseen – the Activiti engine, the FIWARE Orion context broker[2] and the FIWARE IoT agent[3]. Some modules such as the scheduler are marked with a dotted line and are still under analysis to select the best tool.

---

2 https://fiware-orion.readthedocs.io/en/master/.

3 http://fiware-iot-stack.readthedocs.io/en/latest/device_gateway/.

43.4. Conclusion and future work

This chapter presents the work that is being developed in the CPMSinCPPS project, which is developing and experimenting a set of tools to support the manufacturing processes of a factory through CPPS models. Modeling begins with the development of business models, which are then transformed into technical models that, when executed, allow to coordinate what is happening at each step of the production process. At the same time, it is possible to simulate the process identifying potential problems that occur, whereas in real time, the company is supported by tools that allow a monitoring and adjusting of the production plan and schedule. Future work foresees the analysis and selection of the tools still missing to instantiate the presented architecture.

43.5. Acknowledgments

The research leading to these results has received funding from the EC H2020 Program under grant agreement no. BEinCPPS 680633.

43.6. References

[AGO 15] Agostinho C., Sesana M., Jardim-Gonçalves R. *et al.*, "Model-driven Service Engineering Towards the Manufacturing Liquid-sensing Enterprise", *MODELSWARD 2015*, Angers, France, 2015.

[BUR 01] Burlton R.T., "Business process management: profiting from process", Sams Publishing, Indianapolis, IN, 2001.

[CAR 17] Cardoso J., Pereira C., Aguiar A. *et al.*, "Benchmarking IoT middleware platforms", *WoWMoM. 2017*, Macau, China, DOI: 10.1109/WoWMoM.2017.7974339, 2017.

[CPM 17] CPMSinCPPS, "D1 – Requirements and Architecture" deliverable, BEinCPPS, 2017.

[DUC 14] Ducq Y., Agostinho C., Chen D. *et al.*, "Generic methodology for service engineering based on service modelling and model transformation state of the art in model-driven approaches and model transformation", *Manufacturing Service Ecosystem: Achievements of the European 7th Framework Programme FoF-ICT Project MSEE: Manufacturing SErvice Ecosystem*, pp. 41–49, 2014.

[HAM 12] Hamri M., Zacharewicz G., "Automatic generation of object-oriented code from DEVS graphical specifications", *WSC'12*, Berlin, Germany, 2012.

[MAR 17] Marques M., Agostinho C., Zacharewicz G. *et al.*, "Decentralized decision support for intelligent manufacturing in Industry 4.0", *Journal of Ambient Intelligence and Smart Environments*, vol. 9, pp. 299–313, DOI: 10.3233/AIS-170436, 2017.

[MOL 17] Molina E., Lazaro O., Sepulcre M. *et al.*, "The AUTOWARE framework and requirements for the cognitive digital automation", *PROV'17*, available at: https://doi.org/10.1007/978-3-319-65151-4_10, 2017.

[MON 14] Monostori L., "Cyber-physical production systems: roots, expectations, and R&D challenges", *Proceedia CIRP*, vol. 17, pp. 9–13, 2014.

[MOZ 17] Mozzaquatro B.A., Jardim-Gonçalves R., Agostinho C., "Model-driven implementation of security management process", *MODELSWARD 2017*, Porto, PT, pp. 229–238, 2017.

[SAN 12] Santucci G., Martinez C., Vlad-câlcic D., "The Sensing Enterprise", *FInES Workshop at FIA 2012*, Aalborg, Denmark, 2012.

[SEM 06] Semini M., Fauske H., Strandhagen J.O., "Applications of discrete-event simulation to support manufacturing logistics decision-making: a survey", *WSC'06*, Monterey, CA, pp. 1946–1953, 2006.

[THI 16] Thiede S., Juraschek M., Herrmann C., "Implementing cyber-physical production systems in learning factories", *Proceedia CIRP*, vol. 54, pp. 7–12, 2016.

[UM 17] Um J., Fischer K., Spieldenner T. *et al.*, "Development of a modular factory with modular software components", *Procedia Manufacturing*, vol. 11, pp. 922–930, 2017.

[WAI 13] Wainer G., DEVS TOOLS, Carleton University, Ottowa, Canada, available at: http://www.sce.carleton.ca/faculty/wainer/standard/tools.htm, November 2013.

[WHI 14] Whittle J., Hutchinson J., Rouncefield M., "The state of practice in model-driven engineering", *IEEE Software*, vol. 31, pp. 79–85, 2014.

[ZAC 17] Zacharewicz G., Pirayesh-Neghab A., Seregni M. *et al.*, "Simulation-based enterprise management; model-driven from business process to simulation", Mittal S., Durak U., Ören T. (eds), *Guide to Simulation-based Disciplines*, Springer, Cham, Switzerland, pp. 261–289, 2017.

[ZAN 15] Zanni A., "Cyber-physical systems and smart cities", IBM, available at: https://www.ibm.com/developerworks/library/ba-cyber-physical-systems-and-smart-cities-iot/, accessed: March 4th, 2015, 2015.

[ZEI 00] Zeigler B.P., Praehofer H., Kim T.G., *Theory of Modeling and Simulation*, 2nd edition, Academic Press, 2000.

Modeling and Simulation of Decision Systems

Modeling decision systems has been always a challenging activity as it involves human decision-makers which means there is a need for modeling complex behaviors. Simulating such decision systems adds levels of complexity. This chapter presents the DGRAI model and software tool which extend the GRAI model allowing the simulation with GRAI nets.

44.1. Introduction

Enterprise modeling is the art of externalizing enterprise knowledge, representing its structure, organization and behavior, which adds value to the enterprise [VER 03] by providing a semantic unification space where shared concepts can be properly defined, mapped to one another and widely communicated in the form of enterprise models [GOR 92]. Modeling and enterprises are not only related with understanding each other but in analyzing, reengineering and optimizing operations to improve efficiency. Enterprise models should include function aspects (business processes, enterprise activities), information aspects (enterprise objects, relationships, flows), resource aspects (human, technical), organization aspects (organizational unites, decision centers) and temporal and causal constraints [AMI 93] providing abstract representations of the real enterprise components and being analyzed in order to improve its business processes, automate critical processes, to tune enterprise performances and support the decision-making using "what if" scenarios. In order to support the evaluation of analyzed or designed enterprise models, a link between enterprise modeling and simulation is needed [REI 97]. Although different

Chapter written by Raul POLER, Beatriz ANDRES, Guy DOUMEINGTS and Amir PIRAYESH.

enterprise modeling techniques have been proposed over the last few decades, not many of them provide simulation engines for running the enterprise models.

This chapter presents a software tool for modeling and simulating decision systems based on the GRAI model [DOU 84] extended to the DGRAI model [POL 02]. DGRAI allows for the execution of the decision-making processes, providing valuable information for analyzing the dynamic behavior of an enterprise system.

44.2. Decision systems modeling: the GRAI model

The GRAI model, with the GRAI Integrated Methodology (GIM) [CHE 97], aims to provide a generic description of a production system, focusing on the management and control point of view, called the decision system, and a methodology to use the GRAI model to capture the characteristics of the real decision model. In order to structure the decision system, two axes of decomposition are defined: the vertical one is the co-ordination axis, and horizontal one is the synchronization axis (Figure 44.1).

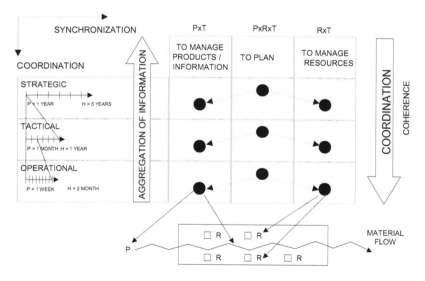

Figure 44.1. *Co-ordination and synchronization axes in the GRAI model*

The co-ordination criterion is a timed one. A couple of time features define each level: "horizon" (the interval of time over which the decisions extend) and "period" (the interval of time after which the set of decisions is reconsidered). Decision levels are: strategic, tactical and operational. Strategic and tactical levels are period-driven (decision activities are launched when a new period starts), while operational levels are event-driven (activities are launched by the appearance of events). Information is aggregated from the bottom to the upper level and decisions are disaggregated from the top to the bottom level. The synchronization criterion is a functional one, with three basic types of functional activities: product management activities, planning activities and resource management activities. The resulting matrix from the two dimensions is the GRAI grid. For each coordination level and each synchronization level a decision centre is set, containing one or several GRAI nets, composed of decision and execution activities.

44.3. Decision systems simulation: the DGRAI model

The first approaches to decision systems simulation in the framework of the GRAI method were presented in [AKI 91, CAR 96, WAD 98, ALA 98], however, simulation has been defined only at the GRAI grid level. Recent research for use simulation in decision systems propose an approach for coupling decisional modeling with the simulation in the frame of model-driven service engineering architecture [ZAC 17]. The novelty of the DGRAI model was to simulate the decision flows at GRAI net level maintaining the GRAI formalism and extending it for modeling the dynamicity of decision-making flows. The DGRAI model formalisms and parameters are:

– Horizons and periods: according to the simulation point of view, periods will set the events' evolution; horizons will have influence on the quality of supports. The review period for the updating of decisions already made is directly related with the time parameter of the decision system simulation model. The horizon used to make the decisions and will determine the higher or lower quality of such decisions. Horizons and periods can be defined using different time scales, the most common ones are: "year", "month", "week", "day", "hour", "minute" and "second".

– Activities: these are the main components of the GRAI nets. Activities are the starting points for structuring the execution and decision flows and for building the nets. The most important parameter at this level is the time required to carry out a particular activity. This time duration is modeled by a parameterized probability distribution (e.g. normal, beta, Weibull, etc.). The parameters for this distribution may be altered depending on the decision-maker and the quality of supports, in concordance with a previously established formula.

– Supports: starting from the static design of the GRAI nets, different types of supports are identified (information, objective, decision variables, constraints and criteria). Two different types of time are associated with supports: searching time and processing time. The human resource in charge of executing an activity must first collect and understand all the activity supports. A corrective factor for each Human Resource is used to model the differences between them regarding their speed for searching and processing supports. An activity can be executed only when all supports are ready, therefore, taking into account that some supports are generated by activities, a precise order of execution should be considered in the simulation process. On the other hand, in order to model the quality performance in the activities execution, supports also have a quality parameter associated. Each generated support starts with a quality calculated by [44.1].

$$QS_s = \frac{\sum_{i=1}^{ns} QS_i}{ns} \cdot \frac{\sum_{j=1}^{nhr} QHR_j}{nhr} \cdot \varphi(nhr) \qquad [44.1]$$

Where: QS_s is the quality of the generated support s; QS_i is the quality of the used support i; ns is the number of supports used in activity a to generate support s; QHR_j is the quality of the human resource j taking part in the generation of support s; nhr is the number of human resources taking part in the performance of activity a to generate support s; $\varphi(nhr)$ is the quality increase formula due to the contribution of several human resources in the performance of activity a.

– Human resources are essential for simulating the decision-making processes. Each activity should be executed by one or several human resources, who have a finite capacity and cannot execute more than one activity at same time. When an activity is activated (period-driven or event-driven), it is allocated to the corresponding human resource queue of activities to be executed. Such a queue will be managed by the human resource using different criteria: decision level, priority, waiting time and so on. Human resources are characterized by quality indicators that keep in mind the difference between decision-making at different levels (strategic, tactical and operational), whilst keeping in mind that a good strategic decision-maker may not be as good making operational or tactical decisions and vice versa. The human resource quality factor is used in [44.1] to calculate the quality obtained in the resulting support. Concerning the support search and process time and the activity execution time, human resources are parameterized with time factors, representing the different speeds. In order to model the interruption behavior of a human resource executing an activity, a beta probability distribution is used for simulation the interruptions and the time spend. As activities which should be executed by several human resources at the same time (e.g. a meeting) are particularly complex when it comes to putting together all participants, some abort parameters used in each human resource: the first is the percentage of activity completion for accepting the abortion, the second is the maximum time waiting for other human resources and incomplete meetings, also the human resource level in the organization is taken into account. The abortion rules are: (1) a human resource with certain organization level (e.g. level 1 correspond to the CEO) can oblige other human resources with below level (e.g. level 2 correspond to the production manager) to abort their current activity execution, no matter the percentage of completion; (2) a human resource can ask another one of the same organization level to abort the current activity execution if he/she has not reached the percentage of completion; (3) when various meetings are competing for human resources, the meeting with more human resources present has priority to be completed. Finally, cost parameters are associated at each human resource for the decision system total cost calculation.

During the decision system simulation execution, different performances can be observed, as time of completion of activities, nets, decision centers, costs of participating human resources, decision processes and so on. Nevertheless, an aggregated parameter is used for analyzing the simulation evolution and to compare different configurations of the decision system (particularly the as-is and to-be situations): the total quality of the decision system, represented by [44.2].

$$QT = \frac{\sum_{s=1}^{ngs} \rho_s \cdot QS_s}{\sum_{s=1}^{ngs} \rho_s} \qquad\qquad [44.2]$$

Where: QT is the total quality of the decision system; QS_s is the quality of support s; ρ_s is the relative weight of support s; nsg is the number of generated supports in the system.

The quality of a support is a time function which depends on the quality of that support at a given moment (at the time of its last regeneration) and on the horizon assigned to the decision centre at which the net containing the activity generates such support. Such quality has a descended behavior with time, which represents its deterioration due to having been generated some time ago, without taking into account the more recent information. The support quality recovers when the activity generating such support is re-executed.

44.4. The DGRAI software tool

The DGRAI model has been implemented in the DGRAI© software tool by the Research Centre on Production Management and Engineering of the Universitat Politecnica de Valencia and has been transferred to the Spin-off UPV EXOS Solutions which use it for the analysis and redesign of decision systems in private companies and public administrations. DGRAI© has been used in industrial companies of different sectors (automotive, textile, ceramic, etc.) to stimulate companies and supply chains. The current version of DGRAI$^©$ is 5.0 and future development work is oriented to the development of the DGRAI$^©$ Cloud which will provide Cloud services to its customers.

44.5. References

[AKI 91] AKIF J. C., "Consistency analysis of P.M.S. based on GRAI modelling", *Computer Applications in Production and Engineering: Integration Aspects*, Elsevier, Noth, Holland, 1991.

[ALA 98] AL-AHMARI A., "GI-SIM (GRAI/IDEF SIMulation)", *5th International Workshop AUGRAI*, Glasgow, August 1998.

[AMI 93] AMICE, "CIMOSA: open system architecture for CIM", 2nd edition, Springer-Verlag, 1993.

[CAR 96] CARRIE A., SUPARNO O., "Evaluation of computer aided production management by process modelling of GRAI grid", *3rd International Workshop AUGRAI*, Bordeaux, April 1996.

[CHE 97] CHEN D., VALLESPIR B., DOUMEINGTS G., "GRAI integrated methodology and its mapping onto generic enterprise reference architecture and methodology", *Computers in Industry*, vol. 33, nos 2–3, pp. 387–394, 1997.

[DOU 84] DOUMEINGTS G., Méthode GRAI: méthode de conception des systèmes en productique, Thesis, University of Bordeaux 1, 13 November 1984.

[GOR 92] GORANSON H.T., "Dimensions of enterprise integration", in PETRIE C. (ed.), *Enterprise Integration Modeling*, MIT Press, pp. 101–113, 1992.

[POL 02] POLER R., LARIO F.C., DOUMEINGTS G., "Dynamic modelling of decision systems (DMDS)", *Computers in Industry*, vol. 49, no. 2, pp. 175–193, 2002.

[REI 97] REITHOFER W., NAEGER G., "Bottom-up planning approaches in enterprise modeling – the need and the state of the art", *Computers in Industry*, vol. 33, nos 2–3, pp. 223–235, 1997.

[VER 03] VERNADAT F.B., "Enterprise modelling and integration. From fact modelling to enterprise interoperability", in KOSANKE K., JOCHEM R., NELL J.G. et al. (eds), *Enterprise Inter- and Intra-Organizational Integration*, Springer, Boston, MA, 2003.

[WAD 98] WADHWA S., "Simulation study of shop floor control systems under decision and information delays using GRAI macro reference model", *5th International Workshop AUGRAI*, Glasgow, August, 1998.

[ZAC 17] ZACHAREWICZ G., PIRAYESH-NEGHAB A., SEREGNI M. et al., "Simulation-based enterprise management", in MITTAL S., DURAK U., ÖREN T. (eds), *Guide to Simulation-Based Disciplines: Simulation Foundations, Methods and Applications*, Springer, Cham, 2017.

Methods and Tools for Product-Service Systems

Part 9 Summary: Methods and Tools to Support the Development of Product-Service Systems

Servitization or moving from a product economy towards a service economy is a confirmed change in the business environment of manufacturing enterprises. Servitization leads to the design and development of Product-Service Systems (PSS) which are based on innovative combinations of products and services to increase the market share. This part of the book discusses the supports for enterprise management in the evolution towards servitization. The main focus is on the prevailing challenges in Product-Service System (PSS) development and how they have been addressed in academic and industrial domains, particularly in the European research era. Solutions supporting PSS design, development and implementation are presented as well.

Pezzotta *et al's*. chapter underlines that external drivers are nowadays affecting manufacturing companies' business models [ROM 16]. In this context, following the growing importance of services in the last decades, companies are forced to change their business model, moving it from a product-oriented model to a new one where the product and the service are bundled and co-created. Consequently, new challenges are raised for the companies due to the lack of methodologies for the creation of PSS in accordance with both the consumers and companies' needs. In this chapter, starting from the PSS Lean Design Methodology, the Product-Service Concept Tree (PSCT) method and tool are presented. These propositions are intended to support companies in identifying PSS concepts valuable for the customer and profitable for the company.

Chapter written by Guy DOUMEINGTS, Sergio GUSMEROLI, Amir PIRAYESH and Giuditta PEZZOTTA.

Pirayesh *et al's*. chapter mentions that to support servitization, enterprise management can be guided with a structured innovation process. For this purpose, the PSS Innovation Process (PSS-IP), developed in the frame of the PSYMBIOSYS European research project, is globally presented. This paper then focuses on the first phase of this process, called Innovation Orientation, which underlines the significant role of Enterprise Strategy. Finally, to increase the understanding of the addressed subject, industrial examples were developed, performed with different industrial pilots in the frame of the aforementioned research project.

In Sopelana *et al's*. chapter, the focus is on the "Tap Request Product-Service Platform" developed in the frame of PSYMBIOSYS European research project. Using an industrial case from the tooling industry, the change in the business model of the company and the adopted operational solution are presented. The advantages of the product-service platform and its devoted methodology are also underlined in this chapter: (1) decrease in the average time between the first iteration with customers and the technical offer, (2) decrease in the average stock level in the customers' facilities, (3) increase in the frequency of control of the customers' stock, (4) increase in the time for the detection of unusual consumption rate of the cutting tools, and (5) decrease in the average time between order and final design, planning.

Decubber *et al's*., in their chapter, describe the "Collaborative Product-Service Factory" persona which is identified by the Connected Factories H2020 project as one of the most promising scenarios for the 2025 Factories of the Future. In addition, two main H2020 projects of the Product-Service Systems PSS cluster (ICP4LIFE and PSYMBIOSYS) are discussed, which identify technological and organizational challenges in order to implement a 360 degree interoperability between Products and Services in a Manufacturing Industry. Organizational challenges, being mainly related to Knowledge-Sentiment and Business-Innovation dichotomies, are currently limiting the adoption of PSSs in Manufacturing. Regarding the technological challenges, the interoperability between Design-Manufacturing and Real-Digital world are mentioned.

Considering the chapters collected in this part of the book, it is possible to conclude that the development of PSS benefits at the same time research development and industrial application through several European Projects in the frame of H2020. The last chapters shows also how to link these developments with Factories of the Future.

45

Identifying New PSS Concepts: the Product-Service Concept Tree

45.1. Introduction

Nowadays, a lot of manufacturing companies facing commoditization of offering and intense competition have been attracted by the possibility of differentiating themselves from competitors by introducing product-related services in their traditional portfolio [OST 15]. This change in their offering is due to the modification of their customers' behaviors and their increasing interest in companies' services [REX 09, BAI 13]. As a result, manufacturers are changing their business models by delivering a Product-Service System (PSS), incorporating service-related activities in their value proposition. Therefore, the evolution towards a new business model where products are integrated with services creates a strong need for methods and tools supporting all the design and development phases [CAV 12].

However, most of the methodologies available today do not support the definition of new PSSs considering at the same time the customers' perspective and the companies' performance. Indeed, the actual design methodologies only frugally focus on the understanding of real customer needs and identifying suitable solutions to satisfy them. To fill these gaps, within the project "DIVERSITY", a new methodology called PSS Lean Design Methodology (PSSLDM) and a related set of methods has been proposed [PEZ 18]. Starting from the PSSLDM and the related methods a design platform has been developed. Among the different methods developed within the methodology a specific one, called the Product-Service Concept Tree (PSCT), has been created with the aim of supporting the translation of customer needs into marketable solutions. In addition, a PSCT tool has been developed and

___

Chapter written by Giuditta PEZZOTTA, Fabiana PIROLA, Roberto SALA, Antonio MARGARITO, Paulo PINA and Rui NEVES-SILVA.

included in the DIVERSITY platform to support the PSS concept phase. In the following, a short introduction to the PSSLDM methodology is provided and then an in-depth explanation of how the PSS concept is identified and evaluated within the PSCT tool is reported in section 45.3, while conclusions are reported in section 45.4.

45.2. The PSSLDM methodology

"Company" and "customer" are the core elements of the PSSLDM, highlighting the main objective of the methodology, namely the trade-off between customer satisfaction and company performance [PEZ 18]. To this purpose, the PSSLDM encompasses the following four phases: (1) customer analysis, (2) solution concept design, (3) solution final design, and (4) offering analysis. This chapter focuses on the "solution concept design" phase of the methodology, presented in the remainder of the chapter.

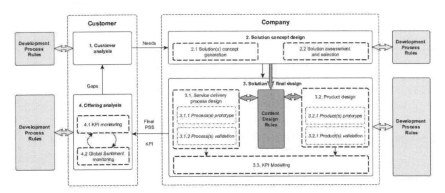

Figure 45.1. *DIVERSITY PSS Lean Design Methodology. For a color version of this figure, see www.iste.co.uk/zelm/enterprise.zip*

45.3. Solution concept design

Considering the gap in the literature and the practical issues concerning PSS methods and tools in industry, the Product-Service Concept Tree (PSCT) method [RON 16] and the related tool have been proposed to be carried out in this phase. This method aims at identifying promising PSS concept solutions and evaluating them starting from the customers' needs. In particular, once the customers' feedbacks are collected, the PSCT aims at proposing a structured approach to transform needs into PSS concepts.

In synthesis, the PSCT method and tool aim at suggesting a possible way to:

– identify PSS solutions capable of fulfilling customers' needs;

– represent solutions in a structured approach;

– manage the selection of the "best" PSS to implement, considering the company perceived impact and difficulty and the prediction of the customer opinion.

Indeed, to make the method and tool industry-oriented, they have been developed in a tight relationship with industrial environments through an iterative approach to the DIVERSITY business cases. In the following sections, the two main sub-phases of the PSCT method and the related tool are explained.

45.3.1. *Solution(s) concept generation*

This sub-phase aims to identify new PSS(s) that can answer customers' latent or declared needs and associate the resources required to deliver the product-service. PSCT concept generation is based on a four-level structure according to the elements described in Figure 45.2 [RON 16]:

– needs: elements that customers consider essential or desirable;

– wishes: represent the needs of customers in relation to company business;

– solutions: possible solutions (products, services or a bundle of them) that the company can identify to fulfill customers' wishes and needs;

– resources: the main human/software resources and/or products and related features necessary to implement the identified solutions.

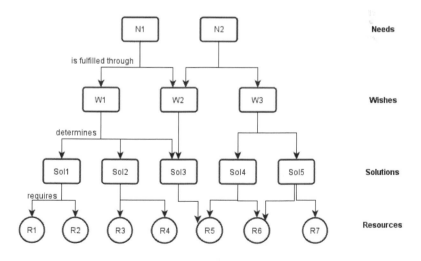

Figure 45.2. *PS Concept Tree (PSCT) method structure*

Based on this method, the tool shown in Figure 45.3 has been developed. In the black box on the right side of the tool, the steps needed to define the PSCT are listed. The first phase is related to the needs identification and description which consists of determining the name of the need and, if necessary, entering a description of the need. Interfaces for needs, wishes, solutions and resources are structured similarly, with three main areas:

– a data entry section made up of text fields that the user must fill to complete the creation of a new object;

– a summary section where all created objects are shown as a list. From the list the designer can access the editing and deleting functionalities;

– a preview area in which the final treemap appearance can be shown in a graphic form.

The last step of the sub-phase is related to the resources input which consists of the definition of the product and the service needed to compose the PSS. Resources are labelled in terms of *Name, description, resource type* (existing product, existing service, new product or new service). In case of an existing product or service, the developed tool allows one to link such resources with product and service data managed on the DIVERSITY platform and PLM systems. Otherwise new product-services can be created and an existing resource can be linked as a parent.

All the items must be connected to each other according to their relationship. In the tool the user visualises all the boxes and creates the TreeMap (Figure 45.3) by linking the boxes representing the needs, wishes, solutions and resources.

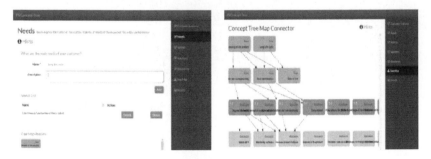

Figure 45.3. *PSCT Tool. For a color version of this figure, see www.iste.co.uk/zelm/enterprise.zip*

45.3.2. *Solution(s) concept selection*

The second sub-phase of the PSCT is a first evaluation of the identified PSS concepts (or solutions) to avoid late reworks and revisions during the concept development. The solution(s) identified through the PSCT previously developed should be evaluated and finally the one(s) worth being implemented is selected. The selection of PSSs is related to the value creation opportunities generated by the identified solution(s). The analysis of the value is based on the classification framework proposed by [BER 17]. The PSCT concept relies on measuring value in an easy and intuitive approach. As reported in Figure 45.4, it considers:

– the difficulty that the company could encounter during the implementation;

– the possible impact that the implementation of a solution can have on the customer and on the company's value;

– the customer opinion prediction, based on the sentiment analysis algorithms, which provides information on the customer acceptance of the proposed solution in terms of global sentiment (Figure 45.4) [NEV 17].

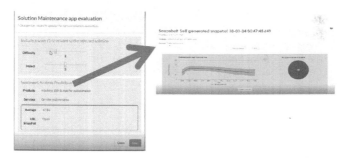

Figure 45.4. *PSCT Tool – Solution Evaluation and Opinion prediction.*
For a color version of this figure, see www.iste.co.uk/zelm/enterprise.zip

Once the scores for "impact" and "difficulty" are assigned and the global sentiment is calculated, the preferred solutions are summarized and a value summarizing the prediction is also provided (Figure 45.4). Once the solution is selected, the detailed design of product(s) and service(s) can start by implementing the next step of the DIVERSITY Platform.

45.4. Conclusion

Many external drivers are nowadays affecting manufacturing companies' business models [ROM 16]. In this context, the growing importance of services in the last decades has forced companies to change their business model, moving it from a product-oriented model to a new one where the product and the service are bundled and co-created along the lifecycle. This has caused new problems for the companies because of the lack of methodologies for the creation of PSS compliant with the consumers' requests and the companies' necessities. Starting from the PSS

Lean Design Methodology, this paper presented the PSCT method and tool. The ambition of the PSCT is to support companies in identifying PSS concepts valuable for the customer and profitable for the company.

45.5. Acknowledgements

This project has received funding from the European Union's Horizon 2020 research and innovation programme under grant agreement No 636692. The content of this publication does not reflect the official opinion of the European Union. Responsibility for the information and views expressed therein lies entirely with the author(s).

45.6. References

[BAI 13] BAINES T.W., LIGHTFOOT H., "Servitization of the manufacturing firm: Exploring the operations practices and technologies that deliver advanced services", *International Journal of Operations & Production Management*, vol. 34, no. 6, pp. 2–35, 2013.

[BER 17] BERTONI M., RONDINI A., PEZZOTTA G., "A Systematic Review of Value Metrics for PSS Design", *Procedia CIRP,* vol. 64, pp. 289–294, 2017.

[CAV 12] CAVALIERI S., PEZZOTTA G., "Product–Service Systems Engineering: State of the art and research challenges", *Computers in Industry*, vol. 64, no. 4, pp. 278–288, 2012.

[NEV 17] NEVES-SILVA R., PINA P., "OpinionSim: modelling and simulating stakeholders' feedback to product-service systems", *International Conference on Engineering, Technology and Innovation (ICE/ITMC)*, Madeira Island, Portugal, 27-29 June 2017, pp. 1473–1478, 2017.

[OST 15] OSTROM A.L., PARASURAMAN A., BOWEN D.E. *et al.*, "Service Research Priorities in a Rapidly Changing Context", *Journal of Service Research,* vol. 18, no. 2, pp. 127–159, 2015.

[PEZ 18] PEZZOTTA G., SASSANELLI C., PIROLA F. *et al.*, "The Product Service System Lean Design Methodology (PSSLDM) Integrating product and service components along the whole PSS lifecycle", *Journal of Manufacturing Technology Management*, Forthcoming, 2018.

[REX 09] REXFELT O., HIORT AF ORNÄS V., "Consumer acceptance of product service systems", *Journal of Manufacturing Technology Management*, vol. 20, no. 5, pp. 674–699, 2009.

[ROM 16] ROMERO D., PEZZOTTA G., MOLINA A. *et al.*, "Strategic Planning Framework for SME Service Organisations: Competitive, Value Chain and Operational Models & Toolkit", *22th International ICE-Conference on Engineering, Technology and Innovation*, Trondheim, Norway, 2016.

[RON 17] RONDINI A., BERTONI M., PEZZOTTA G., "An IPA Based Method for PSS Design Concept Assessment", *Procedia CIRP,* vol. 64, pp. 277–282, 2017.

[RON 16] RONDINI A., PEZZOTTA G., PIROLA F. *et al.*, "How to Design and Evaluate Early PSS Concepts: The Product Service Concept Tree", *Procedia CIRP*, vol. 50, pp. 366–371, 2016.

46

Role of Enterprise Strategy in Product-Service System Innovation Process

Servitization can be considered as a successful strategy to gain competitiveness based on novel combinations of products and services. To support this evolution, enterprise management can be guided with a structured innovation process including measures ensuring the alignment of development actions and their outcomes, Product-Service Systems (PSS), with enterprise strategy as well as market trends. For this purpose, the PSS Innovation Process (PSS-IP) was proposed in the frame of a European research project. This chapter particularly focuses on the first phase of this process, called Innovation Orientation, which underlines the significant role of Enterprise Strategy. It is of utmost importance for all enterprises including SMEs willing to be innovative in a PSS context to analyze servitization according to their global strategy. Considering the generic characteristics of PSS-IP and its phases, its realisation at lower levels can be different due to the particular characteristics of each industrial environment. Therefore, to enrich the description of PSS-IP and also to provide examples of its application, exercises were performed with different industrial pilots in the frame of the aforementioned research project. Among these pilots, the results of two cases are briefly presented in this paper.

46.1. Introduction

The move from product economy to service, called servitization (of business) [VAN 88], has become a practical strategy to achieve competitiveness for manufacturing enterprises [NEE 07]. This movement results in the development of Product-Service Systems (PSS) where innovative combinations of products and

Chapter written by Amir PIRAYESH, Guy DOUMEINGTS, Carl HANS and Maria José NUÑEZ ARIÑO.

services with higher added value are realized [CAV 12]. According to [GRU 15], the PSS innovation process is usually a complex process. Complexity can be due to the multiplicity of influencing determinants [POR 90, ULU 15, CRO 10]. Enterprise strategy is commonly stated as an important determinant of servitization [CRO 10, KEE 13, NYL 15, BAR 13, MSE 14, BIV 12]. Some challenges, related to innovation in servitization, were also identified in the frame of the research project at the origin of this chapter, through exercises with several industrial use cases. The challenges included: a well-defined guideline is missing to support enterprises willing to perform an innovation process in a PSS context; the main issues that should be addressed to be innovative are not completely known, particularly for moving from a product economy to a service economy or vice versa; methodologies and tools are requested to facilitate the innovation process. Considering the above challenges, the research question addressed by this paper is "*how can a global structure for innovation in servitization be provided while considering the role of enterprise strategy?*". Contributing to this question, this chapter presents a structured process for innovative servitization, called PSS Innovation Process (PSS-IP), with a focus on its first phase (Innovation Orientation).

46.2. PSS Innovation Process

To elaborate the global structure of the PSS Innovation Process (PSS-IP), several innovation frameworks adapted to servitization were studied to define the common phases of an innovation process. Among them, the structure of PSS-IP is mainly influenced by the frameworks proposed by the MSEE and BIVEE projects [MSE 14, BIV 12]. Through exercises with industrial use cases, the initial structure of PSS-IP was enriched (with extended activities, information exchanges and resources). Eventually, PSS-IP was described and illustrated[1] to facilitate its understanding. In summary, the three main phases of PSS-IP are: (1) *PSS Innovation Orientation*, highlighting the necessity of starting the innovation process by analyzing the innovation demand according to the enterprise global and innovation strategies; (2) *IPSS Ideation*, proposing a structure for generating and assessing servitization ideas; (3) *PSS Design & Development*, focusing on the combination of the product-related and service-related design and development activities while analysing the interactions.

46.3. PSS Innovation Orientation

The first phase of PSS-IP underlines the role of enterprise strategy while proposing activities that can ensure its alignment with servitization actions all along

---

1 Elaborated using Extended Actigram Star (EA*) language with the support of Manufacturing System Tool Box (MSTB), initially developed in the MSEE European project [MSE 14].

the innovation process to eventually decrease the risks of servitization (see Figure 46.1).

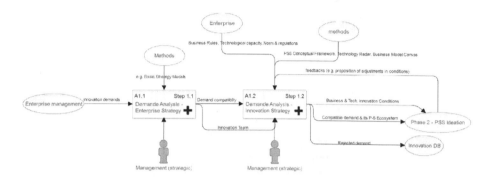

Figure 46.1. *Main steps of Phase 1 (PSS Innovation Orientation) in PSS-IP. For a color version of this figure, see www.iste.co.uk/zelm/enterprise.zip*

46.3.1. *Role of enterprise global strategy*

This step concerns the analysis of innovation demand(s), expressed by the customers (based on the information received from the partners, market analysis, trends, etc.). For this purpose, it is first necessary to analyze the enterprise strategy both for products and services from the early phases when the enterprise is willing to move towards PSS, through *servitization*. In this phase, one of the main issues is the position of the servitization strategy with regards to the enterprise global strategy. Moreover, the links between the strategies for product-service development and their influence on each other should be investigated. Having defined the relation between servitization and enterprise strategy, the management at strategic level should verify the compatibility of the preliminary demands for innovative PSS with that strategy. The results will be reported in the next step of the PSS-IP.

46.3.2. *Role of innovation strategy and innovation conditions*

After analyzing the compatibility of demand(s) for innovative PSS with enterprise strategy, the management should perform a deeper analysis which requires a well-defined *Innovation Strategy* aligned with the enterprise global strategy. Contrary to the global strategy, which covers long-term plans, actions and decisions, the innovation strategy might be more dynamic since it depends on market changes. Thus, the timeline of the innovation strategy is shorter. After this analysis, management will decide on the pursuit of the innovation process.

As the next task in the analysis of innovation strategy, the enterprise should define the *innovation conditions* to be respected all along the innovation process and verify their correlations: (1) *Technological Innovation Conditions*: high-level technical requirements to be respected by a P-S; emerging technologies can be a part of these conditions. Such conditions can be defined through investigation of prevailing technological developments. Collaboration with Research and Technology Organizations (RTOs) and Competence Centers and so on can strongly support the definition of such conditions; (2) *Business Innovation Conditions*: these conditions mainly include the business rules and key resources; the way the enterprise is willing to co-exist with other entities such as partners or competitors in the P-S ecosystem and so on. In order to define these conditions, the performance of a Business Model (BM) analysis is proposed. The idea is to avoid any conflicts between the current BM and the BM of a new PSS or to be able to detect and analyze the conflicts and similarities. In a simplified example, the enterprise might have strict business rules regarding the "Key Relationships" which can raise the following business innovation condition: "a new PSS should not affect the key relationships, particularly the suppliers".

46.4. Case study

Despite the generic structure of PSS-IP, including its first phase, it can be conducted in different ways at lower levels due to the specific characteristics of each industrial environment. Therefore, to illustrate the propositions and to facilitate their understanding, examples are provided from two servitizing industrial use cases (use cases 1 and 2 in the Furniture and Aircraft Video Surveillance domains respectively). Regarding the first step of the Innovation Orientation Phase, the use cases indicated that they have different approaches in the definition or analysis of the servitization situation with regards to their enterprise strategy. Hence, two situations were observed. As the current markets for products are full of competition, the first situation is to create new uncontested market space. Use case 1 can be categorized here since beside the manufacturing of office furniture, they are willing to provide additional services. Since value innovation is identified as a driver for new markets, the second situation is to create more value for the customer and the enterprise, for example by complementing the products with services which correspond to the P-S approach. Use case 2 can be considered in this category since it is willing to provide additional video archiving and analysis services besides their Aircraft Video Surveillance Systems.

Concerning the innovation strategy in use case 1, through brainstorming meetings, new products and services to be offered by the company are discussed, taking into account the experience of previous research projects and the needs of the industry collected in workshops and specific events as well as company visits. In use case 2, due to the advancement of existing technologies and the invention of new technologies as well as continuously increasing customer expectations, the innovation strategy is regularly adjusted to ensure that the objectives still fit with market demands.

With regards to innovation conditions, use case 1 defines *strategic lines* (e.g. developing and optimizing products with IoT connectivity). If an innovative idea is out of the scope of these guidelines it is usually rejected or re-evaluated. This avoids the incompatibility of a developed PSS with the innovation strategy which itself is mainly based on a higher value proposition for the customer. Here, we recall the possible correlations between innovation conditions. In use case 2, the business conditions are more dominant since they search for new ideas to improve customer benefits without being limited by the technology. Regarding Technological Innovation Conditions, in use case 2, a so-called Technology Radar approach is adopted. It should be noted that technological innovation in the final product-service might require technological changes in the development process (Product-Service Lifecycles). Therefore, technology radar is necessary for both product-service and processes. To define Business Innovation Conditions for the use cases, the Canvas approach proposed by [OST 09] was chosen. The reason is its comprehensiveness and ease of application. In addition, it is well-known and established in research and business areas. However, for the application in servitization it will be necessary to adapt and take a more differentiated view on some of the canvas elements.

46.5. Conclusion and discussion

This paper presents the PSS Innovation Process (PSS-IP), developed in the frame of a European project, with a focus on its first phase (Innovation Orientation). PSS-IP is proposed as a structured, modeled and tooled process to globally guide the researchers working in the PSS domain or enterprises willing to perform an innovation process in servitization. With a focus on phase 1 of PSS-IP, Innovation Orientation, it is highlighted that it is of upmost importance for all enterprises including SMEs willing to be innovative in a PSS context to analyze the enterprise situation concerning their global strategy. It is also essential to define an innovation strategy compatible with the global one. In addition, it is necessary to define innovation conditions, early in the process, to be respected all along the process. It should be mentioned that besides the generic aspects of PSS-IP, due to the complexity of each industrial environment, the realization of these phases might require adjustments. According to the industrial use-cases, the transition from a product manufacturer to a service provider comprises various risks and stumbling blocks each of which can have tremendous effects. From the technical point of view everything is available to realize attractive product-service combinations (pervasive internet, embedded systems, efficient data storage and analytics etc.). However, there are many issues a service provider has to deal with and which can endanger the market success of a product-service. A product-service requires significant investments before it can be placed on the market. Thus, companies have to face serious risks – taking a wrong decision (e.g. for a product or service which is not accepted by the customers) can be critical in the end. Concerning future work and development, it is mainly proposed: (1) to continue the decomposition of PSS-IP phases while increasing the methodological and IT support and analyzing the sequence of the steps, and (2) to illustrate the concepts and the methods with additional examples. It is also proposed to exploit the results in the PSS Cluster for further validation and enrichment of the results.

46.6. Acknowledgments

This work has been partly funded by the European Commission through PSYMBIOSYS project: Product-Service sYMBIOtic SYStems (H2020 FoF-05-2014, No. 636804).

46.7. References

[BAR 13] BARQUET A.P.B., DE OLIVEIRA M.G., AMIGO C.R. et al., "Employing the business model concept to support the adoption of product-service systems (PSS)", *Industrial Marketing Management*, vol. 42, no. 5, pp. 693–704, 2013.

[BIV 12] BIVEE PROJECT, Deliverable D2.2-Specification-of-business-innovation-reference, 2012.

[CAV 12] CAVALIERI S., PEZZOTTA G., "{Product–Service} Systems Engineering: State of the art and research challenges", *Computers in Industry*, vol. 63, no. 4, pp. 278–288, 2012.

[CRO 10] CROSSAN M.M., APAYDIN M., "A multi-dimensional framework of organizational innovation: A systematic review of the literature", *Journal of Management Studies*, vol. 47, pp. 1154–1191, 2010.

[GRU 15] GRUENEISEN P., STAHL B., KASPEREK D. et al., "Qualitative System Dynamics Cycle Network of the Innovation Process of Product Service Systems", *Procedia CIRP*, vol. 30, pp. 120–125, 2015.

[KEE 13] KEELEY L., PIKKEL R., QUINN B. et al., *Ten Types of Innovation: The Discipline of Building Breakthroughs*, John Wiley & Sons, New York, 2013.

[MSE 14] MSEE, "Manufacturing Service Ecosystem", WIESNER S., GUGLIELMINA C., GUSMEROLI S. et al. (eds), *Achievements of the European 7th Framework Programme FoF-ICT Project*, Bremer Schriften zur integrierten Produkt- und Prozessentwicklung, Aachen, Mainz, 2014.

[NEE 07] NEELY A., "The servitization of manufacturing: An analysis of global trends", *Proceedings of 14th European Operations Management Association Conference*, Ankara, Turkey, pp. 1–10, June 2007.

[NYL 15] NYLEN D., HOLMSTROM J., "Digital innovation strategy: A framework for diagnosing and improving digital product and service innovation", *Bus. Horiz.*, vol. 58, pp. 57–67, 2015.

[OST 09] OSTERWALDER A., PIGNEUR Y., *Business Model Generation: A Handbook for Visionaries, Game Changers, and Challengers*, John Wiley and Sons, New York, 2009.

[POR 90] PORTER M.E., "The Competitive Advantage of Nations", *Harvard Business Review*, vol. 68, pp. 73–93. 1990.

[ULU 15] ULUSOY G., KILIÇ K., GÜNDAY G. *et al.*, "A determinants of innovativeness model for manufacturing firms", *International Journal of Innovation and Regional Development*, vol. 6, no. 2, pp. 125–158, 2015.

[VAN 88] VANDERMERWE S., RADA J., "Servitization of Business: Adding Value by Adding Services", *European Management Journal*, vol. 6, no. 4, pp. 314–324, 1988.

47

Technological and Organizational Pathways towards 2025 Collaborative Product-Service Connected Factories of the Future

This paper describes the "Collaborative Product-Service Factory" persona identified by the ConnectedFactories H2020 project as one of the most promising scenarios for the 2025 Factories of the Future. Two main H2020 projects of the Product-Service Systems PSS cluster (ICP4Life and PSYMBIOSYS) are identifying technological and organizational challenges in order to implement a 360-degree interoperability between Products and Services in the manufacturing industry. Organizational challenges are mostly concerned with the Knowledge-Sentiment, Business-Innovation dichotomies which are currently limiting the adoption of PSSs in Manufacturing. Technological challenges are mostly concerned with the interoperability between Design-Manufacturing and the Real-Digital world where PLM systems need to be integrated with after-sales systems (e.g. CRM) and data generated along the lifecycle of a PSS need to be semantically interoperated with traditional PLM data. The 2025 challenges identified are going to drive PSS interoperability research actions such as FIWARE for Industry, Industrial data space and Industry 4.0 in general.

47.1. Introduction

The ConnectedFactories project[1], carried out under the European H2020 Factories of the Future cPPP (contractual Public Private Partnership), aims to

Chapter written by Chris Decubber, Sergio Gusmeroli, Guy Doumeingts, Domenico Rotondi, Fenareti Lampathaki and Luis Usatorre Arazusta.
1 http://www.effra.eu/scenarios-personas-pathways.

develop pathways towards advanced digitization of manufacturing processes from different perspectives. Now what is a pathway? As an example, here below you can see a draft pathway, which focuses on digitalization within the so-called "Automation Pyramid". In the ConnectedFactories project, this pathway is associated to the "persona" Autonomous Smart Factories, which is a projection into the future of what Factory Automation will look like in 2025.

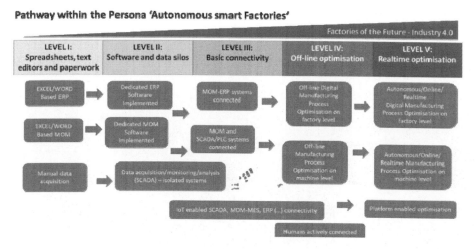

Figure 47.1. *Pathway associated to the Autonomous Smart Factories "persona". For a color version of this figure, see www.iste.co.uk/zelm/enterprise.zip*

A pathway is composed of different levels of digitization that are associated with a number of milestones. These milestones indicate practices of digitization that, while evolving to the right-hand side of the pathways, become more advanced. Ultimately, the milestones on the right fit within the vision of digital manufacturing within that persona. These pathways should not be seen as blind cookbooks or strict recipes, where a milestone should be 100% fulfilled in order to progress to the milestones on the right. In reality, milestones could be also implemented partially in small pilot cases and there could be iterations back and forth.

It is clear that examples and industrial cases are needed to show how milestones have been achieved. This applies to cases and demonstrators from research and innovation projects, but also cases that reflect the current state of play in manufacturing companies. Also, there are many solutions on the market that can be associated with either lower level milestones or even the most advanced milestones in the pathway (even though some of these commercial solutions are still at the beginning of industrial implementation). Associating the advanced use cases of commercial solutions with the milestones of the pathways will also give us a clearer view of how the results of research projects are complementary to solutions that are already on the market. In order to describe different perspectives and associated pathways, we have chosen to use the concept of "personas" with different personas being primarily associated with different domains of manufacturing:

1) *Autonomous Smart Factories*: with a focus on intra-factory manufacturing automation and optimization, including advanced human-in-the-loop workspaces;

2) *Hyper-connected Factories*: with a focus on networked enterprises in complex, dynamic supply chains and value networks;

3) *Collaborative Product-Service Factories*: with a focus on data-driven product-service engineering in knowledge-intensive factories;

4) *Small-scale Digitized Factories* which take into account the need for light solutions that focus on low-hanging fruit.

The persona "Collaborative Product-Service Factories" is a persona which is more lifecycle-oriented, or in which different lifecycles intersect each other in a very dynamic and complex way. Contributions for the development of these 2025 scenarios could come from different domains, giving different interpretations to the PSS concept. This chapter contributes to the development of the pathways within the persona "Collaborative Product-Service Factories", from the viewpoint of the PSYMBIOSYS[2] and ICP4Life[3] research projects.

47.2. The Product-Service persona: challenges and solutions from the PSYMBIOSYS project

Written in 2014, the PSYMBIOSYS Description of Action addressed Product-Service Systems as a quite independent research domain with respect to Industry 4.0. At that time, in fact, Industry 4.0 was still almost exclusively focused on factory automation, on the adoption of innovative technologies based on the CPS concept for the production of physical goods. Starting from 2014, and in particular with the World Manufacturing Forum (WMF) in Milan organized by Politecnico di Milano, the Industry 4.0 concept was redirected more towards manufacturing business objectives, where factory automation was re-thought as a means and not as the major aim of the fourth industrial revolution. New production models (like mass customization or agile value networks of flexible micro-plants ecosystems) were in fact proposed together with new organizational and social production paradigms

---

2 http://www.psymbiosys.eu/.
3 http://www.icp4life.eu/.

(like human-machine/robot collaboration, smart workspaces, blue collar worker empowerment) to support the creation and development of new business models. Servitization of manufacturing business is then identified not just as the most promising way to meet customers' needs and discover unprecedented revenue opportunities, but also as the most important factor to sustain workers' wellbeing and to create new jobs to compensate excessively extreme automation action. Roland Berger in fact during WMF 2016 in Barcelona envisaged 6.7 million new jobs created by 2035 in Europe, which would recover a loss of 7.4 million jobs due to factory automation. Now, at the end of the project, PSYMBIOSYS assumes an even more important role inside the fourth industrial revolution, envisaging an organizational and technological roadmap towards the complete elimination of the five most important barriers limiting service innovation inside the manufacturing industry, identified since the very beginning of the project:

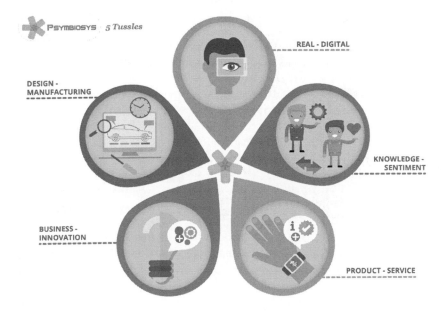

Figure 47.2. *The five PSYMBIOSYS challenges for PSS adoption. For a color version of this figure, see www.iste.co.uk/zelm/enterprise.zip*

In particular, the Product-Service challenge is very much related to the ConnectedFactories "Collaborative Product-Service Factory" 2025 persona. The Product-Service barrier is most probably the highest and most difficult to eliminate, as it represents a mix of technological and organizational issues, but mostly because it goes against deeply rooted traditions and business models and being often disruptive. Manufacturing organizations have been structured around product design, engineering and manufacturing especially in the case of high-tech products. It is not rare for highly specialized manufacturing SMEs, like for instance in the domain of avionic video surveillance systems, to "abandon" their products at the selling time. More than simply extending PDM and PLM systems to the digital service world, this challenge implies a deep change of mindset and require a strong commitment by the top managers and decision makers. Methods and tools to assess the PS maturity of a manufacturing company are extremely useful here to identify areas for improvement define migration pathways and discover new business opportunities and new business models. The major obstacles, especially for SMEs, are the lack of awareness in terms of how product and service departments and people collaborate.

From a more conceptual viewpoint, the most important finding of the PSYMBIOSYS project is the impossibility to clearly define proper lifecycle intersections between products and services, so that we believe that it is not convenient to speak of a PSS lifecycle as a whole. While it is well-recognized that the product lifecycle intersects the production system lifecycle in the "Product Manufacturing" and "Factory Operations" phases, the same situation does not usually apply to products and systems. This is especially true for the design/engineering phase where time-to-market of a new product is usually incompatible with the time-to-market of a service, which implies not designing products and services simultaneously, but designing products as service platforms, so that they can embed different generations of services along their lifecycles. Software-defined product renovation (rejuvenation) is one of the major research topics in this field (e.g. for white goods, cars and machine tools and this does not imply just the user interface or the supported colors) as well as continuous updating of the provided services (e.g. cyber protection or operating system) as in the case of mobile phones or PCs. Saying that there is no exact intersection between product and service lifecycles, we could however see that in the operational real world we see products and services working together, so we can argue that an intersection exists at the operations time, when we perform predictive maintenance on a machine tool or energy management on a washing machine. Again, it is not as sharp as in the product-factory lifecycles intersections.

Finally, in a PSS system we have the symbiotic co-existence of professional knowledge and crowd sentiment. Knowledge denotes the professional cross-organizational expertise, typically extracted from manufacturers' systems and associated with products, while sentiment embraces the crowd-oriented opinions and feelings, typically expressed in relation to services in social media and in manufacturers' customer support systems. Although knowledge and sentiment are acknowledged as key added-value assets of a manufacturer, they remain largely unexploited when it comes to product-service design. Through its knowledge-sentiment symbiotic methodology, PSYMBIOSYS has demonstrated that knowledge extraction and crowd sentiment analysis need to co-exist with collaborative ideation and mapping of skills to product-service needs in order to effectively bring data-driven manufacturing intelligence to product-service design. The convergent knowledge-sentiment perspectives focus on achieving desirability of products and services from a human perspective, yet they are to be treated with different attention depending on various criteria (e.g. the availability of resources at the time, the requirements for analysis of such resources in the future, and the PSS strategy readiness of a manufacturer).

A collaboration with the ConnectedFactories H2020 CSA has just started in order to define migration pathways towards the Collaborative Product-Service Factory 2025.

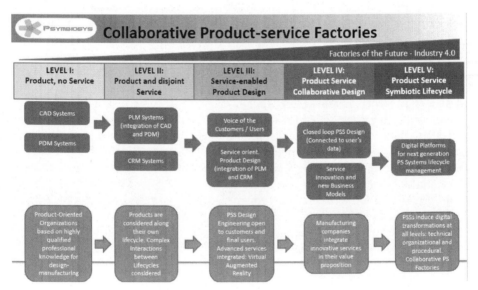

Figure 47.3. *The PSYMBIOSYS contribution to connected factories. For a color version of this figure, see www.iste.co.uk/zelm/enterprise.zip*

47.3. The Product-Service persona: challenges and solutions from the ICP4LIFE project

ICP4LIFE is developing a collaborative platform for the design and support of PSS. Moving from "product" towards "Product-Service System" (PSS) is challenging for companies that want to maintain a distinctive position on the market.

PSS is not a simple addition of separate elements to an existing product, for example, adding "a couple of sensors", but an integrated system of systems to provide an agreed-upon functionality for customers according to a certain business model.

Product mechatronics, including mechanical, electrical and cybernetic engineering must be linked with *intangible service* modules, enabling a system characterized by an integrated design development process and function allocation. As stated before, a profound digital transformation of the company is therefore necessary. Design is no more a mechatronic task, but involves business models and, at the same time, new worker skills.

Obviously, depending on the type of PSS, the type and level of integration between service and product components are different and standard solutions are not feasible considering the different involved stakeholders. In previous paragraphs, it was determined that product and service design/engineering are usually not simultaneous. The ICP4Life project approach to this statement promotes the concepts of "pattern" and "instance" to represent the features of both "generic" and "customized" PSS, considered as shared knowledge to be stored in a common repository.

A pattern is a "general, proven, and beneficial solution to a common, recurring problem in a specific domain" [REC 11]. Then, the refinement of the pattern to reach a detailed solution is fulfilled case by case at the "instance" level [BEL 17]. The ICP4Life approach is valid either for new products or for product renovation (rejuvenation).

Products (and/or PSS) in ICP4Life can be either a final product or an industrial manufacturing good, meaning that the service can be provided from manufacturers to customers, from customers to customers and from customers to users. This concept addresses a complex task involving the exchange of data all along the product and manufacturing process supply chain and lifecycle.

In ICP4Life we have machine manufacturers and machine users, covering the whole lifecycle. Considering this, a new service like "machine health monitoring" can be implemented in a machine by the machine manufacturer, the service can be exploited either by the machine manufacturer or transferred to its customers to be exploited by them. These options, that in any case will have a strong impact in the customer production, lead to different business models in both the manufacturer and the customer. This situation definitely affects the production line design of the customer.

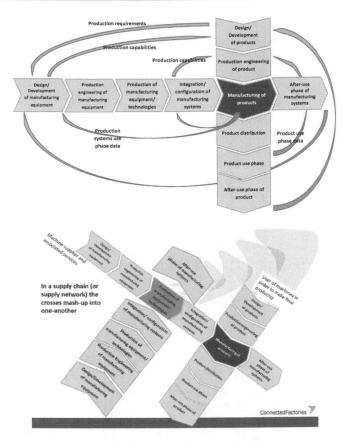

Figure 47.4. *The ICP4Life contribution to Connected Factories. For a color version of this figure, see www.iste.co.uk/zelm/enterprise.zip*

Considering that product lifecycle intersects the production system lifecycle in the "Product Manufacturing" and "Factory Operations" phases, ICP4Life supports it by means of two separate information "folders": on one hand the "data repository" supporting the services lifecycle and on the other the "knowledge repository" supporting the design and engineering of new PSS along the lifecycle of the product and integrating COTS repositories like CAD or PLM systems.

Regarding the definition of the 2025 pathways of the Collaborative PS persona, and according the ICP4Life and Connected Factories projects, the Collaborative Product-Service persona should focus on networked global-oriented manufacturers (regional, national, international) that deliver unique personalized products as a service or production as a service. PSS means working 24/7 on the basis of product, production and open data, and in some cases in real time, so a fully automated inter-, intra- and external communicational and informatic system. The PSS design and lifecycle means flexible and changing ad hoc collaborations and close interactions with users/clients/customers/partners. The PSS design process means a close collaboration with users/clients/customers/partners/suppliers considering the services supporting a complex hardware-software product depend on the individual product configuration a customer requires. PSS financial administration is fully automated and adapted to each PSS.

The digital platform's characteristics for this PS persona are:

– fully tailored, simple, newly developed digital platform;

– collaborative platform for PSS design process digital platform;

– enabling automated real-time monitoring and exchange of data;

– permitting highly advanced Internal/open data modeling and analytics.

47.4. Conclusion

The Collaborative Product-Service Factory persona is one of the 2025 scenarios proposed by the Connected Factories project. The PSYMBIOSYS project is contributing to the definition of technological and organizational pathways: from the technological viewpoint, PSYMBIOSYS is identifying the need for data-driven open platforms inspired by the Industrial Internet Consortium and the Industrial Data Space reference architectures; from the organizational viewpoint, PSYMBIOSYS introduced the concept of SLM and explored its impact on processes, organization, roles and competencies of a manufacturing enterprise. The ICP4Life project, on the other hand, has been more focused on the design and development of the PSS engineering platform, contributing to the Connected Factories with the application of the PSS in the manufacturing supply chain and the Product and Services different lifecycle approach.

47.5. References

[CHE 17] CHENG B., SOLMAZ G., CIRILLO F. et al., "FogFlow: Easy Programming of IoT Services Over Cloud and Edges for Smart Cities", IEEE Internet of Things Journal, vol. PP, no. 99, p. 1, 2017.

[EUR 17] EUROPEAN UNION, Digitising European Industry - Working Group 2 Digital Industrial Platforms (Final Version, Aug 2017), 2017.

[IND 17] INDUSTRIAL INTERNET CONSORTIUM, Industrial Internet Reference Architecture V1.8, 2017.

[NIS 17] NISHIOKA Y., Industrial Value Chain Reference Architecture, Industrial Value Chain Initiative, Hannover Messe, April 2017.

[PAP 15] PAPAGEORGIOU A., CHENG B., KOVACS E., "Real-time data reduction at the network edge of Internet-of-Things systems," *2015 11th International Conference on Network and Service Management (CNSM)*, pp. 284–291, 2015.

[SCH 16] SCHWEICHHART K., Reference Architectural Model Industrie 4.0 (RAMI4.0), Platform Industrie 4.0, 2016.

[SHI 2017] SHI-WAN L., MURPHY B., CLAUER E. *et al.*, Architecture Alignment and Interoperability, Industrial Internet Consortium, White Paper, https://www.iiconsortium.org/pdf/JTG2_Whitepaper_final_20171205.pdf, 2017.

Circular Engineering and Product-Service Systems in the Machine Tool Sector: the PSYMBIOSYS Approach

48.1. Introduction

By 2020, the value chains of the manufacturing sector will be organized in symbiotic forms of collaboration in which, thanks to the adoption of intelligent technologies of advanced manufacturing, the barriers to adopt the next generation of sustainable product-service system (SPSS) will be considerably reduced. However, there are a lot of gaps and lack of knowledge in relation to these new concepts and a need to develop integrated IT frameworks and methodologies to operate an integrated product and service lifecycle. In this sense, PSYMBIOSYS is a project funded by the European Commission within the area of the Factory of the Future, whose objective is to improve the competitiveness of the European manufacturing industry through the development of an innovative environment of product-service engineering, that allows the reduction of the time-to-market of sustainable product-service solutions considerably. The project is based on comprehensive and unified collaboration across the dichotomies identified in the design environment of products and services, such as design-manufacturing, product-service, knowledge-feeling, true-digital world and business-innovation. In this sense, NECO and the Innovalia Association, with other companies, participate in this ambitious project through the development and application of this business model that supports the product-service systems in a real manufacturing environment such as cutting tools manufacturing companies.

Chapter written by Nerea SOPELANA, Lara GONZALEZ, Oscar LAZARO, Andoni LASKURAIN and Rikardo MINGUEZ.

The aim of this chapter is to present the sustainability aspects that motivate the incorporation of the PSS concept in the machine tool sector. Secondly, the chapter will focus on NECO, a Spanish cutting tool manufacturer. This company has developed a new business strategy for PSS in the context of the PSYMBIOSYS European project. Finally, the main challenges, solution adopted and the obtained improvements will be detailed.

48.2. PSS and sustainability

In 1987, the World Commission on Environment and Development defined sustainable development as a "development that meets the needs of the present without compromising the ability of future generations to meet their own needs" [WCE 87]. This development seeks a balance among the economy, the environment and social aspects.

According to this, some authors declared that it is necessary to analyze the evolution of industry sustainability based on three pillars: the current economic situation, the changes in the customers' needs and requirements, and the environmental situation [TRA 14].

From an economic point of view, as a consequence of the economic crisis, during the last decade there has been an increase in competitiveness between manufacturers in general and in the machine tool industry in particular. Moreover, production has been outsourced to low-wage countries and as a consequence of the fact that they can offer the same products for a lower cost, the European manufacturers' sales have decreased considerably.

From an environmental perspective, environmental problems are growing, mainly due to the rapid technological change [GUI 14]. Up until now, developed products had a short lifecycle. As a result of this, companies could increase their income by selling a great quantity of products that had this new technology.

However, manufacturers must take into account that in addition to the increase in the available raw materials' price, actual resources are limited and industry has been consuming more than the Earth's own capacity, so there is a serious need to reduce consumption of raw materials, as has been exposed by Tran and Guidat [TRA 14, GUI 14].

Finally, the current demand of social welfare, as an evolution of the needs and expectations of the client, will generate a change in the type of economy [SAL 15]. The current industrial economy based on the purchase and sale of products is going to lead into a functional economy in which the products are mere providers of functions that seek to satisfy the needs of those who use them [CES 13, GAI 14].

Therefore, in order to overcome these continuous changes, improve competitiveness, meet environmental and economic objectives, and ensure customers' retention [TRA 14, BET 08, BEU 13, SAK 09], firms must offer integrated solutions of products and services, based on a functional economy [CES 13].

These solutions, defined as innovative combinations of products and services that are oriented toward creating a greater added value and unifying responses to customers, would allow companies to improve their position in the value chain, improve their innovative potential and highlight the added value of their offers [ADR 15, GOE 99, MON 02].

In addition to this, this integration of products and services will become increasingly evident in industrialized countries [YOO 11]. Proof of it, will be that more and more manufacturers will tend to put less attention on the manufacture of products and focus more on providing the added value for customers through the provision of services that will eventually generate a lower impact on the environment without compromising the customers' needs.

This idea related to the environment was also presented by Arnold Tukker [TUK 13]. Some environmental researchers have determined that it would be easier to design a system that meets the needs of the end user or customer with a considerable reduction in the environmental impact associated with it if manufacturers' focus on the needs of the end customer or the service that a user requires instead of thinking exclusively of the manufacture of products. The idea behind the Product-Service System (hereinafter PSS) concept is that consumers do not specifically demand products but look for the utility associated with these products along with their associated services [GOE 99, MON 02]. As Arnold Tukker and Ursula Tischner point out, its real strength is that PSS advocates for focusing on the final needs, demands, or functionalities that are needed to achieve a particular end instead of selling more products.

48.3. Cutting tool challenge and PSS approach

Cutting tools are an integral part of any manufacturing process, such as advanced machining or drilling processes in aeronautics or automotive sectors. The use of this kind of tool is at the very core of achieving the end look and feel and functionality of the product. Nowadays, there is a clear trend in the manufacturing of cutting tools to deliver customized solutions, taking into consideration the specifications that respond to the needs of a specific manufacturing processes.

In this sense, NECO, as part of the TIVOLI Group, is one of the main Spanish cutting tool manufacturers. NECO has accumulated a diverse portfolio of cutting tools and services around the world that are focused on the machining and drilling industry. The aim of this portfolio is to face the pressure that the company encountered to maintain their offer of high quality services.

Figure 48.1. *NECO cutting tools. For a color version of this figure, see www.iste.co.uk/zelm/enterprise.zip*

On one hand, the process to deliver a machining tool begins with the selection of the workpiece material and the coating type such as Chemical Vapor Deposition (CVD) or Physical Vapor Deposition (PVD). This suitable solution must be selected taking into account the type of material to be machined. On the other hand, in the case of drilling tools, the coating is not as helpful to drill flutes, due to the fact that it creates additional friction and slows down the chip flows. So, in this type of tool, the geometry of the flute is important for the stability in the cut and the finish of the surface.

These design processes of cutting tools show that, in general, NECO begins considering the material to machine. Thus, it is not enough to develop a simple "client-provider" relationship, rather a more collaborative relationship is required to deliver the most suitable solution. In this sense, the role of NECO should evolve from providers of cutting tools to provider of cutting solutions focused on the requirements of their customers to develop a customized cutting solution and taking into consideration all the stakeholders that take part along the lifecycle of a machine tool.

48.4. PSS NECO

To offer the cutting tool solution, a collaborative relationship among the different stakeholders alongside the lifecycle is needed to share different types of information and offer the most suitable solution. It is well known that during the last few years Product Lifecycle Management tools have emerged and allow the presentation of information to the machine tools manufacturers. However, the effort to link and collect all knowledge related to the lifecycle of a machine tool component is still too laborious and costly.

This lack of a full lifecycle knowledge management system focused on the product-services that are somehow limiting the capabilities of the development of cutting tools that meet the customers' demands for a specific sector is such as the machining of hard-to-machine materials, is every day more common in aeronautics and other sectors. In the end, with PSYMBIOSYS, NECO developed a new Product-Service Platform, named "Tap Request Product-Service Platform". This Platform allows the linkage of the information about customer machining process, cutting tools engineering and production planning along a digital thread for the complete lifecycle. The aim is to develop new product-service system offerings to the market and to ensure a consistent design of the tools in increasingly customized machining applications. This solution will allow interoperability between their design, manufacturing and inspection tools and the PLM systems of the company.

Among the main challenges that NECO had to face were the provision of a design, the maintenance of a cost-effective supply of advanced cutting tools, the management and synchronization of the embedded product-services and the transition from a cutting tool provisioning to a cutting performance service. However, NECO expected to improve their business competitiveness through the creation of some circular benefits related to the following processes: engineering collaboration with customers in the provision of a customized cutting tool, engineering and manufacturing thanks to the collaboration with the 3D metrology service provider and improvement of the drilling performance in aeronautics industries.

48.5. Conclusion

Finally with the "Tap Request Product-Service Platform", NECO offered a change in the business model and an operational solution for tool design, the budget and delivery date, an agile remote stock control with smart cabinets and quality reports on customized precision cutting tools performance. The product-service platform and PSYMBIOSYS methodology deliver clear competitive advantages summarized as follows: (1) decrease from 1 week to 24 h in the average time between the first iteration with customers and the technical offer, (2) decrease from 8 weeks to 4 weeks in the average stock level in the customers' facilities, (3) increase from monthly to daily in the frequency of control of the customers' stock, (4) increase from monthly to daily in the time for the detection of unusual consumption rates of cutting tools, 5) decrease from 1–2 weeks to 1–2 days in the average time between order and final design planning.

48.6. References

[ADR 15] Adrodegari F., Alghisi A., Ardolino M. *et al.*, "From ownership to service-oriented business models: a survey in capital goods companies and a PSS typology", *Procedia CIRP*, vol. 30, pp. 245–250, 2015.

[BET 08] Bettencourt L., Ulwick A., "The customer-centered innovation map", *Harvard Business Review*, vol. 86, no. 5, pp. 109–114, 2008.

[BEU 13] Beuren F., Ferreira M., Miguel P., "Product-service systems: a literature review on integrated products and services", *Journal of Cleaner Production*, vol. 47, pp. 222–231, 2013.

[CES 13] Ceschin F., "Critical factors for implementing and diffusing sustainable Product-Service Systems: insights from innovation studies and companies' experiences", *Journal of Cleaner Production*, vol. 45, pp.74–88, 2013.

[GAI 14] Gaiardelli P., Resta B., Martinez V. *et al.*, "A classification model for product-service offerings", *Journal of Cleaner Production*, vol. 66, pp. 507–519, 2014.

[GOE 99] Goedkoop M., van Halen C., te Riele H. *et al.*, *Product Services Systems, Ecological and Economic Basics*, VROM, The Hague, 1999.

[GUI 14] Guidat T., Barquet A., Widera H. *et al.*, "Guidelines for the definition of innovative industrial product-service systems (PSS) business models for remanufacturing", *Procedia CIRP*, vol. 16, pp. 193–198, 2014.

[MON 02] Mont O., "Drivers and barriers for shifting towards more service-oriented business: analysis of the PSS field and contribution from Sweden", *The Journal of Sustainable Product Design*, vol. 2, pp. 89–103, 2002.

[SAK 09] Sakao O., Birkhofer H., Panshef V. *et al.*, "An effective and efficient method to design services: empirical study for services by and investment machine manufacturer", *International Journal of Internet Manufacturing and Services*, vol. 2, no. 1, pp. 95–110, 2009.

[SAL 15] Salazar C., Lelah A., Brissaud D., "Eco-designing Product Service Systems by degrading functions while maintaining user satisfaction", *Journal of Cleaner Production*, vol. 87, pp. 452–462, 2015.

[TRA 14] Tran T.A., Park J.Y., "Development of integrated design methodology for various types of product-service systems", *Journal of Computational Design and Engineering*, vol. 1, no. 1, pp. 37–47, 2014.

[TUK 13] Tukker A., "Knowledge collaboration and learning by aligning global sustainability programs: reflections in the context of Rio+20", *Journal of Cleaner Production*, vol. 48, pp. 272–279, 2013.

[WCE 87] WCED, *Our Common Future*, Oxford University Press, Oxford, 1987.

[YOO 11] Yoon B., Kim S., Rhee J., "An evaluation method for designing a new product-service system", *Expert System with. Applications*, vol. 39, no. 3, pp. 3100–3108, 2011.

Interoperability for Crisis Management

Part 10 Summary: Interoperability for Crisis Management: Increasing Resilience of Smart Cities

The workshop on Interoperability for Crisis Management: Increasing Resilience of Smart Cities – ICRIM 2018 is the third of the workshop series promoted and organized by the *TG2 Enterprise Interoperability for Crisis Management* of *InterOP-VLab* group. It aimed to provide an outlook of the research on how interoperability solutions for crisis management could increase the resilience of smart cities.

The call for papers invited research addressing topics related to: big data analytics and management in crisis management; communication infrastructures, technologies and services for crisis management; crisis and emergency ontologies; coordination, collaboration and decision support technologies and systems for crisis management; decision-making under uncertainty; humanitarian logistics; evacuation and rescue geo-planning; geo-information technologies for crisis management; interoperability in crisis management; meta-models for crises; modeling and simulation tools for crisis and disaster situations; prediction and early warning systems; querying and filtering heterogeneous, multi-source streaming disaster data; reasoning with uncertainty in crisis management; resilience engineering; risk, damage and loss assessment; situation awareness; smart cities resilience; social media for crisis management; and participatory activities.

Five multidisciplinary papers were accepted. All of them consider crisis management as a specific context where expectations about collaboration and interoperability are drastically exacerbated. In fact, the criticality of consequences

Chapter written by Antonio DE NICOLA and Frédérick BENABEN.

on the one hand increases time constraints and the obligation to act, and, on the other hand, implies we should imagine specific collaborative approaches fitting with specific domains and specific actors.

The workshop covered a half-day programme and gave space for a wide and open debate on new emerging ideas addressing crisis management to increase the resilience of smart cities. The workshop was organized into two sessions: a paper session, organized with highly interactive style and a session on EU project calls to discuss ideas for new project proposals on the theme of crisis management and interoperability.

We wish to remind the reader that the workshop had important support from Martin Zelm and David Chen, respectively, chair and co-chair of the IESA 2018 workshops, from *InterOP-VLab*, and from the local organization of the conference.

Finally, we wish to acknowledge the work of the program committee who supported us in the scientific success of the event. In particular, we thank Bernard Archimède (ENIT, FR), Vincent Chapurlat (IMT Mines Ales, FR), Alex Coletti (SM Resources Corporation, US), Nicolas Daclin (ENIT, FR), Daouda Kamissoko (IMT Mines Albi, FR), Hedi Karray (ENIT, FR), Aurélie Montarnal (IMT Mines Albi, FR), Riccardo Patriarca (Sapienza University, IT), João Luiz Rebelo Moreira (University of Twente, NL), Francesco Taglino (IASI-CNR, IT), Marianthi Theocharidou (Joint Research Centre, IT), Maria Luisa Villani (ENEA, IT), and Jingquan Xie (Fraunhofer IAIS, GE).

49

Assessment of Climate Change-related Risks and Vulnerabilities in Cities and Urban Environments

Climate change and related extreme weather events in particular threaten urban population centers as they impact citizens, critical infrastructure systems, as well as interregional and global value chains. The combination of climate change-related impacts and the trend towards increasing urbanization necessitates improvements to municipal climate change adaptation planning processes, which are already ongoing. Towards that goal, this chapter reports on the ongoing development of a standardized risk-oriented vulnerability assessment method, supported by dedicated software tools, as a first step of adaptation processes. The software tools include a web-based application to develop impact chain diagrams as well as a toolset for the automatic processing of climate change relevant indicators for quantitative assessments. Integrating close feedback provided by end-users, called "co-creation", is a continuous part of the development process, assuring a broader acceptance and adaptation by the city administrations in charge.

49.1. Introduction

Extreme weather events resulting from climate change are severe threats to urban population centers with their high density of residents and economic assets [COL 16]. The increasingly complex dependencies of infrastructure components combined with the ongoing trend towards urbanization (see [UNI 14]) make it necessary for local authorities to develop proactive crisis management strategies

---

Chapter written by Jingquan XIE, Manfred BOGEN, Daniel LÜCKERATH, Erich ROME, Betim SOJEVA, Oliver ULLRICH and Rainer WORST.

against climate change-related extreme weather events. One of the prerequisites for designing effective management and adaptation strategies is a comprehensive understanding of the specific risks and vulnerabilities in the local or regional context. However, not many standardized methods or toolsets exist today that enable municipal decision-makers to consider, analyze, and evaluate risks and vulnerabilities under specific extreme weather events and climate change-related scenarios. International standardization bodies have only recently started their work in the field of climate change adaptation. A standardized approach to vulnerability assessment would enable comparison and benchmarking between cities with similar make-ups, ensure interoperability between methods and tools, and enable the establishment of data standards, as well as facilitate monitoring and reassessment.

This chapter reports the ongoing development of a standardized process for the assessment of climate change-related risks and vulnerabilities in cities and urban environments, based on the well-established approach by the German Federal Ministry for Economic Cooperation and Development [GER 14]. Seven interconnected modules guide practitioners and end-users through the risk-oriented vulnerability assessment process, beginning with a systematic selection of hazards and drivers in their local context, and ending with a standardized presentation of the resulting outcomes to decision-makers and stakeholders. The described vulnerability assessment process is developed as part of the EU project "climate RESilient cities and INfrastructures – RESIN" [RES 17]. The project develops practical and applicable methods and tools to support municipalities in designing and implementing adaptation and mitigation strategies for their local contexts. Other interdisciplinary, practice-based research projects investigate climate change-oriented resilience in European cities too: the recently concluded project "Reconciling Adaptation, Mitigation and Sustainable development for citiES – RAMSES" [RAM 17] developed methods and tools to quantify the impacts of climate change and the costs and benefits of adaptation measures to cities. The ongoing project "Smart Mature Resilience – SMR" [SMR 17] aims to develop a resilience management guideline to support city decision-makers in developing and implementing resilience measures.

This chapter continues with an overview of the vulnerability assessment method in development (see section 49.2), and then describes the software tools developed to support its users (see section 49.3). It concludes with a short summary of lessons learned and an outlook on further steps (see section 49.4).

49.2. A risk-oriented vulnerability assessment method

Figure 49.1 depicts the main stages of the vulnerability assessment process (for a more detailed description see [ROM 17]), starting with a systematic analysis and selection of hazards, drivers, and stressors relevant to the region or urban area under examination (module M0). This serves as a base for the detailed planning of the assessment and ensures that the limited resources and budgets available for the assessment are spent on the most pressing current and future hazards, and that no other threats or possible dependencies between different hazards are overlooked. In addition, a thorough documentation of the rationale for selecting hazards, drivers, and stressors ensures that future (re-)assessments can follow the same methodology, thus enabling results comparison.

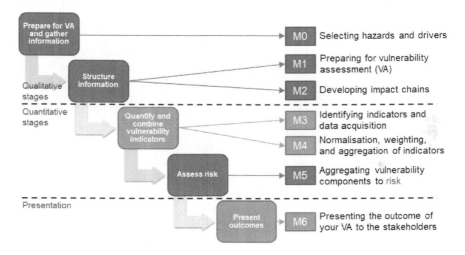

Figure 49.1. *Steps of the vulnerability assessment process (source: see [ROM 17]). For a color version of this figure, see www.iste.co.uk/zelm/enterprise.zip*

As part of module M1, a common taxonomy is defined and communicated, and the overall objectives, scopes, participants and their roles and responsibilities, as well as the target audiences, have to be defined in agreement, and ideally, in cooperation with the relevant stakeholders. M1 also serves to identify and gather relevant information to form a detailed implementation plan. The information needed for this step includes a list of relevant stakeholders including both institutions and individuals, measures and strategies that are already in place or are being considered (e.g. sector strategies, community or national development plans, and ongoing adaptation measures), climatic, socio-economic and sectoral information to be included, and a list of climate and city development scenarios to be examined.

Based on this foundation for the vulnerability assessment, impact chains are developed (module M2, for a more detailed description see [LÜC 18]). These impact chains describe cause-effect-relationships between the elements that contribute to the consequences of a given combination of hazard and the exposed objects. Each element of an impact chain is and has to be described in a *qualitative* way by specifying attributes. Usually, impact chain diagrams are developed during collaborative workshops with domain experts. As a result, impact chains are not exhaustive, but describe the common understanding of these experts. An important rule-of-thumb is: keep it simple!

Module M3 is about the identification and definition of measureable indicators for identified elements of the generated impact chains. The indicator identification and data collection processes are highly dependent on each other. The availability of data is of critical importance for M3: Without a feasible method of data acquisition, the best indicator would be inoperable. To this end, it is extremely important to include domain experts with extensive knowledge about data availability. To ease the indicator selection process, established directories of standard indicators can be employed, for example, the annex of the Vulnerability Sourcebook (see [GER 14, pp. 14–17]) or the annex of the Covenant of Mayors for Climate and Energy Reporting Guidelines (see [NEV 16, pp. 61–67]).

Communicating a multitude of complex, multi-dimensional indicators in a comprehensive way is extremely complicated. Therefore, the calculated indicator values should be normalized (e.g. via Min-Max normalization), weighted, and aggregated (e.g. using weighted arithmetic mean) to composite scores for different risk components (module M4). The calculated indicator values most likely employ different measurement units and scales, and thus cannot be aggregated into composite scores without being normalized. The selected indicators may not necessarily have equal influence on their corresponding risk component, which should be reflected by assigning weights to them when combining them into composite scores. Weights can be assigned based on existing literature, participatory approaches including stakeholders and experts, and statistical procedures.

Module M5 covers the risk assessment, which is based on the well-established risk analysis process by the German Federal Office of Civil Protection and Disaster Assistance (see [GER 11]), assuring organizational, legal, and political interoperability. In this approach, consequences and probabilities are classified using discrete, ordinal classes (e.g. "insignificant", "minor", or "disastrous" for consequences and "very unlikely", "likely", and "very likely" for probabilities). The resulting consequence and probability pairs, that is, the risk scores, are then assigned to discrete, ordinal risk classes using a risk matrix. This matrix has one axis for the consequence classes and one axis for the probability classes, and thus defines risk classes for every combination of the two.

The last module, M6, concerns the systematic presentation of outcomes to all relevant stakeholders, including external risk analysis experts to assure external result validation. Best practices are shared and supporting material, that is, report and presentation templates, are being provided, as well as graphs exported by the developed software tools.

49.3. Tool support for risk-based vulnerability assessment

It has emerged during several workshops with stakeholders that generating, updating, and documenting impact chain diagrams with feature-laden general-purpose tools, for example MS PowerPoint, is perceived as quite cumbersome. Therefore, a web-based graphical Impact Chain Editor (ICE+) was developed in the RESIN project that automatically arranges and colorizes the diagram components. ICE+ facilitates structured annotations and most importantly, it provides a rule engine for checking the validity of diagrams (e.g. hazard elements can only link to exposed objects or other hazard elements).

As the elements and internal relationships of the generated impact chains are represented as JSON objects[1], the captured information is automatically available for further processing, and thus does not have to be manually converted to an appropriate format for transmission and storage. In addition to managing JSON objects, the tool also imports and exports XML, CSV, as well as MS Excel files, and provides standard graphics formats for presentation and print. ICE+ is accessible with all major web browsers; and includes comprehensive user management, providing each user or user group with their own account and workspace.

In addition to ICE+, software tools for the automatic calculation, normalization, weighting, and aggregation of indicators are under construction at present. Based on raw spatial data stored in a custom database, indicator values are calculated using in-database techniques. The resulting indicator values are fed into another software tool, which automatically normalizes all indicator values, employs statistical methods to calculate indicator weights lowering the correlation between indicators, and aggregates the resulting values to composite risk.

49.4. Conclusions

To facilitate the development of local crisis management strategies regarding climate change-related extreme weather events, a standardized process for the assessment of climate change-related risks and vulnerabilities in urban environments has been developed. A set of software tools is being developed to support local authorities during the process. In further steps, the vulnerability assessment process will be validated in co-creation workshops between the developers, city stakeholders, and domain experts. These will result in a number of documented best-practice use cases regarding the tier-1 cities in the RESIN project, namely Bilbao (Spain), Bratislava (Slovakia), Greater Manchester (United Kingdom) and Paris (France).

---

1 Using JSON-LD to provide a higher-level of semantics in terms of data and system interoperability is an interesting extension of the system. This will be further explored in the next version of the software system.

49.5. Acknowledgements

The authors thank their partners in the RESIN consortium for their valuable contributions during the development and test process. This chapter is based in part upon work in the framework of the European project "climate RESilient cities and INfrastructures – RESIN". This project has received funding from the European Union's Horizon 2020 research and innovation programme under grant agreement no. 653522. The sole responsibility for the content of this publication lies with the authors. It does not necessarily represent the opinion of the European Union. Neither the EASME nor the European Commission is responsible for any use that may be made of the information contained therein.

49.6. References

[COL 16] COLETTI A., DE NICOLA A., VILLANI M.L., "Building climate change into risk assessment", *Natural Hazards*, vol. 84, no. 2, pp. 1307–1325, 2016.

[GER 11] GERMAN FEDERAL OFFICE OF CIVIL PROTECTION AND DISASTER ASSISTANCE, "Method of Risk Analysis for Civil Protection", *Wissenschaftsforum*, vol. 8, 2011.

[GER 14] GERMAN FEDERAL MINISTRY FOR ECONOMIC COOPERATION AND DEVELOPMENT, *The Vulnerability Sourcebook: Concept and Guidelines for Standardised Vulnerability Assessments*, Deutsche Gesellschaft für Internationale Zusammenarbeit, Bonn, Germany, 2014.

[LÜC 18] LÜCKERATH D., BOGEN M., ROME E. *et al.*, "The RESIN climate change adaptation project and its simple modeling approach for risk-oriented vulnerability assessment", *Workshop STS/GMMS 2018*, March 8–9, 2018.

[NEV 16] NEVES A., BLONDEL L., BRAND K. *et al.*, *The Covenant of Mayors for Climate and Energy Reporting Guidelines*, EUR 28160 EN, doi:10.2790/586693, 2016.

[RAM 17] RAMSES, "RAMSES: Reconciling adaptation, mitigation and sustainable development for cities", available at: http://www.ramses-cities.eu/, 2017.

[RES 17] RESIN, "RESIN: Climate Resilient Cities and Infrastructures", available at: http://www.resin-cities.eu/, 2017.

[ROM 17] ROME E., BOGEN M., WORST R. *et al.*, *Deliverable D2.3 Realisation and Implementation IVAVIA*, EU H2020 Project RESIN, Sankt Augustin, Germany, available at: http://www.resin-cities.eu/, 2017.

[SMR 17] SMR, "SMR: Smart Mature Resilience", available at: http://smr-project.eu/, 2017.

[UNI 14] UNITED NATIONS, DEPARTMENT OF ECONOMIC AND SOCIAL AFFAIRS, POPULATION DIVISION, *World Urbanization Prospects: the 2014 Revision, Highlights*, United Nations, 2014.

50

Semantic Interoperability of Early Warning Systems: a Systematic Literature Review

An Early Warning System (EWS) is a system-of-systems that is able to detect emergency risks and warn different stakeholders. Semantic interoperability is crucial in these systems because it enables unambiguous data exchange, so that different data sources can be integrated with EWS'. This chapter presents the results of our systematic literature review on EWS interoperability. The research questions targeted existing interoperable EWS' and their architecture and components' functions, emphasizing the role of data representation mechanisms, for example, data/message models, protocols and ontologies. Since semantic models rely on syntactical models, this review also includes these data representation approaches. This chapter also analyzes the main issues concerning the improvement of EWS interoperability, stressing the role of the Internet of Things in smart situation-aware emergency services. We conclude by proposing topics for follow-up research.

50.1. Introduction

An Early Warning System (EWS) is an integrated system that supports accident prevention, when a seizure is eminent, and accident recovery, when the accident already occurred, by monitoring physical entities, detecting situations of interest and warning relevant parties. The UN agenda for disaster risk reduction (Sendai) aims to improve risk identification through a holistic approach for EWS integration. It emphasizes the need to share disaster risk information and to increase availability towards multi-hazard EWS. This leads to challenges in all interoperability levels, for example, technical, semantic and organizational. Semantic interoperability is crucial

Chapter written by João Luiz Rebelo Moreira, Luís Ferreira Pires, Patricia Dockhorn Costa and Marten van Sinderen.

for EWS integration because it focuses on terminology and deals with human interpretation of heterogeneous information, enabling unambiguous data exchange, ensuring that the information is understood in the same way by data producers and receivers, thus, avoiding misunderstandings when communicating about delicate issues. Semantic interoperability also enables a seamless integration of different data sources and leverages risk identification. This chapter presents the results of a systematic literature review on interoperability issues when developing a multi-hazard EWS, emphasizing the semantic level. The research questions targeted interoperable EWS architectures, their components' functions and their data representation mechanisms. The chapter is further structured as follows: section 50.2 presents the SLR in terms of its research questions and results, section 50.3 describes a common architecture for interoperable EWS, section 50.4 identifies open issues and trends in data representation and section 50.5 presents lessons learned and future work.

50.2. Systematic literature review

Our Systematic Literature Review (SLR) was performed in the scope of software engineering design science, problem investigation [KIT 07]. In this chapter we describe the results of the knowledge questions listed in Table 50.1, which were transformed into queries performed on eight digital libraries: ACM, Science Direct, Springer, Google Scholar, IEEExplore, CiteSeer, Scopus and Wiley. Technical specifications (e.g. reports) from projects and standardization initiatives were also considered.

#	Description
KQ1	Are there surveys or literature reviews on EWS?
KQ2	What are the main initiatives (e.g. projects) for emergency interoperability?
KQ3	What are the common EWS architectures and their components' functions?
KQ4	What are the data representation mechanisms (e.g. data models, lexicon standards, ontologies) in emergency services that (may) interact with EWS?
KQ5	What are the main issues or mechanisms that produce them and current solutions?

Table 50.1. *Knowledge questions on EWS interoperability*

The identification phase of our SLR process resulted in 2917 papers from digital libraries and 261 from other sources, according to our inclusion criteria. The framing phase resulted in 3082 merged, having 2715 discarded by our exclusion criteria, resulting in 367 works assessed. Seventy-five technical specifications (reports and standards) and 292 papers, from 18 journals and 12 conference proceedings, were fully revised.

We identified several EWSs and the most popular EWS survey reported by the UNISDR [UNI 06] lists more than 50 EWSs at that time (2006). The United Nations Environment Programme report [UNI 12] updates this list and classifies EWSs according to rapid/sudden-onset and slow-onset environmental threats. The World Health Organization [WHO 14] describes the guidelines to develop multi-hazard EWS to improve monitoring risks for public health by mixing indicator-based and event-based surveillance techniques. The review on chemical EWS for public health highlights the problem that "currently interoperability and cross posting between alerting and reporting systems during an incident rely on human vigilance and interactions" [ORF 14]. Additionally, it enforces the relevance of intelligent automated EWS that are able to interoperate with other EWS, and timely legislation to facilitate cross-border communication. A historical perspective including the main initiatives (e.g. GITEWS, TRIDEC and IDIRA projects) is described in [MOR 18].

50.3. Interoperable EWS architecture

The concept of EWS as a system-of-systems (SoS) is exploited in many references. Waidyanatha [WAI 10] proposes a chain of subsystems as functional EWS components: sensor, detection, decision, broker and response activities. Similarly, a conceptual high level architecture of an interoperable EWS was described in [WÄC 14] (Figure 2). In this architecture, data are acquired from sensor systems (upstream data), which are represented with interoperability standards (e.g., OGC SWE and W3C SSN). These data are pre-processed and stored in an internal context database (e.g., relational and NoSQL). Models represent the mechanism to identify the emergency situations, which can be either specification-based (e.g., rule-based approaches) or learning-based (e.g., machine learning approaches). A "decision and action" module applies the rules over the context data and enables decision-making through the brokering of messages (downstream information) towards different target groups. Usually each target group has specific information requirements for message content, thus, the EWS must include the adequate content according to these requirements. The target groups can either be humans, receiving alerts through different technologies (e.g., mobile application and low-frequency radio), or actuators. OASIS EDXL is the common standard used for downstream data representation, as in GITEWS, IPAWS and several other EWS. This architecture allows EWS to integrate with each other through event-based message-oriented middleware (MOM), as a service broker.

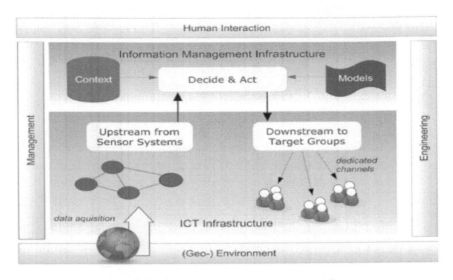

Figure 50.1. *Standard-based EWS architecture, from [WÄC 14]. For a color version of this figure, see www.iste.co.uk/zelm/enterprise.zip*

A "semantic EWS" extends this architecture by using semantic technologies to represent data (upstream and downstream), taking advantage of inference capabilities. Performance tends to be a drawback, which makes scalable time-sensitive data exchange and the processing of data from heterogeneous data sources quite challenging. The "semantic IoT EWS approach" [POS 15] deals with this challenge by providing a balanced way of lightweight and heavyweight ontologies. Current EWS tend to use informal models, while only a few use lightweight or heavyweight semantic models.

The "semantic IoT EWS" represents upstream data by annotating sensor data with the W3C SSN ontology, which is the lightweight approach to represent OGC SWE standards. Annotation is applied at the gateway level, since sensors only need to interoperate with a control center via a sensor's access node. Data acquisition is supported by a publish/subscribe MOM, which manages data import in the knowledge base (i.e., the implementation of the context database as an ontology management service that can be accessed through a semantic registry UI). A rule-based approach is adopted for decision and action, which is implemented through a decision support workflow service that applies the rules to the stored data. Heavyweight semantics are added and linked through additional metadata after the sensor data is imported in the context database. Downstream data generated by the execution of the workflows have the semantics enriched in order to better address the information requirements of the targets.

50.4. Data representation for crisis management

A fundamental aspect of interoperability is the mechanism to represent data. Numerous data representations have been proposed for crisis management, including lexicon standards and ontologies. The OASIS Emergency Data Exchange Language (EDXL) and the OGC Sensor Web Enablement (SWE) are the most popular lexicon and ready-to-use standard initiatives for the interoperability of emergency services.

In DEWS [LEN 12], the role of EDXL-CAP in logistics accidents is exploited. EDXL-CAP is one of the core elements of IPAWS and is a key standard for the representation of alerts for multi-hazards [KEE 12]. Moreover, EDXL allows for the representation of emergency situations (EDXL-SitRep) and tracking emergency patients (EDXL-TEP). EDXL standards support requirements engineering for emergency interoperability, as in the profile-based approach [BOŽ 15]. Although EDXL is not implemented as a semantic model, it allows the inclusion of controlled vocabularies serialized as RDF/XML through the *ValueListURIType* element.

OGC SWE standards are often used for sensor data representation, and have been applied in diverse types of EWSs (e.g., for floods, earthquakes and tsunamis) [ZAM 15]. For example, Emergency Management Victoria (Australia) uses these standards for multi-agency sensor data integration [ALA 16]. OGC SWE consists of four information models and four service models. Information models focus on the representation of sensor data with a sensor modeling language (SensorML) and Observations and Measurements (O&M). Services include observation and notification.

Several data models and ontologies for emergency/crisis/disaster management were proposed. For example, Othman and Beydoun [OTH 16] use an extensive list of information sources for disaster management metamodeling and included the term *EarlyWarningSystem*. In semantic approaches, terminology regarding events and *situation-awareness* is widely exploited, probably because it is often necessary to represent dynamic temporal aspects of emergencies. For example, the *Event-Model-F* [SCH 12] was developed to address the requirements of sharing event interpretations in emergency responses, exploiting the role of causality of events and situations.

We also observed that it is often necessary to match equivalent terminologies in order to provide a higher level of interoperability for EWS with multiple data sources. For example, EDXL-TEP provides mappings to HL7 standards regarding the overlapping terms about patients. The W3C SSN ontology and several other ontologies in the context of IoT (e.g., ETSI SAREF) provide mappings to OGC SWE, especially SensorML and O&M. The "semantic IoT EWS" approach introduced the Decision Support Ontology (DSO), which uses some W3C SSN predicates and incorporates terms from O&M. Although DSO's goal is "to aggregate and align multiple ontologies to support compound EWS semantics and ontology commitments", it lacks the support for multiple domain ontology alignments at runtime (i.e., it does not provide a mechanism for describing and executing ontology alignments at runtime). Besides this, efficiently publishing large volumes of semantically rich sensor data is a major architectural challenge [MID 13], mainly due to the inefficient data transfer (throughput) of the current semantic technologies.

50.5. Conclusion

This chapter presents the main outcomes of our systematic literature review about interoperable EWS architectures and their data representations. We highlight the importance of the semantic approaches for the development of interoperable EWS, emphasizing the "semantic IoT EWS". Unfortunately, due to space limitations we could not discuss our survey results in more detail, though they can be found in [MOR 18].

Our research aims to improve the semantic interoperability of IoT EWS for smart emergency services (i.e., we aim to improve the semantic integration capacity of components of an IoT EWS and enable seamless integration with other EWS). To achieve this goal, we concluded that the following three challenges must be addressed: (C1) the semantic integration of a variety of data sources, avoiding loss of semantics when multiple data representations from multiple domains are involved, considering their syntactic and semantic alignments; (C2) processing in time- and safety-critical applications to provide the required performance for data acquisition, risk detection and message brokering, in terms of scalability and total transaction time; (C3) data analysis for effective responses to enable high quality situation awareness (perception, comprehension and projection) to improve emergency decision support.

50.6. References

[ALA 16] Alamdar F., Kalantari M., Rajabifard A., "Towards multi-agency sensor information integration for disaster management", *Computers, Environment and Urban Systems*, 2016.

[BOŽ 15] Božić B., Gençtürk M., Duro R. *et al.*, "Requirements engineering for semantic sensors in crisis and disaster management", *Environmental Software Systems: Infrastructures, Services and Applications*, 2015.

[KEE 12] Keeney J.H., Buan S., Diamond L., "Multi-hazard early warning system of the United States National Weather Service", *Institutional Partnerships in Multi-Hazard Early Warning Systems: a Compilation of Seven National Good Practices and Guiding Principles*, 2012.

[KIT 07] Kitchenham B., Charters S., "Guidelines for performing systematic literature reviews in software engineering", *Engineering*, 2007.

[LEN 12] Lendholt M., Hammitzsch M., "Towards an integrated information logistics for multi-hazard early warning systems", *The Open Environmental Engineering Journal*, 2012.

[MID 13] Middleton S. E., Zlatev Z., Mossgraber J. *et al.*, "The seven main challenges of an early warning system architecture", *Information Systems for Crisis Response and Management*, 2013.

[MOR 18] Moreira J., "SEMantic model-driven engineering for IOT Interoperability of emergenCy serviceS", available at: http://semiotics-iot.eu, 2018.

[ORF 14] Orford R., Crabbe H., Hague C. *et al.*, "EU alerting and reporting systems for potential chemical public health threats and hazards", *Environment International*, 2014.

[OTH 16] Othman S. H., Beydoun G., "A metamodel-based knowledge sharing system for disaster management", *Expert Systems with Applications*, 2016.

[POS 15] Poslad S., Middleton S. E., Chaves F. *et al.*, "A semantic IoT early warning system for natural environment crisis management", *IEEE Transactions on Emerging Topics in Computing*, 2015.

[SCH 12] Scherp A., Franz T., Saathoff C., "A core ontology on events for representing occurrences in the real world", *Multimedia Tools and Applications*, 2012.

[UNI 06] United Nations, "Global survey of early warning systems: an assessment of capacities, gaps and opportunities toward building a comprehensive global early warning system for all natural hazards", United Nations, 2006.

[UNI 12] United Nations Environment Programme, "Early warning systems: state-of-art analysis and future directions", United Nations, 2012.

[WÄC 14] Wächter J., Usländer T., "The role of information and communication technology in the development of early warning systems for geological disasters: the tsunami show case", *Early Warning for Geological Disasters: Scientific Methods and Current Practice*, 2014.

[WAI 10] Waidyanatha N., "Towards a typology of integrated functional early warning systems", *International Journal of Critical Infrastructures*, 2010.

[WHO 14] WHO, "Early detection, assessment and response to acute public health events: implementation of early warning and response with a focus on event-based surveillance", WHO, 2014.

[ZAM 15] Zambrano A. M., Pérez I., Palau C.E. *et al.*, "Sensor Web Enablement applied to an earthquake early warning system", *International Conference on Internet and Distributed Computing Systems*, vol. 9258, 2015.

51

Towards Semantic Generation of
Geolocalized Models of Risk

We present the architecture of a tool suite that aims to generate geolocalized conceptual models of risk to be used for the risk assessment of a geographical area, such as a city, a district or a country. This suite consists of three main components: CREAM, a tool for the automatic generation of conceptual models of risks, leveraging semantic and computational creativity techniques; TERMINUS, a domain ontology that gathers knowledge concerning environment, critical infrastructures and related risks; and CIPCast, a GIS-based tool for critical infrastructures protection, enhanced with forecasting and decision support functionalities. Then, we describe the interoperability issues we considered to design this suite of tools. Finally, we discuss usage scenarios for the risk assessment of an urban area.

51.1. Introduction

Different geographical areas are characterized by their specific Critical Infrastructures (CI), and services targeted at populations individual needs. Given a specific area, natural hazards (e.g. flash floods, earthquakes), anthropic hazards (e.g. terrorist attacks, cyber attacks), and threats related systems, and vulnerabilities and stakeholders define a potential risk of given severity [1]. Hence, each zone could be subject to different risks. An open research problem is to conceive the possible risks of a given geographical area and quantify them. Associating risks with geographical areas could support the work of risk analysts. These risks can be used before a crisis event to assess the potential impact on a specific area (i.e. a prevention phase) or during a crisis event to assess its possible consequences

Chapter written by Alex COLETTI, Antonio DE NICOLA, Antonio DI PIETRO, Maurizio POLLINO, Vittorio ROSATO, Giordano VICOLI and Maria Luisa VILLANI.

(i.e. a response phase). To this purpose we propose a phased approach supported by a suite of tools. In the first phase, possible risks of a given geographical area are automatically generated as fragments of conceptual models. In the second phase, such risks are quantitatively assessed by the means of mathematical functions of risk. In this chapter, we face the first phase of the problem and, in particular, we aim at geolocalizing fragments of automatically generated conceptual models of risks and showing them on a map.

We propose a suite of tools consisting of three main components: CREAM (CREAtivity Machine), a software application able to automatically generate conceptual models of risks by leveraging semantic and computational creativity techniques [2]; TERMINUS (TERritorial Management and INfrastructures ontology for institutional and industrial USage) [3], a domain ontology that gathers territorial knowledge concerning environment, critical infrastructures and related risks; and CIPCast [4], a GIS (Geographical Information System)-based tool for CI protection, enhanced with forecasting and decision support functionalities. We discuss how such geolocalized fragments of risks, termed risk mini-models [2], are generated and the interoperability issues we faced to design the architecture of the tool suite.

Localizing vulnerabilities and hazards is a fundamental aspect of risk assessment [7]. However, existing approaches mainly focus on information systems for quantitative estimates and only a few approaches address the conceptual problem of supporting the identification of new risks [6]. To the best of our knowledge, our solution, which integrates quantitative and conceptual risk assessment by leveraging semantic and computational creativity techniques and a GIS interface, is novel and unprecedented.

The rest of the chapter is organized as follows. Section 51.2 presents the system architecture for geolocalized risk assessment. Section 51.3 describes the interoperability issues. Section 51.4 presents a usage scenario of geolocalized risk assessment. Finally, section 51.5 provides some conclusions.

51.2. System architecture for geolocalized risk assessment based on semantics

Traditional systems for risk assessment consider a limited number of predefined vulnerabilities of systems and compute the level of related risk based on some mathematical risk functions. Even if the accuracy of these systems is increasing, a limitation is that the corresponding mathematical models do not consider the overall complexity of the problem but address only some of the aspects of a potentially harmful situation. To overcome this limit, we consider risk assessment from a wider perspective where traditional quantitative risk assessment methods are enriched by semantic reasoning mechanisms that generate likely and unlikely risks. To this purpose we propose a suite of tools that is configurable according to location.

Figure 51.1 illustrates the architecture of the tool suite and the related process flow. Accordingly, institutional operators (e.g. civil protection) interact with the suite through a WebGIS interface to select an area of interest and other contextual information as systems, services or possible hazards. This information is used by CREAM to generate possible risk situations for the area and by CIPCast to compute the level of risks for the area. Reasoning performed by CREAM is based on the TERMINUS domain ontology. In what follows, we briefly describe the overall architecture.

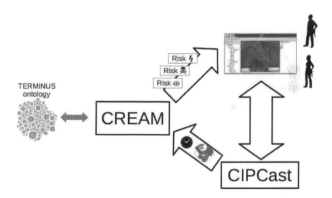

Figure 51.1. *Architecture of the tool suite for the semantic generation of geolocalized models of risk. For a color version of this figure, see ww.iste.co.uk/zelm/enterprise.zip*

The TERritorial Management and Infrastructures ontology for institutional and industrial USage includes knowledge representing environment, CI and related hazards, risks and threats. At the current stage, TERMINUS is built deriving concepts from the vulnerability upper model (VUM) and from the system aspect design pattern presented in [3]. It also includes knowledge related to interdependencies between critical infrastructures [5].

The CREAtivity Machine is a software application that automatically generates models of risks; more specifically, it creates conceptual representations of risk situations by means of a combination of semantic and computational creativity techniques. Conceiving new risks requires involving operators with interdisciplinary technical expertise that are not always available or accessible. CREAM overcomes the problem by autonomously suggesting new risks to institutional operators. Such risks are extracted as risk mini-models from the TERMINUS domain ontology by means of SPARQL queries based on some predefined system design patterns and logic rules.

CIPCast is a novel Decision Support System (DSS) [4] able to produce a real-time operational risk forecast of CI in a given area due to natural hazards. The main functionalities of CIPCast are: (1) real-time monitoring of natural phenomena; (2) *prediction of natural events (if predictable);* (3) *prediction of damage scenario* on critical infrastructure components; (4) *prediction of impacts of critical infrastructure services and impacts on citizens*; and (5) *definition of efficient strategies* to support decision-making operator processes.

51.3. Interoperability issues

In this section we briefly discuss the interoperability levels concerning the interoperation of the CREAM software with the CIPCast DSS. We identified four levels: *risk assessment, process, model,* and *data.* These are represented in Figure 51.2.

The *risk assessment level* concerns the system risk. In our case, CREAM deals with identifying some of the types of risks whereas CIPCast deals with the quantitative assessment of risk by associating a severity value to a predefined type of risk. Ensuring interoperability at this level means to define how these two approaches for risk assessment can be used together. The *process level* deals with the interoperability of the processes implemented by two systems. In our case, for instance, it is dedicated to the interoperability of the process that CREAM uses to generate risk mini-models with CIPCast processes to make simulations and forecasting and vice versa. The *model level* concerns semantics. For instance, here, the challenge is to specify how to map the CIPCast data model to TERMINUS by identifying the possible clashes between software applications. The *data level* deals with identifying the technical aspects concerning the information exchange between the two systems. In our case, for instance, the problem is to define which data should be passed from CIPCast to CREAM and how these data should be managed (e.g. syntactic format of data).

51.4. Usage scenarios

Usage scenarios of the combined CREAM-CIPCast systems serve to demonstrate the enhancement of the risk assessment functions and to validate the CREAM ability to identify risks relevant to a given spatiotemporal context.

Generally, we envisage two phases for systems' interoperation to support risks analysts: (1) *prevention phase* from potential crisis events that pose risks to a specific area; and (2) *early response phase* during some crisis event to foresee and assess its direct and indirect consequences on the given area for the purpose of decision-making. An example of the latter usage is water distribution management after an earthquake in a nearby area. Such analysis requires the availability of dynamic data updates on environmental conditions, infrastructure failures and so on. In such a setting, CREAM can be set to select risk situations possibly appropriate for the new context.

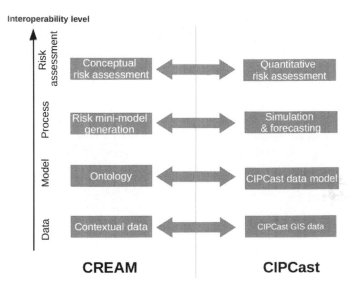

Figure 51.2. *Interoperability levels concerning the tool suite*

The following scenario illustrates the usage of CREAM-CIPCast in the prevention phase:

> A risk analyst wants to assess the consequences of an earthquake for a zone of an urban area. The analyst specifies the hazard and selects the city area by interacting with a map by means of the WebGIS interface of the CIPCast system. Relevant geographic information for the area include: points of interest such as schools, hospitals and public places; and CI components such as water pipes, road characteristics, the position of electric substations, etc. These entities can be automatically identified using CIPCast and this information will be exploited by CREAM to generate semantic descriptions of possible damage scenarios for the selected area. Results include both direct damages (e.g. on the buildings) and cascading effects (e.g. a broken water pipe interfering with a school evacuation). Damage scenarios can be quantified through CIPCast functions, and the results are supplied to the risk analyst on the WebGIS interface. The analyst is also supported by the system in the identification and browsing of all relevant risk situations, with the final aim to improve completeness, and hence reliability, of the risk assessment.

51.5. Conclusion

Risks identification in socio-technological systems is a complex activity due to uncertainties of hazards, to an increased interdependence of CI, and to the limited ability to foresee cascading failures. To this aim, CREAM is a novel software system to support risk analysts by projecting relevant risk situations with semantic reasoning and computational creativity techniques [2] based on a formal description of the scenario. On the other hand, risk assessment requires data on the geographical areas and on the societal and infrastructures' characteristics of the specific system under analysis. This problem is addressed by CIPCast [4], which is a GIS-based tool for CI protection, enhanced with forecasting and decision support functionalities. In this work, we proposed an architecture that enables these two systems to interoperate and complement the newly developed CREAM risk assessment system with location specific risk descriptions and analysis capabilities.

51.6. References

[1] COLETTI A., DE NICOLA A., VILLANI M. L., "Building climate change into risk assessments", *Natural Hazards*, vol. 84, no. 2, pp. 1307–1325, 2017.

[2] COLETTI A., DE NICOLA A., VILLANI M. L., "Enhancing creativity in risk assessment of complex sociotechnical systems", *Computational Science and its Applications – ICCSA 2017. LNCS*, vol. 10405, Springer, Cham, pp. 294–309, 2017.

[3] COLETTI A., DE NICOLA A., VICOLI G. *et al.*, "Semantic modelling of cascading risks in interoperable sociotechnical systems", *Proc I-ESA*, 2018.

[4] GIOVINAZZI S., POLLINO M., KONGAR I. *et al.*, "Towards a decision support tool for assessing, managing and mitigating seismic risk of electric power networks", *Computational Science and its Applications – ICCSA 2017 LNCS*, vol. 10405, Springer, Cham, 2017.

[5] RINALDI S. M., PEERENBOOM J. P., KELLY T. K., "Identifying, understanding, and analyzing critical infrastructure interdependencies", *IEEE Control Systems*, vol. 21, no. 6, pp. 11–25, 2001.

[6] MAIDEN N., ZACHOS K., LOCKERBIE J. *et al.*, "Establishing digital creativity support in non-creative work environments", *Proceedings of the 11th ACM Creativity and Cognition Conference*, ACM, 2017.

[7] VAN WESTEN C. J., CASTELLANOS E., SEKHAR K. L., "Spatial data for landslide susceptibility, hazard, and vulnerability assessment: An overview", *Engineering Geology*, vol. 102, nos 3–4, pp. 112–131, 1st December 2008.

52

An Ontology-based Emergency Response System for Interoperability in a Crisis Situation in Smart Cities

In a crisis situation, the emergency response process becomes very critical. Various emergency responders have to coordinate their activities and react together to save peoples' lives and properties. However, this makes the challenges of information sharing and interoperability among emergency management systems highly substantial. Therefore, to solve the deficiency of interoperability and to overcome the semantic heterogeneity of data so as to guarantee a consistent shared understanding of the meaning of information, we propose in this chapter, POLARISC, an ontology-based operational emergency response system for smart cities. We developed a common modular ontology towards defining emergency responders' knowledge in order to solve semantic interoperability issues in emergency management. In addition, POLARISC offers a set of services for smart cities including alerting smart actors, the evacuation of victims, providing Emergency Detour Route and so on.

52.1. Introduction

In recent decades, people have been confronted to a notably increasing number and types of disasters. Whether they are natural or human-made, they engender the occurrence of major harmful events. Lives can be lost and property can be damaged. The need to face these problems makes disaster management processes becomes more critical and challenging [DEV 06]. As a process, emergency response can be divided

Chapter written by Linda ELMHADHBI, Mohamed-Hedi KARRAY and Bernard ARCHIMÈDE.

into three phases: (1) pre-crisis, which is about prevention and preparation, (2) crisis response, which is when management must actually respond to a crisis, and (3) the post-crisis phase, which looks for better ways to prepare for the next crisis [COO 07]. In this context, we will focus on the crisis response phase. In fact, there are two levels of intervention in the conduct of a crisis, namely, the crisis management level that includes political, strategic and tactical stages and the operational management (firefighters, gendarmerie, police, health care services and civil security services) [COS 13]. In this chapter, we will focus specifically on the operational level. The major challenge at this stage is that the involved Emergency Responders (ERs) should have access to the appropriate information and share it with the right stakeholder at the right time in order to guarantee an efficient coordination between ERs and to accomplish a real time common operational picture of the field situation. Although, since each ER has deployed its own information system and uses different vocabularies and graphical charters to represent the same term, as a consequence, a main issue of semantic heterogeneity arises. So, to overcome semantic heterogeneity and to guarantee a consistent shared understanding of the meaning of information, the use of ontologies is crucial [ANT 13]. Thus, they offer the richest representations of machine-interpretable semantics for systems and databases [OBR 03]. They serve as both knowledge representation and as mediation to enable heterogeneous systems interoperability [SON 13]. However, the question that arises is how to match these ontologies in order to provide the semantic interoperability of multiple information systems. The key way to integrate heterogeneous knowledge across various ontologies is to make use of upper level ontologies. It provides a common ontological foundation for domain ontologies which describe the most general domain independent categories of reality as: time and space, individuals, objects, events, processes, instantiation and so on [DEG 01].

For this purpose, in this chapter, we present a novel solution, POLARISC (Plateforme OpérationnelLe d'Actualisation du Renseignement Interservices pour la Sécurité Civile), an ontology-based operational emergency response system for large-scale situations. It is a new project which started in 2017. It is an interoperable inter-services software solution for reliable and timely information sharing for the operational management of large scale crisis situations. The focus is about offering to all ERs a real-time operation picture of the situation in order to enable coordination within the ERs. Once the common operating platform is established, various smart cities services can be enabled. The rest of this chapter is organized as follows. The next section goes into detail regarding the proposed solution and the system architecture. Section 3 delivers an overview of the proposed ontology. Finally, the conclusion and the future work are presented.

52.2. The proposed solution

Information accessibility and availability is vital during a large scale emergency response. For this purpose, POLARISC aims to offer a common operational picture, timely access to the needed information, data sharing and coordination between stakeholders. Figure 52.1 illustrates the architecture of POLARISC as a whole system. POLARISC is mainly a software solution that plays the role of mediation between ERs. It is composed of four layers. First, the user's layer is composed of the different stakeholders that will use the system (firefighters, police, healthcare services, etc.). Second, the mediator's layer is responsible of transforming the data according to the appropriate vocabulary and graphical charter (color codes and graphical symbols) of the stakeholder. It is a gateway between end-user systems. As a result, each stakeholder perceives information in accordance with their vocabulary and checks the operational picture of what exactly happens in the field according to their graphical charter. Third, the data layer is the core of the proposed system. To overcome semantic heterogeneity among stakeholders, the definition of a common terminology among the ERs is essential.

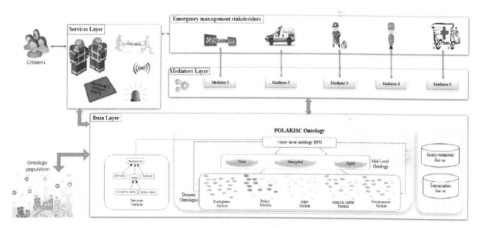

Figure 52.1. *POLARISC architecture. For a color version of this figure, see www.iste.co.uk/zelm/enterprise.zip*

At last, the services layer is about suggesting a set of services designed to support the smart cities vision – "It is the utilization of networked infrastructures to improve economic and political efficiency and enable socio, cultural and urban development" [KUM 17]. Among these services, once the emergency scene is defined, an emergency detour route aims to send messages, using sensing capabilities and GPS, to vehicles in proximity of the emergency field. The aim is to alert citizens and pre-determine the egress route to help them bypass emergency road closure and to go around the affected route. Then, the evacuation of victims' service allows finding as quickly as possible the appropriate health care institutions and reserves according to the patient state [MHA 15].

52.3. POLARISC ontology

To develop our proposed modular ontology (a module for each stakeholder), we used an upper level ontology. Indeed, the use of upper level ontologies facilitates the alignment between several domain ontologies. In addition, upper level ontologies play the same role as libraries in software programming tasks. Once they are used, one could reuse the defined concepts and relationships and so inherit the inferencing capabilities furnished by them. In this way, developing a domain ontology is an easier task that requires less time than usual. Moreover, the aim is to avoid having several incompatible domain ontologies [BAU 06].

To select the appropriate upper level ontology, we first looked for a realist upper ontology that represents the world as is. Then, to ensure that the upper level ontology can be extended to an emergency management ontology, it should be universal. Universal classes are often characterized as natural classes that abstract or generalize over similar particular things. Person, location, process and so on, are examples of universals [SEM 04]. Accordingly, we employed the Basic Formal Ontology (BFO) as an upper level ontology [SEP 14]. We might say that the ontology encapsulates the knowledge of the world that is associated with the general terms used by scientists in the corresponding domain [ARP 15]. As a starting point, BFO uses the term "entity" as a common representation of anything that exist in the world. Then, it incorporates two categories of entity – "Continuants" and "Occurrents" – as top-level distinction between entities. Continuants are entities that persist through time. Occurrents are entities that happen or develop over time, such as processes.

As a mid-level ontology, Common Core Ontology (CCO) is adopted for building the ontology. It meets most of our requirements since it inherits from BFO and defines a set of extensible modules that can be connected to our domain ontology. In our work, we only reused three modules of ten that will be extended according to the domain level needs which are agent ontology, time ontology and geospatial ontology. Concerning the domain ontologies and to develop the different modules, interviews were conducted with stakeholders so as to capture their needs and to identify their technical vocabulary (commandment hierarchy, means, types of intervention, roles, etc.). We started first by firefighters' module. In order to ensure a better understanding of the created ontology, an overview of the firefighters' module is shown in Figure 52.2.

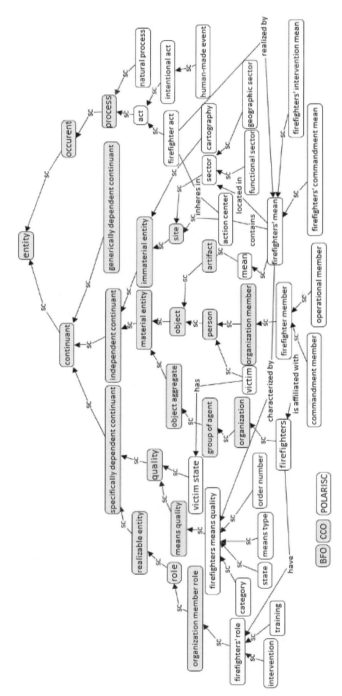

Figure 52.2. *An overview of POLARISC ontology (firefighters module).*
For a color version of this figure, see www.iste.co.uk/zelm/enterprise.zip

In the firefighters' module, as regards to the continuant part, we extended the agent ontology to cover the different members of firefighter organization. Under agent quality, we incorporated the firefighter hierarchy of commandment and we attributed a grade for each member. In addition, we affected the role of each member of firefighters. In the class artifact, we classified firefighter different with means by specifying their functions. Each mean is characterized by category, state, type and order number. Immaterial entities include the different types of sector and firefighters' action centers. Concerning occurrent entities, we added, on the one hand, the different types of firefighters' interventions, which is related to its needs in terms of means and staff, and on the other hand, the possible types of processes (natural process or human made event). At the end of this stage, the firefighters' module had around 429 classes and 246 relations. The classes are labeled in English and in French. The final step consists on the evaluation of the proposed ontology by domain experts in terms of inconsistency, incompleteness and redundancy. To summarize, the ontology we created, once it is complete and all the emergency responders' modules are integrated, will be instantiated to test it by means of a concrete use case and it will be used by the POLARISC platform as a common shared vocabulary. Domain experts and users should then evaluate and validate the obtained results.

52.4. Conclusion and future work

This chapter addresses real issues that cause slower and inefficient decision-making in responding to emergency situations such as the semantic heterogeneity of data and the deficiency of interoperability in emergency management systems. An inter-services operational emergency response system for data sharing among heterogeneous ERO in large scale situations has been proposed. It offers a real-time common operating platform in order to enable data exchange within the EROs. For all we know, the modular ontology proposed in this chapter is the first ontology based on the BFO and CCO that aims to define the ERs knowledge. In future, we will exploit the rest of the ERs' modules. Once POLARISC ontology is done and the common operating platform is established, the cited smart cities services can be enabled.

52.5. Acknowledgments

This research was conducted as part of the POLARISC project. It was funded by the regional operational program, FEDER/FSE "Midi-Pyrénées et Garonne 2014–2020" as part of the call for "Easynov2016" projects.

52.6. References

[ANT 13] ANTUNES, G. *et al.*, "Using Ontologies to Integrate Multiple Enterprise Architecture Domains", *International Conference on Business Information Systems,* Springer, Berlin, Heidelberg, 2013.

[ARP 15] ARP, R., SMITH, B., SPEAR, A. D., *Building Ontologies with Basic Formal Ontology*, MIT Press, 2015.

[BAU 06] BAUMGARTNER, N., RETSCHITZEGGER, W., "A Survey of Upper Ontologies for Situation Awareness", *Proceeding of the 4th Iasted International Conference on Knowledge Sharing and Collaborative Engineering*, St. Thomas, VI, pp. 1–9, 2006.

[COO 07] COOMBS, W. T., Crisis Management and Communications, Institute for Public Relations, 2007.

[COS 13] COSTE, F., NEXON, E., DAGUZAN, J. F., ANVIL: Analysis of Civil Security Systems in Europe, Country Study, France, 2013.

[DEG 01] DEGEN, W. *et al.*, "GOL: Toward an Axiomatized Upper-Level Ontology", *Proceedings of the International Conference on Formal Ontology in Information Systems*, ACM, 2001.

[DEV 06] DEVLIN, E. S., *Crisis Management Planning and Execution*, CRC Press, 2006.

[JAQ 06] JAQUES, T., "Issue Management and Crisis Management: an Integrated, Non-Linear, Relational Construct", *Public Relations Review*, vol. 33, no. 2, pp. 147–157, 2006.

[KUM 17] KUMMITHA, R. K. R., CRUTZEN, N., "How do we understand smart cities? An evolutionary perspective", *Cities*, vol. 67, pp. 43–52, 2017.

[MHA 15] MHADHB, L., AKAICHI, J., KARRAY, M. H., *et al.*, "Ontologies for location-based services quality enhancement: the case of emergency services", *Second International Conference on eDemocracy & eGovernment*, IEEE, pp. 90–97, 2015.

[OBR 03] OBRST, L., "Ontologies for Semantically Interoperable Systems", *Proceedings of the Twelfth International Conference on Information and Knowledge Management*, ACM, 2003.

[RUD 16] RUDNICKI, R., *An overview of the common core ontologies*, CUBRC, 2016.

[SEM 04] SEMY, S. K., PULVERMACHER, M. K., OBRST, L. J., Toward the use of an upper ontology for US government and US military domains: an evaluation, Report, Mitre Corp Bedford, MA, 2004.

[SEP 14] SEPPÄLÄ, S., SMITH, B., CEUSTERS, W., "Applying the Realism-based Ontology-versioning Method for Tracking Changes in the Basic Formal Ontology", *FOIS*, pp. 227–240, 2014.

[SON 13] SONG, F., ZACHAREWICZ, G., CHEN, D., "An Ontology-driven Framework Towards Building Enterprise Semantic Information Layer", *Advanced Engineering Informatics*, vol. 27, no. 1, pp. 38–50, 2013.

53

Analyzing Interoperability in a Non-functional Requirements Ecosystem to Support Crisis Management Response

53.1. Introduction

The *"ilities are desired properties of a system [...] that often manifest themselves after a system has been put into its initial use"* [DEW 12]. In other words, "*-ilities*" are non-functional requirements to be reached and that provide a "special" capacity to a system to support the achievement of its mission. Numerous -ilities are identified in the literature, such as robustness, resilience, reliability and interoperability [ROS 12]. These non-functional requirements are clearly identified as requirements that have an impact on the functioning, the achievement of the mission and the performances of a system that must be mastered. This is typically the case of interoperability in a crisis context where it stands as a requirement that plays a major role between actors that develop plans, actions and processes to build an adapted crisis response. In this context and like any other requirement, interoperability is developed through technological (e.g. enterprise service bus), organizational (e.g. collaborative processes) or else conceptual (e.g. data management) aspects [ISO 09]. A part of these developments is related to the evaluation of interoperability in order to know its degree of satisfaction and further, if a given interoperability solution is fully adapted. Indeed, the evaluation of interoperability allows actors to either build a response before a crisis occurs or else, adjust their plans, actions or processes during a crisis. Thus, various methods are developed to evaluate interoperability guiding the actors in its implementation and further, in their monitoring and control of the situation. Whether formal (e.g. mathematical operators) or informal (e.g. maturity model), as well as quantitative (e.g. numerical scale) or qualitative (e.g.

Chapter written by Nicolas DACLIN, Behrang MORADI, Vincent CHAPURLAT.

truth value), these methods are often dedicated to the evaluation of interoperability without necessarily considering its impact on other -ilities that are also developed and vice-versa. The purpose of this chapter is to present the interest to analyze the interoperability not only in an isolated manner but also as a part of a complex non-functional requirements "ecosystem[1]". This chapter is structured as follow. Following this brief introduction, the problem statement and expected outcomes will be provided and discussed in section 53.2. Section 53.3 will then lay out the proposed investigation and the concepts on which it relies.

53.2. Problem statement and expected outcomes

Different means and methods (Table 53.1) to evaluate interoperability exist [REZ 14] in order to have a vision of an interoperability level whether qualitative or quantitative [BOT 16].

Quantitative	Qualitative
Interoperability modes [FOR 08], Quality attributes [KAS 04], Semantic interoperability [YAH 12], Ratio of interoperability [ELM 11]	LISI [C4I 98], OIM [FEW 03], LCIM [TOL 07], EIMM [ATH 05], MMEI [GUÉ 15], Formal Verification [MAL 15]

Table 53.1. *Interoperability evaluation*

Quantitative evaluation mainly relies on mathematical formalization and gives accurate results (e.g. numerical results) based on measurable and quantifiable data. Conversely, these approaches are difficult to manipulate – for unaccustomed actors – according to their degree of formalization. Qualitative evaluation can be less accurate (e.g. binary results) but offer powerful means to evaluate interoperability. The maturity models stand as the most accomplished means, providing not only a means to evaluate interoperability but also recommendations and good practices to improve interoperability. Nevertheless, quantitative evaluation is strongly related to human expertise with possible misinterpretation or else, time to get a result. In the limited frame of interoperability in crisis contexts, the work developed in [MAL 15] proposes a set of tools based on formal verification (model checking) to evaluate interoperability within a response collaborative process but only offers a result such as satisfied/not satisfied without more information. Although these methods show the importance to handle interoperability and are fully adapted, they only focus on the evaluation of interoperability without the consideration of possible impacts on other requirements

---

1 The "*-ilities*" ecosystem is defined as "*a set of '-ilities' that interact with each other and with the other requirements (functional, non-functional) of the system in which they are developed*" [DAC 17].

and further, without considering the impact of *other* requirements on interoperability. It results in a partial vision of the interoperability level since the different results do not include the possible impact of other requirements that disturb interoperability. In this case, actors are likely to focus their analysis and investigation on a problem that only relates to interoperability and that does not consider the influence of other *-ilities*. Thus, as stated in [DEW 12], a given -ility is *"often treated in isolation"* without including the possible relationships that could exists amongst other *-ilities "including complements, substitutions or others tradeoffs"* between *-ilities* [ROS 12]. Once more, in the frame of crisis management, the work developed in [BIL 15] does not focus, strictly speaking, on -ilities relationships but attempts to highlight the link between interoperability and its impact on the performance of a collaborative system that engages means to solve a crisis. It proposes a matrix of impact showing the influence of interoperability according to its lifecycle (compatibility, interoperation, autonomy and reversibility). More recently and related to the context of -ilities analysis, [MOR 17] establishes a link between resilience and interoperability, highlighting the influence between these requirements. As a consequence, the expected outcome of this research is to develop an approach that allows the evaluation of interoperability, taking into account its relationships with other non-functional requirements on which it can have an impact, or else, can be impacted. This research relies on the work initiated in [DEW 12] that proposes a set of -ilities and their possible relationships. The main goal is to have a set of means that allows the evaluation of interoperability independently (existing means in literature, see Table 53.1) and to evaluate interoperability in its ecosystem.

53.3. Interoperability analysis in an -ilities ecosystem

The relationship aspect between *-ilities* is clearly identified, especially in [DEW 12]. From web-based queries about -ilities that play a major role in systems, they establish a relationship graph between all *-ilities* as shown in Figure 53.1. For example, the graph shows that reliability, evolvability or else extensibility are related to interoperability. That means the study of these requirements is related to interoperability and vice versa. The thickness of the link shows the intensity of the co-occurrence of the -ilities – for instance between safety and interoperability – but does not give any indication about the nature of the link. Nevertheless, this graph has a particular importance since it highlights the relationship between non-functional requirements and allows one to identify a set of questions to address. Thus, this graph acts as a base to develop a deeper investigation concerning non-functional requirements considered as an ecosystem. The purpose is not to address interoperability in isolation, but to consider it according to different aspects that make it possible to bring out its relationships and its nature with its environment, namely *influence*, *direction* and *intensity*.

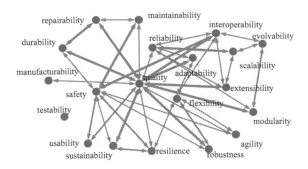

Figure 53.1. *Graph of ilities dependencies [DEW 12]*

The **influence** entails an identification of the existing relationship between interoperability and other -ilities. The influence means that a modification of an -ility can modify that with which it is linked. For instance, the previous graph shows that reliability has an influence on interoperability. This is the case since, for instance, a given organization in charge of a crisis management can rely on technical systems (e.g. a communication system) that are fully interoperable, but if these systems are not reliable, interoperability can hardly be achievable (e.g. an impossibility to exchange information). However, this graph is currently incomplete in terms of relationship exploration. Some relations are not yet identified either because they are not yet formally identified or because the study on a given -ility is still relatively new. This is the case for interoperability (even if it has been studied for the last two decades), which can be assumed to be related to other requirements but without this link being discovered and studied because of the novelty of the domain. For instance, it can be assumed that interoperability is related to the resilience since it can – in a collaborative system – participate with *"the capacity of a system to absorb disturbance and reorganize while undergoing change so as to still retain essentially the same function, structure, identity, and feedbacks"* [WAL 04]. In the same vein, some works establish the link between agility and interoperability [BÉN 12] without this link being visible. The **direction** informs us of the existence of the influence from an -ility onto another - ility. In the case of the study of interoperability, it allows one to know the set of -ilities which influence interoperability (inputs) but also the -ilities that are directly influenced by the interoperability (outputs). Thus, the interoperability is influenced by compatibility (interoperability does not exist without compatibility) on the one hand, and it influences quality (in terms of mission achievement for instance) on the other hand. As a consequence, the graph that allows one to analyze interoperability has to consider both directions (*impacts interoperability* and *impacted by interoperability"*). Lastly, the **intensity** expresses the strength of an -ility onto another. More precisely, characterizes the notion of influence. Moreover, this intensity can be variable during the lifecycle of an -ility. For the interoperability life cycle [MAL 11], the compatibility strongly influences the creation of the relationship between organizations and less in the phase of interoperation. The reliability strongly influences the interoperation phase and less in the phase of compatibility. In terms of output, the interoperability strongly influences resilience in each phase of its lifecycle (anticipation, mitigation, recovery).

53.4. Conclusion and prospects

The three components defining the nature of the link between interoperability and -ilities must be implemented that means the influence, the direction and the intensity between interoperability and -ilities must be identified. This should lead to getting a graph dedicated to interoperability and allowing a development of the means for an advanced analysis. To this aim, the different means presented (i.e. qualitative or quantitative as well as formal or not formal) can be investigated to make available suitable tools that allow actors to accurately and quickly analyze interoperability to be reactive and to adjust their actions if needed. Likewise, the notion of effects will have to be fully integrated into the analysis to precisely know the result of the relationships between -ilities that influence interoperability but also between the interoperability and -ilities that would be, in turn, impacted.

53.5. References

[ATH 05] Athena I.P., "Framework for the Establishment and Management Methodology", Project, ATHENA Deliverable DA1.4, 2005.

[BÉN 12] Bénaben F., "Conception de Système d'Information de Médiation pour la prise en charge de l'Interopérabilité dans les Collaborations d'Organisations", Habilitation à Diriger les Recherches, INP Toulouse, October 2012.

[BIL 15] Billaud S., Contribution à l'ingénierie de système de systèmes : modélisation multi points de vue et analyse de l'impact de l'exigence d'interopérabilité, PhD Thesis, University of Montpellier II, 2015.

[BOT 16] Botelho Espadinha Da Cruz P.E., Business interoperability: a methodology to analyse and re-design interoperable buyer-supplier dyads, PhD Thesis, University of Lisbon, 2016.

[C4I 98] C4ISR, "Levels of Information Systems Interoperability (LISI)", USA Department of Defense, 1998.

[DAC 17] Daclin N., "Formalisation et évaluation des exigences non fonctionnelles pour l'ingénierie des systèmes collaboratifs", Habilitation à Diriger les Recherches, University of Montpellier II, 2017.

[DEW 12] De Weck O., Roos D., Magee C., "Life-Cycle Properties of Engineering Systems: the Ilities", *Engineering Systems: Meeting Human Needs in a Complex Technological World*, MIT Press, p. 232, 2012.

[ELM 11] Elmir B., Bounabat B., "A Novel Approach for Periodic Assessment of Business Process Interoperability", *International Journal of Computer Science Issues*, vol. 8, no. 4, pp. 298–306, July 2011.

[FEW 03] Fewell S., Clark T., "Organisational Interoperability: Evaluation and Further Development of the OIM Model", *Proceedings of the 8th International Command and Control Research and Technology Symposium*, Washington, DC, 2003.

[FOR 08] Ford C.T., Interoperability measurement, PhD Thesis, Air Force Institute of Technology, 2008.

[GUÉ 15] Guédria W., Naudet Y., Chen. D., "Maturity Model for Enterprise Interoperability", *Enterprise Information Systems*, vol. 9, no. 1, pp. 1–28, 2015.

[ISO 09] ISO, "Part 1: Framework for enterprise interoperability", *Advanced automation technologies and their applications*, ISO/DIS 11354-1, ISO/TC 184/SC 5/WG, 2009.

[KAS 04] Kasunic M., ANDERSON W., Measuring Systems Interoperability: Challenges and Opportunities, Technical note, CMU/SEI-2004-TN-003, 2004.

[MAL 12] Mallek S., Daclin N., Chapurlat V., "The application of interoperability requirement specification and verification to collaborative processes in industry", *Computers in Industry*, vol. 63, no. 7, pp. 643–658, 2012.

[MAL 15] Mallek S., Daclin N., Chapurlat V. *et al.*, "Enabling model checking for collaborative process analysis: from BPMN to Network of Timed Automata", *Enterprise Information Systems*, vol. 9, no. 3, pp. 279–299, 2015.

[MOR 17] Moradi B., Daclin N., Chapurlat V., "Formalization, evaluation of non functional requirements for system of systems engineering: application to resilience", *Doctoral symposium of the 14th International Conference on Information Systems for Crisis Response and Management*, 2017.

[REZ 14] Rezaei R., Chiew T.K., Lee S. P. *et al.*, "Interoperability evalution models: a systematic review", *Computer in Industry*, vol. 65, no. 1, pp. 1–23, 2014.

[ROS 12] Ross A.M., Beesemyer J.C., Rhodes D.H., "A Prescriptive Semantic Basis for System Lifecycle Properties", SEAri Working Paper Series, WP-2011-2-2, 2012.

[TOL 07] Tolk A., Diallo S.Y., Turnitsa C.D., "Applying the Levels of Conceptual Interoperability Model in Support of Integratability, Interoperability, and Composability for System-of-Systems Engineering", *Systemics Cybernetics and Informatics*, vol. 5, pp. 65–74, 2007.

[WAL 04] Walker B., Holling C.S., Carpenter S.R. *et al.*, "Resilience, adaptability and transformability in social–ecological systems", *Ecology and Society*, vol. 9, no. 2, 2004.

[YAH 12] Yahia E., Aubry A., Panetto H., "Formal measures for semantic interoperability assessment in cooperative enterprise information systems", *Computers in Industry*, vol. 63, no. 5, pp. 443–457, 2012.

I-ESA 2018 Doctoral Symposium

Part 11 Summary: Current Research in Enterprise Interoperability

The goal of the Doctoral Symposium of i-ESA'2018 was to provide a forum for PhD students with topics in the context of enterprise interoperability. It was intended to deliver an opportunity to interactively discuss their findings, issues or ideas with experienced participants from the industry and research. This symposium aimed at exchanging knowledge to encourage new findings. Furthermore, the PhD students could get exclusive feedback from members of the research community and all participants to boost their own thesis. This chapter summarizes the content of the accepted and presented work and reports issues brought up during presentation and discussion at the symposium.

Providing the flexibility of the shop floor to information systems for monitoring tasks (Alexander Dennert)

This chapter addresses the flexibility of modern production systems and its influence on monitoring solutions for production information systems, relevant for managing the production process. To ease these managing tasks, the information shall be represented in the structure of the production process. The challenging aspect is that a change in the production process also requires a change in several or all information providing systems. This paper presents a flexible solution relying on business processes that describe the value adding processes of a company, in order to configure the information system to provide the correct information. This paper uses two use cases, one for providing KPIs the other for providing condition monitoring information.

Chapter written by Martin WOLLSCHLAEGER.

The discussion focused on the definition and usage of key performance indicators, KPIs. The modeling of potential objectives and actions has been discussed, including solutions for measuring the success of using a KPI. Potential sources for KPI definition were evaluated, considering integrating KPI definitions directly into a production model. It would be supported to identify and to model appropriate roles for KPI definitions and for their usage. The paper proposes to use Business Process Model and Notation (BPMN) as a suitable description. It was discussed whether there was the need for extending this notation. A clear example for each use case would strengthen the proposal. Finally, potential measures to evaluate the success of the proposal have been sketched.

Shop floor management systems in the case of increasing process variation (Wolf Schliephack)

In this chapter, a holistic view on shop floor management systems is discussed, focusing on the production processes and their performance visualization using a shop floor board. The importance of standardization of such processes is outlined. This is particular important for recognizing deviations of performance indicators, and for identifying problems and inefficiencies. Standardized processes and modular approaches may sometimes contradict. The chapter shows how the use of process modeling can support a methodological approach towards a system architecture for performance boards.

During the discussion, product-centric and globalized production approaches and their influence on the efforts of shop floor management systems came into focus. The author was encouraged to discuss this in the thesis, together with transparency topics provided by KPIs on suitable screens. Furthermore, migration aspects have been discussed, caused by a replacement of traditional boards by those proposed by the author. An interesting topic raised by discussing abilities of representing the KPIs in the process model. Such a model should include objectives and actions for each KPI and offer a method for modeling interdependences of single KPIs. It was proposed to evaluate library-based approaches for the deployment of the results.

Comprehensive function models for the management of heterogeneous industrial networks as an enabler for interoperability (Santiago Soler Perez Olaya)

The scope of this chapter is on industrial networks as integral part of modern production systems. A digital factory, following the proposed structure of Industry 4.0, requires interoperability in a heterogeneous landscape of networking technologies.

The concept proposed in the work is to use comprehensive function models for the management of such industrial networks. This will set up a core of a holistic network management system, guaranteeing interoperability in the business processes of the future industrial sector. The roadmap to evolve from legacy industrial systems to future-ready productive environments is indispensable to guarantee the success of this evolution.

In the discussion, the process of defining network functions was addressed, with the intention of finding similarities between IT and industrial applications. The integration processes along the horizontal domain have been discussed. A specific example would be helpful for dealing with the abstraction level shown in the paper. There should be a short view on localized versus globalized management approaches. The idea of the mapping of logical network structures to physical ones led to discussions of equivalency of physical system and environment. Furthermore, aspects of reactive and self-adapting systems came into the focus, specifically for distributed system approaches. Hierarchy levels inside ERP have been discussed, indicating the need for strategic, tactic and operation definitions. It was proposed to consider applying concepts of systems theory to the approach. Finally, the relation of the approach to message-oriented communication standards and to semantics have been discussed, concluding with the future required steps to bring the ideas to reality.

54

Providing the Flexibility of the Shop Floor to Information Systems for Monitoring Tasks

Modern production systems have to be highly flexible and reliable. This requirement must also apply to the systems that provide monitoring information about the production system. This information is relevant for managing the production process. To ease this challenge, the information shall be represented in the structure of the production process. The challenging aspect is that a change in the production process also requires a change in all the information-providing systems. This chapter presents an approach to use business processes that describe the value-adding processes of a company to configure the information system to provide the correct information. This approach uses two use cases, one for providing KPIs the other for providing condition-monitoring information.

54.1. Introduction

Producing companies are faced today with various customer demands. On one side, the customer requires a highly flexible production. On the other side, the products shall be cheap. To support the production processes or at least to support the worker, normal IT hardware, for example a tablet or smartphone, is used.

In order to detail my work, I have set up two use cases. The first use case is called "Condition Monitoring", the second "Key Performance Indicators". The monitoring of a production system's health is essential for a production without interruption. Many manufacturers of production machinery integrate functionality into their devices that

---

Chapter written by Alexander DENNERT.

provides information about the machine's health status. The German Mechanical Engineering Industry Association (VDMA) describes in its guideline 24582 [VDM 14] structures that are manufacturer and field bus-independent and allow condition monitoring for factory automation devices. A central part of this definition is a function block which defines all relevant information for condition monitoring. This monitoring will be extended for IT devices. This allows an overview of all relevant systems, not only focusing the automation devices. The second use case deals with key performance indicators. They are used to infer statements about the production process. One example is the turnover rate of the total goods inventory. Definitions for KPIs on MES Level can be found for example in [VDM 10]. Machines providing their own KPIs provide them via the production network. Assembling these KPIs to systems of KPIs for production processes is the aim of this use case.

The global target of the two use cases is to provide information based on the production process. This target becomes challenging if the production processes become more and more flexible. The flexibility for producing goods requires also a flexibility for the monitoring. In current situations, each system needs to be reconfigured by itself to be aligned to the current situation of production system. This flexibility is also relevant for modular plants. Here the system needs to be able to integrate new information from probably different network protocols or interfaces. This also includes the usual IT systems that become more relevant for the production process.

The aim is to reach interoperability on different levels. The first one is the level of data access. The information that shall be provided usually comes from a heterogeneous set of systems that are typically not compatible to each other. All this data needs to be provided to the user without these technical barriers. The second one is that structural configuration in terms of the value adding process needs to be transferred to the structures of the information. The provided information needs to represent the current situation of the production process to allow a process based monitoring of relevant data.

54.2. Related Work

In [FRI 12], an approach is described that extends the BPMN structures for KPIs. This approach is limited to the requirement that the relevant information needs to be representable as KPIs. Information not compatible with KPIs are out of scope of this approach.

Approaches that create digital twins of the shop floor like [TAO 17] are not focusing on structural changes of the processes but on different recipes that are executed by the plant. Here the request on integrating changes of the process into information systems is not given.

54.3. Used technologies

This section describes the technologies that provide functionality for solving the described challenges. An evaluation of relevant technologies is not part of the abstract. The functionalities that have been identified for this abstract are: network management, condition monitoring, key performance indicators and business processes.

54.3.1. *System management*

System management is an extension of network management, which has been developed to ease the management of heterogeneous devices of a computer network. The system management extends the standardized approach to all kind of computer systems.

One part of the network management is the performance management. Following Hegering *et al.* this activity is the "Collection of statistical data and recording of the network history to improve the performance of resources" [HEG 94]. This is strongly related to the requirements described in the two use cases. Since network management only focuses on networks, an extension to the area to all kind of IT systems has been done. For this kind of activities the term systems management has been established. It contains amongst others data security, monitoring and management of data, installation and configuration of software and performance management.

54.3.1.1. *Web-based Enterprise Management.*

The technology used to provide a proof of concept is web-based enterprise management (WBEM). The WBEM specifications are developed under the umbrella of the Distributed Management Task Force (DMTF). The basis of the WBEM is an architecture that consists of five parts [THO 98]. The architecture is displayed in Figure 54.1.

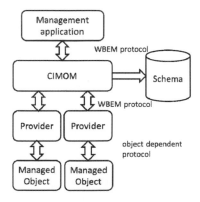

Figure 54.1. *WBEM architecture following [THO 98]*

According to [THO 98], a client application (management application) accesses the WBEM Server by generating requests to the CIM Object Manager (CIMOM). The interface that is used therefore is defined by the DMTF for example by using HTTP [DMT 18]. The CIMOM is responsible for providing the objects. It stores information about instances of classes. The providers provide the information about the instances. These providers work as an interface between the managed objects and the CIMOM as they are encapsulating the managed objects dependent protocols and technologies. The schema storage is responsible for storing the information model definitions. The basic structure for the information model is the common information model (CIM) meta-model [DMT 14].

54.3.1.2. Common information model

The Common information model (CIM) is used to describe the classes that are used to manage systems with the WBEM. It is an object-oriented model also defined by the DMTF [DMT 14]. The CIM schema now defines (in version 2.50) more than 1600 classes. These classes are separated into the core schema and the common schemas like the metrics schema or the network schema. Classes can only be part of one schema. These schemas help to overview the huge amount of classes. The functionality provided by the classes and their connections is described by the CIM Profiles. These profiles describe the interconnection of classes and their usage. While one class can only be part of one schema one class can be part of many profiles.

54.3.2. Key performance indicators

According to [ISO 14] key performance indicators (KPIs) are used "to improve the value creation process of an enterprise". In ISO 22400 a neutral structure for KPIs in industrial usage is given. The basis for the KPIs is a three-tier model consisting of the parts KPI definition, KPI instance, and KPI value. Part two of the standard defines certain KPIs for example scrap ratio, allocation ratio, throughput rate or overall equipment effectiveness index. Following [MEY 06], performance figures are figures that describe business facts. This allows visualization of the existing situation and its management. KPIs can be connected to each other, logically or calculational. These KPIs and their connections are forming KPI systems.

54.3.3. Condition monitoring

As stated in the introduction the informational basis of the VDMA condition monitoring approach [VDM 14] is a function block that defines the information structures to achieve vendor independent environment in the automation world. Their demand is that all devices will integrate such function blocks and by this provide their "health data". This also allows hiding the algorithms that calculate the statement about the health of the device. For brown field situations it is also possible to deploy such a function block on third-party infrastructure that uses the process data from a device to calculate the same statement.

54.3.4. *Business processes*

The organization of companies work can be described via business processes. These processes describe the workflow of all activities that are necessary for the companies business. Since 2005, the Object Management Group (OMG) maintains the Business Process Model and Notation (BPMN) [OMG 11], a graphical notation for modeling business processes. BPMN defines five categories of elements. These are flow objects, data, connecting objects, swimlanes, and artifacts. The flow objects are specialized into activity, gateway and event. To connect the flow objects, the connecting objects are used. In the first proof of concept only the sequence flow was selected. Figure 54.2 shows the selected objects and their graphical representation.

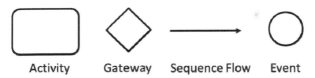

Activity   Gateway   Sequence Flow   Event

Figure 54.2. *Used elements of BPMN*

54.4. Solution approach

The presented technologies will be used to provide a highly flexible environment for providing information originated in IT and automation world. Therefore the BPMN models of the company's business are used to adopt the flexibility of the production processes. These processes provide the structure of the value chain including the assets that are used within the single process steps. The KPI model provides the structures necessary for calculating and presenting statements about the efficiency of a certain point of view. The condition-monitoring approach provides structures and methodologies for deriving information about the health of a machine.

These three parts are integrated into the CIM as a schema. The schemas and their classes can be used uncoupled to the others. This usage would provide their functionality inside an open accessible system. The big benefit arises by coupling the KPI and condition-monitoring models with the BPMN model. This linkage reduces the configuration effort for modeling the structures of a production company for each information system. This benefit increases with increasing flexibility of the processes inside a company. Each change in the process structures would require a reconfiguration of the single models that shall provide the process information. Figure 54.3 shows the models in the CIM. The connection between the models is displayed with "A" and "B".

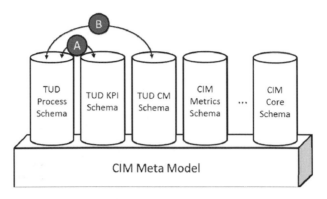

Figure 54.3. *Models extending the CIM*

The used WBEM/CIM system allows the creation of solutions that are extensible and accessible using standardized techniques. The models for monitoring that have been presented in the use cases can be extended by others. This would lead to new pillars in Figure 54.3. The main part of work is to integrate the BPMN model into the CIM. Therefore the CIM and BPMN meta-models need to be compared and their compatibility needs to be proven. This models needs to be adapted to the monitoring models. This will be done using link models see "A" and "B" in Figure 54.3.

54.5. Conclusions

The presented approach, increasing interoperability in terms of reducing configuration efforts for flexible systems by using business processes, has three main aspects. The first is that the different measuring models need to be integrated into the management system. The second is that the meta-models of the management system and the business process model need to be compatible. The third is that the connections between the process model and the measuring models need to be created, ideally automatically. First solutions for these three aspects are made. The complete comparison for the meta-models is ongoing work, but the models seem to be compatible.

This approach will reduce the set up time for production companies and allow them to become more flexible in regards to their monitoring software.

54.6. References

[DMT 14] DMTF, DMTF – Distributed Management Taskforce, *Common Information Model (CIM) Metamodel*, Online, available at: http://www.dmtf.org/sites/default/files/standards/documents/DSP0004_3.0.1.pdf, 2014.

[DMT 18] DMTF, DMTF – Distributed Management Taskforce, *CIM Operations over HTTP*, Online, available at: https://www.dmtf.org/sites/default/files/standards/documents/DSP0200_1.4.0.pdf, 2018.

[FRI 12] FRIEDENSTAB J.-P., JANIESCH C., MATZNER M. *et al.*, "Extending BPMN for business activity monitoring", *45th Hawaii International Conference on System Science (HICSS)*, Maui, 2012.

[HEG 94] HEGERING H.-G., ABECK S., *Integrated Network and System Management*, University of Michigan, Addison-Wesley, 1994.

[ISO 14] ISO 22400-1, Automation systems and integration — Key performance indicators (KPIs) for manufacturing operations management Part 1: Overview, concepts and terminology, Standard, ISO, 2014.

[MEY 06] MEYER C., *Betriebswirtschaftliche Kennzahlen und Kennzahlen-Systeme*, Sternenfels, Verl. Wissenschaft & Praxis, 2006.

[OMG 11] OPEN MANAGEMENT GROUP, *Business Process Model and Notation (BPMN) Version 2.0*, Online, available at: http://www.omg.org/spec/BPMN/ 2.0/PDF, 2011.

[TAO 17] TAO F., ZHANG M., "Digital twin shop-floor: a new shop-floor paradigm towards smart manufacturing", *IEEE Access*, vol. 5, pp. 20418–20427, 2017.

[THO 98] THOMPSON J.P., "Web-based enterprise management architecture", *IEEE Communications Magazine*, vol. 36, no. 3, pp. 80–86, 1998.

[VDM 10] VDMA, Verband Deutscher Maschinen- und Anlagenbau e. V., *Einheitsblatt 66412: Manufacturing Execution Systems (MES) Kennzahlen*, VDMA, 2010.

[VDM 14] VDMA, Verband Deutscher Maschinen- und Anlagenbau e. V., *Einheitsblatt 24582: Feldbusneutrale Referenzarchitektur für Condition Monitoring in der Fabrikautomation*, VDMA, 2014.

Shop Floor Management Systems in Case of Increasing Process Variation

55.1. Introduction and shop-floor management

Most of the German production companies use shop floor management systems, which are built on holistic production systems. The standardization of processes helps to recognize deviations of performance indicators to identify problems and inefficiencies. However, latest developments illustrate that companies use higher modularization in their production systems to face the increasing complexity through the individualization of products. The resulting transition of the underlying production system towards more process variation counteract the focus on one standardized process and a clear holistic process view. According to this, a new generation of performance boards have to provide new methods and services to prepare data of the changed complex production environment in a more efficient way to support the daily shop floor meeting with well-selected analyses and overviews.

Holistic production systems were developed on single lean methods to get a global process optimisation instead of just a local implementation of single tools. To stabilize and improve these processes a new leadership and improvement culture was necessary [NYH 13]. With an implementation quote of 90% in manufacturing companies in Germany, holistic production systems are industry standard [DOM 17]. Many big companies and costumers of Fraunhofer IPK use the mentioned shop floor management in their production too.

According to the literature comparison of Hertle *et al.* there is no uniform definition of shop floor management [HER 17]. Following Peters, shop floor

Chapter written by Wolf SCHLIEPHACK.

management serves to lead the production according to strategic business goals as well as supporting the independent leadership of organizational units according to operational departmental targets [PET 09]. In doing so, the three main objectives are process operation, process improvement and training involved employees [HER 17]. In order to archive these objectives and based on a holistic view on the production system a cascade of shop floor meetings on different management levels forms the organizational structure. Thereby strategic corporate objectives are derived for the single subgroup and communicated top down. At the same time the communication cascade illustrated in Figure 55.1 promotes a culture in which the higher management level supports the problem-solving process with the worker with methodical knowledge and bigger organizational reach [DOM 14].

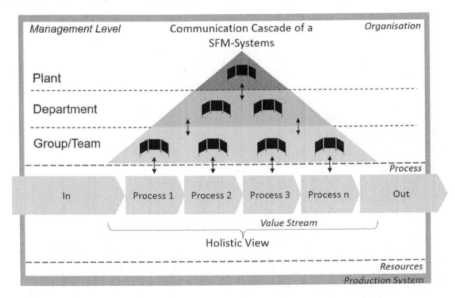

Figure 55.1. *Organizational structure of shop-floor management and the use of performance boards (see [NYH 13, DOM 14])*

A shop floor or performance board is used in the daily meeting as a supporting tool. To support the achievement of the main objectives of shop floor management the performance board has basic characteristics, which are complemented regarding individual needs of different production types, organizational levels or preferences. The first characteristic is to achieve transparency for all participants. Furthermore it includes the visualization of trends and deviations as base to be able to identify problems and to track continuous process improvements as well as structured problem solving functionalities. Additionally it should support the optimization of used process resources (e.g. a worker) on the short term [DOM 16, HER 17]. First industry applications and research activities aim to digitalize these performance boards and their functionalities for more efficient data usage and more specific data analysis [BOS 18, PWT 18, SHO 18].

55.2. Fundamental change towards cyber physical production systems

On a more development-related view, lean production and the described holistic production systems were created to achieve customer individual mass production. Reason is that in saturated markets the satisfaction of individual customer wishes helps to improve the market position. This trend is intensifying and existing production systems have to deal with strong increasing complexity [JOV 03, BAU 14]. The fix chain of production steps in existing systems is in case of different process times of individual products a big challenge. To break up these fix linked processes in order to increase the flexibility a more modular approach is required [BAU 14].

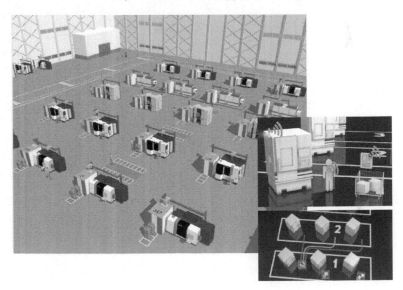

Figure 55.2. *Agent based self-organization of a gear production [IWE 18]. For a color version of this figure, see www.iste.co.uk/zelm/enterprise.zip*

The research project "iWePro" of an intelligent workshop production addressed this issue. In that context Fraunhofer IPK developed with further research organizations and industry partner an approach for the gear production of a German OEM where products route independently through the production system. The agent-based control enables each product to negotiate with the respective machines to find free production capacities according to their individual work plan. The objective is to open the fixed link of flow lines during high utilization of production equipment

[IWE 18]. A basic prerequisite is the communication of assets. In order to achieve this, machines, products, components etc. need embedded systems to be able to communicate via the Internet as so-called cyber physical systems (CPS) [BAU 14]. Initial approaches like this illustrate new possibilities of flexibility as well as a challenge of new upcoming complexity. However, if the cyber physical production system (CPPS) provides more opportunities within the system to map processes, the variation will increase significantly. Examples concerning this matter are different routing between parallel resources, the use of different modules in case of deviating process requirements or the use for various durations. At the same time full digitalized workshops and model-based engineering provide a solution to limit and handle the complexity. This illustrates at the same time that methods and functionalities of existing analogue shop-floor boards are not far-reaching enough to address the objectives of shop-floor management on this basis anymore. Only a digital performance board is able to prepare data of such a complex environment efficiency and is able to support the daily shop-floor meeting with well selected analysis and overviews.

55.3. Characteristics for digital performance boards on CPPS

Referring to the basic role of workers in the digital factory, there are two funda-mental scenarios described in the literature. In the "specification scenario" the worker will be supported by machines and information of the digital production to fulfill the work task and to make better decisions in that complex context. In contrast, in the "automation scenario" the worker has no bigger understanding over processes and is controlled by the decisions of the production system that the worker can no longer understand [BAU 15]. Over the mid and long-term the shop floor management objectives of process improvement and the training of worker are mutually dependent. The basic assumption for shop floor management in cyber physical production systems is that companies want to use the special capabilities and knowledge of their employees for improvements in their production. Based on that, shop floor management is at least as necessary as in existing production systems.

While the initially described overall objectives of shop floor management [HER 17] and the characteristics of the supporting performance board [DOM 16, HER 17] helping to achieve these objectives will remain unchanged, the specifies of how to reach these requirements (e.g. transparency) will change as a function of the production system. Out of these specifications the combined use of existing methods [DOM 15] and new services [REI 17] is required and illustrated in Table 55.1. At the same time the organizational structure as to be addressed by the system architecture of an integrated digital shop floor management system. In this connection the use of enterprise modeling, consisting of business, information and production processes, is able to define a basic structure. At the same time the upcoming process variation can be mapped by a modular process approach to reach the flexibility of the production system. The enterprise model can help to set up shop floor management from a global perspective down to the individualized process execution. A next important aspect is the visualization of processes for all participants on different management levels to archive the needed transparency. Furthermore it can be used to link data to different process steps to organize context-based analyses and higher-level aggregation. Additionally it could be used for context-based problem identification along the integrated net of business and production processes.

Objectives			Characteristics	Specification	Method, Service
Process Operation	Process Improvement	Development of Employees	Optimization of used resources	Understanding of next products and their effects	Predictive production management e.g. forecast of individualized cases by simulation and integrated digital twins
			Transparency	For processes, connections, routings, decisions	Process visualization, process mining/digital shadow
			Performance visualization	Trends and deviations for customer specific orders	KPIs, automatic configured reference level for individualized processes
			Problem identification	Out of data correlations	Integrated SPC Big data analytics
			Structured problem solving	Specific problem allocation, responsibilities, traceability	A3-method, process visualization
			Continuous improvement	Context-based planning and control of changes	Model-based configuration of PDCA activities (plan, do, check, act)

Table 55.1. *Methods and services for digital performance boards in CPPS (see [HER 17, DOM 17, DOM 15, REI 17])*

55.4. Research question and outlook

Next step is to analyze state-of-the-art of industrial solutions on digital performance boards and to inspect their ability to promote these methods and services or to define differences. At the same time the specific need of these services should be investigated in industrial environment. Regarding this the actual process variation and the benefit of the respective use of single services should be tested and evaluated. If there is action required, a first research question could be how to develop a first method chain to set up shop floor management for individualized processes. The following question is how these different services could work together to support the shop floor meeting in that new digital production environment.

55.5. References

[BAU 14] BAUERNHANSEL T., TEN HOMPEL M., VOGEL-HEUSER B., *Industrie 4.0 in Produktion, Automatisierung und Logistik: Anwendung – Technologien – Migration*, Springer Vieweg, Wiesbaden, 2014.

[BAU 15] BAUER W., "Arbeitsorganisation in der Fabrik 4.0, Anwendung – Technologien – Migration", *Future Tracks: Gute Arbeit in der Fabrik 4.0*, Aktiengesellschaft, Hannover, Germany, pp. 16–21, 14 April, 2015.

[BOS 18] BOSCH REXROTH AG, *Active Cockpit*, available at: www.boschrexroth.com, 2018.

[DOM 14] DOMBROWSKI U., BELZ T., JÄGER F., "Shopfloor Management im Regelkreis der GPS-Implementierung, Mit durchgängigen und standardisierten Kennzahlsystemen das Lean Leadership unterstützen", *Zeitschrift für wirtschaftlichen Fabrikbetrieb (ZWF)*, vol. 109, nos 1–2, pp. 20–25, 2014.

[DOM 15] DOMBROWSKI U., MIELKE T., *Ganzheitliche Produktionssysteme, Aktueller Stand und zukünftige Entwicklungen*, Springer Vieweg, Berlin Heidelberg, 2015.

[DOM 16] DOMBROWSKI U., BELZ T., JÄGER F., "Einsatz von Shopfloor Management zur Unterstützung von Qualitätsmanagementsystemen, Operative Umsetzung der Anforderung aus der ISO 9001:2015 in produzierenden Unternehmen", *Zeitschrift für wirtschaftlichen Fabrikbetrieb (ZWF)*, vol. 111, no. 4, pp. 169–173, 2016.

[DOM 17] DOMBROWSKI U., RICHTER T., KRENKEL P., "Wechselwirkungen von Ganzheitlichen Produktionssystemen und Industrie 4.0, Eine Use-Case-Analyse", *Zeitschrift für wirtschaftlichen Fabrikbetrieb (ZWF)*, vol. 112, no. 6, pp. 430–433, 2017.

[HER 17] HERTLE C., TISCH M., METTERNICH J., ABELE E., "Das Darmstädter Shopfloor Ma-nagement-Modell", *Zeitschrift für wirtschaftlichen Fabrikbetrieb (ZWF)*, vol. 112, no. 3, pp. 118–121, 2017.

[IWE 18] IWEPRO, *intelligente selbstorganisierende Werkstattproduktion*, available at: www.projekt-iwepro.de, 2018.

[JOV 03] JOVANE F., KOREN Y., BOËR C.R., "Present and future of flexible automation: towards new paradigms", *CIRP Annals – Manufacturing Technology*, vol. 52, no. 2, pp. 534–560, 2003.

[NYH 13] NYHUIS P., DEUSE J., REHWALD J., *Wandlungsfähige Produktionen, Heute für morgen gestalten*, PTZ Verlag, Garbsen, 2013.

[PET 09] PETERS R., *Shopfloor Management: Führen am Ort der Wertschöpfung*, LOG_X Verlag, Stuttgart, 2009.

[PTW 18] PTW, TU DARMSTADT, PROZESSLERNFABRIK (CIP), *Digitales Shopfloor Management*, available at: www.prozesslernfabrik.de, 2018.

[REI 17] REINHART G., *Handbuch Industrie 4.0, Geschäftsmodelle, Prozesse, Technik*, Carl Hanser Verlag, München, 2017.

[SHO 18] SHOPFLOOR MANAGEMENT SYSTEMS, available at www.sfmsystems.de, 2018.

56

Comprehensive Function Models for the Management of Heterogeneous Industrial Networks as an Enabler for Interoperability

The future of the industrial sector relies on the viability of the evolution towards the digital factory proposed by the platform Industrie 4.0. This digital factory requires the interoperability in a heterogeneous landscape of network technologies. The concept proposed here is the use of the comprehensive function models for the management of heterogeneous industrial networks as core of the holistic network management system that can guarantee the interoperability in the business processes of the future industrial sector. The roadmap to evolve from legacy industrial systems to future-ready productive environments is indispensable to guarantee the success of this evolution.

56.1. Problem formulation

The current industrial production plant evolution is tending to a more flexible and interconnected production environment. This trend is one of the reasons for the existence and one of the aims of the platform "Industrie 4.0" [BMW 15]. The use of new technologies like data analytics and of approaches like plug and produce demands the integration of heterogeneous network technologies [WOL 17]. This integration can be solved at different levels.

Typically, a person provides interoperability to heterogeneous systems that are working together. The person managing the different systems is aware of the application relations that are needed to let the system work as a whole and

---

Chapter written by Santiago SOLER PEREZ OLAYA.

configures the different subsystems, which need to interoperate in the appropriate way. In this traditional approach, the management of the different systems remains isolated and the flexibility and integration depend directly on the human worker.

Imagine a heterogeneous industrial system composed by three different network technologies, for example Profinet, TCP/IP over Ethernet, and Industrial Internet of Things (IIoT) [GEN 17], where the collaboration of the elements living in different network technologies could be an improvement of the productivity (see Figure 56.1). This scenario is likely to appear in the future when the added new technology, network C, stops being an interesting add-on regarding predictive maintenance and/or monitoring to become an integral part of the optimized business process of the productive system. At that point, it will be necessary to enable the interoperability of the heterogeneous systems by implementing holistic management systems, including the network management of heterogeneous industrial networks.

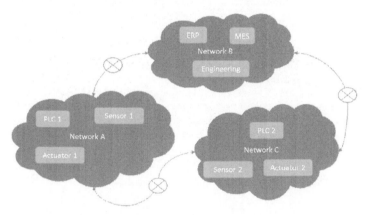

Figure 56.1. *Example of a heterogeneous industrial system with three different network technologies. For example, Network A could be a Profinet, Network B TCP/IP over Ethernet, and Network C an IIoT. The round symbols interconnecting the three networks can be seen as adapters of any kind, e.g. bridges or gateways.*

56.2. Research hypothesis

The management operations that the person runs are perhaps the same for all three systems, but the realization of those is different for different systems. An example of such an operation list can be found in [DMT 15]. The person understands the goal of the management operations and runs the adequate functions with the adequate parameters on each system management interface. This knowledge of the different management operations is what I call the comprehensive function model. It describes the function's goal as well as the information, input and output, exchanged with the function in an abstract way (see Figure 56.2).

By using this knowledge about management operations, it is theoretically possible to create holistic management systems capable of dealing with heterogeneous industrial networks as a whole with automated procedures and without the intervention of humans.

These holistic management systems will enable the interoperability not only inside one enterprise in a vertical integration, but also the horizontal integration of legacy technologies with state-of-the-art communication and computation systems. This interoperability ensures also future interoperability with technologies yet to come and boosts the flexibility of the productive environments by allowing the implementation of the Industry 4.0 [RAU 16] philosophy with retrofitting measures, without requiring brand new systems to substitute the legacy ones.

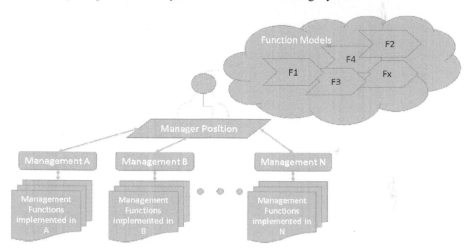

Figure 56.2. *Concept of the comprehensive functions models for the management of heterogeneous industrial networks. The different networks, A, B...N, implement their own management, A, B...N, with a subset of the management functions, F1, F2 ... Fx. These functions are represented as comprehensive function models in the intellect of the network manager.*

A first step to conceive of comprehensive function models for the management of heterogeneous industrial networks is to classify the management functions of existing network management systems by the goal of the function. Under the premise that the functions of different network management systems can have different granularities, it is logical to assume that a set of management functions of a network management system A can be equivalent in goal to a different set of management functions of a network management system B, including the possibility of single functions in a function set.

Another assumption is that a set of management operations common for all network management systems exists and can be abstracted from the comparison of the equivalent function sets mentioned above. This common set of management operations builds the core functionality of the holistic network management system. Identifying this core set and its requirements regarding information is the second step to conceiving the comprehensive function models needed for the holistic network management system.

56.3. Proposed solution

Full-functional interoperability can be addressed by intelligent adapters between the different networks. Depending on the capabilities of these networks, the intelligent adapters will be more or less complex. The intelligent adapters shall guarantee not only interoperability in the management plane but also interoperability at all functional levels. This requires deep knowledge of the different network systems and its capabilities. Future network technologies [ITU 11] will have interfaces to communicate with other networks. These future networks are interoperable per design at the communication level. A device inside one of this future networks can be reachable from outside, and the device itself can reach other devices outside its own network. In the legacy industrial systems [IEC 14] there is no provision for heterogeneity. Even the interconnection of similar industrial communication systems require the use of a gateway to perform some interoperability. In the case of the example presented here, the interoperability can be achieved when every device living outside the network A that is required in network A for productive purposes needs to be reflected by the intelligent adapter as it was an actual field device pertaining to network A. With the appropriate information, the adapter can perform as a proxy and respond to network A, translating the information supplied by the actual devices in network B or C.

The architecture based on the intelligent adapters is a network of networks, where the interoperability with future communication technologies depends on the possibility of developing a new intelligent adapter. In fact, it is expected to be a seamless integration as new technologies will address the interoperability themselves.

The interoperability at the management plane [ITU 04] relies on the core of comprehensive function models described in the previous section. With a holistic management system, the person responsible for network management does not require a deep knowledge of every management system. This person can rely on a holistic approach and manage the heterogeneous industrial network as a whole, focusing on the optimization of the productive environment.

Another important aspect for the holistic network management approach is the capability for dealing with dynamic changes in the network. The origin of the network changes can be of different character going from degradation of the communication channel typical in wireless communication to pre-engineered dynamic changes in the productive environment. This capability aims to enable future-proofing and to ultimately deliver more robust network management. Other enablers are the application requirements-oriented management of resources. However, the fundamental challenge is at the core of comprehensive function models.

56.4. Expected contributions

An analysis of different network management systems [PI4 16, 5GP 16, DIN 16] is in progress and is expected to deliver information related to the management functions belonging to network technologies like Profinet, Sercos III, and TSN among others. The classification of these management functions and their grouping in functional sets will deliver the comprehensive function models for the management of heterogeneous industrial networks. The full-functional core of comprehensive function models will allow the discussion of management architectures and approaches that can ensure the future-ready character of the holistic management system based on intelligent adapters. The paradigm of requirements-based management will also be addressed by this architectural approach.

The industrial sector requires a graceful evolution from legacy systems, which usually are isolated solutions, to a heterogeneous industrial network landscape. The required steps towards the future digital factory [EUC 13, PI4 16] need to be planned carefully and tacking the retrofitting of existing solutions as the point of departure. There will be many milestones needed to guarantee the viability of the roadmap towards interoperable productive environments. This roadmap will be planned for the given example, paying attention to the above-mentioned issues as a proof of viability of the holistic management system for heterogeneous industrial networks that will deliver the desired interoperability. The success evaluation of this approach is planned as a KPI matrix that shows the interoperability status between every two different communication technologies. The KPI list, yet to be defined, will include not only parameters regarding the management of the networks but also parameters regarding communication, identification, plug and produce capabilities, and other industrial systemic aspects.

56.5. References

[5GP 16] 5G PPP ARCHITECTURE WORKING GROUP, *View on 5G Architecture*, Available at: https://5g-ppp.eu/wp-content/uploads/2014/02/5G-PPP-5G-Architecture-WP-July-2016.pdf, 2016.

[BMW 15] BMWI, *Industrie 4.0 und Digitale Wirtschaft*, Federal Ministry for Economic Affairs and Energy (BMWi), Berlin, Available: http://www.bmwi.de/, 2015.

[DIN 16] DIN SPEC 91345:2016-04, *Reference Architecture Model Industrie 4.0 (RAMI4.0)*, Beuth Verlag, Berlin, 2016.

[DMT 15] DISTRIBUTED MANAGEMENT TASK FORCE, INC., *DSP0223 Generic Operations Specification v2.0.0*, 10 March 2015, Available at: https://www.dmtf.org/standards/wbem, 2015.

[EUC 13] EUROPEAN COMMISSION, *FACTORIES OF THE FUTURE - Multi-annual roadmap for the contractual PPP under Horizon 2020*, Publications Office of the European Union, Luxembourg, 2013.

[GEN 17] GENG, H., "The Industrial Internet of Things (IIoT)", *Internet of Things and Data Analytics Handbook*, Wiley Telecom, pp. 816, doi: 10.1002/9781119173601.ch3, 2017.

[IEC 14] IEC 61158-1 *Industrial communication networks - Fieldbus specifications - Part 1: Overview and guidance for the IEC 61158 and IEC 61784 series*, International Electrotechnical Commission, 2014.

[ITU 04] ITU-T Y.2001 *Next Generation Networks – Frameworks and functional architecture models*, ITU-T, 2004.

[ITU 11] ITU-T Y.3001 *Future networks: Objectives and design goals*, ITU-T, 2011.

[PI4 16] PLATFORM INDUSTRIE 4.0, *Structure of the Administration Shell*, 2016.

[RAU 16] RAUCHHAUPT, L. *et al.*, *Network-based Communication for Industrie 4.0 - Proposal for an Administration Shell*, Federal Ministry for Economic Affairs and Energy (BMWi), Berlin, 2016.

[WOL 17] WOLLSCHLAEGER M., SAUTER T., JASPERNEITE J., "The Future of Industrial Communication: Automation Networks in the Era of the Internet of Things and Industry 4.0", *IEEE Industrial Electronics Magazine*, vol. 11, no. 1, pp. 17–27, November 1, 2017.

List of Authors

Carlos AGOSTINHO
CTS
UNINOVA
New University of Lisbon
Portugal

Abderrahim AIT-ALLA
Bremer Institut für Produktion und
Logistik (BIBA)
University of Bremen
Germany

Panagiotis AIVALIOTIS
Laboratory for Manufacturing Systems
and Automation (LMS)
University of Patras
Greece

Raquel ALMEIDA
KnowledgeBiz
Caparica, Portugal

Víctor ANAYA
Research Centre on Production
Management and Engineering
Universitat Politècnica de València
Spain

Beatriz ANDRES
Research Centre on Production
Management and Engineering
Universitat Politècnica de València
Spain

Dimitris APOSTOLOU
Institute of Communication and
Computer Systems (ICCS)
National Technical University of Athens
and
Department of Informatics
University of Piraeus
Greece

Bernard ARCHIMÈDE
LGP Laboratory
University of Toulouse
France

Giacomo BALDI
Zerynth
New York City, USA

Dian BALTA
Fortiss
Munich, Germany

Manuele BARBIERI
RINA Consulting
Genoa, Italy

Matteo BARBIERI
Department of Electrical, Electronic and
Information Engineering
University of Bologna
Italy

Caio Martins BARBOSA
Federal University of Espírito Santo
Vitoria, Brazil

Andrea BAÙ
Zerynth
New York City, USA

Frédérick BENABEN
IMT Mines Albi
France

Jesús BENEDICTO
ATOS
Barcelona, Spain

Gash BHULLAR
Control 2K
Bridgend, UK

Manfred BOGEN
Fraunhofer–IAIS
Sankt Augustin, Germany

Markus BÖHM
Technische Universität München
Garching, Germany

Andrea BONACCORSI
Department of Engineering of Energy,
Systems, Territory and Construction
University of Pisa
Italy

Yvar BOSDRIESZ
University of Twente
Enschede, Netherlands

Alessandro BOSSO
Department of Electrical, Electronic and
Information Engineering
University of Bologna
Italy

Alexandros BOUSDEKIS
Institute of Communication and
Computer Systems (ICCS)
National Technical University of Athens
Greece

Bernd BREDEHORST
Pumacy Technologies
Bremen, Germany

Christopher BREWSTER
TNO
Soesterberg, Netherlands

Kay BUROW
Universität Bremen
Germany

Jacopo CASSINA
Holonix
Milan, Italy

Vincent CHAPURLAT
LGI2P
IMT Mines Alès
France

David CHEN
IMS
University of Bordeaux
Talence, France

Sang-Je CHO
École Polytechnique Fédérale de
Lausanne (EPFL)
Switzerland

Matteo CIPRIANI
Zerynth
New York City, USA

Alex COLETTI
SM Resources Corporation
Ashburn, USA

Christian CONFICONI
Department of Electrical, Electronic and
Information Engineering (DEI)
University of Bologna
Italy

Pedro CORISTA
CTS
UNINOVA
New University of Lisbon
Portugal

Eva Coscia
Holonix
Milan, Italy

Carlos Coutinho
ISTAR-IUL
Instituto Universitário de Lisboa
and
Caixa Mágica Software
Lisbon, Portugal

Anna Maria Crespino
University of Salento
Lecce, Italy

Nicolas Daclin
LGI2P
IMT Mines Alès
France

Davide Dalle Carbonare
Engineering S.P.A.
Milan, Italy

Laura M. Daniele
TNO
The Hague, Netherlands

Antonio De Nicola
ENEA
Rome, Italy

Stefano De Panfilis
FIWARE Foundation
Berlin, Germany

Chris Decubber
European Factories of the Future
Research (EFFRA)
Brussels, Belgium

Quan Deng
University of Bremen
Germany

Alexander Dennert
Institute of Applied Computer Science
Technische Universität Dresden
Germany

Carla Di Biccari
University of Salento
Lecce, Italy

Antonio Di Pietro
ENEA
Rome, Italy

Konstantinos Dimoulas
Laboratory for Manufacturing Systems
and Automation (LMS)
University of Patras
Greece

Roberto Diversi
Department of Electrical, Electronic and
Information Engineering
University of Bologna
Italy

Patricia Dockhorn Costa
Federal University of Espírito Santo
Vitoria, Brazil

Guy Doumeingts
INTEROP-VLab
Brussels, Belgium

Yves Ducq
IMS
University of Bordeaux
Talence, France

Alexander Egyed
Johannes Kepler University
Linz, Austria

Linda Elmhadhbi
LGP Laboratory
University of Toulouse
France

Gualtiero Fantoni
Department of Civil and Industrial
Engineering
University of Pisa
Italy

Alena V. FEDOTOVA
University of Bremen
Germany

Florian FELLER
Fortiss
Munich, Germany

Alba FERNÁNDEZ
Universidad Politécnica de Madrid
Spain

José FERREIRA
CTS
UNINOVA
New University of Lisbon
Portugal

Luís FERREIRA PIRES
University of Twente
Enschede, Netherlands

Cristiano FERTUZINHOS
CRISTEMA
Braga, Portugal

José Luis FLORES
Dependable Embedded Systems
IK4–Ikerlan Technological Research
Centre
Arrasate-Mondragón, Spain

Francisco FRAILE
Research Centre on Production
Management and Engineering
Universitat Politécnica de Valéncia
Spain

Marco FRANKE
Bremer Institut für Produktion und
Logistik (BIBA)
University of Bremen
Germany

Michael FREITAG
University of Bremen
Germany

Raúl GARCÍA CASTRO
Universidad Politécnica de Madrid
Spain

Oscar GARCIA PERALES
Information Catalyst
Valencia, Spain

Konstantinos GEORGOULIAS
Laboratory for Manufacturing Systems
and Automation (LMS)
University of Patras
Greece

Sudeep GHIMIRE
CTS
UNINOVA
New University of Lisbon
Portugal

Zied GHRAIRI
University of Bremen
Germany

Joao GIAO
CTS
UNINOVA
New University of Lisbon
Portugal

Roberta Lima GOMES
Federal University of Espírito Santo
Vitoria, Brazil

Helder Oliveira GOMES FILHO
Federal University of Espírito Santo
Vitoria, Brazil

Lara GONZALEZ
Innovalia
Bilbao, Spain

Paul GOODALL
Wolfson School of Mechanical, Electrical
and Manufacturing Engineering
Loughborough University
UK

Sergio GUSMEROLI
Politecnico di Milano
and
Engineering S.P.A.
Milan, Italy

Carl HANS
OHS Engineering
Wildeshausen
and
FTI Engineering Network
Wildau, Germany

Nina-Mareike HARDERS
Fortiss
Munich, Germany

Matt HECKMAN
Zuyd University of Applied Science
Maastricht, Netherlands

Bjørnar HENRIKSEN
SINTEF Technology and Society
Trondheim, Norway

Tobias HINZ
Innovation and Product Development
Ascora
Ganderkesee, Germany

Karl HRIBERNIK
Bremer Institut für Produktion und
Logistik (BIBA)
University of Bremen
Germany

Maria IACOB
University of Twente
Enschede, Netherlands

Massimo IPPOLITO
Comau
Torino, Italy

Nenad IVEZIC
NIST
Gaithersburg, USA

Frank-Walter JAEKEL
Fraunhofer Institute for Production
Systems and Design Technology IPK
Berlin, Germany

Kai JAKOBS
RWTH Aachen University
Germany

Ricardo JARDIM-GONÇALVES
CTS
UNINOVA
New University of Lisbon
Portugal

Mohamed-Hedi KARRAY
LGP Laboratory
University of Toulouse
France

Yves KERARON
ISADEUS
Paris, France

Dimitris KIRITSIS
École Polytechnique Fédérale de
Lausanne (EPFL)
Switzerland

Gerrit KLASEN
Innovation and Product Development
Ascora
Ganderkesee, Germany

Ernö KOVACS
NEC Lab Europe
Heidelberg, Germany

Helmut KRCMAR
Technische Universität München
Garching
and
Fortiss
Munich, Germany

Boonserm KULVATUNYOU
NIST
Gaithersburg, USA

Fenareti LAMPATHAKI
Suite5 Data Intelligence Solutions
Limassol, Cyprus

Andoni LASKURAIN
NECO – Tivoly
Elorrio, Spain

Oscar LAZARO
Innovalia
Bilbao, Spain

Mariangela LAZOI
University of Salento
Lecce, Italy

Marianna LEZZI
University of Salento
Lecce, Italy

Luís LOPES
Caixa Mágica Software
Lisbon, Portugal

Daniel LÜCKERATH
Fraunhofer–IAIS
Sankt Augustin, Germany

Heinz LUGO
Wolfson School of Mechanical, Electrical
and Manufacturing Engineering
Loughborough University
UK

Michael LÜTJEN
Bremer Institut für Produktion und
Logistik (BIBA)
University of Bremen
Germany

Babis MAGOUTAS
Institute of Communication and
Computer Systems (ICCS)
National Technical University of Athens
Greece

Sotirios MAKRIS
Laboratory for Manufacturing Systems
and Automation (LMS)
University of Patras
Greece

Luís MANTEIGAS DA CUNHA
Almende
Rotterdam, Netherlands

Antonio MARGARITO
EKA
Università del Salento
Bari, Italy

Gökan MAY
École Polytechnique Fédérale de
Lausanne (EPFL)
Switzerland

Daniele MAZZEI
Department of Computer Science
University of Pisa
Italy

Gregoris MENTZAS
Institute of Communication and
Computer Systems (ICCS)
National Technical University of Athens
Greece

Rikardo MINGUEZ
Department of Graphic Design and
Engineering Projects
University of the Basque Country
Bilbao, Spain

Nejib MOALLA
Université Lumière
Lyon, France

Gabriele MONTELISCIANI
Zerynth
New York City, USA

Behrang MORADI
LGI2P
IMT Mines Alès
France

Ali MOUSAVI
Brunel University
London, UK

Eitan NAVEH
Faculty of Industrial Engineering and
Management
Technion
Haifa, Israel

Artem A. NAZARENKO
CTS
UNINOVA
New University of Lisbon
Portugal

Markus NEUHAUS
FFT Produktionssysteme
Fulda, Germany

Rui NEVES-SILVA
CTS
UNINOVA
New University of Lisbon
Portugal

Nikolaos NIKOLAKIS
Laboratory for Manufacturing Systems
and Automation (LMS)
University of Patras
Greece

Maria Jose NUÑEZ ARIÑO
AIDIMME
Valencia, Spain

Apostolos PAPAVASILEIOU
Laboratory for Manufacturing Systems
and Automation (LMS)
University of Patras
Greece

Danny PAPE
Innovation and Product Development
Ascora
Ganderkesee, Germany

Sarogini PEASE
Wolfson School of Mechanical, Electrical
and Manufacturing Engineering
Loughborough University
UK

José Gonçalves PEREIRA FILHO
Federal University of Espírito Santo
Vitoria, Brazil

Olaf PETERS
Pumacy Technologies
Berlin, Germany

Giuditta PEZZOTTA
Università degli Studi di Bergamo
Italy

Paulo PINA
CTS
UNINOVA
New University of Lisbon
Portugal

Simona PIRA
Department of Civil and Industrial
Engineering
University of Pisa
Italy

Amir PIRAYESH
INTEROP-VLab
Brussels, Belgium

Fabiana PIROLA
Università degli Studi di Bergamo
Italy

Raul POLER
Research Centre on Production
Management and Engineering (CIGIP)
Universitat Politècnica de València
Spain

Maurizio POLLINO
NEA
Rome, Italy

María POVEDA
Universidad Politécnica de Madrid
Spain

Primoz PUHAR
HELLA Saturnus Slovenija
Ljubljana, Slovenia

Matthijs PUNTER
TNO
Soesterberg, Netherlands

João Luiz REBELO MOREIRA
University of Twente
Enschede, Netherlands

Marc Allan REDECKER
University of Bremen
Germany

Alice REINA
Holonix
Milan, Italy

Anibal REÑONES
CARTIF
Boecillo, Spain

Tobias RIASANOW
Technische Universität München
Garching, Germany

Raffaele RICATTO
Fidia
San Mauro Torinese, Italy

Jorge RODRIGUEZ
ATOS
Barcelona, Spain

Erich ROME
Fraunhofer–IAIS
Sankt Augustin, Germany

Vittorio ROSATO
ENEA
Rome, Italy

Carl Christian RØSTAD
SINTEF Technology and Society
Trondheim, Norway

Domenico ROTONDI
Fincons Group
Milan, Italy

Oscar J. RUBIO
IK4–Ikerlan Technological Research
Centre
Arrasate-Mondragón, Spain

Eduardo SAIZ
Operations and Maintenance
Technologies
IK4–Ikerlan Technology Research Centre
Arrasate-Mondragón, Spain

Oscar J. SAIZ
IK4–Ikerlan Technology Research Centre
Arrasate-Mondragón, Spain

Roberto SALA
Università degli Studi di Bergamo
Italy

Matteo SARTINI
LIAM Lab
Vignola, Italy

Joao SARRAIPA
CTS
UNINOVA
New University of Lisbon
Portugal

Nicolas SCHEIDL
Technische Universität München
Garching, Germany

Wolf SCHLIEPHACK
Fraunhofer Institute for Production
Systems and Design Technology IPK
Berlin, Germany

Richard SHARPE
Wolfson School of Mechanical, Electrical
and Manufacturing Engineering
Loughborough University
UK

Prince M. SINGH
University of Twente
Enschede, Netherlands

Betim SOJEVA
Fraunhofer–IAIS
Sankt Augustin, Germany

Santiago SOLER PEREZ OLAYA
Institute of Applied Computer Science
Technische Universität Dresden
Germany

Nerea SOPELANA
Innovalia
Bilbao, Spain

David SOTO SETZKE
Technische Universität München
Garching, Germany

João SOUSA
CT2M, Department of Mechanical
Engineering
University of Minho
Guimarães, Portugal

Andries STAM
Almende
Rotterdam, Netherlands

Ludo STELLINGWERFF *
Almende
Rotterdam, Netherlands

Michele SURICO
Fidia
San Mauro Torinese, Italy

Klaus-Dieter THOBEN
Bremer Institut für Produktion und
Logistik (BIBA)
and
Faculty of Production Engineering
University of Bremen
Bremen, Germany

Andrea TILLI
Department of Electrical, Electronic and
Information Engineering
University of Bologna
Italy

Jan TORKA
Fraunhofer Institute for Production
Systems and Design Technology IPK
Berlin, Germany

Leonello TRIVELLI
Department of Civil and Industrial
Engineering
University of Pisa
Italy

Giovanni UGUCCIONI
RINA Consulting
Genoa, Italy

Oliver ULLRICH
Fraunhofer–IAIS
Sankt Augustin, Germany

Luis USATORRE ARAZUSTA
Fundacion Tecnalia R&I
Bilbao, Spain

Kate VAN-LOPIK
Wolfson School of Mechanical, Electrical
and Manufacturing Engineering
Loughborough University
UK

Marten VAN SINDEREN
University of Twente
Enschede, Netherlands

Pieter VERKROOST
CAPE Group
Enschede, Netherlands

Jeroen VERSTEEG
FFT Produktionssysteme
Bremen, Germany

Vítor VIANA
Caixa Mágica Software
Lisbon, Portugal

Giordano VICOLI
ENEA
Rome, Italy

Maria Luisa VILLANI
ENEA
Rome, Italy

Bastian VON HALEM
Innovation and Product Development
Ascora
Ganderkesee, Germany

Moritz VON STIETENCRON
Bremer Institut für Produktion und
Logistik (BIBA)
University of Bremen
Germany

Georg WEICHHART
Profactor
Steyr-Gleink, Austria

Andrew WEST
Wolfson School of Mechanical, Electrical
and Manufacturing Engineering
Loughborough University
UK

Roel WIERINGA
University of Twente
Enschede, Netherlands

Martin WOLLSCHLAEGER
Institute of Applied Computer Science
Technische Universität Dresden
Germany

Rainer WORST
Fraunhofer–IAIS
Sankt Augustin, Germany

Jingquan XIE
Fraunhofer–IAIS
Sankt Augustin, Germany

Bob YOUNG
Wolfson School of Mechanical, Electrical
and Manufacturing Engineering
Loughborough University
UK

Gregory ZACHAREWICZ
IMS
University of Bordeaux
Talence, France

Davide ZANARDI
RINA Consulting
Genoa, Italy

Martin ZELM
INTEROP-VLab
Brussels, Belgium

Index

C

C2NET, 24
canonical model, 51
capability maturity model integration
  (CMMI) framework, 325
case study, 52, 163, 187, 193, 210, 240,
  248, 275, 279, 315, 345, 376
class diagram, 346
climate change, 401–406, *see also*
  environmental issues
Climate Resilient Cities and
  Infrastructures (RESIN) project, 402
coffee production, 222
cognitive robotics, 57
collaborative product-service factory, 381
common core ontology, 424
common data model (CDM), 213
common information model, 444
competitiveness, 153, 373, 393
complex event processing (CEP), 292
computer numerical control (CNC), 194,
  258
condition monitoring, 263, 272, 441
condition-based maintenance (CBM), 292
connected smart factories (CSA), 181
ConnectedFactories project, 182, 366,
  381
construction industry, 209
consumer energy manager (CEM), 202
containerization, 96
context-aware ontology, 272
CPMSinCPPS, 353
CPS adaptor, 21
CPSization, 343
crawler, 229
CREAM (Creativity Machine) software,
  416
CREAM–CIPCast interoperability, 417
CREMA project, 24
crisis management, 399, 421, 429
critical infrastructure, 416
current research in EI, 437–462
cutting tools, 393
cyber attacks, 80, 416

cyber-physical
  artifacts, 58
  systems (CPS), 17, 43, 99, 343, 349,
    452

D

data
  aggregation, 23
  analytics, 27, 104, 255, 412
  distribution service (DSS), 46
  -driven architecture, 175, 258
  economy, 179
  harmonization, 103
  integration, 187–190, 217–222, 411
  management component (DMC), 99
  mining, 281, 294
  platform, 210
  privacy, 278
  stream processing, 292
  transformation, 104
decision-making, 310, 357
decision-support system (DSS), 4, 23,
  359, 417
demand–supply flow, 174
denial of service (DoS) attack, 80
design, 188, 352, 394
device driver, 92
DGRAI, 334, 361
dichotomies, 391
digital, 382
  factory framework, 204
  "human twin", 4
  performance board, 452
  single market, 152
  transformation, 209
Digital Agenda for Europe, 193
digitally-charged product pattern, 66
directed decision support, 10
discrete event specification (DEVS), 351
DIVERSITY project, 368–371
Docker (platform), 85, 115, 228
document-oriented data, 103

Printed and bound by CPI Group (UK) Ltd, Croydon, CR0 4YY